Children of Separation and Divorce

Management and Treatment

Children of Separation and Divorce

Management and Treatment

Edited by

Irving R. Stuart, Ph. D.
and
Lawrence Edwin Abt, Ph. D.

 VAN NOSTRAND REINHOLD COMPANY

NEW YORK   CINCINNATI   ATLANTA   DALLAS   SAN FRANCISCO
LONDON   TORONTO   MELBOURNE

Van Nostrand Reinhold Company Regional Offices:
New York   Cincinnati   Atlanta   Dallas   San Francisco

Van Nostrand Reinhold Company International Offices:
London   Toronto   Melbourne

Library of Congress Catalog Card Number: 81-958
ISBN: 0-442-24431-2

Manufactured in the United States of America

Published by Van Nostrand Reinhold Company
135 West 50th Street, New York, N.Y. 10020

Published simultaneously in Canada by Van Nostrand Reinhold Ltd.

15   14   13   12   11   10   9   8   7   6   5   4   3   2   1

Library of Congress Cataloging in Publication Data
Main entry under title:

Children of separation and divorce.

    Includes bibliographical references and index.
    1.   Children of divorced parents—United States.
2.   Divorce—United States.   I.   Stuart, Irving R.
II.   Abt, Lawrence Edwin.   [DNLM: 1.   Child psychology—
Popular works.   2.   Divorce—Popular works.   3.   Parent-
child relations—Popular works.   4.   Child psychiatry.
WS   105.5.A84   C537]
HQ777.5.C45 1981   306.8'9   81-958
ISBN 0-442-24431-2   AACR2

LIST OF CONTRIBUTORS

Maria de Lourdes Arguelles Ph. D.
Director, Outpatient Mental Health Services, La Frontera Center, Inc., Tucson, Arizona

Joan Beir, M.S.W.
Remarried Consultation Service of the Jewish Board of Family and Children's Services, Inc., New York City

Kenneth K. Berry, Ph. D.
Associate Professor of Medical Psychology, Department of Psychiatry, College of Medicine, The University of Nebraska, Omaha, Nebraska

Stephen Billick, M.D.
Fellow in Child Psychiatry, St. Vincent's Hospital, New York City and former Chief Fellow in Forensic Psychiatry, University of Pennsylvania

Dorothy D. Bolding, M.S.W., A.C.S.W.
Assistant Professor of Neurology, School of Medicine, Coordinator of Social Work Services, Developmental Disability Center for Children, School of Allied Health Professions, L.S.U. Medical Center, New Orleans, Louisiana

Holly Brown, R.N.
Remarried Consultation Service of the Jewish Board of Family and Children's Services, Inc., New York City

Daniel A. Calvin
A policy analyst for the Health Services Administration, Department of Health, and Human Services

Helen Crohn, M.S.W.
Remarried Consultation Service of the Jewish Board of Family and Children's Services, Inc., New York City

Ellen A. Drake, Psy. D.,
  Educator-Clinician, College of Medicine and Dentistry of New Jersey, Rutgers
  Medical School, Community Mental Health Center, Piscataway, New Jersey;
  Field Supervisor, Rutgers University, Graduate School of Applied and Profes-
  sional Psychology, Piscataway, New Jersey

Robert M. Friedman, Ph. D.
  Adolescent Project, Child, Adolescent, and Community Program, Florida
  Mental Health Institute, Department of Health and Rehabilitative Services,
  Tampa, Florida.

Enid Gamer, Ph. D.
  Director of Children's Programs, Norwood-Medfield Area, Massachusetts
  Department of Mental Health

Joanne G. Greer, Ph. D.
  Deputy Chief, National Center for the Prevention and Control of Rape, National Institute of Mental Health, Rockville, Maryland

Judith A. Harris, M.D., F.A.A.P., F.C.C.P.
  Associate Professor of Pediatrics, School of Medicine, Director, Developmen-
  tal Disability Center for Children, School of Allied Health Professions, L.S.U.
  Medical Center, New Orleans, Louisiana

Nancy R. Haslett, M.D.
  Assistant Professor of Psychiatry & Neurology, School of Medicine, Coor-
  dinator of Clinical Services, Developmental Disability Center for Children,
  School of Allied Health Professions, L.S.U. Medical Center, New Orleans,
  Louisiana

Marla B. Isaacs, Ph. D., Director,
  Division of Counseling Services for Children and Families, Philadelphia Child
  Guidance Clinic, Philadelphia, Penn.

Joan B. Kelly, Ph. D.
  Co-Principal Investigator, California Children of Divorce Project and Director
  Northern California Mediation Center Greenbrae, California

Sharon Lardieri, A.C.S.W.
  Adolescent Project, Child, Adolescent, and Community Program, Florida
  Mental Health Institute, Department of Health & Rehabilitative Services, Tam-
  pa, Floria.

Don McNair, M.S.W.
  Social and Economic Services, Department of Health & Rehabilitative Services,
  Tampa, Florida.

Cynthia R. Pfeffer, M.D.
  Assistant Professor of Psychiatry, Cornell University Medical College, and
  Chief, Child Inpatient Service, New York Hospital-Cornell Medical Center,
  Westchester Division, White Plains, New York

Judith Quick, M.S.
  Adolescent Project, Child, Adolescent, and Community Program, Florida

Mental Health Institute, Department of Health & Rehabilitative Services, Tampa, Florida.

Carla Repetosky, M.S.W.
Social and Economic Services, Department of Health & Rehabilitative Services, Tampa, Florida

Dorothy I. Riddle, Ph. D.
Department of Psychology, University of Arizona, Tucson, Arizona

Evelyn Rodstein, M.S.W.
Remarried Consultation Service of the Jewish Board of Family and Children's Services, Inc., New York City

Robert L. Sadoff, M.D.
Clinical Professor of Psychiatry, University of Pennsylvania; Lecturer in Law, Villanova University School of Law

Clifford J. Sager, M.D.
Remarried Consultation Service of the Jewish Board of Family and Children's Services, Inc., New York City

Ann K. Schrader, A.C.S.W.
Principal Clinical Social Worker, Erich Lindemann Mental Health Center, Boston, Massachusetts

Daniel C. Schuman, M.D.
Director of Psychiatry, Norfolk County Probate and Family Court; Assistant Clinical Professor of Psychiatry, Tufts University School of Medicine, Massachusetts

David Stoops, B.A.
Personnel Office, Department of Health & Rehabilitative Services, Tampa, Florida

Libby Walker, M.S.W.
Remarried Consultation Service of the Jewish Board of Family and Children's Services, Inc., New York City

Mary F. Whiteside, Ph. D.
Children's Psychiatric Hospital, University of Michigan Medical Center, Ann Arbor, Michigan, Clinical Assistant Professor of Psychology in Psychiatry, University of Michigan Medical Center, Ann Arbor, Michigan, and Staff Member, Ann Arbor Center for the Family, Ann Arbor, Michigan

Preface

Since 1972, when the first edition of this book was published, the problems and trends identified—and considered at some length—concerning the effects of separation and divorce upon children have clearly intensified. For example, in 1970, approximately three-quarters of a million couples sought divorce; in 1979, the latest year for which we have reliable information, well over a million couples terminated their marriages. Thus, problems for children, which arise as a result of dissolved marriages, have grown greatly, both in number and in severity.

The first edition of *Children of Separation and Divorce* looked at problems and issues from the point of view of parents dissolving their marriages and the effects of such actions as seen through the eyes of their children for whom new problems and tensions were generated. In contrast, the present edition directs its attention to matters of management and treatment since these issues have greatly increased in recent years and offer strong professional challenges to all of the disciplines that may contribute to their resolution. The first and second editions clearly are meant to complement each other, although each, at the same time, is separate and offers its own point of view.

This volume is divided into four parts that examine management and treatment from different viewpoints. Part I provides insight into the legal problems and issues faced by children of divorced parents; that is, what their legal rights and responsibilities are and the attitude of courts and their professional staffs toward such matters. Both Dr. Robert L. Sadoff and Dr. Stephen Billick are psychiatrists specializing in the legal aspects of that discipline, and they are unusually well qualified to write in this area. Their contribution arouses our interest and respect.

Part II on Psychodynamics commands a broad range of considerations in the areas of emotional and psychological factors involved in understanding and providing for children whose parents have ended their marriages.

Dr. Cynthia R. Pfeffer examines the developmental issues affecting children whose parents have separated and are now divorced, providing the reader with an appreciation of the long-range developmental changes that are important in dealing in professionally effective ways with such children.

Dr. Kenneth K. Berry offers a very useful, and timely, statement of the opportunities and the difficulties facing male single parents who are carving out new social roles for themselves and the children in their custody. His treatment is forthright, the issues and problems are faced squarely, and his view is largely optimistic.

It has long been recognized that there are psychiatric aspects of custody loss, and Dr. Daniel C. Schuman provides a helpful theoretical view of how such losses are experienced and their effects. As a sensitive director of psychiatry in a Massachusetts Probate and Family Court, the contributor makes explicit the counter-transferential aspects of psychiatrists and attorneys working with such angry parents, offering a new dimension of understanding.

Part III, entitled "Management of Behavior Associated with Marital Discord," directs the reader's attention to a number of different management problems growing out of divorce and separation.

The chapter on "Placement of Children in Foster Care: Uses, Abuses, Risks, Realities, and Myths," by Robert M. Friedman and other contributors, offers suggestions for recognizing, and thus avoiding, placement opportunities and the problems they may involve.

Daniel A. Calvin suggests a family and social policy in relation to joint custody that is both long and thoughtful and full of interesting and helpful insights.

Dr. Ellen A. Drake in her chapter invites the interest of the reader in considering the role of the school in helping children cope with issues and problems of divorce, and her contribution sets forth some of the direct ways in which schools may be helpful.

Dr. Dorothy I. Riddle and Dr. Maria de Lourdes Arguelles concern themselves with children of gay parents about whom, they suggest, relatively little is known. Their own survey, conducted with eighty-two gay parents, is one of the few on record, and their contribution offers new information and understanding of a growing social process.

In "Children of Incarcerated Parents: Problems and Interventions," Dr. Enid Gamer and Ms. Ann K. Schrader address a socially sensitive issue that has frequently been overlooked; that is, what happens to children when one of their parents is imprisoned? Their chapter is enlightening and highly informative.

The final chapter in Part III, by Dr. Joanne G. Greer, invites the reader's attention to an increasingly common occurrence, that of problems associated with adolescent pregnancy in a disrupted family. She indicates that the very young daughter of divorced parents is probably at greater risk of pregnancy than the girl in an intact family, and she discusses the reasons for this difficulty and some of the problems of its management.

Part IV, "Treatment Within the Family Unit," consists of chapters addressed to a wide variety of problems confronting professional workers and others who deal with fractured families.

Dr. Marla B. Isaacs considers the effects of stress upon children without psychopathology when their parents separate. In doing so, she provides a systems model for looking at and seeking to resolve the many difficulties that arise.

In an interesting and useful chapter that concentrates on the nonorganic factors involved in children's "failure to thrive," Dr. Judith A. Harris and Dr. Nancy R. Haslett, together with Ms. Dorothy D. Bolding, offer the reader a new conceptual framework for understanding, detecting, preventing, and treating such problems.

Ms. Helen Crohn and her fellow contributors examine the plight of the child, and the large range of his/her new relationships, in the remarried family. Their considerable experience in this area is both helpful and enlightening, especially in relation to management.

In a related chapter, Dr. Mary F. Whiteside sets forth a family systems approached with similar remarried families that offers further understanding of their treatment.

The final chapter, by Dr. Joan B. Kelly, gives an outline of the research findings and their clinical implications from the California Children of Divorce Project which she codirected with Dr. J. S. Wallerstein. The focus of the chapter is on the problems and opportunities that children face in developing visiting relationships with the noncustodial parent after divorce.

I. R. S. and L. E. A.

Contents

Children of Separation and Divorce

Management and Treatment

Part I

Medico-Legal Considerations

The single chapter of Part I, written by two psychiatrists whose specialty is the legal rights of children of separation and divorce, and the difficulties they encounter, makes clear that the legal status of such children differs significantly from that of their parents.

Moreover, Dr. Robert L. Sadoff and Dr. Stephen Billick suggest that the handling of children differs somewhat from one state to another; and in reviewing the history of changing roles of the father, they suggest how modern legal rights and responsibilities have evolved.

The chapter that follows brings the reader something of the history and background of the emerging legal rights of children when their parents divorce. Dr. Robert L. Sadoff and his coauthor, Dr. Stephen Billick, also provide a helpful outline of the difficulties, in the eyes of the law, that such children face and how courts seek to alleviate or minimize their problems.

As the authors indicate, with the changed status of women in American society, custody of the child, once the pre-eminent right of the father, is now a shared responsibility of both parents. Courts increasingly recognize changed mores and social relationships and have, over the years, provided what amounts to a doctrine of child custody that is treated in some detail in the following chapter.

1

The Legal Rights and Difficulties of Children in Separation and Divorce

Robert L. Sadoff, M.D.
and
Stephen Billick, M.D.

I. INTRODUCTION AND HISTORY

At one time there was no dispute about the legal custody of children since children were considered to be chattels, or the property, of the father, and the state and society had no valid interest in this relationship. However, today the state definitely has an interest in the welfare of children and in the outcome of childhood. Healthy children usually make healthy and productive adults; unhealthy children often make unproductive and sometimes violent, dangerous adults. Consequently, the state clearly has an interest in the child and his care and welfare. Thus, children have been ascribed certain rights along with their more apparent and obvious needs.

One difficulty the state has in determining children's rights is that they cannot exactly parallel the rights of adults. It is important that children be accorded legal rights and legal safeguards on a similar basis as adults. However, this decision must be tempered with the reality of the developing child. Different children have different levels of maturity at different stages of development. One cannot give a two-year-old child, as one might give to a sixteen-year-old adolescent, the right to his or her own decisions. Clearly, the rights of children and the expectation that their needs will be met correspond closely with the inherent interest of the state in producing an orderly and nonviolent society.

It is important to differentiate between the rights of children and their needs. Needs are much more universal and transcultural: the need for food, shelter, caring, protection from physical and mental harm and abuse, and the need for education to function in an increasingly complex society. It should be apparent that over and above these basic needs children can be provided with additions and supplements. The basic minimum, however, should be met by the parents or guardians according to their ability and resources. In our society, when these cannot be met by the parent or the guardian, the state intervenes to supplement through financial allocations and/or special programs.

On the other hand, the rights of children are usually protected by the courts. These include privacy, religious freedom, and the chance to have an individual rather than a group choice made for the child's future. The child also has the right to self-determination within his/her expertise, experience, and level of judgment maturity. It is within this framework that the legal rights of children in separation and divorce proceedings will be approached.

As previously noted, throughout history children have been the property of the father. The father had exclusive rights to the children and the determination of their future. Children within this context virtually had no rights at all. The question of custody of children, raised by the Anglo-American legal system, in a male-dominated society, turned on the ability of the parent to care for the children. In the seventeenth and eighteenth centuries, women had little opportunity to be financially independent. Thus, the father, who could support the children, and best provide for their basic needs, was invariably granted custody. No concern was given at that time to the rights of the children.

With the rise of women's rights in the late nineteenth and early twentieth centuries, however, there began also a concern for the rights of children. This concern was reflected in the concept of the "tender years" doctrine of granting custody of young children to their mother rather than to their father. The basis of this doctrine was that children in their "tender" or early years were best satisfied by being raised by their mother. This became possible for a number of reasons:

1. Women had new opportunities to earn income;
2. Women were gaining civil rights including the right to vote;
3. Women were granted the right to alimony and child support as a result of divorce and separation from their husbands.

The "tender years" doctrine of child custody introduced the psychiatrist and psychologist into the domestic relations court to present expert testimony regarding parent-child relationships, emotional needs of developing children, and predictions of outcome of various parent-child arrangements. Child psychiatrists, psychologists, and family therapists began to influence court decisions, raising questions of children's rights, optimal parental environment, and the basic needs of growing children. Courts began to scrutinize the behavior and stability of parents before awarding custody. Thus, the "tender years" doctrine may appear to be biased in favor of the mother being awarded custody in most cases, but in fact, the court often appointed experts to investigate the emotional stability and behavior of the mother. What seemed relevant for the court was not so much evidence of mental disorder, but whether the mother acted in a moral fashion, such as not introducing other men to the children, or, in fact, not dating at all. If the court was satisfied that the mother did not meet all requirements of the stable, moral person, the children were almost automatically awarded to the father. Little psychiatric or moral scrutiny was paid to the father as the double standard of morality and sexuality has persisted until very recently.

In Painter v. Bannister, [1] the court awarded the child to the grandparents on the recommendation of the psychologist, Dr. Hawkes, who established that the grandparents were more stable in their Iowa home than Mr. Painter was in his. Matters of religion and lifestyle were raised with an indication that there was no emotional instability in either home. The court concluded, "We do not believe it is for Mark's best interest to take him out of this stable atmosphere in the face of warnings of dire consequences from an eminent child psychologist and send him to an uncertain future in his father's home. Regardless of our appreciation of the father's love for his child and his desire to have him with him, we do not believe we have the moral right to gamble with this child's future." With some further understanding the court said, "He should be encouraged in every way possible to know his father. We are sure there are many ways in which Mr. Painter can enrich Mark's life." The issue in this case appears to be the welfare of the child as against the rights of the father, and marks the transition in the legal thinking about child custody.

The "tender years" doctrine has been progressively replaced by the "best interest of the child" concept. Buttressed with new clinical data from the psychiatric community, the legal profession has moved to further recognize the child's inherent rights. At present, the primary concern is what is best for the child, with only secondary regard to what is best for the parents. In Garvey v. Garvey[2] the court said, "the welfare of the child itself will be the first consideration. . .the child's own welfare is superior to the claims of either parent whose wishes and personal desires must yield, if opposed to such welfare." Thus the child has moved from a state of being property or a chattel to that of being an individual in the law who has primacy in child custody proceedings. His/her needs having been assured, the child is now accorded his/her rights under law.

THE ROLE OF THE COURTS

It is essential when discussing child custody that the issues and conflicts be clarified and distinguished from those of divorce and separation. They need to be separated because they have different purposes and entirely different end points. Divorce splits the family, separates one parent from the other, dividing two individuals for a variety of reasons. The ability of a human being to maintain marital object relations is not the same as the ability of that human being to parent a child. Further, it is generally accepted that the bond of parenting is a far stronger one than is the bond of marriage. This is supported statistically since divorce and separation rate is far higher than parent-child separation rate. Divorce and custody cannot be entirely separated, however, since divorce inevitably precedes the issue of custody. In order to ensure the best outcome for the child, divorce counseling for the separating parents may be recommended. By working through their differences in a professional, therapeutic atmosphere, the parents afford the children less chance of abuse during the process of divorce with its inevitable emotional crises. Further, the child has a right to treatment if he/she shows signs of emotional or behavioral difficulties during this transitional period.

It is often difficult for children to experience the disruption of their family; they often wish parents would reunite and re-establish the family integrity as previously existed. However, children do not have the right to prevent parents from divorcing. They do have the right, however, to be spared the guilt for parents' separation or divorce. Further, they have the right to be free from exploitation by one parent over the other. Parents often use children inappropriately in their arguments and disputes with one another. This abuse may lead to further conflicts within the child and to emotional or behavioral disorders which will require therapeutic intervention.

It should be noted that the legal system in which the separation, divorce and custody proceedings occur may tend to foster emotional difficulties within the child. In many states divorce is based on fault or blame by one party to another. Even where no such fault exists, the spouse is encouraged to provide evidence for wrongdoing by the other spouse. In some states the law says divorce can only be granted when there is an innocent and injured spouse and the other is to blame. Thus husbands or wives are often encouraged to make up stories about their spouses even when they wish to divorce amicably. This type of thinking often leads to negative feelings which can be conveyed to the children as well. No-fault divorce has certainly aided in this difficulty but has not resolved it entirely.

Parents battling their way through the system of divorce often cause great conflict within their children by using them as pawns in their own conflicts. The system does nothing to protect the children from such abuse. Perhaps greater abuse occurs after separation and during custody and visitation proceedings. Parents often take out their residual anger toward the other parent on the children by denying visitation with the other parent or by obstructing such visitation proceedings. They often put the child in the middle as a means of communication to the other parent. Perhaps the worst abuse of all comes within the courtroom where the child is put in a position of making the choice. Some children are just not able to express a choice of parental option and should not be made to do so. Others have very definite choices and often are not allowed the privilege of expressing their choice. One fifteen-year-old girl, who was seen for evaluation in the Forensic Psychiatry Clinic at the University of Pennsylvania, absolutely refused to make a choice about living with her mother or father. She believed the nonselected parent would become violent toward her and would abandon her for life. No amount of discussion with her and her parents would alter her decision. It was believed that in her best interest the court ought to make the decision without consulting her and putting her in a position where she would feel anxiety and subsequent guilt.

In another family situation that was evaluated at the Forensic Psychiatry Clinic, difficulties arose when the mother was required to be hospitalized for a nervous breakdown. She had a serious depression with suicidal ideation. The children, all boys, opted to live with their father when the parents separated. They had a pact with the father not to yield to the mother's demands. The father also believed that his sons would be harmed if they lived with their mother. Even in the face of the mother's psychological improvement and the increasing positive feelings toward the mother, the boys would not relent. It was only through professional intervention that the true wishes of the boys to be with their mother and visit with their father was brought to the surface that an optimal solution occurred. The boys returned to live with their mother without the guilt of abandoning her when she needed them most and visited their father frequently. This result was obtained primarily through the use of divorce counseling, which is highly recommended when children are involved and especially where disputes occur between parents which involve the welfare and best interests of the children.

OPTIONS AVAILABLE

Given a situation where two parents separate with or without a divorce, the first choice for custody of the child should be joint custody. This is especially true for parents who both have a loving interest in their children and are able amicably to work out a system for continuing healthy parental relationships.

The state does not usually intervene in the normal nuclear family without a dispute between marital parties or where third-party allegation of abuse is raised. Within accepted norms of society (educational requirements and health laws) and within the understanding of behavioral science, parents have the right to raise their children without the state's intervention. Thus, even with separation and divorce, should the parents be able to continue their parental relationship with the child in joint custody, the state need not intervene. Such intervention by the state in an amicable joint custody arrangement may be disruptive and be against the best interests of the children.

In a single custody agreement which is uncontested by the other party, the state may have an interest in the outcome. Because of the nature of the legal adversary system, two adults who are separating from their marital bonds may, for purposes of achieving a divorce settlement, yield certain custodial grounds which are not in the child's best interest. If one parent is to have custody and the other parent has agreed to relinquish his or her rights to custody, the court may need to review this agreement to ensure that the child's rights and needs are being met. It is imperative that the court pay particular attention to the child's right to visitation with the non-custodial parent. Often these uncontested custody agreements will be found to be more than adequate; however, since there will not be joint custody, which was the pre-existing state prior to separation and divorce, the child's rights need to be safeguarded by the court's review. In practice, the court rarely, if ever, intervenes in such agreements.

In contested custody cases the usual arrangement is for two parents and two lawyers. The child in the majority of cases does not have legal representation. However, there has been a growing change in this regard. It is not unusual currently in many states for a guardian *ad litem* to be appointed. Child advocates can become involved to help safeguard the rights of minors, and in complex custody matters courts have appointed attorneys to represent the rights of the children. In 1974 the American Bar Association published the Uniform Marriage and Divorce Act which included suggested statutory court-appointed representation of the children.[3] It has been suggested that this makes economic sense because society pays the cost of possible resultant long-term psychiatric treatment or community care for disturbed individuals. A court-appointed attorney enjoys all the privileges of the parental attorneys. He has the right to subpoena expert witnesses, and has access to evaluation of the parents and to home assessments. In this situation a psychiatrist and/or other competent mental health professional can conduct an evaluation and aid the child's search for a proper custody arrangement.

With the increasing use of psychiatrists and psychologists in these custody cases, the focus is moving from assessment of the individual psychodynamics of the two contesting parents to a more appropriate stance of family dynamics and children's emotional interests. The child is evaluated for his/her needs and the parents are evaluated for their ability at parenting. It is imperative that the psychiatrist recognize the difference between individual morality and the psychological fitness to care for children. This is particularly true where separating parents have begun to engage in new coupling relationships which do not yet have legal standing. It is not the appropriate role of the psychiatrist to pass religious, ethical, or moral judgments upon parental behavior. Rather, it is the role of the mental health expert witness to evaluate the ability to parent. Within this context more has been done towards identifying the psychological parent. No longer is it assumed necessarily that the psychological parent is the biological mother or even the biological father. Frequently it is found that an aunt, grandparent or adoptive parent may be the true psychological parent. Within this regard it may be important in some cases to demonstrate the superiority of the psychological parent to the parenting ability of the biological parent. In a case in New Jersey the court awarded custody to the psychological adoptive couple over the wishes of the biological mother where the child's intrinsic worth and his own rights were considered.[4] It should be noted that in most cases the psychological parent is also the biological parent.

Even where psychosis exists, a parent may be appropriate to care for the children. One particular case seen at the Forensic Psychiatry Clinic involved a thirty-seven-year-old paranoid schizophrenic male who had four children. His wife had died and he maintained his paternal relationship with his children. The neighbors were concerned because he would often dress in a white sheet and would light candles and chant various unusual phrases. There was a petition to remove the children from their home and place them in foster care. The father petitioned to maintain custody of his children, arguing that he was a good father and was able properly to care for their emotional and physical needs. Psychiatric examination revealed that the father was in fact paranoid schizophrenic but did not impose his delusional system upon his children. He had a confined paranoid system regarding religious beliefs and restricted his delusional thinking to his daily religious behavior. He was able to provide food, clothing, and educational opportunities for the children. Interview of the children revealed that they wished to stay with their father and they knew he was "weird" but this did not bother them. They described his religious behavior and often chuckled at it, realizing that it was their father's particular idiosyncracy and that they were not involved in his delusional system. They were able to carry on fairly normal conversations with him in areas other than religion.

Within the evaluation of the contested custody suit, the child should have a choice appropriate to his or her age of development and level of maturity between which parent or parental options he wishes. It should be emphasized to the child, however, that he/she can state his/her preference, but the decision rests with the court; in this way the child can have an active, valuable input into the decision but be free of guilt for having one parental option over the other. The child should accept responsibility for his/her choice, but not the guilt for the court's decision. It is important that the child, given the stage of development and the level of maturity, have a right to self-determination and self-development.

Reference has been made to the child's developmental stage and level of maturity. It is obvious to even the least psychologically minded person that a two-year-old child is in no position to actively determine the best parental option. However, the majority of fourteen-year-old adolescents are in such a position. Particular attention needs to be paid to the child's reasons for choosing one option over the other, and an understanding of these reasons needs to be seen within the developmental framework in the varying levels of maturity. The evaluating psychiatrist has the unique opportunity to see the underlying reason for the choice. Similarly, if the child wishes not to make a decision or choose one parent over the other, no coercion should be imposed upon him/her to do so.

Much of the foregoing discussion has pertained exclusively to "the child." However, many separation and divorce proceedings involve multiple child families. What is the right of a child either to live with or live apart from his other siblings? And what are the rights of the other siblings, vis à vis a particular child? The psychiatrist must be tuned in to the delicate balance between sibling interactions. Children should have both the right to not be separated from their siblings and also the right to be apart from their siblings, should they so choose. Each case must be individualized and no clear-cut formula can be drawn in this regard. Most people believe that it is better to keep children together even if one particular child will suffer from the decision. It is better to avoid generalizations and deal with each family individually. It may be necessary to take one child out of the family and place either with the noncustodial parent or in a foster home or with a relative. Some children may need to be with their mother whereas their siblings may need to be and wish to live with their father. Great care needs to be taken in determining each case on an individual basis, demonstrating the need for comprehensive psychiatric assessment.

Certain biases and myths have developed in custody matters that need to be discussed: in the past it has been assumed that a working parent would be inferior to the parent who stayed at home. This has prevented many working women from pursuing both a career in the marketplace and a career as a mother. It has been used as an argument for supporting maternal rights over paternal rights. Behavioral science clearly shows it is not the quantity of parenting, but the quality and consistency of parenting that is important. With the multiple support systems now available to a working parent, children can be raised with the most appropriate parental option while the parent continues to be employed. Public and private day-care centers are numerous. It is important to examine the child's understanding of the situation and to note the level of functioning of the person assuming the parental role.

Probably even more controversial than the working parent or the unmarried couple in parenting is the homosexual parent. Clearly, in the past the homosexual parent was granted no custodial or visitation rights. The American Psychiatric Association sees sexual orientation no longer as an illness but rather as an option within the normal range of human behavior. The changing legal atmosphere concerning homosexuals in America further demonstrates the difficulty in distinguishing between the status of psychiatric knowledge and the slower changing cultural norms. The homosexual parent should have equal rights to custody as a heterosexual parent. Custody of the child should be concerned with the ability to parent, not with the ability of the parent to couple with a person of the same or different sex. Studies have shown that homosexual parents usually produce heterosexual children. The child has the right to live with the homosexual parent equally as with the heterosexual parent. It has also been shown that sexual abuse toward children is not more prevalent by homosexual parents than by heterosexual parents. Heterosexual pedophilia is more prevalent than homosexual pedophilia. Nevertheless, the child has the right to be free of sexual, physical, or mental abuse regardless of whether it comes from the heterosexual or homosexual parent. Individuals should be evaluated for their ability to parent regardless of their sexual orientation.

One particular case, also seen at the Forensic Psychiatry Clinic, at the University of Pennsylvania, involved a twenty-nine-year-old woman who was fighting her mother for custody of her nine-year-old daughter. The argument by the grandmother was faulty in that she assumed that if her daughter raised the nine-year-old girl her daughter would introduce homosexuality into the home and influence the child toward that orientation. What she neglected in her argument was the fact that she, as a heterosexual, had raised a homosexual daughter and the court might not allow her the opportunity of raising another daughter who could become homosexual. This argument, of course, was not valid, but neither was the grandmother's concern for taking her daughter's nine-year-old girl away from her.

POSTCUSTODY ARRANGEMENTS

After a custody determination has been made, the child should feel that the arrangement is permanent. Stability and continuity, more than anything, are important for the developing child.[5] Just as any drastic changes in conditions could again present cause for litigation and change of the custodial decree, neither of these should be emphasized to the child. In the usual nuclear family, a child may be removed if his welfare is jeopardized; so too, can any "permanent" custodial decree be changed when the need arises. In the usual nuclear family one does not emphasize the fact that the state can, upon just cause, intervene to disrupt the family; neither, after a custodial decree is announced, should the emphasis be placed upon possible change in the future. It is imperative that permanency be maintained and emphasized unless circumstances absolutely require otherwise.

As custodial and noncustodial parents move from state to state and children visit their parents in various states, jurisdictions may change depending upon where the child resides. Mental health professionals need to encourage various state jurisdictions to come in conformance with one another. Perhaps a federal standard may be applied to custody arrangements in the future. Fewer things are more disconcerting or confusing for the child than to be awarded custody to one parent in one state and at the same time to the other parent in another state. It has been shown that two of the major reasons for interstate custody conflicts have been the separated parent's anger at the other parent or the frustration at not receiving visitation rights as decreed. Parents must learn this fact, and it is hoped that by divorce counseling conflicts can be resolved that will avoid the use of children as pawns in parental battles.

Custodial parents should not try to thwart the just needs of the children to visitation of their noncustodial parent. Visitation by a noncustodial parent to the child should be guaranteed unless it is clearly proved that the relationship is dangerous, physically or emotionally. It is a clear abuse of the child for one parent to intentionally alienate the child from the other parent. It is unfair, unwise and should be discouraged both by mental health professionals and by courts. The child has an absolute right to neutral or positive posture of one divorced parent toward the other. It is confusing for a child who lived with both parents at one time to hear the battles of the parents and the accusations made against the other parent whom the child continues to love and to respect. It should be remembered as stated in Smith v. Smith[6] that visitation is a right given by the court and is not determined by the custodial parent.

Child-napping by one parent or the other should have severe legal penalties because it places the child in psychological harm. Children become frightened when they are whisked off even by the noncustodial parent to another state or even another country. Child-napping further alienates one parent from the other, negating the child's right to neutral or positive posture between parents. Child-napping also destroys the sense of permanency, stability, and continuity which is needed for the child to be secure within himself or herself.

In some cases, child-napping is either unconsciously encouraged by the system or is the result of significant flaws in the system. One flaw is the lack of a federal rule regarding custody cases. In one particular case, also seen in the Forensic Psychiatry Clinic, a family separated, the mother taking a four-year-old child from Virginia to Pennsylvania. Several months later the father decided that he wanted to have custody of the child and did not believe the mother had legal custody. There had only been a verbal agreement that the mother would leave with the child during the period of separation. The father went to Pennsylvania and took the child from her playground. He called the mother, indicating that the child was safe and that he was going to keep the child in Virginia. The father then instituted a court proceeding in Virginia to obtain custody of his daughter. Since the jurisdiction of the court resides where the child resides, the court in Virginia assumed jurisdiction. At the first hearing the court could not come to a decision and delayed the final decree for thirty days, allowing the child to return to Pennsylvania with her mother. During those thirty days the mother obtained legal custody by the courts in Pennsylvania. She was then advised by her lawyers not to return to Virginia for the final hearing since she already had custody in Pennsylvania and need not return to Virginia. Father, however, returned to Pennsylvania and took his child once more, this time from in front of her home, and whisked her to Virginia. The court in Virginia awarded the father custody since the mother was in contempt of the Virginia court by not appearing at the stated time. The court in Virginia did not give credence to the argument that custody had already been granted in Pennsylvania nor was that custodial decree in Pennsylvania honored by the judge in Virginia. The mother was told by friends and relatives that she should go to Virginia and take her child back in the same way that the child's father obtained his daughter, i.e., by child-napping.

The mother refused to do so because she believed that even though she wished to have custody of her daughter, that child-napping would harm her daughter more. In effect, the court in Virginia encouraged the kidnapping by not questioning how the child was returned to Virginia but only by granting custody to the father who had child-napped his daughter. It is that type of decision making by courts and the lack of honoring of other states' decisions that leads to confusion and further difficulty within the system whereby children are abused.

Only in the most extreme situations and where all parental-biological and psychological-parental options are inappropriate should foster home placement be considered. The potential harm of foster home placement or institutionalization is simply so great that every effort should be made to obtain a more appropriate custody situation. Similarly, adoption should only be made because of the severe mental or physcial neglect and/or abuse that would result from continuing parental care. Before the state undertakes to move the child to foster home placements or adoptions, other family alternatives through blood relatives should be pursued. For example, the court in *In Re: Mark*[7] awarded custody of a child to its illegitimate father rather than accepting adoption as an alternative.

It is imperative that in these settings the child have representation. The child's interests do not necessarily equal the interest of the state and it should not be assumed that the judge will weigh the child's interest more heavily than the interest of the state. The child in our adversary legal system needs adequate legal counsel to ensure a just and equitable outcome. Custody determinations are court-decreed placements of the child in a setting other than the usual nuclear family. Because the child's environment is being changed by legal decree, the child has a right and an absolute need to be represented by adequate counsel. The child's right should be paramount in custody proceedings. He/she should not be allowed to be placed in the middle of the parents' dispute. Serious sanctions ought to be placed where the child's rights are abused by battling parents. Sanctions are imposed on parents who neglect or abuse their children. It is suggested that in divorce and separation proceedings without proper legal safeguards, the child is subject to serious emotional neglect and/or abuse which should be avoided. Only through zealously guarding the rights of the children in these delicate and often violent legal battles can we protect the child from further abuse. He/she must have legal counsel in any proceeding that affects his/her future and life. The difficulties faced by the child may be overwhelming and may be seriously destructive for further growth and development.

Separation and divorce will continue and child custody proceedings and visitation debates will occur. These need not be destructive to the child if proper safeguards are instituted. Regardless of the adversary system, the mental health professional should maintain a neutral standard of assessment, utilizing comprehensive techniques of examining all parties concerned for the true best interest of the child.

REFERENCES

1. *Painter v. Bannister,* SC Iowa, 140 NW 2d 152 (1966).
2. *Garvey v. Garvey,* 233 SW 2d 48, 50–51.
3. Foster, H. H., Jr. Divorce reform and the Uniform Act. *Family LQ.* 7:170–210 (1973).
4. 114 NJ Super. 584, 277 A 2d 566 (1971).
5. Goldstein, Freud, and Solnit. *Beyond the Best Interest of the Child.* New York: Free Press, Macmillan, 1973.
6. *Smith v. Smith,* 142 NW 2d 421,425 (1966).
7. *In Re: Mark,* 154 NW 2d 27.

Part II

Psychodynamics

Psychodynamics is usually considered as any psychological process that changes or is a cause of change. The three chapters that constitute Part II share a common concern for the underlying motives and drives that effect such change. Each chapter addresses this larger issue in its own way and within its own focus so that together they suggest something of the developmental issues among children whose parents have divorced as well as the roles of the parents in the changed and changing status of the child.

Dr. Cynthia R. Pfeffer, after reviewing the greatly accelerating incidence of divorce, proceeds to interpret the relevant literature in light of her clinical experience on the Child Inpatient Service of a large New York City hosptial, where she is Chief of Service.

Dr. Kenneth K. Berry seeks to bring together and critically review the developing information concerning the role of the male single parent, who is emerging more and more frequently as the parent of custody choice.

The psychodynamic factors that may represent loss or injury by parents are examined by Dr. Daniel C. Schuman, and are considered by him as among the more distinctly psychiatric aspects of loss of custody.

Part II goes from a consideration of the genetic and developmental issues to a view of the newer role of the male as a single parent, and finally to an appreciation of the effects of custody loss that is seen as having possible psychological and emotional outcomes for divorced parents that may issue in clear psychiatric symptoms.

Dr. Cynthia R. Pfeffer looks upon divorce as a process that starts with a period of marital disharmony, or "emotional divorce," and proceeds through a series of crises that result in final dissolution of the marriage. As part of this process, she sees the child or children going through a period of grief or something akin to grief that may or may not be different from bereavement that occurs when a parent is lost through death.

In light of what is frequently a long, drawn-out process, the author raises many developmental issues about children upon whom such new stresses are placed. Since divorce is viewed as a process, many factors are involved in the child's learning to cope with new arrangements and tensions, and these are understandingly examined in the chapter that follows.

2

Developmental Issues Among Children of Separation and Divorce

Cynthia R. Pfeffer, M.D.

The rapidly rising divorce rates in the United States have produced a relatively recent but necessary concern about the effects of divorce on children and their parents. This chapter will utilize a literature review and the author's experience working with children whose parents were divorced to highlight developmental issues for parents and children when separation or divorce has occurred.

INCIDENCE OF DIVORCE

In 1950, the United States divorce rate was 2.6 per thousand; in 1970 it was 3.5 per thousand; and in 1977 it was 5.1 per thousand.[24] An estimated 103,000 divorces were granted in July 1979 and during the twelve months ending in July 1979 there were 1,151,000 divorces.[19] This was an increase of 40,000 over the total twelve months, ending with July 1978. The divorce rate in 1979 was 5.3 per thousand. There are no clear estimates of how many divorces involved families with children, how divorced persons remarry, or how many remarriages involved children in the household.

Problems following divorce were estimated in an investigation of 148 consecutive divorce cases in the Dane County Family Court in which 71 percent (105 cases) involved children.[28] In this study, among cases not involving children, only 5 percent were followed by legal complaints but 52 percent of the divorces involving children were followed by legal contests. Furthermore, in 31 percent of the divorces involving children, there were continued intensive interactions between the divorced couple during the two years after divorce. When problems occurred, they centered around finances (50 percent of the cases) and disputes about the children (50 percent of the cases). However in two-thirds of the cases, divorce was not followed by turbulence necessitating court action. In most of these cases, the divorce was followed by either complete separation of the couple or by a mutually satisfactory resolution of financial and child care arrangements.

The reported incidence of divorced families of children seen in child psychiatric clinics is 8 to 28 percent with a median of 15 percent.[11] In one study, 153 consecutive cases entering the University of Wisconsin Child Psychiatry Clinic were evaluated.[28] Fifteen percent (23 families) experienced divorce. Fifteen children were totally separated from one parent and eight children were troubled by postdivorce turbulence between divorced parents. These cases of residual parental conflicts were characterized by disturbed parental personalities and problematic parent-child relationships.

Another study of 400 children referred to the Child and Adolescent Psychiatric Inpatient, Psychiatric Day Treatment, and Psychiatric Outpatient Clinic of the Department of Psychiatry at the University of Michigan during a ten-month period from October 1974 to July 1975 concluded that the rate of occurrence of divorce in this psychiatric population of children was twice that in the general population of children.[11] In that sample, 41.1 percent of the children experienced parental divorce or separation. This percentage may be high because the population included a range of seriously disturbed children who may have intense family turmoil including not only divorce or separation but severe parental psychopathology. Furthermore another reason for the high percentage of histories of divorce among this disturbed group may be the phenomenon that a significantly higher frequency of girls than boys were living in stepparents' households usually with a stepfather. One observation of the study was that living with a stepparent constituted an especially stressful life experience for these girls. This may have contributed to the need for intensive psychiatric intervention.

Data about the ages of children at the time of divorce may facilitate planning a preparatory phase of explanation about the divorce that will suit the developmental needs of the child. In the course of such preparation the parents and child can work through fears, fantasies, and practical considerations for the future changed family system. In one study, younger children predominantly constituted the sample with separated parents.[11] Furthermore, children from stepparent families were usually older. Several implications of this ought to be considered. For example, the stress of parental loss by separation may be too intense for a young child's immature ego to integrate. Furthermore, the introduction of a stepparent especially during adolescence may stimulate the child's sexual and aggressive impulses and interfere with maintenance of appropriate generational boundaries. Further research is necessary to assess whether there are specific phases of development in which separation, divorce, and remarriage may be particularly stressful to the child.

Many of these issues stimulate the need for additional investigation. For example, are children whose parents divorced more vulnerable to serious psychiatric conflicts and disabilities? Second, what are the most vulnerable periods in a child's life for divorce to occur? Third, is there a sexual difference for the degree of risk of psychiatric disturbance when parents divorce? Fourth, are other racial/ethnic factors operative in determining the rate of parental divorce and its effects upon children? Fifth, what is the relationship between the increased divorce rates and our cultural and societal conditions? Sixth, what are the factors that are associated with why some divorces result in resolution of conflict and adequate developmental growth of the child and other divorces result in continued discord and childhood disturbances? Seventh, what are the long-range effects of divorce upon future family structures and parent-child relationships?

THE IMPLICATIONS OF DIVORCE FOR CHILD DEVELOPMENT

Divorce is a process whereby the marital partners plan and implement arrangements for the dissolution of their marriage. Divorce can be viewed as a crisis which starts with marital disharmony and reaches a potential resolution with the divorce decree. Despert[7] spoke of the period of marital disharmony as "emotional divorce."

For children, one effect of divorce is either a permanent, a total, or a partial separation from at least one parent. As a result, it may be expected that a period akin to grief for the child may ensue. The child's reaction, however, may be different from bereavement occurring after the death of a parent. There may be several reasons for this. First, divorce as willfully determined separation by the parents, has the potential to be adequately planned, discussed, and worked through before and after the divorce. Kelly and Wallerstein[13] believed that the choice intervention for preschool children whose parents divorce are those interventions that are made on behalf of the children with their parents. Second, each parent has a possibility of maintaining continued involvement with the child. The child has the potential to express his/her anger, anxiety, sadness, pleasure, questions and opinions to the parent who is separated from the child. As a result, this provides a potential for working through the loss and a possibility of reestablishing a new form of relationship with the parents. Finally, divorce may have positive beneficial effects on the child by diffusing a previously and intensely malevolent family environment. The parents may then be more capable role models and ego supports that positively promote the growth of their child's personality[26].

Divorce is not a specific entity or event. Instead, it is a process within the family's history that works parallel to the developmental phases in a child's life. The ingredients of such a process include a crisis period of marital tension. Such stress may include characteriological incapability between the parents, serious psychopathology of one or both parents, financial pressures, sexual disturbances, and parental career goals. The child, no matter how old, is involved in these dynamic aspects within the family. At times, the child may actually be blamed by the parents for their problems. Often, children unrealistically blame themselves for their parents' difficulties. The child may be terrified by witnessing chronic parental arguments and violence. The child may feel confused, hopeless, and abandoned by the negative, ambivalent, and hostile emotions expressed by the parents. During the time of marital tension, the child may actually be neglected or his/her needs may not be sufficiently gratified. Sara, age eight, is an example of such a stressful phenomenon. Her parents repeatedly argued when her father came home from work. Sara retreated to her room and wept by herself. She had no one to talk to about her sadness over her parents' disagreements. Often, Sara could not finish supper because her parents began to fight. She left the supper table to go to her room. Within two months, Sara lost ten pounds. This was not noticed by her parents but instead the school nurse discovered this on a routine physical checkup.

The resolution of parental conflicts after divorce either may be complete or result in continuing stress of varying degrees. For example, in many cases the parent may have been unable to focus his/her support and empathy upon the child owing to the intensity of the marital conflict, but once divorced, the parent may be better able to invest his/her time and energy in the parental role and respond to the needs of the child. In other cases conflicts after divorce may continue or intensify. Several forms of conflicts after divorce have been observed.[28] One is the parents' postdivorce turbulence in which they continue the same conflicts and relationships that existed before the divorce. Another is the child's sense of turbulence in which the child manipulates the parents to perpetuate continued conflict or to prompt reuniting the parents. A third conflict is when a parent and child join forces to undermine the other parent. A fourth conflict arises when the support system, such as friends and relatives, provokes and influences one parent to continue being dissatisfied with the divorce arrangements.

As can be noted, divorce results in a specific re-equilibrium of the family system and creates a different network of communication, visitation, support, and potential entry of additional people, such as lawyers, judges, therapists, spouses, and stepparents into the family schema. Therefore, to understand the effects of divorce on children, it becomes essential to assess the environmental setting in which the child lives as well as the intrapsychic state of the child before, at the time of, and after the divorce. These variables require a systematic investigation which may elucidate types of intervention programs that may assist a smooth transition around divorce. Since very little is known about the long-range effects of divorce upon a child's development, research of the specific components of environmental and intrapsychic factors that contribute to a child's healthy adjustment to separation and divorce is necessary.

THE CHILD'S ENVIRONMENT IN RELATION TO DIVORCE

Developmental theorists, clinicians, and research investigators have been intrigued by the delicate balance between a child's environment and the specific state of the child's physical and psychological achievement. Divorce specifically alters the environmental structure so that the nuclear family becomes a more open type of family system. The diffusion of spouse interaction and parental support has ramifications for the child's development that are as yet unknown. Divorce produces issues such as new roles of the parent in raising the child, the effects of single-parent households, effects of remarriage and the addition of a stepparent, the type and implementation of appropriate visitation rights of parents, the structuralization of the custody arrangements, the psychological meaning of divorce for the parents, parental adjustment to divorce, and parental adjustment to an altered parental role. Most of these concerns have not been sufficiently analyzed.

An adequate family environment should provide basic life supports for the physical survival of the child, stimulation of the child's emotional, social and cognitive achievements, promotion of stability of intrapsychic development of the child to ensure adequate control over impulses, reality testing, affect regulation and moral stability, and the ability to disengage from the family constellation as part of a process of life-long individuation.[16]

Kelly and Wallerstein[13] noted that during the divorcing period parent-child relationships are fluid and subject to radical changes in character. In fact, sometimes the role of the child in providing support to the distressed parent becomes magnified. McDermott[18] noted that identification with the absent parent was a frequent reaction of children of divorced parents. McDermott used a quotation from Anna Freud who stated that "the reason why a broken home is destructive for a child's development is less in the absence of a parental figure of identification than in the fact that the remaining parent will tend to cast the child into the absent parent's place" (page 425).[18]

Support from siblings may be stabilizing. It has been noted that only children may be more vulnerable to stress and conflicts from divorce because they receive the undiluted parental hostility.[13] The effects of other support systems such as extended family, peers, and teachers must be investigated.

While effects of parenting have been a major interest in understanding child development, there have been few studies of the challenges, vicissitudes, and problems of the single parent. Yet, the rapidly rising divorce rate indicates that the prevalence of one-parent families is increasing. Klebanow[15] believed that there are many universal psychological stresses and pathology associated with single parenthood. Special parental responsibilities include meeting the emotional and nurturing need of the child, providing financial security and furnishing a model for self-esteem and social adjustment of the child. One of the main difficulties for the single parent is preoccupation with these tasks and inability to provide sustenance to the child who is coping with the loss of a parent and the uncertain availability of the other parent. As a result, a major task of the single parent is to provide a state of object constancy and to furnish figures for identification for the child. The role of a single parent requires that the parent take on responsibilities that may have been shared by their spouse. For example, for either a male or a female single parent, motherly functions have to be combined with increased work responsibilities to support the household. There is need to study the differences between the adaptation of single fathers and mothers. This was excellently depicted in the film *Kramer vs. Kramer*. The necessity for the custodial parent to take on responsibilites and parenting tasks which had been previously shared with the spouse was explicitly represented in the film.

There is need to study the effects of divorce upon the parent who does not have primary caretaking responsibilities. One of the only studies of the effects of divorce on fathers pointed out that fathers experience a decrease of influence on the emotional and moral development of their child, on their ability as parents to teach their child appropriate social behaviors, and on financial decision-making functions. These parameters were affected by the degree of separation and absence from their child[10] Another finding of the study was that fathers with contact with their child had increased responsibilities to provide recreational activity for the child. Finally, when the father's involvement with the child was intense, the father felt more satisfaction about his perception of his parental role.

The aftermath of divorce entails plans for continuity of care for the child as well as continuity of the relationship with the parent. It also establishes a realignment of the relationship of the parents to each other. Many believe that it is in the best interest of the child to maintain a meaningful relationship with both parents.[1,2,3,4,6,29] Other studies have concluded that the noncustodial parent should have no right to see his or her child except on the prerogative of the custodial parent.[9] Some believe that a joint custodial arrangement in which both parents have equal custodial privileges and a child moves back and forth between two households is most feasible.[21] Still others emphasize that it is important to determine the preference about the custodial arrangements.[22] In any event, the role of visitation must be systematically addressed as well as the best types of custodial arrangements. It may be that each of the above approaches is valid and the arrangements must be determined on the basis of the specific factors within the family. Furthermore, in many cases at the time of divorce parents are not aware of the full significance of establishing visitation rights, so that it may be helpful to have available predivorce and postdivorce counseling to discuss these issues. Benedek and Benedek[3] suggested that studies be undertaken to evaluate the particular effects of total parental absence and partial parental absence resulting from divorce, the effects of various visitation plans on the parents and the child, and to assess the age of the child in relation to the decision for custodial rights and visitation privileges.

Divorced parents are often stressed by an additional readjustment of remarriage and integration of previous unhappy family experiences into a new family structure. Often in remarriage, a parent may feel a deep sense of uncertainty about his or her ability to sustain a satisfactory family. One of the most dramatic and typical problems of reconstituted families is of the stepparent being excluded from his or her role function.[9] For example, in the fatherly role of disciplinarian, a stepfather may be reluctant or unable to provide discipline for the stepchildren. Similarly, a stepmother functioning to provide nurturing may be inhibited by the time it may take to gain the trust and acceptance from the stepchildren. Often the stepmother may be seen as competing with the natural mother for the child's affection. Finally, the relationship between the stepparent and the child's natural mother and father must find a satisfactory state of equilibrium. This may vary from intense hostility or noninvolvement to empathy, friendship, and agreement upon parental role function. The most appropriate types and methods of psychotherapeutic treatment for reconstituted families are in need of systematic study.

THE EFFECTS OF DIVORCE UPON THE CHILD'S INTRAPSYCHIC DEVELOPMENT

Since the divorce agreement provides for a plan of long-range rearrangement of the family unit, one would expect effects upon the child to be evident throughout the child's formative years. Nevertheless, there have been very few studies of the specific influences of divorce upon symptom development, ego functioning, and moral development of children. Lacking are the systematic investigational approaches of the relationship of divorce to the specific age and sex of the child at the time of divorce. Among the studies already reported, the results are not conclusive and have led to controversy.[8] However, these studies have provided striking findings which may point out new approaches for research, means of planning and working out divorce procedures, and methods to provide psychotherapeutic intervention.

McDermott[18] studied the intake records of 1487 children up to age fourteen who were evaluated at the Michigan Children's Psychiatric Hospital from 1961 to 1964. The children were divided into two groups: those whose parents were divorced (116 children) and those whose parents' marriages were legally intact (1349 children). It seemed that divorce was a special stress for which the children coped by acting out rather than by neurotic symptomatology. There was a cluster of symptoms including running away and poor home and school behavior which was associated with higher rates of delinquency in the divorced group. Furthermore, there was a greater incidence of depression (34.3 percent of the children) in the divorced group. In many cases the children believed that they had caused the divorce by their own wrongdoing. Some children even justified the parents' divorce by believing it was due to the child's acting out behavior and symptoms. Other complications of the divorce process were noted to be aberrations in the child's moral development. The children found it difficult to internalize parental moral demands over impulse expression while the parents were splitting up and acting out towards each other. These problems were reflected in the child's expression of sadistic impulses which were similar to those witnessed and expressed by the parents in their marital disagreement.

Another study of 400 children referred to the University of Michigan Youth Services from October 1974 to July 1975 found that children of divorce living in single parent homes did not differ in symptoms from children of divorce living in stepparents' homes.[12] However, significantly higher proportions of children from the divorced single parent and stepparent group exhibited overt aggression towards parents and sexual behavior problems than children from intact families. This study did not fully distinguish these effects for different ages or sexes of the children. Indications were, however, that adolescent girls with stepparents had significantly higher incidences of aggression, sexual behavior, drug involvement and school difficulties, than girls from intact families. Additional studies with large sample sizes and appropriate comparison groups are needed to assess the types of developmental deviations associated with sequellae of divorce.

The methodology and results of one large-scale study are worthy of special note since this study attempted to evaluate children's reactions to divorce when it occurred at different phases of the child's life.[13,14,26,27,28] The entire sample included 131 children between the ages of two and one-half and eighteen years from sixty families. The children and the parents were studied after the initial separation of the parents and one year later. All children were considered to be within normal developmental range prior to the separation.

In one phase of the study, thirty-four preschool children were evaluated. Among the youngest children who were two and one-half to three and one-quarter years old, all the children responded to the separation with acute regression in toilet training, irritability, whining, acute separation anxieties, sleep problems, cognitive confusion, increased autoerotic activities, return to transitional objects, escalation of aggressive behavior and tantrums. Regression occurred most precipitiously for the children who had not been given an explanation for the parent's departure. However, by follow-up time one year later, the regression, enhanced aggression, and fearfulness disappeared in most children. The children who still manifested symptoms were in families in which there was continued parental discord and the parents were unable to adequately administer to their children.

Among the middle preschool children who were three and three-quarters to four and three-quarters years old, regression was less apparent although the children were irritable and cried. Aggression increased and separation anxiety were expressed as specific thoughts and ideation. The children voiced a desperate desire for a father. The children played out threats to their survival and intense helplessness. There was explicit expression of self-blame for the separation of their parents.

In the oldest preschool group who were five to six years old, they exhibited heightened anxiety and aggression. They seemed to have a reasonable understanding of the changes in the family constellation. They were able to express sadness, longing for their fathers, and a wish to restore the unbroken family. Among the more vulnerable children there was intensive expression of depression, low self-esteem and prolonged investment in oedipal fantasies.

Among the group of fifty-seven latency age children, ages seven to ten years, there were two distinct groups. One group was of twenty-six children who were seven and eight years old and the other was of thirty-one children

who were nine and ten years old. The younger group was severely immobilized by suffering while the older latency group shared greater capacity to understand the consequences of the family destruction. The younger
group most strikingly showed sadness and was aware of their suffering and
had difficulty obtaining relief. Many of the younger group denied responsibility for causing the separation. At follow up, the younger latency group
had modified responses. The intense pain disappeared and children were
resigned and realistically accepted the divorce.

The older latency age children seemed to perceive the family reality with
a soberness and clarity and were actively struggling to master their conflicts, fears, and their need to have continuity. Their coping devices were
activated to the maximum to defend against painful feelings. Feelings of
shame of divorce were common. To overcome their painful feelings, activity and play were frequent modes of coping. A marked distinguishing
feature of this group of children was their conscious intense anger expressed
at their mothers and fathers. The anger was expressed in temper tantrums,
diffuse demandingness, and dictatorial attitudes. About one half of the
children experienced a deterioration in school achievement and school
behavior patterns.

Among the adolescent group, who were thirteen years or older, there were
twenty-one boys and girls. The adolescents experienced the divorce as an
extraordinarily painful event, felt intense anger at the parents, sadness, a
sense of loss, and feelings of betrayal by the parents. Intense feelings of
shame prevented the adolescents from sharing their feelings with peers. Of
significance were the adolescents' fears about their own future as a marital
partner. Fortunately, in the follow-up one year later, most of the turmoil
engendered by the divorce was beginning to subside.

Sorosky[24] in a review of the effects of divorce on adolescents summed up
significant problems for adolescents as (1) fear of abandonment, rejection
or loss of love; (2) an interference with the resolution of adolescent conflicts; and (3) an intense fear of personal marital failure. He noted that
what the adolescents wanted most was a re-establishment of generation
boundaries in which to relate to parents as authority figures not as friends.
As a result the parents must work together to provide loving support and
firm limits. Based on these dramatic observations, specific recommendations may be developed for parents planning to divorce. These recommendations would be based on the specific issues of the age of the child and his
developmental needs. The recommendations would take into consideration
the appropriate best time for the separation and divorce, specific tasks required of each parent, and a prediction of the long-range developmental
needs of the child.

Reactions of children in single parent households and reconstituted family situations deserve attention. Neubauer[21] focused on the relationship be-

tween the single parents and the child. He noted from a case report of a girl whose father abandoned the family after the child's birth that the child was unable to master the oepidal conflict. The relatively healthy adjustment of the child was credited to the mother's influence. However in contrast to this case, there may be a vast difference in the psychological development of children who have never known their father in comparison to those whose relationship to the father was severed after attachment was formed. Such differences in the child's reactions may include the types of fantasies the child has about the absent parent, the degree of the idealization of the long lost parent and simultaneous quality of ambivalence, trust, empathy, and adjustment with the remaining parent, whether the effects are different from those when a parent is lost by death, the quality of interaction with early loss with the constitutional factors of the child, and the effects of race/ethnicity and socioeconomic class on the psychological and environmental adjustment of the child and family.

Kestenbaum and Stone[15] studied the clinical cases of thirteen girls who lost their fathers by death, separation or divorce between the periods of infancy and adolescence. In each case, the missing father and the girl's intense longing for him were key dynamic issues. The girls thought about their ideal loving and protective father who if he returned to the family would create an idyllic home life. Devaluation of the mother following the departure of the father was present to varying degrees. Failure to complete oedipal resolution and impairment of feminine identification were noted in all cases. All the girls repeatedly talked of wanting their fathers to be reunited with the rest of the family. This study pointed out the need for more systematic study which could elucidate a means of planning therapeutic intervention. For example, could the effects of father loss be modified in cases where the father could maintain close relationship with the daughter?

A contrasting issue is that very few studies have been done on the effects of children raised in single parent households by the father. Recently, more fathers are being granted custody of the children. Berlin[5] examined special developmental problems experienced by daughters living with their fathers in single parent families. In infancy, single father-female infant couples face critical issues of attachment and bonding because the father must work and find a parent substitute and in many cases there are several surrogate caretakers. This may distort development of object relations and the separation-individuation process which may lead to character problems, neurotic, and psychophysiologic symptoms throughout childhood and adolescence. In the oedipal stage the young girl may have no female models which may create a "triumphant attitude" in the oedipal triangle in which she has the father as lover. The exclusive relationship with the father may make relationships with women difficult. An advantage may be that the daughter's talents, abilities, and intellectual development may be recognized early and encouraged in the extreme. In adolescence, the problem can become extreme. Rebellion and striving for independence may not be possible because of the close relationship between the father and daughter. Often in these relationships the father tends to gratify the daughter's wishes. As a result, the girls may be unable to accept boys their own age because of comparisons with their idealized fathers.

IMPLICATIONS AND CONSIDERATIONS FOR FUTURE INVESTIGATIONS

No doubt, study of divorce can be challenging, fascinating and imperative. Not only must issues of age and sex of the child be described as a factor for risk from divorce, but social class in relation to cultural expectation and ability to provide stable family life must also be evaluated. There are, to date, no systematic studies of the long-term effects of divorce upon children. For example what are the effects of divorce upon the child's future ability to be an adequate parent and marital partner? Is there a higher frequency of divorce in families where the parents of one or both partners were divorced? A group of at-risk children which should be studied are second-generation offspring of parents who divorce.

In conclusion, understanding developmental factors relevant to divorce may help families plan the time and arrangements of divorce more adequately. It may provide a better means of offering counseling and psychiatric intervention to children and their parents. The wisdom derived from such developmental understanding may promote greater sensitivity within the legal channels that execute divorce arrangement. Finally, it is hoped that divorcing parents may be better able to "divorce their own conflicts with each other from their understanding of the developmental needs of their children." In this way, the best interests of the child may be accomplished.

REFERENCES

1. Abarbanel, A. Shared parenting after separation and divorce: A study of joint custody. *American Journal of Orthopsychiatry*. **49**:320–329 (1979).
2. Anthony, E. J. Children at risk from divorce: A review, *In: The Child in His Family*. Anthony, E. J., and Koupernik, C. (Eds.). New York: Wiley and Sons (1974).
3. Benedek, R. S., and Benedek, E. P. Postdivorce visitation. *Journal American Academy of Child Psychiatry*. **16**(2):256–271 (1977).
4. Benedek, E. P., and Benedek, R. S. Joint Custody: Solution or illusion? *American Journal of Psychiatry*. **136**(12):1540–1544 (1979).
5. Berlin, I. Vicissitudes of father and daughter relations in single-parent families. *Psychiatric Opinion*. **16**(9):9–11 (1979).

6. Buxton, M. Controversy in child psychiatry: Non-custodial parent visitation rights. *New Jersey State Bar Journal.* **82**:18–21 (1978).
7. Despert, J. L. *Children of Divorce.* Garden City, New York: Doubleday, (1962).
8. Farson, R. Parental divorce: A growth experience for children? *American Journal of Orthopsychiatry.* **48**:183–184 (1978).
9. Goldstein, H. S. Reconstituted families: The second marriage and its children. *Psychiatric Quarterly.* **43**(3):433–440 (1974).
10. Goldstein, J., Freud, A., and Solnit, A. J. *Beyond the Best Interests of the Child,* New York: Macmillan Publishing Co. (1973).
11. Greif, J. B. Fathers, children, and joint custody. *American Journal Orthopsychiatry.* **49**:311–319 (1979).
12. Kalter, N. Children of divorce in an outpatient psychiatric population. *American Journal of Orthopsychiatry.* **47**(1):40–51 (1977).
13. Kelly, J. B., and Wallerstein, J. S. The effects of parental divorce: Experiences of the child in early latency. *American Journal Orthopsychiatry.* **46**(1):20–32 (1976).
14. Kelly, J. B., and Wallerstein, J. S. Brief interventions with children in divorcing families. *American Journal Orthopsychiatry.* **47**(1):23–39 (1977).
15. Kestenbaum, C. J., and Stone, M. H. The effects of fatherless homes upon daughters: Clinical impressions regarding paternal deprivation. *Journal American Academy of Psychoanalysis.* **4**(2):171–190 (1976).
16. Klebanow, S. Parenting in the single parent family. *Journal American Psychoanalysis.* **4**(1):37–48 (1976).
17. Lewis, M. The latency child in a custody conflict. *Journal American Academy of Child Psychiatry.* **13**:1635–647 (1976).
18. McDermott, J. F. Divorce and its psychiatric sequelae in children. *Archives of General Psychiatry.* **23**:421–427 (1970).
19. Miller, E. Psychotherapy of a child in a custody dispute. *Journal American Academy of Child Psychiatry.* **15**(3):441–452 (1976).
20. Dept. of Health, Education and Welfare. Monthly vital statistics report–National Center for Health Statistics, DHEW Publication **28**(7):2.
21. Neubauer, P. B. The one-parent child and his oedipal development. *The Psychoanalytic Study of the Child.* **15**:286–309 (1960).
22. Roman, M., and Haddad, W. *The Disposable Parent.* New York: Holt, Rinehart and Winston (1978).
23. Siegel, D. M., and Hurley, S. The role of the child's preference in custody proceedings. *Family Law Quarterly.* **11**:1–58 (1977).
24. Sorosky, A. D. The psychological effects of divorce on adolescents. *Adolescence.* **12**(45):123–136 (1977).
25. *Statistical Abstract of the United States.* Washington, D.C.: U.S. Department of Commerce–Bureau of the Census (1978).
26. Wallerstein, J. S., and Kelly, J. B. "The effects of parental divorce: The adolescent experience." *In: The child in His Family* Anthony, E. J., and Koupernik, C. (Eds.) New York: Wiley and Sons pp 479–505 (1974).
27. Wallerstein, J. S., and Kelly, J. B. The effects of parental divorce: Experiences of the preschool child. *Journal American Academy of Child Psychiatry.* **14**:600–616 (1975).
28. Wallerstein, J. S., and Kelly, J. B. The effects of parental divorce: Experiences of the child in later latency. *American Journal of Orthopsychiatry.* **46**(2):256–269 (1976).
29. Westman, J. C., Cline, D. W., Swift, W. J., and Kramer, D. A. Role of child psychiatry in divorce. *Archives of General Psychiatry.* **23**:416–420 (1970).
30. Wooley, P. Shared custody. *Family Advocate.* Summer: 6–9 (1978).

This chapter briefly reviews the small amount of research literature available on the male single parent and attempts to pull together the most salient points from information now presently available. Most of the problems experienced by the male single parent are very similar to those encountered by the female single parent. However, there are some problems which appear to be unique to the newly developing role of the lone father. At the heart of this is the fact that there is a lack of social sanction and a lack of institutionalization of the single male parent role. He is still viewed as an anomaly by society and this life-style seems to make people uncomfortable. As a result the male single parent encounters a good deal of difficulty arising from the biases and prejudices of the courts, the current institutions, and society in general. The male single parent has little community support and has a good deal of difficulty in achieving individual supportive relationships as compared with the female single parent today. In spite of these handicaps, current research generally indicates that the male single parent does well and that the problems he encounters are not insurmountable. There are a number of needs which the mental health professional can meet. These range from the development of classes and support groups for single parent fathers, encouraging changes in the legal system, both in the courts and through legislative action and through advocating for the male single parent. Much further research is needed on motherless families involving a wider range of individuals from all socioeconomic levels.

3

The Male Single Parent

Kenneth K. Berry, Ph. D.

For a father, divorce generally means the loss of custody of his children. Estimates of contested custody awards to mothers vary from 85 to 90 percent. However, as a result of the feminist movement, the increasing divorce rate, and some changes in the courts' attitudes, there are increasing numbers of children being reared primarily by their fathers. Recent figures indicate that close to 900,000 children under the age of eighteen live with their fathers alone. To date, there have been only a few studies of single fathers and their children, but those that have been done are generally positive, concluding that the problems faced by the male single parent are not insurmountable. The sole negative voice has been that of Arnold Katz[9] from his study of an Australian sample of fathers, but his data were derived only from a questionnaire and did not include a comparison with a like sample of female single parents.

This chapter will review the relevant research, examine the problems faced by the male single parent, and look at the role of the mental health professional in meeting his needs. The discussion will be limited to those families which have been disrupted through separation or divorce and will not include families which are motherless as a result of maternal death. It would appear that there may be differences between those fathers who actively seek custody of their children and those who have it thrust upon them as a result of mother desertion; unfortunately, however, none of the research examines this variable nor distinguishes between these two groups.

The bulk of the extensive literature on the single-parent family has dealt primarily with the female single parent. However, since 1970 there have been a number of studies in the United States and abroad which have examined the male-headed family. The significant studies have been those of George and Wilding,[7] which used an English sample; Todres,[21] Schlesinger and Todres[18] in Canada; Mendes,[15] Orthner, Brown and Ferguson,[16] Smith,[20] Gasser and Taylor,[6] Keshet and Rosenthal,[11] Schlesinger,[19] Bartz and Witcher,[1] DeFrain and Eirick,[5] and Katz.[9] There has been a spate of other papers written, but these are representative of those examining and presenting research data.

All of the studies have a number of shortcomings, resulting primarily from sampling problems. The recent samples are generally small, with the exception of Katz,[9] and may not be representative. Some of the data have been derived from questionnaire studies, but most of the studies have relied primarily upon interviews with nonrandom samples. Some studies such as Katz[9] and DeFrain and Eirick[5] relied solely upon questionnaire data.

In general, the studies indicate that fathers are doing at least as well as, and perhaps better than, their female counterparts carrying out the dual role of wage earner and primary parent. However, the methodological weaknesses of the research must be borne in mind. The samples do not appear to be cross-sectional, but this may be the result of the fact that less skillful and more poorly educated fathers do not have the opportunity, financially or in terms of job flexibility, to seek custody of their children. Katz's Australian sample appears to represent a better cross-section of that population than have previous studies. His results present the gloomiest picture of the male single parent, but it appears that most of the difficulties he found are those most often reported by female single parents. Unfortunately, Katz did not collect any comparative data.[9]

With these methodological weaknesses in mind we will examine the problems of the fathers and the children, make recommendations, and point out directions for future research, as well as examining the role of the mental health worker in dealing with single fathers and their families.

THE FATHERS

The majority of the studies of male single parents yield very similar results. Virtually all report demographic data indicating that single fathers are at the higher socioeconomic levels. They have higher than average incomes, are frequently employed in professional managerial positions, and their educational level is high. The fathers rate very high on economic and social stability, as shown by their incomes, job stability, and the fact that they usually live in their own homes and move infrequently.

It is clear that these fathers are not representative of the general population. There are probably a number of reasons for this. First is that locating a representative sample of single fathers is most difficult. In finding subjects most researchers depend upon word of mouth and requests for subjects through the popular media. It seems highly probable that those fathers at the lowest socioeconomic levels are not likely to volunteer as research subjects. Probably a more important variable is that the courts may be much more willing to grant custody to individuals of higher socioeconimic status. Thus, it may well be that at least in the United States and Canada, these subjects *are* representative of the present population of male single parents. As greater equality is achieved in the courts, this picture may change. (Katz presents the only study in which these are not the demographic findings.)[9]

Regarding personality variables, there are no data available which would separate male single parents from other males. However, there are suggestions in most of the studies that the fathers are highly nurturant, highly assertive, confident, and at least give lip service to a high degree of structural organization in their daily lives. It is clear that with most of the fathers their motivation to do well is extremely high.

With the assumption of single parenthood the fathers report far-reaching changes in their living routines, roles, and shifts in their life's priorities. There are changes in attitudes toward their careers and many of them report shortened working hours and decreased opportunities for job change and promotion. Any of the necessary flexibility present in their work clearly depends upon the good will of their supervisors and coworkers, since, as Mendes[15] points out, the male single-parent role has not yet become institutionalized and systems do not make allowances for the life style.

Virtually all the studies find that in the first year the fathers experienced withdrawal and disengagement, during which they spent much of their time at home. This was of relatively short duration, and soon after they began going out socially. Most fathers reported feelings of loneliness and depression; some reported somatic symptoms. The first year of single fatherhood appears to be a generally stressful one; however, most of the fathers at the time of the studies presented themselves as being well-adjusted. This finding may in part be a result of the high desirability of presenting an image of competence, partially because of the continual threat of court custody change hanging over the heads of many of the fathers. Katz[9] believed that the personal and child management problems reported by his Australian fathers represented only the "tip of the iceberg" (p. 527) and that a lone father does not fare any better, and perhaps fares worse, than the female single parent. However, his sample was drawn from the organization,

Parents Without Partners, and it may well be that these men were participating in this group in order to further their search for a new mother because of the very fact that they were doing poorly at the job of parenting.

It is clear that the assumption of the dual role of primary parent and wage earner is a very stressful one and that the role strain and adjustments are not easy. These difficulties may be greater for the male single parent than for the female single parent because of the lack of role models in our society, combined with problems of societal prejudice which the female single parent does not face today. This is discussed in greater detail below.

Smith[20] found that men made a successful and relatively easy transition to single parenthood provided they had earlier experienced sufficient anticipatory socialization, low levels of role strain, and had personal goals which could be reasonably easily obtained. He concluded that fathers found it much easier to make the transition to single parenthood when they:

1. Had actually gained experience in child rearing;
2. Had received some education about children and child development;
3. Had participated earlier in household responsibilities;
4. Had actively been involved in discipline of their children prior to the separation, and
5. Had nurturing supportive interaction with their children.

He reported that the transition to single parenthood was enhanced by a high degree of confidence, if the father had no need to prove that he was a successful parent, and had adequate knowledge and resources necessary for meeting both his children's needs and his own emotional needs.

Readjustment of life priorities appears to be one of the more salient changes which occurs in the father that moves from the traditional role into the single parent role. As one of Levine's fathers said, "It was an attitude. People at my level didn't run out the door at 5 o'clock. It's not really that there was so much work to do. My boss was a man with a penchant for working long hours. I think he wanted me and everybody else to create the impression that we were killing ourselves the way he was. I could have maintained that job if I could have worked two or three nights a week until 7 P.M. But there was no way I could do that. It was true that I was always running out the door at 5; the daycare center wasn't too keen on parents who didn't pick their kids up at 6." Or, as another father stated, "I'd be sitting there at the end of the day in these meetings worrying if I was going to be able to get out in time to pick Stephanie up. Nothing we were talking about seemed as important to me as that."[13] (p. 32)

THE CHILDREN

Some studies have found that boys exceed the number of girls in male single-parent families. In a few cases fathers had custody of sons while mothers had custody of their daughters. It appears that courts tend to operate on the assumption that fathers perform better at raising male children. The number of male and female children is almost evenly divided in the majority of studies; however, most of the families consisted of about two children.

Virtually all the research examining the impact of the father upon children's development comes from studies of father absence. Separation from the father consistently appears to result in difficulties for the children, regardless of their sex.[3] We have almost no research data examining the effects of mother absence. The older material from deprivation studies was not actually examining so much mother absence, as *parent* absence. In most of the studies the children were not only deprived of "mothering," but also of "fathering" or rather "parenting."

It would seem logical to assume that the children of male single parents undergo experiences and consequences much like those of children who reside solely with their mother following separation or divorce. The bulk of the data would suggest that the children of single fathers experience some transitory problems involving insecurity and some behavior problems ensue immediately following the family break-up. The reason for the lower incidence of reported child problems from the fathers is apt to be a result of the two variables mentioned above, namely a high need to present an image of competence, and/or the fact that the fathers, particularly those in the United States, have gone through a highly selective process as a result of the biases of the courts.

Two areas in which fathers most often express concerns about their children are in the areas of their own ability to meet their children's emotional needs (i.e., to engage in expressive behaviors as opposed to instrumental ones, and sex and sex-role identification). The sexual concerns were expressed primarily by those fathers who were faced with rearing daughters alone. Mendes[15] found that fathers over forty were reluctant to discuss sexuality and sexual mores with their daughters. One of the fathers had requested the daughter's fourth-grade teacher to discuss the "facts of life." In anticipation of his daughter's developing sexuality, this father had bought sanitary napkins and a sanitary belt which he left in the bathroom. The father and his daughter never openly discussed this, but since that time he replenished the supply in the bathroom whenever needed. Single fathers in the studies also seem to be much more aware of their daughters' than their sons' sexuality.

Lowenstein and Koopman[14] did do a comparison of the self-esteem of boys living with single-parent mothers and those with single-parent fathers. They examined the sons of twenty female single parents and twenty male single parents. The results indicated that there were no significant differences in self-esteem between these two groups. There were no correlations between the self-esteem of the boys, the length of time they had lived in a single-parent home, and the quality of the parental relationship. Of interest, however, was the fact that they reported that the self-esteem of the boys who had frequent contact with the noncustodial parent was higher than that of those boys who saw the noncustodial parent less than once a month.

A considerably higher number of fathers in Katz's Australian study reported difficulties. Slightly over one-third of the fathers reported concerns about their children. Approximately 31 percent felt that their children were having "school or health problems" and about 24 percent of that group said that they were having problems with disobedience. These fathers felt responsible for the children's difficulties, slightly less than half admitted that they were experiencing too much pressure in the dual role, and about 36 percent felt that the job was too much for one person.[9]

In regard to personality variables, other than self-esteem, we can say very little about personality variables and the effects of mother absence upon children's development at this time.

LIFESTYLE

Although a large percentage of the fathers in the studies had actually participated in household activities and child care prior to their divorce, only a very few of them had carried the responsibility alone. Thus, for most of the fathers a complete change in lifestyle was necessary. Fathers, like mothers, when faced with the necessity of assuming all the tasks previously shared, tend to move in one of three directions: They will reduce the quality of the tasks performed, reduce the number of tasks, or hire outside assistance. The popular picture of the male single parent is that of one who hires a housekeeper. All the studies found that only a minority of fathers do this. Some of the fathers attempted it, but were displeased with the quality of the work done, or found themselves unable to meet this expense. Most of the fathers in the studies assume the responsibility themselves for all the household tasks. A large percentage of them do share the responsibilities for some of the work with their children. The statistics from the studies indicate that 80 to 90 percent of the fathers reported that they themselves performed the household functions of cleaning, preparing meals, food shopping, laundry and ironing. The household tasks which they found most difficult were clothes shopping and clothing repair. Some fathers reported that although they enjoyed meal preparation, the necessary regularity of this brought about some degree of pressure. A large percentage of the fathers reported that they already had expertise in areas of cleaning and cooking. One study did find that almost half of the fathers indicated that they obtained some assistance in food preparation.[11]

CHILD CARE

Many of the fathers reported that they had engaged in a significant amount of child care prior to their divorce, but there were some who indicated that they had not engaged to a great extent in such activities as bathing and dressing of the children.

Virtually all the fathers reported the necessity of utilizing others for daily child care. A number of fathers hired babysitters during the first year, but most became somewhat dissatisfied with this and the bulk of them preferred using daycare for their younger children. When the fathers began going out in the evenings, locating evening sitters did present problems for some of the fathers. Most had not had the responsibility for contacting babysitters during their marriage and many felt somewhat uncomfortable in doing this. Many of the fathers reported that some mothers were reluctant to let their teen-age daughters sit for them. As the fathers became more active socially and developed relationships with women, one might expect them to use their women friends for child care. This does not appear to be the case and in fact it appears that fathers tend to be somewhat protective of their children in terms of the adults with whom they permit them to spend time. In the studies which examined this area, it was found that they rarely permitted adults other than themselves time with their children.

Most of the fathers regarded their time with their children very positively. In fact, one gains the impression that their children and their relationship with them rapidly become the top priority in their lives. Although it is a fictional account, the development of the parent-child relationships depicted in *Kramer vs. Kramer*[4] appears to accurately reflect what occurs in the lives of many fathers when faced with the situation of rearing their children alone. They move from peripheral parental involvement to making their children the first priority in their lives.

FRIENDS AND SOCIAL LIFE

It is commonly reported by female single parents that following divorce they find that their old friends who are married tend to move away from them and their relationships become less important as newer relationships are developed. This does not appear to be as clear-cut for fathers since many of them do not report this as a problem. However, they do tend to drift toward the development of new relationships with single people. Seemingly, they feel that single people and particularly single parents have more understanding of their situation. Although there is an initial disengagement, the larger percentage of the fathers begin active dating well within a year of their divorce. Most of them maintain active sexual activity, but some do report dating problems. Although one would expect single parenthood for fathers to be fairly short-lived, this does not appear to be the trend and many of the fathers studied seemed satisfied with their lifestyle and were not anxious to enter a new marriage. As one father said, "I would never get married to satisfy my son." Another father from the same group stated, "I would love to be married again, to have someone help me with the family and household chores. I get tired at times of doing it all. But, I am not going to rush into another marriage." And a third stated, "We are definitely a whole family."[1] (p. 6)

In regard to their sexual activity, they seemed to strive to protect their children from knowledge of this and generally engaged in sex in settings other than their home. DeFrain and Eirick[5] reported that the majority of the single fathers felt the children were unaware of their sexual activities.

It is clear that in general the fathers do maintain relationships and continue social life; however, they may not have the level of activity that would be present if they did not have their children. Most of the fathers did not express any great degree of dissatisfaction with their social life.

The single fathers report that living with the children alone had a strong beneficial effect upon the parent-child relationship. Bartz and Witcher[1] reported that their fathers were almost unanimous in describing the relationship between themselves and their children as "affectionate," "close," and "better than before the divorce." One of their fathers commented (page 5) "I would have never known the girls as well as I know them now had I stayed in the marriage," and "having the sole responsibility opens up all kinds of opportunities for having a closer family." Another father said "We've worked on things like 'I love you,' which we hadn't done in the past. We are working at showing affection."[1]

PROBLEMS

It is clear from all the studies that becoming a single parent requires a far-reaching shift in lifestyle and priorities for the father. With these drastic changes, it is not surprising that there are problems. Most of the fathers tend to downplay difficulties and, as stated before, it may well be that because of the biases of the courts and their selection processes, at least in the United States and Canada, the fathers do exceed the average parent's competency. However, almost all the fathers do report some problems, particularly during the first year of their parenthood.

The most frequently cited problem is that of finances. The expenses are greater because of the necessity for child care and because of the pressure of time. Many of the fathers must depend upon already-prepared foods from the market, most of them have little time to shop for "bargains," thus there are increases in their general budget. Another factor is that many of the fathers have large legal bills since they are not only responsible for their own legal fees during the divorce and custody suits, but generally also responsible for those of their ex-wife. As one of Bartz's and Witcher's fathers told them, "It cost me 22 pounds, $18,000 and six months' total effort."[1]

Most of the fathers continue working, but a very small number elect to stay home. This brings about some serious financial problems. Although there are government-assistance programs available, such as Aid to Families of Dependent Children (AFDC), funds from such programs are much more likely to go to single-parent mothers than fathers. It seems highly probable that using such programs also would tend to jeopardize some fathers' maintenance of custody since many courts would tend to view this as a lack of independence and competence of fathers.

One of the topics which one hears discussed most frequently at single fathers' meetings, and at men's rights groups, is bias in the courts. In 1975, a New York family court judge, in denying a father's petition for custody of his four-year-old son, stated "Fathers don't make good mothers."[13] On January 2, 1974, the Utah Supreme Court rejected a claim by a father for continuing custody of his child, and observed that the father's "contention might have some merit to it in a proper case if the father was equally gifted in lactation as is the mother." This was the oft-cited Arends case.[13] In states which have passed statutes giving fathers equal rights in custody proceedings, the same high rate of awarding children to mothers appears to be continuing. Even after custody is awarded, single fathers' legal difficulties frequently continue. In some cases, fathers who are strapped financially, following expensive divorce and custody suits, must pay their wives alimony even in cases where the ex-wives' and the fathers' incomes are equivalent. Rarely is child support awarded to a single father. Fathers frequently complain there is a period of legal harassment following the award of custody. The ex-wife is usually free to utilize the courts, because in most states, often even years later, the father may still be responsible for his ex-wife's attorney's fees when she applies to alter the custody or divorce decree.[12]

Rena Uviller, who is now a judge on the bench of the New York State Supreme Court, recalls during her days as Director of the Juvenile Rights

Division of the American Civil Liberties Union, getting many calls from men who wanted to know if it were legally possible for them to get custody of their children. She said that many of them believed that they had no rights at all under the law. Judge Uviller was one of the two attorneys who filed a petition for a *writ of certiorari* to the United States Supreme Court on the Arends' case but was unsuccessful in having it even reviewed by the Supreme Court.[2]

Rorris published a paper in the *Minnesota Law, Minnesota Practice Manual,* in 1971, in which he stated

> Except in very rare cases, the father should not have the custody of the minor children of the parties. He is usually unqualified psychologically and emotionally; nor does he have the time and care to supervise the children. A lawyer not only does an injustice to himself but he is unfair to his client, to the state, and to society if he gives any encouragement to the father that he should have custody of his children. A lawyer who encourages his client to file for custody, unless it is one of the classic exceptions, has difficulty collecting his fees, has a most unreasonable client, has taken the time of the court and the welfare agencies involved, and has put a burden on his legal brethren.[17]

In the midst of the ongoing legal harassment of the male single parent frequently encounters, he often complains that he is forced to deal with prejudice in his neighborhood, day-care centers, school, and from professionals such as pediatricians and dentists. One father reported that at his first teacher conference the first question his son's teacher asked was "Why would the judge give *you* the children?"[2] In his book, *Who Will Raise the Children?* Jim Levine tells of a father from Manhattan's Upper West Side who was looking for day-care and was asked questions such as, "Why do *you* have him?" "Why can't he be with his *mother*?" and, "Why can't he be with *your mother*?" This father said that he dealt with it by going into what he refers to as his histrionic welfare routine: "I just started screaming, 'God damn it, if you don't give me day-care, I'm going to write to the governor and say I had to quit my job and go on welfare because you wouldn't give me day-care!" His son was accepted. Announcements which the day-care center sent home are all addressed "Dear Mother." However, "this whole thing has really made me a feminist!" the father said (pages 31–32).[13] Bartz and Witcher reported that several of their fathers said schools tend to assume that when the primary parent is a male he will not be able to do the things mothers do, such as send cookies or serve as "room mother." One of their fathers became a Cub Scout "Den Mother" and reported that people expressed uncertainty about his ability to do the job.[1]

Recently a teacher called the author in response to a newspaper article to tell him that she felt that the children that she had taught during her many years of teaching who lived only with their fathers definitely had more emotional problems, did poorly in school, and suffered from lack of supervision at home as demonstrated by their chronic sleepiness, because the fathers rarely had set bedtimes for them. When teachers are aware that a child lives alone with his or her father, it appears that they frequently seem to keep a close eye for signs of emotional disturbance, poor nutrition, and ill health. One father recalled how, after being advised by the teacher to take his child to a physician because she felt the child was sick (he dutifully took the child each time to a pediatrician) asking the pediatrician if she would write a letter to the school reporting her findings that the child was in good health and growing properly. It was not until then that the teacher stopped the calls to him complaining about his son's health.[2]

Neighbors often seem to present difficulties for the male single parent. One father reported that after his wife left and he had obtained custody of his two sons, neighbors in his middle-class neighborhood did not speak to him and there were occasions when garbage was dumped on his front lawn. Some fathers who have remained in their old neighborhoods report that neighbors refuse to speak or in some cases to even let their children interact with his. However, it appears that these fathers are a minority. Other parents are frequently uncomfortable in letting their daughters spend the night with his since there is no woman in the house. In the case of the female single parent they would think nothing of letting a daughter or a son do this.[2]

Because of the lack of social sanction and lack of institutionalization of the single male parent role, he is still viewed as an anomaly by society and this lifestyle seems to make people uncomfortable. At the National Conference on the Male Single Parent, held in Omaha in 1978, one father reported housing difficulties in a midwest city. He told of apartment managers making statements such as, "We don't want your kind here." He said that they were not able to elaborate upon what they felt "his kind" was. Many people, of course, want to be helpful, but do not realize the effects of the attitude they convey. Relative strangers, or acquaintances (generally older females), are free with advice about children's nutritional needs, emotional needs, food preparation, and child rearing. One midwestern father observed that negative responses from people (both men and women) are common. As he said, "They view a man's wanting to rear his children as an irresponsibility."[2]

Female single parents develop feelings of solidarity and willingness to provide mutual support and help, but this is not often the case with men. Many of the men expressed feelings of isolation and oftentimes didn't even know of the existence of other male single parents in the community. The lack of the "buddyship" relationship which Goldberg[8] discusses may in part be responsible for this. In current society, men are not permitted to have the same kind of supportive "buddy" relationship which women are able to enjoy, perhaps because of the fear of homosexual overtones.

Although part of this tendency toward isolation may be self-imposed, much comes from others' attitudes. For example, one young single father, who upon arriving in a new town was instrumental in setting up a babysitting cooperative, became concerned about the apparent failure of the enterprise until he discovered it was thriving, but that he was being excluded by never being called to sit. Difficulties in locating evening child care are common in that most middle-class mothers of female teenagers are uncomfortable in letting their daughters sit for a single male.[2]

These attitudes and biases are not without their effects upon the single father. From observation of groups discussing problems, it appears that the father may have a tendency to become somewhat suspicious and may tend to be overprotective and overcautious with his children. Many fathers report that even though they try to avoid it, they find themselves thinking, "What will the teacher, the neighbor, the dentist, say?" Some appear to feel personally responsible for each dental cavity in their children's mouths. They seem to feel, perhaps realistically so, that they are being continuously judged.[2]

Many problems experienced by the male single parent are a result of the overwhelming time and role demands placed upon the single parent. As one father who failed to anticipate the weight of day-to-day responsibilities said: "Most men don't appreciate the logistical problems of the suburban housewife. The problem of coordinating the laundry, chauffering, and food purchasing was a nightmare. It was the biggest shock of my life, especially because it interfered terribly with my relationship with the kids. We had screaming, raging, and crying until I broke down and pleaded helpless and realized I didn't have to do everything. Now I pay lots more attention to what my five-year-old wants to do to help out."[13]

About half of the fathers report stress in trying to coordinate all of the various jobs of caring for the home, and the children, as well as meeting the responsibility of being the sole wage earner. As noted above, most of the fathers reported they did not rely upon hired help and received little or no help from their extended family. It appears that the children provide the father with a good deal of assistance in carrying out the daily responsibilities of life. As Levine[13] reported, the fathers discover that their children are capable of assuming a good deal more responsibility than they, or their ex-wife, ever believed or allowed. One father reported "I give them more freedom and responsibility now." (p. 38). Another of Levine's fathers with sons age twelve, ten, and eight, said, "In order to have some time for myself, and in order to spend a better quality of time with them, I had to enlist more of their cooperation. Bruce vacuums on weekends, Richard and Todd clean the bathrooms and they all help out during the week. I can't understand why we didn't share more before. The kids don't begrudge it; they understand that they are part of the team, part of a family." (p. 39).

Children still face the problems of postdivorce adjustment whether they live with their father or their mother. Most of the fathers reported some child problems during the first year, but most felt these were transitory and in most of the studies most of the fathers reported that at the time of the data collection their children were doing well.

The kinds of problems which fathers reported shortly after divorce included children's feelings of possessiveness toward the father, fear that the father would leave, also the development of bedwetting and frequent crying. Some fathers whose marriages had been particularly stressful on the children reported that they found that their children became more relaxed and seemed happier.

Katz's Australian sample presented a slightly different picture in terms of problems with the children. Thirty-seven percent indicated that they were having difficulty with the children. Approximately 35 percent felt that the problem was related to household difficulties; apparently many felt that they had difficulty in getting their children to assist them with household responsibilities. Twenty-four percent of the group reporting problems stated that the problems were related to the child's behavior, principally relating issues of noncompliance. A slightly greater number (32%) of the fathers reported school or health problems. Only a small percentage of this group (9.5%) felt that there were role model problems. It is of interest to note that almost 70 percent of this group reported that they had sought help primarily from relatives, friends, social workers, and physicians. In most cases only approximately half of the people seeking help felt that they had been helped.[9] DeFrain's and Eirick's study, which to date is the only matched comparison of male single parents with female single parents, found that the majority of parents of both sexes felt that the initial effects of the divorce were quite stressful to the children. However, seemingly the children did make an adjustment and the parents felt that their performance in school and their physical health were unchanged. A few of the parents, both male and female, reported higher grades, but none reported lower grades following the divorce. Essentially, they found no differences between the male and female single parents on any of their variables.[5]

In those studies in which the children's peer relations were explored it was felt that there had been little change. There were only a few cases in which any degree of stigmatization was felt. Even Katz's Australian sample did not report difficulties in peer relationships. However, Bartz and Witcher[1] reported that one father told of a comment made to his child, "You live with your daddy. Something wrong with you?" (p. 6)

Some fathers were concerned about sex role problems. This was generally in regard to their daughters. At this time, the only parent-child gender variables which have been explored are those involving the effects of father absence upon role development of children. To date we have no data available on gender identity of children reared in motherless homes. One of Levine's fathers reported an anecdote about his four-year-old indicating that some children did learn early that males, too, can be nurturant. "Looking at a mare and a colt in a meadow, he tugged at his father's sleeve and said, 'Look at the daddy horse taking care of his baby.'"[13] (p. 136)

REWARDS

Most of the studies have been oriented toward exploration of the problems of single fathers. However, most of them do indicate that there are rewards and satisfactions reported by the fathers.

Keshet, Finkelstein, and Rosenthal concluded that instrumental responses, e.g., cooking, cleaning, bathing the children, and meeting their affective needs successfully, serve as proof to the father of his parental adequacy and, by extension, his personal adequacy. In most of the studies, fathers report a good deal of joy and satisfaction in meeting the responsibilities to the children and come to recognize strong nurturing abilities within themselves. They come to derive satisfaction in the feelings of accomplishment as a parent.[10] Orthner, Brown and Ferguson drew the following conclusions: "If there is one most impressive conclusion we can make from our interviews with single-parent fathers, it is this: These fathers feel quite capable and successful in the ability to be the primary parent of their children. The confidence they express and the satisfaction they derive in fatherhood is very difficult to deny. . . .Their sense of pride in being able to cope with the challenge of parenthood and in seeing their children mature under their guidance is a major compensating force (for any problems of role strain and adjustment).[16]

Many fathers reported greater feelings of autonomy since the single parent doesn't have to consult with another adult on the issues of parenting and managing a home. Some fathers were very pleased not to have to deal with intrafamily conflicts around discipline. Most of the fathers had expectations of children sharing in the responsibilities and tasks of running a home and felt that their children had developed positive feelings about the acceptance of responsibility.

Keshet and Rosenthal summed up the positive aspects of single father-hood:

> The experience of marital separation has brought the men into the sphere of what is commonly considered the woman's world—of being responsible for children's growth and satisfying children's needs. The men responded by restructuring their daily lives in order to care directly for their dependent children. As a result, fathers felt more positive about themselves as parents and individuals. A majority of the men reported that being a single parent had helped them to grow emotionally. They felt they had become more responsive to their children and more conscious of their needs, a responsiveness they reported as reaching out to other adults as well.[11]

NEEDS

Many of the single fathers' difficulties arise from the fact that male parenting roles have not been given social legitimacy. The following appear to be the primary needs of the male single parent. Some of these are unique to single fathers, but many of them reflect the needs of single parents regardless of their sex.

1. *Child care.* Most of the fathers find it difficult to obtain adequate day-care facilities at the time of day when they are needed. Most would find it quite helpful if services were extended into the evening hours and if transportation were provided to and from the facility for the children. Some type of formalized care after school hours is also needed. Orthner, Brown, and Ferguson recommended the placement of child-care facilities in shopping centers to assist fathers who have small children in order to decrease the frustration involved with shopping with small children and in shortening the time required for this.[16] Many fathers would be able to benefit from assistance in setting up babysitting cooperatives.

2. *Classes and groups for single-parent fathers.* Many of the fathers could make use of classes with a focus on parenting and household management from their viewpoint. Some fathers have reported that books and advice from female single parents are of limited value. The area in which many new fathers feel uncomfortable is that of dealing with the emotions of their children. Specific education on child development and the handling of emotional crises would be of great benefit. Because of the isolation which many of the fathers have

reported, a mutual support group would be most helpful. Orthner, et al. advocated the counterpart to "big brothers" as being needed for these fathers who are rearing daughters alone.[16] This would be especially helpful where there is little or no relationship between the daughter and her mother either on the part of the mother or through mutual choice. Although there are probably many females available to the daughters of single fathers, many of the fathers have reported that it is not easy to locate one who wants a relationship with their daughter rather than using the daughter as an entrée into his life in her search for a husband. As one daughter said to her father, "How can I tell if a woman likes me for me, or likes me for you?"

3. *Changes in the legal system.* The legal area continues to present problems for fathers before, during and after divorce. Courts continue to be affected by the so-called "tender years presumption." In general, all things being equal, the mother is considered to be the better parent. Many of the fathers who had engaged in custody suits had had to prove the mother unfit and have had to present evidence supporting themselves as "super fit." It is rarely true that mothers must prove their "super fitness" and the father unfit to gain custody. Although some states do have statutes calling for equal consideration of mothers and fathers in regard to child custody, many states do not have this. Even in those states which do have equality written into their laws, it is frequently not practiced in the courts.

4. *Financial assistance.* Financial help needs to be made as readily available to the single father as it is to the single mother. A double standard continues to exist in most countries.[19] Fatherless families usually find it much simpler to obtain government financial assistance, but motherless families are frequently not included in family benefits. The assumption underlying this is that a man should not stay home to care for his children, but should go out to work. There should be some changes in the attitude of courts in awarding child support to motherless families from the mother when she is capable of paying this.

5. *Public education.* Fathers often report that there is little community support for them and their families. The male single parent is still considered an anomaly by most people. Public education would go a long way toward combating the prejudices about motherless families. Most individuals' first contact with the court system is through divorce proceedings. One of the most common reactions heard by the author from fathers (and mothers too) is shock and disbelief at the rules, procedures, and difficulties encountered in obtaining "justice." Thus, we need public education not only about the role of the male

single parent, but also about the law. Newspaper articles, factual realistic movies and novels such as *Kramer vs. Kramer* can go a long way toward educating and raising the consciousness of the public and legislators to the problems faced by fathers in their attempt to remain parents to their children.

THE ROLE OF THE MENTAL HEALTH PROFESSIONAL

There are a number of activities which can be carried out by the mental health professional to be of assistance to the male single parent and his children. Perhaps a prerequisite to these is examination of, and development of, awareness of their own prejudices and biases when they are providing assistance to the single father and his family. The professional must be open to alternative life styles and parenting alternatives. Woody feels that the professional should maintain an objective stance, offer evaluative information from a scientific base, should as a family advocate help the more able parent "vigorously pursue a legal decision," when faced with a custody suit (p. 62).[22] As part of his or her special role as a family advocate, the professional should see to it that biases and prejudices do not prevent the utilization of professional services as a result of institutional restrictions. Mendes[15] recommended that professionals should work toward the formation of parent education groups specifically for fathers.

Our society in general should be assisted by professionals to become more aware of the needs of the single father and should work toward creating opportunities to provide education of young males in developing child care and home management skills. We need the development and funding for more programs such as that sponsored by the Federal Office of Child Development, "Exploring Childhood." In this program students in high schools and junior high schools can gain academic credit for work done in preschools, elementary schools, and day-care centers. Through these programs, junior high and high school students, both male and female, gain knowledge about child development as well as experience in dealing with young children. However, it would seem that only a few males have the courage to take advantage of this program.[13] The males who did take advantage of the program apparently responded quite favorably. As one whom Levine[13] interviewed (p. 157) said, "It was a fantastic experience. I guess I didn't just learn about kids. I learned about myself. That I was really good at teaching them. You know, this is the only class in high school where I ever felt successful—where I've really done something."

The professional also has additional responsibilities for the generation of more research data. Our knowledge of the children growing up in motherless families is presently indeed very small. We need comparative studies of motherless families and fatherless families. We need data to determine what the effects upon child development are of growing up in a motherless home. Being reared in a fatherless home apparently can have disastrous effects upon children. Does growing up without a mother have similar consequences? We also need to examine such variables as social, class, and cultural differences of the male single parents and their children.

Single fathers have demonstrated their competence and willingness to carry out successful parenthood. It appears very reasonable to assume that they can rear responsible, healthy children. None of the writers doubt that the number of single fathers will increase. The time has come to develop appropriate programs to assist fathers to assume their changing roles and responsibilities to society's children.

REFERENCES

1. Bartz, Karen W., and Witcher, Wayne C. When father gets custody. *Children Today*. 7:2–6 (1978).
2. Berry, Kenneth K. The male single parent: Experiences and prejudices. Presented at the symposium: *The Male Single Parent: An Emerging Parent Role,* the American Psychological Association Annual Convention: New York, September 3, 1979.
3. Biller, Henry B. *Father, Child, and Sex Role*. Lexington, Massachusetts: D. C. Heath and Co. (1971).
4. Corman, Avery. *Kramer vs. Kramer*. New York: Random House (1977).
5. DeFrain, John, and Eirick, Rod. Coping as divorced single parents: A comparative study of fathers and mothers. Presented at the symposium: *The Male Single Parent: An Emerging Parent Role,* the American Psychological Association annual convention: New York, September 3, 1979.
6. Gasser, Rita D., and Taylor, Claribel M. Role adjustment of single parent fathers with dependent children. *The Family Coordinator*. 25:397–401 (1976).
7. George, Victor, and Wilding, Paul. *Motherless Families*. London: Routledge and Kegan Paul (1972).
8. Goldberg, Herb. *The Hazards of Being Male*. Plainview, New York: Nash Publishing Co. (1976).
9. Katz, Arnold J. Lone fathers: Perspectives and implications for family policy. *The Family Coordinator*. 28:521–528 (1979).
10. Keshet, H. Finkelstein, Harry, and Rosenthal, Kristine M. Fathering after marital separation. *Social Work*. 23:11–18 (1978).
11. Keshet, Finkelstein, Harry, and Rosenthal, Kristine M. Single parent fathers: A new study. *Children Today*. 7:13–17 (1978).
12. Levine, David I. *How to Get a Divorce With Or Without a Lawyer*. New York: Bantam Books (1979).
13. Levine, James A. *Who Will Raise the Children?* New York: J. B. Lippincott (1976).
14. Lowenstein, Joyce, S., and Koopman, Elizabeth J. A comparison of the self-esteem between boys living with single-parent mothers and single-parent fathers. *Journal of Divorce*. 2:195–208 (1978).
15. Mendes, Helen A. Single fathers. *The Family Coordinator*. 25:439–444 (1976).

16. Orthner, Dennis K., Brown, Terry, and Ferguson, Dennis. Single-parent fatherhood: An emerging family life-style. *The Family Coordinator*. **25**:429–437 (1976).
17. Rorris, James T. Separation agreements—Support for the spouse and minor children: Minnesota family law. *Minnesota Practice Manual*. Minneapolis: University of Minnesota, (1971).
18. Schlesinger, Benjamin, and Todres, Rubin. Motherless families: An increasing societal pattern. *Child Welfare*. **55**:553–558 (1976).
19. Schlesinger, Benjamin. Single parent fathers: A research review. *Children Today*. **7**:12 (1978).
20. Smith, Richard M. Single-parent fathers: An application of role transition. (EDRS No. ED 151 719) Tucson, Arizona: The University of Arizona (1976).
21. Todres, Rubin. Motherless families. *Canadian Welfare*. **51**:1–13 (1975).
22. Woody, Robert H. Fathers with child custody. *The Counseling Psychologist*. **7**:60–63 (1978).

This chapter takes as a starting point the clinical reality of almost universal anger in custody cases and presents a theoretical formulation for its etiology. The basic postulate is that a guiding parenthood fantasy as a personal introject serves as a part of each individual's psychic structure. Loss of custody through divorce or contested visitation damages such psychic structure and leads to re-emergence of primitive feelings of loss or injury. These primitive affects constitute a regressive pull which is in dynamic balance with self-restorative narcissistic fantasies which give resilience to the personality under stress.

Inability to accept and to take responsibility for emerging affects leads contesting parents into power struggles and almost inevitable tendencies to project responsibility for the dilemma onto external sources. Such alloplastic focus creates "manipulative" custody contests with the common psychiatric experience of two parents acting like character disorders, each blaming the other for it. When denial of affect becomes dense in these situations, it is functionally/dynamically psychotic, though such diagnosis is usually not warranted formally.

Psychiatric expertise is the ability to bring clarity to the network of motivations in a case, not necessarily to decide the outcome of the case administratively. Countertransference problems are inevitable in psychiatrists and attorneys working in child custody cases, especially the impulse to control outcomes. Nonpsychiatric factors are important as well as psychiatric evaluations of attachments and motivations. No doctrine has yet been evolved as a reliable single decisional criterion, but a new decisional concept of patterns of parenting is suggested as an attempt to synthesize important factors including parenthood fantasies, behavior, and reciprocal attachments among parents and children.

4

Psychiatric Aspects of Custody Loss

Daniel C. Schuman, M.D.

A startling clinical reality emerges from psychiatric work with families involved in custody disputes. This is the phenomenon of a quality of bitterness and anger between parents which is rare in most of their other human contacts. Such feeling is often oddly "out of character" and is accompanied by a dramatic, qualitative, negative shift in the way one parent views the other one.

Why does this happen, and how does it work; and ultimately, how can people thus engaged be worked with? Concepts like pride, shame, greed, and revenge are certainly involved in this phenomenon, but such concepts are only descriptive; they fail to explain causes or to advise on strategies. This chapter presents a theoretical formulation of the etiology of parents' emotional reactions to custody losses, with the intent that understanding the causes will lead to more reasoned responses by decision-makers.

Custody loss is a frontal assault on parenthood, and parenthood status per se is a major intangible, structural, integrative force in day-to-day personality function. To be sure, tangible bulwarks of social function are also shaken in divorce and custody disputes. The importance of parenthood as a status or role does not dispute the fact that "real" objects are lost as well, including children, money, or property. Indeed, even the nuclear family itself is a real object which is similarly lost in divorce. But the thesis in this chapter distinguishes parenthood as a crucial introject quite apart from children as "real" objects.

The psychiatric viewpoint on custody provides insight into intangible, elemental inner forces which forge attachments to real objects; these inner forces invest such objects with their meaning for the individual and make the objects "worth fighting for" when their possession is threatened. Parenthood itself assumes the emotional reality of a tangible object when a custody dispute erupts.

A custodial conflict exaggerates the personal issue of what it means to be a parent. Must custody always be "lost" or "won?" For this discussion, yes; because custody here is defined as possession of a child or children. That implies that even when there are visits between a noncustodial parent and the child, that the custody is temporarily lost, at least on some level of fantasy in the mind of the custodial parent.

In a custody "battle" one may try to consider who the winner or the loser is. Lost custody is, after all, lost and gone even if it is regrieved over and over again. But the paradox is that custody "won" is then lost over and over, because often the custodial parent feels a renewed sense of threat, injury, and loss with every visitation. That is one of the major shocks and disillusionments to parents who "win" bitter custody disputes. They find that they then have to refight the struggle all over again on the issue of visitation. As a result, often the presumed winners are losers too. The crisis recurs and recurs.

So custody is always lost by everyone, at least temporarily, or ar least as a felt threat. It follows that a custody dispute or its twin, a visitation dispute, is each individual's nightmare and each individual's projectional screen. The felt threat entangles everyone involved, including the parents, the psychiatrist, the attorneys, and also the judge. Frequent blurring of roles and customary ego distance contributes to countertransference.

Countertransference particularly affects attorneys as well as psychiatrists. Both professionals become members of the family, with attendant regressive potential that they ought to be aware of. But each profession has characteristic defenses which obscure the intensity of emotional involvement.

The people who are most likely to be overlooked as emotionally entangled parties are the attorneys. Attorneys are central characters because they are charged with acting on the case; that is, they at least have to act up if not act out. If they must act, they can encourage spite, greed, obstinacy, and externalization of blame; but they can also soothe, console, and act with a calm voice as a real friend of the family. The attorneys' respective transferences and countertransferences are almost impossible to study because of the way the rules of legal process are established. Attorneys "have no feelings" themselves. They are specifically charged with acting, and the action orientation of the attorneys protects them from having to deal with their own feelings.

Psychiatric countertransference in custody cases is inevitable and powerful. It is not always positive. The impulse to polarize is virtually irresistable for everyone; this should serve to remind psychiatrists in custody cases to be alert to their mission, which is to offer a psychiatric point of view as discussed below. Countertransference helplessness, guilt, or anger leads evaluating psychiatrists to assume authority over their patients by attempting to dictate what ought to happen. At such times, psychiatrists become directive toward their patients or haughty about Family Courts not doing the "appropriate thing." In fact, these are cases that the courts often cannot control either. Family Court presides over family process, but cannot dictate to it. The families are stronger than the courts.

To discuss the inner psychiatric basis for emotional reactions to a custody dispute, this chapter first considers the dispute as a crisis. As such, it evokes a potential regression which taxes an individual's resiliency. The psychiatric point of view then becomes very useful in translating between the inner world of injured fantasy and the courtroom or other "real world" where contemporary custody issues are forged.

CUSTODY LOSS AS A REGRESSIVE CRISIS

Crises can be opportunities for growth and development. Divorce is sometimes described like this, especially when it is a response to a destructive marital relationship. But the crisis involved in the loss of custody is almost always disruptive because it threatens the security of major family and personal systems that have served to sustain individual parents' self structures.

The disruption is potential rather than inevitable because the crisis creates a regressive *pull*, not necessarily a regression in *itself* or not necessarily regressive behavior, and this distinction is important. The distinction is made manifest by the puzzle of why some families wilt under the stress of custody/visitation disputes, while others brace tensely but master the crisis. Usually those masterful families don't come to mental health referral and the nature of their crises often goes unexamined.

Jaques[3] makes the point that when a social organization fails, people have to reabsorb their depressive/hopeless or their bad/persecutory and angry objects back into themselves; they have to take back ownership of these kinds of primitive concepts of objects that the social system somehow bound up. Parenting is a social system or contract that faces failure in custody disputes.

The quality or the degree of intensity of the need for a fantasy resolution of primitive disappointments, failures or injuries partially indicates the likelihood of *giving in* to a regressive pull in the face of a custody dispute. At least, it indicates the potential strength of the regressive pull on an individual. It does not reveal much about the individual's strengths in resisting that pull, but it indicates what the individual is going to be up against in facing loss of custody if an examiner can only obtain understanding of what those fantasies are, of what the possession of the child "solved" for the parent.

The existence of a marriage binds or solves "bad feelings" via a marital fantasy that is covert but magically restorative against the early wounds. Similarly, parenthood has even more powerful restorative fantasies attached to it that confer hope and optimism for some kind of new life through the child.[1] Just as divorce challenges and destroys the marriage fantasy, the more magically restorative parenthood fantasies are destroyed by a custody dispute. Since the parenthood fantasies are structurally reparative, the loss of parent status in a socially unacceptable way is an actual injury to the psychic structure of the person's self.

Losing a child in a custody dispute is socially unacceptable. At best, it elicits sympathy, but more likely a covert social stigma pertains: "There must have been something wrong with that person that he or she did not prevail." The impact of such a groundswell of social pressure and expectation shows how pervasive in our culture is the sustaining nature of the parenthood role or fantasy.

One pointed example involved an Italian immigrant man who had built up a successful business. Complaining of his old world domination and abuse, his immigrant wife petitioned for custody of the children and to have him evicted. This turn of events impacted on the man as an intolerable afront to his manhood, which he experienced as being identical with *paterfamilias*. If he could not be given social charge of his family and children, he would only be a child himself. Thus, he stated his personal reality that if evicted, he would have to return to his parents in Italy. The court ordered him out of the house, and he did leave his business and children. The children's loss of their father was culturally impelled by his rigid inner concept that the shame of loss of head of household status destroyed his adulthood.

More frequent examples involve women who unexpectedly lose custody of their children and precipitously decompensate to frank depression or even grossly disordered thinking. On recovery, many have revealed their lack of anticipation of how socially devalued they would feel if stripped of the honor of being maternal custodians. (It is equally true that often the covert resentment involved in "winning" custody proves to be a major stress after custodial obligations become more apparent.)

Socially repugnant loss of legal custody stands in contrast to socially acceptable ways of losing parent status. For example, the death of a child is a very poignant and tragic occurrence, but with no social opprobium attached. Unless the child who dies has been invested with some covert or denied evil or angry aspects of the self, death or some other such loss of parent status usually leads to grief with idealization rather than a sense of injury with retaliatory, spiteful hate as the reaction.

There is a loss of parenthood status through any custody fight or through any reappearance of the other parent during visits. This loss of parenthood status is at best an insult, more likely a threat, and very possibly a felt injury to the parenthood fantasy which restores the psychic self. The regressive pull which drags every parent involved in a custody dispute *toward* feeling injured or wounded or maimed through the destruction of that particular parent's unique parenthood fantasy is an entirely different kind of regressive pull from the kind involved in almost every other loss.

It is completely socially unacceptable to have "your" child "taken away" and it is more personally grievous and injurious than almost any other loss. Rightly or not, custody or visitation disputes are usually perceived by the parent involved as having this "taking my child away" flavor. Though a parent involved in a custody dispute always feels that he or she is acting in the best interests of the child, the threat to the parent's self leads the parent to relinquish her or his customary ego distance from the child. Interests and needs come to be perceived as identical; this is a regressive drift toward a symbiotic point of view. It is quite rare for a parent faced with a custody dispute genuinely to consider the possibility that the children's best interests may be best served by being elsewhere than with her or him.

As noted above, the strength of an individual's regressive tendency or pull is dependent on the intensity of the parent's need for parenthood status (or the parenthood fantasy) as a means of restoring or sustaining the self against old (forgotten), early problems. Put another way, the tendency to regress is inversely proportional to the ability to believe in one's own intactness despite the injury. Or, alternatively, the regression is inversely proportional to one's fantasy or ability to repair by oneself the damage of the injury to one's self.

It may be that the belief in such self-sustenance is akin to a retreat into narcissism. This is especially true if the process of turning inward to one's self leads to the abandonment of external commitments and responsibilities. At such points, the self-repair has become rigid and brittle, as was the case cited of the Italian immigrant man above. (A paradoxical reversal of narcissistic flight may be the need to preserve the self by fighting for custody of a child whose possession the parent does not genuinely desire—as though "for the principle of it.")

If a parent who faces potential loss of custody lacks such (magical) belief in self-sustenance or self-repair, then there is a very powerful likelihood of regression to a power struggle in order to win, so as to retain or regain the structural and magically restorative power of the parenthood fantasy. One such case involved a maternal custodian whose child had genuinely undergone some abusive overstimulation by the father which the mother had helplessly permitted and even participated in. Faced with a custody fight, she became desperate, and genuinely came to believe her own polarized description of the former situation, a variant of the "Little Red Riding Hood" fable (cf. Bettleheim's thought-provoking analysis of this particular myth in *The Uses of Enchantment*). She emerged from a period of severe psychiatric disorganization with a fixed conviction of her husband's dangerousness. Despite massive continuing psychiatric intervention, she entangled two children in her perceptions of their being beleaguered covictims of paternal assaults. Mother and father came to engage in protracted and inconclusive litigation about custody, visits, schooling, and property that dissipated the family's emotional and financial resources. Father was equally unable to relinquish the struggle, but mother's perceptions and accusations against him were more obviously self-serving in that they helped to ward off major psychiatric decompensation on her part.

The vast majority of parents do not fall to either extreme described above. A parent confronted with potential loss of custody may have sufficient inner resources or other, nonmarital, sources of support to enable her or him to sustain the regressive pull of the threat of loss of custody without resorting to regressive behavior itself. If the (magical) belief in self-sustenance can stop short of narcissistic withdrawal or retaliatory defensive attack against a (projected) perceived external threat, then the parents can negotiate reasonably and constructively within the field of stress that is represented by the potential loss of possession of the child.

If the parents both don't desperately need a parenthood fantasy to achieve intactness of themselves, then they will both be able to resist the regressive pull and will be able to retain control of the child's destiny as their consensus task. They will be able to keep the custody dispute out of the courts. That is the best resolution, the best process in the face of the need for conscious decisions regarding custody.

NATURE OF THE REGRESSION

If parents fall prey to regressive behavior in the face of a custody dispute, it can be helpful to identify certain aspects of the phenomena involved. Everyone who is asked to work with families in such turmoil has to defend himself. It is common to see in helpers a cycle of disbelief (denial), outrage, scapegoating, cajolery (bargaining), depression; and ultimately, despair, futility, or cynical deprecation of the misery involved. Such pained responses often coexist with altruism that is tenaciously and defensively clung to. Such reactions are discernible in all levels of professional competence: judges, attorneys, psychiatrists, probation office personnel, and even court office staff such as secretaries and switchboard operators who have to bear the brunt of the most frequent communications of distress by litigants.

One major characteristic of such parental regression is that in the course of such regression, threats and perceived injury to self or children are magnified. What the parent reacts to is what *may* happen or what the parent fears will happen, not what is happening. A complaint is often *phrased* in terms of what is happening, e.g., what a noncustodial parent is doing during visits, or what the custodial parent is doing to interfere with visits; but such phrasing is a thinly veiled disguise against the anxiety of what is feared will happen or what may happen in the future.

Such altered perception of self in-the-world represents a decrement in ego functioning. The nature of this regression flows from the perception that the experience is at least a threat and more likely is an actual psychic injury that occurs without the person's awareness of his or her own participation in setting the stage for the injury via the idiosyncratic harboring within the self of relatively unrealistic hopes and expectations of either marriage or parenthood.

This injury that flows from the destruction of the parenthood fantasy either inspires or evokes fear or anger. Such feelings are a reflection of concern about further invasion and destruction of the psychic space or are a retaliatory effort to defend oneself. Children literally *are* the psychic space of the parent via the parenthood fantasy. These feelings of fear or anger are essentially emergency responses that tend to be characteristic of that individual, but these emergency responses are all universally desperate. This quality of desperation and anger is remarkably characteristic whether the parents involved are grim, frantic, belligerent, or bitter. They can either be quietly desperate or loudly desperate, but they are all desperate. Few courts are presented with a custody or visitation dispute without a parent's sense of being damaged or without that parent's being angry or desperate about it.

The rare exception to this is when there is denial of a threat, denial of the injury and denial of the anger. Such dense denial usually leads to displacement of the reason for the dispute onto the children. For example, a custodial mother may say, "It isn't that I don't want my ex-husband to see the children on visits, the children don't want to go. I don't blame the children because Daddy locked them in a closet last time, so whatever they want is OK with me." Or a noncustodial father may say, "I realize the children don't want to see me because their mother has brainwashed them against me. It isn't their fault that she is such a liar, but I have tried to save them from her so I will pursue the litigation for their sake. I know that whatever I have done in the past or will do now is only in their interests; they may need some discipline because she is too lax, but I would never harm them."

Such saccharine, bland, displaced affect then leads to a much more intransigent, byzantine battle. From the standpoint of communication analysis, these are skew patterns in which each partner perceives only the other, not the self, and sees the other in dichotomous, negative terms, which may be valid as far as they go. But the percepts are cartoons: caricatures of *parts* of the other's personality which represent the self's worst fears of the other. And such externalized percepts consistently evade and excuse any of the person's own particular participation in or responsibility for the process. Indeed, when parents enmeshed in such skew patterns of communication are confronted with their own responsibilities, they quite often become overwhelmed with anxiety.

This anxiety represents the breakdown of a defensive system based on projection. It is functionally psychotic even in an otherwise intact personality. "Psychosis" is used here in a dynamic sense, not in a diagnostic sense. These people should not be diagnosed (and certainly not in writing) as being psychotic, but they have lost the ability to sense that the place of origin of the affect is inside themselves. The origin of the affect is sensed as being outside, displaced and projected onto the child. "It's not my affect, it's my child's affect;" this is operationally psychotic. Sometimes it leads to a bizarre, truncated folie à deux. Using the case vignettes immediately above, the child really does then present as being afraid of the noncustodial parent and being unwilling to participate in visits, or as parroting the custodial parent with a remarkable appearance of having been brainwashed even without such intent by the custodian.

Such extreme results of parenting fantasies are the *potential* outcome in custody disputes, though thankfully they are relatively rare. It is important to identify such outcomes as the result of a threat to *parenting* fantasies as distinct from *marriage* fantasies because the two processes of divorce and custody disputes often overlap although they are not congruent.

Family courts do see increasing numbers of unwed parents, almost all of them mothers. (It is still very rare to have an unwed father being given custody of his child.) But today it is possible to entertain and to actualize the fantasies of parenthood without going through the formalities of marriage. It is becoming increasingly socially acceptable for women to select men to impregnate them out of wedlock, and what may evolve in the next social cycle is a movement for men to select women to bear them children as single paternal parents. This opens the door to increased numbers of contests about custody of children who formerly were called illegitimate. Unfortunately, this affords the opportunity to study the destruction of parenting fantasies in "pure culture," i.e., in the absence of marriage fantasies that have led to a legal union. From the standpoint of the custodial parent, these would be parthenogenetic children; the parent would believe them to have only a single parent, him or herself.

It is probably impossible to generate a complete list of parenting fantasies that precipitate such regression by virtue of their unrealistically restorative magital powers. Indeed, it is important to realize that the fantasy *itself* does not generate a regression. The fantasy becomes available to examination only when threatened by the circumstance of its being challenged in a custody dispute after it has been reified by childbirth. What generates the regressive behavior is the deeply despairing, helpless, or angry forces deep within the personality which the fantasy assuaged. Nevertheless, it does seem that in clinical practice some particular fantasies are relatively common.

One of these is the quasiconscious notion of maturity and its ally: escape from a childhood that has been fraught with helpless noneffectance. Parenthood confers a presumption of adult status, power, and competence. If the parents were perceived as helpless, stagnant, or inept, parenting may offer a fantasy reaction formation: an opportunity to escape one's own parents' fate or style.

Other parenting fantasies flow from the concept of complementarity: having a child will complete me, make me whole, happy. A child may transform a parent in other ways also: change her/him from bad to good or alter her/him sexually. Parenthood may free the parent from guilt over her/his own sexuality or may relieve her/him of felt pressures and burdens entailed in having sexual feelings.

Some custody fantasies involve symbiotic concepts, i.e., that the child is integral to the parent and that neither one could survive without the other. A related symbiotic concept is that of the parthenogenetic child who has only one parent; that parent denies any need for another parent of the opposite sex by the children. A subvariant of this symbiotic concept is the idea that custody is inherent in the female gender, that loss of custody is equivalent to castration and suddenly not being female any more. This fantasy has been fostered by our cultural practice in the last seventy-five years of automatically giving custody to women. Courts will start seeing an analogous fantasy more and more in men as the culture shifts toward accepting more nurturance in men and a more obvious attachment between men and their children; at the same time, the fantasy in women will sustain quite a realistic threat due to the cultural shift toward "gender neutral" custody determinations.

There are also family fantasies involving custody concerning the child's being the bearer of the family torch or the bearer of the family seed. The child, for example, may protect the family from disintegration. "If we as a family lose this child, we become unimportant or our family name disappears." Some of the vicious custody battles that occur in courts involve litigation not between two natural parents but between parent surrogates, e.g., a maternal aunt and uncle versus paternal grandparents. Not infrequently, the father's parents will have invested their grandchild with the power to continue the family. They become afraid that if the child is raised by someone with a different last name, they and the child will somehow disappear or dissolve.

Perhaps it should be emphasized that the discussion above focuses on more pathologic and pathogenic fantasies. One is much more accustomed to taking for granted altruistic, respectful, and nurturing concepts of parenting as reasons for bringing a child into the world. Custody disputes present an unwelcome opportunity to perform psychiatric autopsies on pathogenic fantasies which have been unable to sustain frightened parents in their desperate need to remain intact and at the same time to share parenting functions.

CASE STUDY

Illuminating fantasies is extremely difficult, especially at a time of crisis, but it can be done. Discerning such fantasies in more or less intact people can provide a sense of orientation about how to approach studying more intensively distressed people who do wind up in custody disputes. This case is unusual in that it emerged as a result of the long-term treatment of two individuals whose marital litigation with other spouses was not the presenting problem; the two patients individually and jointly resolved their individual and network complications without formal resort to adversary process.

Anne, twenty-seven years old, is a college educated senior laboratory technician with credits achieved towards a Master's degree. She was referred for psychotherapy for depression during the breakup of her childless marriage. She had married an ineffectual man who clung to her while she disparaged him. In the process of the divorce, she was propositioned by her own attorney and was relatively promiscuous with several different men. Her motivation for divorce was an increasing sense of impasse and lack of self-fulfillment in her marriage, and an increasing sense that her husband was no longer able to meet her needs. She had married him in her early twenties in a relatively desperate bid to break away from her own strife-torn family. Anne subjected herself to binges of bulimia which led to substantial weight gain.

In initial psychotherapy, she demonstrated considerable desperate isolation of affect, but a therapeutic breakthrough occurred with her growing insight that she repeatedly incorporated a man into herself in an almost literally oral fashion in order to achieve possession of his penis, and thereby a sense of self-identity through him. For her, a penis represented identity, but she remained vulnerable to her own sense of unimportance because the penis could always be taken away from her. This sense of vulnerability to helplessness led her later on to attacks of rage against a man who could not satisfy her, but her eating symptoms and promiscuity decreased remarkably.

Anne met Joe, who was in the process of divorcing his wife, Sue. After a period of courtship, Anne and Joe came to live together and to consider marriage. In the process, Joe's son, Samson, (whom I will also call Sam) became the focus of substantial conflict. Samson had been readily relinquished by Sue to be in Joe's custody, and Sue's visitations were erratic and infrequent with Samson.

Anne came to recognize troubling sexual feelings towards Samson although there was no acting out. She was perplexed and intrigued by her

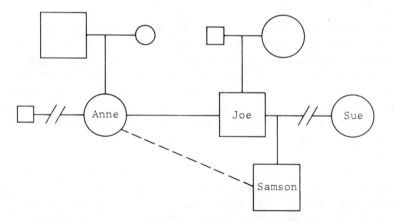

Figure 4-1 Case Study Family Diagram. The reader should note that the sizes of the boxes are meant to convey visually the perceived "mass" of psychological power of each person. That is, Anne perceived her mother as less powerful than her father, and Joe perceived his father as less powerful than his mother; similarly, Anne perceived her first husband as relatively powerless.

own sense of sexual stimulation and pleasure at Sam's curiosity about her body. Sam at this time was five-and-a-half years old. Her sexual feelings towards Sam led her to explore her own childhood sexuality, and to allow herself to uncover a sense of her father's physical intrusiveness toward her which had led her covertly to feel repeatedly raped by him. As she remembered it, her mother did nothing about this intrusiveness, absorbed as she was in her own melancholic involutional period. Anne remembered her father as robust, earthy, alluring and frightening; in essence, fascinating but dangerous. Her anger at her devalued mother led to a sense that femininity and sensuality were dangerous or were to be linked with anger, and these antimaternal feelings led her to reject her own femininity. Sexual identity problems with some acting out were widespread in her family. She worked through feelings of hatred towards her own voluptuous curves with resultant sudden impulses to begin eating, which she managed to suppress. Such ventilation and clarification led her to discontinue her bulimia, but she continued to feel vulnerable to feeling small.

She developed a tenacious reaction formation, wanting a child of her own in order to be a good mother, and then wanting Samson as her child. This led her into competition with Sue and to become angry with Joe for not extruding Sue. Anne's continuing struggle with herself was her own need to be a mother quickly via Sam, and a potentially adversary relationship developed between Joe and Anne. Joe was caught between his ex-wife and his lover. This led Joe to an attorney to counsel both Anne and Joe on their rights; his as a custodial father afraid of his ex-wife, and Anne as a stepmother but de facto custodian of Samson. Anne had to struggle to restrain herself from polarizing Joe vis à vis Sue, to let go of her own fast-food fantasy of motherhood via Samson, and to allow herself to be a better woman than her own mother, enjoying her sexuality with Joe and her own natural motherhood not competitively with Sue.

At around the time that Anne came to realize her inappropriate longings to be Sam's mother, she referred Joe for psychotherapy because she knew that he was dissatisfied with himself, although she didn't know why. Unbeknownst to Anne, Joe had obsessive fantasies regarding women's breasts, much thought blocking, and then transient oral hetero- and homosexual fantasies. He had major problems asserting himself with subordinate women at work, where he was a successful but nondoctoral degree research manager.

His course of therapy was shorter than Anne's, focusing essentially on his hesitancy about masculine identity that had grown out of his identification with a father who was ineffectual in dealing with his mother. His mother had withdrawn from social and family life to be a recluse after a freak accident at home that had left her face scarred. His father came to leer licentiously at other women, but confided to Joe that he had never had an affair.

Joe's therapy focused on his anger at his father for not confronting his mother's refusal to have plastic surgical rehabilitation. Therapy led to his more effectively setting limits on Sue, being less fearful that she would take Sam away, and being more able to put Anne in her place with respect to her realistic legal future with Sam. As this progressed, his obsessions faded.

In psychodynamic terms, the therapy could be conceived as corrective emotional experiences for both parties: Anne with a sexual male psychiatrist who could provide an introduction to intimacy via transference without being sexually threatening, and for Joe an identification with a more confident father figure who could provide permission for him to be assertive. Samson had become the focus of two Delilahs in real life, a biological mother who for unknown reasons relinquished him partially, and a new stepmother who needed him for her own reasons to assuage her own anger at her own mother. Anne came to be able to control her competitive, antimaternal regression toward incestuous loss of sexual identity boundaries so as to provide Samson with a more neutral, benevolent stepmother. Joe had regressed to being like the father he hated, ineffectual with women except in fantasy because of his fear that he might be no more manly than his father was; but he was able to tolerate his own fear at his anger at his father, and then to gain confidence in his ability to deal more effectively with women. The attorney they consulted, unlike Anne's initial one, provided a valid, restrained role model that freed them from fearing both their sadistic opportunities or their castrating legal limitations. In identifying with him, Joe was able to proceed with working out his impotent but enraged identification with his inadequate father.

In retrospect, it seemed that under the stress of marital breakdown and subsequent reattachments in different ways to the single child of these three marriages, both Joe and Anne became vulnerable to characteristic regressions: Anne in a pseudosexualized fashion to obtain an identity for herself as a person and a woman, and Joe in a castrated fashion in an identification with his inept father. Their respective regressions contained the seeds of a major custody and visitation battle with Joe's ex-wife Sue, which was averted by Joe's and Anne's ability to overcome their respective regressive pulls and to refrain from engaging in a spiteful custody and visitation battle with Sue.

THE PSYCHIATRIC POINT OF VIEW

The psychiatrist's contribution to child custody cases is the psychiatric point of view: a unique quality of being able to understand, analyze and clarify regressive tendencies and motivations as well as some regressive behavior. From a treatment standpoint, if one can clarify and help to repair regressive behavior while it is still only a tendency, then there is a real chance to keep the people out of court. This is especially true of the healthy parents who without help would wind up in court, but also perhaps of the unhealthy ones who are more prone to giving in to the regressive pull. Psychiatric expertise is the ability to assess motivation: the interplay of hope, fear, idealism, fantasy, and the effect of elemental sexual and aggressive urges on the individual as he interacts in a family network.

A custody fight or a visitation dispute always focuses on the children. The psychiatrist can see through a child's eyes, with a child's vision, better than anyone else and he or she can articulate the children's fantasies better than anyone else, especially children's sense of urgency due to their shortened time sense and absence of historical perspective. But a child's viewpoint is parochial, immediate, and often erratic. Therefore, the psychiatrist's impulse to provide succor to this hurting child has to be tempered by the realization that children simply do not know their own long-term best interests. The psychiatrist needs to explore the entire network of the child's multiple and conflicting attachments (especially if there is more than one child) to all of the adults and other children in a child's relational field.

Considering a case from the standpoint of the child's attachments operates from the basis of the doctrine of psychological parent. That doctrine has been greatly overvalued as a decisional criterion in family court cases. It is *part* of the psychiatric point of view, but an examination of even the child's entire network is insufficient when taken only from the child's own point of view.

The psychiatrist also can and should evaluate what the parents or the other custodians or guardians (not necessarily the natural parents), can offer to the child in terms of emotional support and growth possibilities. The network of adult attachments to the children expands on the doctrine of the wanted child, which is another part of the psychiatric point of view, although once again that part is incomplete in and of itself.

It follows that no custody evaluation is complete without a reasonable assessment of the entire family as individuals within a network, including the attorneys and the extended family. Many psychiatrists will unfortunately venture a partial opinion based on a truncated evaluation made possible for the psychiatrist by a biased and interested party. One cannot be too careful about this. To quote the Massachusetts Supreme Judicial Court in other contexts, the real need is for a "detached but passionate" explication of the entire network. Otherwise, the psychiatrist is abrogating the truly unique psychiatric manner of formulating data.

The psychiatric mission is to evaluate and explain all of the mixed attachments within the network with illumination of all of the various patterns of motivation and fantasy both from the child's standpoint "up" and from the adults' viewpoint "down." The psychiatric mission is *not* just to advocate *for* the child or to advocate *from* the child's viewpoint. The psychiatrist should *explain how* the family functions, not just what they do; how to understand them, not just what to recommend. This is the concept of an emotional balance sheet.

The psychiatric evaluation ought certainly to speak to custodial strengths, but it should always at least explain the nature of a custodian's parenthood fantasies toward the child, fantasies that will inevitably generate effects on the caretaker's childrearing patterns. The psychiatric evaluation should elucidate the susceptibility of each custodian to the kind of regression analyzed above (in the face of threat of injury involved in loss of custody) because whichever person or people get custody of the children, they will be faced with the continued threat of loss of custody. Therefore, the psychiatrist needs to advise custodial decision makers on how a perspective custodian is likely to handle the continual threat of loss of custody once she or he has custody, extrapolating from analysis of how the adults' feelings and behavior have responded under similar stress before.

The psychiatrist ought to be aware that as a physician and healer, he or she naturally tends to limit or minimize regressive behavior. Such imposed limitation generates increased anxiety. In these cases, the increased anxiety generates evasion or obstruction of the psychiatrist. Parents involved are faced with custody evaluations by psychiatrists and can be extremely provocative, insulting, or threatening. The anxiety-riddled regressive pull induced by the threat of loss of custody can lead to bald-faced lying. Many psychiatrists are taken aback by such developments. At such times, it is helpful to remember that the psychiatric mission is to expand awareness and the option for sentient choice, not to control outcomes. The psychiatric viewpoint is unique and useful, but it is a limited point of view and it is often not wanted or used.

APPLYING THE PSYCHIATRIC VIEWPOINT TO CONTEMPORARY CUSTODY ISSUES

Decisional criteria concerning child custody are in flux. Since the early twentieth century, the maternal presumption or "tender years" doctrine has held sway in the guise of "the best interests of the child." The "best interests" doctrine has provided an umbrella broad enough to encompass increased psychiatric input to the custody decisional process, and more recently, to new sociopolitical movements too.

Psychiatric input has contributed several key concepts which have encouraged the courts to recognize children's emotional functioning. The "wanted child" concept has utilized attachment theory formulations from the parent's viewpoint, just as "psychological parent" has done so from children's viewpoints. More recently, psychiatric understanding has contributed to concepts of continuity and children's expressed interest.

"Continuity" as applied to child custody cases also has its roots in attachment theory, in a child's developmental need for stable relationships in order to obtain stable, benevolent object introjects that in turn ease passage into a generative adult life. In the regressed, heated atmosphere of adversary litigation, "continuity" has often been used synonymously with "sameness" or "consistency" and in that rush to judgment the presumption of benevolent, flexible structure which is inherent in the psychiatric concept of "continuity" has often been lost. Maintaining the "same" circumstances is not necessarily useful for a child's growth. What requires "continuity" is an environment which is firm but responsive to a growing child's changing developmental needs. Thus, the concept of continuity is neutral with respect to the distinction between biologic and psychological parent; it can be asserted by biological parents against each other, or by any presumptive custodian versus a biological parent.

The new doctrine of expressed preference of the child is even more problematic. This emerges from the context of the civil rights movement and even more recently, the children's rights movement. As such, it achieves instant respectability and to be skeptical is lèse majesté. Yet there are genuine problems and complications as this plausible concept comes into play.

Perhaps the least of these complications is that expressed custody preferences by children inevitably conflict with one contending parent's preferences for possession and the right to rear the child. It is no longer deemed proper to consider children as chattels, yet the rush toward according children unfettered expression or even full party status in litigation with separate legal representation ignores more basic children's needs or "psychiatric rights": a right to as intact a family as possible, or a right to the gratification of childhood dependency status which is essential for proper maturity and later citizenship. Granting a child a premature right to engage in litigation may well compromise his or her later rights to function as a fully volitional and mature adult.

A more serious problem with the expressed interest of the child doctrine is that it presumes a rational and competent child.[4] In psychiatric fact, children are rarely either of those. Competency cannot be achieved by attaining a certain age, and it is always painfully compromised in a child who is in loyalty conflict as a result of a custody dispute. Close examination reveals that the child rarely is able to offer a reliable, valid, informed, voluntary expression that is fully moral, i.e., one that weighs two equal possible choices and opts for one on the basis of sober reflection and choice.[2] Yet this question of the child as a typically incompetent witness is rarely faced squarely by child advocates.

From a psychiatric viewpoint, a more valid standard for custody determination would assess *patterns* of parenting as the basis for near-term extrapolations of the parent-child relationship. One essential parameter of parenting style for assessing future custodial suitability is a parent's recognition of the need to change, and the ability to effect such change. The "good enough" parent provides a stage-appropriate relationship to a child which recognizes the child's changing developmental needs; this concept of "continuity" emphasizes a qualitatively consistent relationship with a flexible focus on such issues as trust, autonomy, discipline, independence, sexuality, intimacy, and creativity. Appropriate parental behavior for an infant must change dramatically in order to be equally appropriate for the same child as a toddler or teenager; the child needs "different parents" at different ages.

For such flexible relatedness to flourish on the part of a parent, it is likely that the parent must have an awareness on some level of his/her guiding parental fantasy *and* the ability to objectify such fantasy for the independent welfare of the child. In the context of child custody issues, this dual faculty may express itself as a parent's recognition that the child needs the other parent as well as oneself, with willingness to foster easy *access* to the other parent or parenting figure (e.g., grandparents). Such operational considerations take into account the dynamic reality of families rather than positing a static concept of "continuity" or "attachment."

As always in the child custody field, decisions are rendered increasingly difficult by shifting societal standards. Resorting to an arbitrary decisional criterion will not ease the problem, but will only obscure it behind a facade of certainty. All of the above criteria are worthy, and have their respective historic contexts. One or more will be selected by a decision maker as her or his point of reference, but such selection is best made with full recognition of psychiatric complexities and emotional costs to the parties.

This is equally true for psychiatrists performing custody evaluations with recommendations. In such situations, the psychiatrist should make clear to his audience which presumptions and which processing and decisional criteria he or she has operated with. Such clarity of presentation allows the report or testimony to be immediately more comprehensible, human, and accountable.

The ultimate result of a custody dispute is a custody determination. In recent years, novel custodial formulae have evolved to complement the traditional single custody, in which one parent had possession of all the children all of the time except for noncustodial parental visitations. One such novel concept is that of shared custody, in which each parent has legal custody of the children during times of possession. In this case, the children are usually domiciled with one parent predominantly, but during visits with the other parent, that other parent has full legal custody.

Legal complications aside, this kind of arrangement affords the non-custodial parent a sense of increased presence or impact on the children, thereby softening damage to the noncustodian's parenting fantasy. However, it does demand an increased amount of cooperation between the divorced parents, thereby placing additional strain on the custodial parent's divorce fantasies. This arrangement may imply a need by the noncustodial parent for a gesture of emotional support inasmuch as it seems contrived. Yet such "contrivances" are often pragmatically necessary in order to preserve as many options as possible for the children.

Another novel concept in custody is that of split custody, each parent having domiciliary possession and custody of some of the children all of the time. The cost to the children in ruptured sibling relationships (a regressive phenomenon) is obvious, and inherently this situation connotes a greater need by each parent to have his or her respective parenting fantasies gratified rather than mastered for the children's benefit. Yet this too may be the relationship of choice as the optimum strain acceptable to each parent's sense of injury in the real context of a divorce, if a decision maker's primary value choice is to maintain at least some biparental input to each child.

Perhaps the most publicized custody evolution has been joint custody, in which both parents have legal custody of all children all the time. This is the only essential meaning of joint custody, with the result that many attorneys and parents think that they "know what it means," only to find themselves in dispute with an opponent to whom "it means" something different. Such misunderstanding arises out of confusion between the limited explicit denotation of "joint custody" as a concept vis à vis the logistical and residence arrangements designed to make it work.

These logistics are as varied as the human imagination, ranging from children living in the same house with move-in-move-out parents to children mastering complex domiciliary rotation schedules on weekly, monthly, or yearly cycles. Such logistics can be as consensual as the phrase "as agreed upon" in a custody judgment or as tangled as a 40-page schedule can make it. The flexibility of such arrangements demands substantial cooperation between the parents; this brings home to them the clinical fact of family dynamics that it often takes more work to make a good divorce than to make a good marriage.

Joint custody is such an appealing idea that is seems a facile solution to custody problems for proponents of men's rights *and* women's rights, and joint custody can be made to work well in remarkably diverse economic and geographic circumstances. But such faith may seek to evade or conceal real conflicts between the parents' respective emotional needs regarding themselves as parents, and then the emotions will come to dominate even joint custody's appeal.

And later on? When the emotional distress of a divorce and the injury of threatened loss of custody is scarred over or healed, what has evolved in the family? Current social unrest includes increased social politicization of fragmented groups, all asserting their rights. The epidemic of divorce might well cause despair if we were not mindful of the dictum that "Americans are the marrying kind." In one guise or other, family affiliation does seem to be universal. What seems like the demise of the extended and nuclear families may be a restructuring of families away from those based on extended consanguinity (cousins) and toward those based on legal/marital relationships (my stepbrothers's stepbrother).

Research is painfully needed, but it is too early in the swing of the social pendulum to know which questions to ask. Perhaps many families work it out in ways we cannot yet imagine. Certainly, most of the very acrimonious custody disputes seem to subside if not to settle, possibly under the weight of court-imposed reality, fatigue, financial strain, or even effective emotional resolution. Psychiatrists ought not to be dragged reluctantly toward acceptance of socially valid aspects of human nature by political movements (for example, that women can love *and* work, or that men can work *and* nurture). Instead, the psychiatric viewpoint that explicates inner motives coupled with external challenges should continue to make an enormous positive contribution by studying and illuminating the tumultuous changes that are in process in family life patterns.

REFERENCES

1. Corman, A. *Kramer v. Kramer.* New York: Random House, pp. 39–43 (1977).
2. Gutheil, T. G., et al. Legal guardianship in drug refusal: An illusory solution. *American Journal of Psychiatry.* **137**:(3):347–352 (1980).
3. Jaques, E. "Social systems as defence against persecutory and depressive anxiety" *In: New Directions in Psycho-Analysis.* Klein, M. (Ed.) London: Tavistock (1955).
4. Siegel, D. M., and Hurley, S. The role of the child's preference in custody proceedings. *Family Law Quarterly.* **XI**(1) 216–273 (1977).
5. Goldstein, J., Freud, A., and Solnit, A. J., *Beyond the Best Interests of the Child.* New York: Free Press McMillan, 1973.
6. *Smith v. Smith* 142 NW 2nd 421, 425 (1966).
7. *In Re: Mark,* 154 NW 2nd 27.

Part III

Management of Behavior Associated with Marital Discord

With the large increase in separation and divorce, the management of behavior associated with marital discord has come to represent a professional challenge of increasing magnitude. The six chapters of Part III offer professionals and others insights into and techniques for the more effective handling of the manifold problems encountered.

The contribution by Dr. Robert M. Friedman and his coauthors directly deals with the placement of children in foster care, surveying as it does both the realities and the myths and the opportunities and the risks. In their hands, placement is seen as a rational, careful process of matching children with prospective foster parents by dedicated, aware, and sophisticated professionals.

Daniel A. Calvin presents a major contribution that considers the increasing pressures experienced by families as social institutions. His consideration of the normative American family yields to a better perception of the reality of the average American family and the problems it faces. He considers thoughtfully and fully the many social policy issues involved in joint custody, which he sees as a viable option. His bibliography is particularly complete and helpful, and the whole chapter is a useful and encouraging contribution.

Dr. Ellen A. Drake's chapter presents interesting notions about helping children cope with divorce in relation to the role of the school. Writing as both an educator and clinician, she makes clear that the school, in working with children from ruptured homes, has both a responsibility and an unusual opportunity to aid in the adjustment of such children.

Interesting enough, in her view and based on her experience, it is clear that the work of the school in helping children face divorce and its problems necessitates concurrent sessions with both children and their parents.

Chapter 8, dealing as it does with children of gay parents, deals forthrightly and helpfully with a relatively new phenomenon in our society. In the hands of Dr. Dorothy Riddle and Dr. Maria de Lourdes Arguelles, the full range of issues and problems such children face, and the nature of society's reactions, are set forth with sympathy and understanding.

Many readers may not be aware of the large number of persons incarcerated in American penal institutions and of the fact that such confinement has the very real effect of fracturing a family that is comparable in many ways to that of divorce. Dr. Enid Gamer and Ms. Ann Schrader, in their perceptive chapter, provide an insightful approach to the problems that are special to the circumstances of confinement for children from such families.

The final chapter of Part III, prepared by Dr. Joanne Greer, indicates why young women, and even early teenage girls, are especially susceptible to pregnancy when they live with a single parent whose authority is less than it would have been had the family not been ruptured by divorce. It is well known that many adolescent girls who go to full term with their pregnancies are desirous of retaining their children; others, for many reasons, are prepared to put them out for adoption. The chapter deals with these and other issues in thoughtful and informed ways.

This detailed survey of the realities of foster home placement points to what are considered essential operations if the program is to provide the service for which it has been constructed. Suggestions for recognizing and avoiding common problems accompany each area discussed. There is an emphasis upon the need for careful matching of strengths and weaknesses of placement alternatives for each client. Just as careful a match of child and foster parents, by trained and aware workers, is necessary for optimum results, as is an evaluation of the real intentions of the natural parents in seeking outside placement.

5

Placement of Children in Foster Care: Uses, Abuses, Risks, Realities, and Myths

Robert M. Friedman, Ph. D., Sharon Lardieri,
A.C.S.W., Don McNair, M.S.W., Judith Quick, M.S.,
Carla Repetosky, M.S.W. and David Stoops, B.A.,

INTRODUCTION

The focus of the present chapter will be on foster family care, the system by which substitute families, called "foster families," are used to provide care for children whose own families are unable to care for them. Such a topic has a logical and important place within this book, *Children of Separation and Divorce*. Within foster care, children have to deal with separation from not just one but both parents, a separation that has been referred to as, "perhaps the most tragic occurrence in a child's life".[15]

The task for professionals in child welfare, mental health, and other human services systems who work with youngsters who have undergone this type of separation is a most important and difficult one. In working with youngsters for whom the plan is a return to natural parents, the professionals must help the children deal with the reality of the separation as adequately as possible, and to adjust to a new family living situation while working towards being reunited with their natural parents. In those cases where the youngster has literally or psychologically been abandoned, the task of the professional then becomes one of assisting the youngster to achieve an emotional understanding of this that will not interfere with developing attachments to substitute parents. Many professionals outside the child welfare system are in the especially difficult situation of having a limited knowledge of how foster care operates. The purpose of this chapter is to provide a balanced perspective of foster care today, the risks, realities, and proper uses of it along with myths and abuses, to assist professionals to make effective use of foster care. The chapter represents a combination of general information about foster care with specific suggestions for clinicians who are serving potential or present foster children.

DEFINITION OF FOSTER CARE

The Child Welfare League of America has provided the following specific definition of foster family care: "A child welfare service that provides substitute family care for a planned period for a child when his own family cannot care for him for a temporary or extended period, and when adoption is either not yet possible or not desirable."[3]

This definition distinguishes foster family care from other types of substitute care which are either not within a home (institutional care), or intended to be permanent (adoption). Within this chapter, as well as the general child welfare field, a distinction will be maintained between foster *family* care, and the broader category of foster care which includes substitute care in institutions, group homes, and child care facilities as well as families.

Within the child welfare field, as in the mental health field, the most desired interventions are those which are as nonrestrictive as possible, serve to strengthen the basic family unit, and to keep the family intact. Substitute care, therefore, is designed to be a service only to be provided when there is an immediate and serious danger to a child, which is not likely to be effectively ameliorated through other less restrictive actions.

Child welfare services are generally grouped into three categories of supportive, supplementary, and substitute services. Supportive services include supervision of a child in his/her home by a protective service worker, and treatment in a child guidance, family service, or mental health clinic. Supplementary services include a variety of income maintenance programs, homemaker service, and day care. When supportive and supplementary services have not proven adequate to reduce the danger to a child of staying in his/her home, then the most drastic step of substitute care is taken whereby a child is declared "dependent" and the state assumes responsibility for the child's care.

The need and demand for foster care services is obviously closely related to the availability of adequate supportive and supplementary services. The rate at which youngsters enter foster care can most effectively be reduced through strengthening and intensifying the social, financial, and mental health services designed to prevent family problems, intervene early in their development, or deal with serious problems and crises while still keeping the family intact.

Placement of a child in foster care, by its very nature, is a very serious step involving a change in physical as well as legal custody. The parents give up certain rights in decision making regarding the future of their children, and the child welfare agency assumes control as case manager. Until recent years, after the initial court action was taken placing a youngster in custody of the agency, decisions were made mainly by the particular caseworker assigned to the youngster. Within the 1970s however, there has been an increasing recognition of the need for that control to be shared, and there have developed specific administrative and judicial review procedures designed to ensure that for each youngster, an appropriate case plan is developed and implemented. Similarly, in the last few years there has developed a stronger recognition of the importance of keeping natural parents closely involved with the youngster after placement, and of involving the natural parent in the decision-making process as much as possible.

HISTORY OF FOSTER CARE

The task of providing for children who cannot be cared for by their own parents is clearly not a new one. Prior to the development of the present foster care system, a variety of approaches were tried. One of the earlier forms of foster care, developed with the enactment of the Elizabethan Poor Laws, was the "indenture system." This was typically an arrangement whereby a family agreed to accept a child in its home and provide room and board in exchange for the labor of the child. This type of a system was obviously utilized during times when children were considered an economic asset because of their capability from an early age of performing productive work, in contrast to present times when the financial cost of child care to a family is continually increasing.

The origins of the modern foster care system in the United States began with the New York Children's Aid Society. During the 1850s and 1860s, New York City was experiencing thousands of homeless children living and growing to adulthood in the streets. Based partly on the rationale that the city was an unfit environment for children to be reared in, and the country was much more desirable, the Children's Aid Society developed a system of transporting children hundreds of miles from their home to midwestern rural placements. It is estimated that between 1854 and 1929 over 100,000 New York children were so placed in "free foster homes" in the midwest.[18] This arrangement was based on the exchange of child labor for child care, and did not involve a formal contractual agreement.

Another form of out-of-home care provided within the nineteenth century for children was placement in almshouses. These were typically "mixed" institutions in that they housed adults as well as children. However, toward the end of the nineteenth century, states began passing laws prohibiting the placement of children in mixed almshouses, and thereby providing further impetus for the development of foster family care. In addition, as the unsuitability of mixed almshouses began to be recognized, orphanages and institutions designed only for children began to become more common.

Massachusetts pioneered in paying foster parents for boarding children, during the mid-nineteenth century. These payments were made for youngsters who were too young to be profitably indentured, and who otherwise might have been placed in institutions. Towards the end of the nineteenth century, the Boston Children's Aid Society carried foster care one step further by looking at the needs of individual children rather than just seeking placement. This represented the origin of studying and licensing foster parents, something unheard of until that time. Plans and goals were established for the child placed in care, with the ultimate goal of actually returning the child to his/her natural parents.

At the end of the nineteenth century, as many states began to prohibit placement of children in mixed almshouses, the need for foster care took on a greater prominence. Debate raged between advocates of foster family care and institutional care until the First White House Conference on Children, in 1909, officially endorsed foster family care as the placement of choice for normal children. This Conference also clearly declared that children should not be deprived of their home life except for "urgent and compelling reasons," and that poverty alone was insufficient cause.[18] To help make this declaration more of a reality, states began passing laws providing financial relief to families with no father, and by 1921, forty states had enacted such legislation.

PRESENT STATUS OF FOSTER CARE

At the present time there is no single, unified foster care system in the United States. Rather, each state operates its own system with considerable variability in such areas as contracting with private agencies to provide services, payments to foster parents, case review procedures, and caseworker to child ratio. A recent national study of foster care found that there were such inconsistencies between states in types of information kept that it was not possible to even determine the number of children in foster care.[21] As a result of this variability between states, and the inconsistency in information available, this chapter will not be able to include as many precise data as would be desirable. Instead, the experience of the authors in Florida, a rapidly improving state with regard to foster care, will be drawn upon heavily along with general clinical findings about the process of foster care which tend to be consistent across the country.

The most accurate estimate of the number of children in foster care in the United States seems to be about 502,000. This figure is based on a national survey conducted in 1977.[25] Of this group, 395,000 children were living in foster family homes while 35,000 were in group homes, 29,000 in residential treatment centers, and 43,000 in child care institutions.

The number of children in foster care represents a substantial increase in the 1960s and 1970s. While the general population of children under age eighteen in the United States increased by only 4 percent between 1961, when an earlier national study had been conducted,[16] and 1978, the number of children in foster homes jumped from 132,000 to about three times that many (395,000).

The reasons for this large increase in children in foster family care are many. First there have been large increases in divorce rates. While the rate was 2.2 per 1000 population in 1960, it rose to 5.0 per 1000 in 1977.[30] Remarriage rates are also high. One recent study of referrals of adolescents to foster care indicated that a disproportionately high number came from stepfamilies, suggesting that the high remarriage rate may also be increasing referrals to foster care.[6] Second, there have been very large and dramatic increases in the recognition of the problems of child abuse and neglect. During the four-year period beginning in 1962, legislatures of all fifty states passed statutes against the abuse of children by their caretakers.[24] Laws requiring that both citizens and professionals report suspected incidents of abuse and neglect have also proliferated, and mechanisms to facilitate such reports, such as toll-free phone numbers, have become commonplace. The most dramatic illustration of the effects of the new reporting laws and procedures was in Florida, where the number of reports of abuse and neglect increased from 17 statewide in 1970, to over 19,000 in 1971 after a new reporting system was implemented and widely publicized.[20] Since parental neglect and abuse are two of the major reasons for youngsters entering foster care, the increased attention paid to these problems has naturally had its impact upon the foster care system. Third, the problem of child neglect in particular has been shown to be closely related to income.[25] Although there has been more debate on the relationship between income level and child abuse, the preponderance of recent evidence is that there is a link between these two as well.[23] Therefore, it is to be expected that as the cost of child care increases, and economic conditions worsen, there is likely to be an increase in abuse and neglect with concomitant increases in referrals to foster care. Fourth, there has been a growing disenchantment within the mental health, juvenile justice, and child welfare fields with institutional care. This disenchantment has been based on considerations of cost, effectiveness, and restrictiveness of treatment. As each of these fields has moved towards less expensive community-based placements, foster care has naturally assumed greater importance. Sixth, to some extent the child welfare system has been assigned the responsibility for youngsters who previously might have been more likely to have been handled through other systems, such as mental health or juvenile justice. As people have become dissatisfied with the effectiveness of treatment within these systems, they have taken the approach of reassigning responsibility. This is illustrated in a state like Florida, where 1975 legislation transferred responsibility for status offenders—runaways, ungovernables, and truants—from the juvenile justice system to the child welfare system. The legislation[14] stipulates that these children are to be treated as "dependent" rather than "delinquent," a change which has been endorsed by several notable individuals and organizations in the field.

At the same time as the absolute number of youngsters in foster care has been increasing there have also been trends towards more older children, and more children with serious problems entering foster care.[18] Of those youngsters in foster homes in 1977, for example, 48 percent were eleven years of age or over.[25] Yet, the most problematical area for foster family care has always been recognized as service to adolescents.[7, 18] In Florida, the number of children aged twelve and over in foster care increased by 146.3 percent from 1972 to 1979, while the number in the 0–5 age range increased by 38.8 percent, and the number in 6–11 age range increased by 35.6 percent. As a result, adolescents represented 49.3 percent of the foster care population in Florida in 1979, while constituting only 35.1 percent of the population in 1972. A study of a random sample of adolescents in one county in Florida in 1976 indicated that probably one-third to one-half of the adolescents in foster care had serious problems of a behavioral or emotional nature.[9]

The increase in number of youngsters in foster care has resulted in greater attention being paid to this system. This has often produced great criticism of the foster care system. For example, the National Commission on Children in Need of Parents[21] has reported that, "With some admirable

exceptions, the foster care system in America is an unconscionable failure.
. . ." However, that same report also identifies some positive new
developments in foster care and comments that, "the problem is one which
stems from neglect more than intransigence. The failings of the current
system can be solved. Further, they can be solved by the application of
good sense, rather than huge new outlays of public spending."

Few people familiar with foster care, whether working within the system
or not, would question the general conclusion that there is much that needs
to be changed. However, there is clearly also considerable encouragement
to be found from some of the important and significant new developments
within the system. Primary among these has been the more explicit recognition of the need and right of every child to a permanent home as soon as
possible. Following upon a demonstration project in Oregon[4] which
showed that permanent homes can be found even for youngsters who had
been in foster care for several years, many states have begun multifaceted
programs to ensure that youngsters do not drift in foster care from one
temporary living situation to another but that permanent plans are made
and implemented as soon as possible. These new efforts include the following:

1. Development of case review procedures, either administrative or
   judicial, to ensure that each youngster's specific situation is reviewed
   a short time after admission to foster care and periodically thereafter
   (the experience of South Carolina has been one of the most successful
   in this regard);[2]
2. An examination of laws regarding the termination of parental rights,
   and actions to create new laws and/or act more rapidly to terminate
   parental rights when natural parent involvement is minimal and it is
   in the best interests of the child. The termination of parent rights then
   makes the child available for adoption;
3. The creation of adoption subsidies, thereby facilitating the adoption
   of older children, sibling groups, and children with handicaps, and
   almost doing away with the notion of the unadoptable child;
4. The utilization of more specific contracts between agency and
   natural parents at the time a youngster is placed in foster care, indicating the types of changes needed before the youngster will be
   returned home. This focus is based on a California demonstration
   project;[26, 27]
5. A greater focus on the involvement of the natural parent as much as
   possible and as soon after placement as possible in recognition of the
   fact that as time in placement increases, the likelihood of return home
   decreases;[5]

6. For those youngsters not available for adoption (usually older youngsters), and for whom return home is out of the question, the development of "permanent" placements within foster care to provide a greater degree of security than presently exists;

7. Training of foster care staff and foster parents to orient them to work together as a "team," and to prepare them to work towards the ultimate goal of developing a permanent living situation for youngsters. Excellent training material for foster parents has been prepared by groups such as Child Welfare League of America, Nova University, and Eastern Michigan University.

In addition, there have been increased efforts to develop preventive programs designed to keep youngsters in their own home (such as the Homebuilder program in Washington[19] and the Comprehensive Emergency Service model in Nashville.[1] As is typical in the human services field, the pace at which these preventive programs have developed has dragged behind the pace of progress in services for youngsters already in the system.

RISKS OF FOSTER FAMILY PLACEMENT

The professional considering making a referral to foster care should be aware of the risks involved. Some of these risks are intrinsic to any out-of-home placement while others are particularly related to foster family placement. This next section will discuss some of these while also offering suggestions of ways to minimize the risks.

Short-Term Placement Will End Up Long-Term

As indicated earlier, a major problem of the foster care system has been that youngsters placed in foster care have tended to drift from one year to the next, and one home to the next, without permanent plans being made. Indeed, one study that asked caseworkers what the plan was for youngsters in their caseload found that for 66 percent the plan was foster care until the youngster reached the age of majority.[29] A second study, focusing only on adolescents in foster care, found foster care until reaching the age of majority to be the plan for 82 percent of the youngsters.[9]

There are several reasons why placements initially intended to be temporary and short-term have often ended up being long-term. First, sometimes parents who have indicated at the time of placement that they wish to have their child returned as soon as possible subsequently change their mind and choose not to have them returned. This is not an infrequent event with all types of residential placements, particularly when the children involved have been creating great stress for the parents. This change of decision is sometimes directly communicated by the parents, and sometimes not. When it is directly communicated, then foster care caseworkers can proceed to make other permanent plans for the youngster. When parents either do not express this directly, or remain unsure of whether or not they wish to have their child back, the child often ends up in a temporary living situation and a general state of limbo. Under conditions, for example, of periodic visiting by the parents, even if that visiting is relatively infrequent, courts have traditionally been reluctant to terminate parental rights and free children for adoption, and agencies have been reluctant to initiate termination procedures. This type of situation calls for extremely skillful casework and treatment to help the natural parents in their decision-making process. Oftentimes relatively unskilled caseworkers are reluctant to bring up directly the sensitive issue of a parent considering voluntarily terminating his/her rights, even though natural parents oftentimes respond with relief to such a question.

Second, parents are often not involved in the entire treatment process as early and as fully as they should be. This results from the fact that foster care caseworkers typically have very high caseloads, and end up devoting most of their efforts to dealing with crises, and helping youngsters to adjust within their foster homes. Work with natural parents, as important as it is recognized to be, often ends up taking a back seat to the immediate pressures of youngsters acting-out in foster homes, running away, etc. Natural parents are often reluctant to initiate contacts with social workers, and as a consequence of this lack of close work between caseworker and natural parents, the child often ends up staying in foster care longer than intended.

Third, some youngsters end up spending more extended time in foster care than originally planned because of the worsening of problems. Youngsters, for example, often experience rejection within a foster home. This is most likely to be the case where foster parents have received inadequate training, where the match of foster parents and child has been inappropriate, or where casework procedures to help all the people understand the reasons for placement, and prepare for it, have been inadequate. Under such circumstances, children or foster parents may ask for the placement to be terminated, creating an unfortunate process of bouncing from one foster home to another. This process of being removed from another family inevitably has damaging effects on a youngster, contributing to emotional and/or behavioral problems that make it more difficult to achieve a satisfactory return to natural parents.

There is considerable progress being made across the country in dealing with this problem of foster care drift. As indicated earlier, greater emphasis is being placed on the early development of permanent plans for each child, and this process is being assisted and monitored in many jurisdictions through formal review procedures. The results of these procedures have already been impressive in some areas in reducing the average length of stay of youngsters in foster homes.[2]

The responsibility for ensuring that placements intended to be brief do not end up excessively long rests both with foster care staff and the referring individuals. Foster care staff obviously need to proceed with all haste to develop permanent plans, involving natural parents in the process from the beginning, and getting the specific steps needed to achieve reunification in motion. The referring agent has the responsibility before recommending foster family care of knowing and understanding the agency policy for working with foster children. Since there is so much variability from state to state, and even within states, the referring agent cannot take anything for granted in terms of procedures. Further, the referring agent, particularly if a mental health professional, should be prepared to continue working with the youngster and natural parents to help them deal with the separation and make plans for getting back together. In this regard, the assistance of the referring agent will almost always be appreciated by the foster care caseworker, and planning for the family can and should be collaborative. The referring agent has the special opportunity of being a stabilizing, consistent figure in the life of a child who now finds that he/she is living with different adults, attending a different school, has new siblings, and a new caseworker.

Natural Parents Will Not Cooperate With Treatment Plans

One serious risk not only of foster family placement but all out-of-home placements is that the child's parent(s) will cease to be cooperative with the agency after placement, and as already mentioned, perhaps even decide that they do not wish to have the youngster return to them. This is a special risk with adolescents where a particular child may be especially resented for having raised complaints of abuse, or may contribute to marital difficulties. In some cases, the parents seem to conclude once a child is removed from the home that they now have a better chance of making it in their marriage.

While this is a problem that confronts all out-of-home placement, there are some special features of foster family care that add to it. For one thing, youngsters in foster homes are living with other "parents" unlike youngsters who are placed in institutional care. Parents whose children are in foster homes frequently report how difficult it is to imagine their youngster with other parents, and to visit him/her in the home of others. A sense of competition with the foster parents for the affections of their child sometimes develops. All of this contributes to the natural parents remaining in the background, and eventually reducing contact with their child to a minimum.

Conversely, foster parents often have difficulty dealing with visitation between their foster children and the natural parents. They may fear that the visit will be upsetting to their foster child, or they may carry negative feelings about the natural parents based on the inability of the natural parents to adequately care for the child. The foster parents may communicate their feelings, intentionally or unintentionally, either to their foster children who may perceive it as pressure to not visit often, or to the natural parents, who may perceive themselves as unwelcome. In either case, this may contribute to the natural parents, who typically feel inadequate anyway about having their child in foster care, becoming less involved with their child.

Part of this risk is not only that the parents will decide that they do not want their child returned, but that they will remain undecided for an extended period of time, leaving their child in limbo. With young children, the current emphasis quite appropriately is on decision making within foster care based on what is considered to be in the child's best interest. This represents a shift from earlier times when the rights of parents were given ultimate consideration, even above the right of a child to a stable, loving, permanent home. Now foster care agencies are likely to initiate legal procedings to terminate parental rights and free a child for adoption if the parents have shown minimal interest in the child over a period of time. If the parent remains confused, however, and has relatively frequent contact but is simply unwilling to cooperate fully with the treatment plan or accept the youngster back home, the termination of parental rights procedure is not likely to be initiated, and the child will be left in a temporary situation. Therefore, especially where young children are concerned, the risk that the parent will remain undecided for a period of time is as great as the risk that the parent will decide not to have the child back. If the parent of a young child decides not to have the child back, then termination procedures can typically be initiated and an adoptive home can be found. With older children, however, if the parent(s) decide not to have the child back, the option of adoption is typically quite remote. The child is left to spend many years in a temporary situation, and perhaps to end up bouncing from foster home to foster home.

There is no certain way to ensure that parents will cooperate after treatment, and will in fact follow-through on their earlier indication that they wish to have their child back. One of the most effective ways to minimize this risk, however, is to have the parent closely involved from preplacement to placement, and then after placement has been made. The parents should be involved in determining, without pressure either from the referral agency or the child welfare agency, whether their ultimate goal is to have the child returned or not. They should participate in establishing short-term objectives that need to be achieved in order to make it possible for the child to return home. They need to further be involved in deciding on specific steps to be taken to ensure that these objective are met. The best model for this process is one based on a behavioral contracting procedure, developed in California.[26, 27]

Parents also need to be involved in visitation from the onset of placement. While visitation always needs to take into consideration the effects it will have on the foster home, the primary consideration must be the effect it will have on the ultimate goal of placement—presumably preparing the family for reunification. The natural parent will experience a variety of strong emotional reactions upon placement and also will experience some strong reactions from friends, extended family, coworkers, etc. The parents need assistance either from professional mental health staff, the foster care caseworker, or both, in dealing with this situation so that they will in fact be able to work towards meeting the treatment objectives established.

This whole process can also be greatly facilitated by understanding and nonjudgmental foster parents. Agencies need to provide training to foster parents about this aspect of their role, and, as much as possible, to place youngsters who it is hoped will be returning home soon with those foster parents best able to work with natural families. It takes a special kind of person to be able to open up his home to a child, to care for and give to that child, and at the same time to work towards the return of that child to his/her natural parents.

Children will Bounce from One Foster Home to Another

The horror stories of children who have been in twenty and twenty-five different foster homes are familiar to all professionals who have any dealings with foster care. Unfortunately, these stories are true for the occasional child who has special problems. Even though this is clearly the exception, there certainly remains the risk that placement in a foster home will end up being unstable, and the child will bounce from one home to another. The national study of social services to children found that 22 percent of the foster care population had been in at least three foster family homes.[25]

Children end up being moved from one foster home to another for reasons related to and totally unrelated to their behavior. Some of the unrelated reasons may include illness or death of a foster parent, relocation of foster parents to another city, and marital problems between foster parents. Children in their own home would not typically be moved for any of these reasons. However, there are features of foster family care that make it inherently less stable than care in one's own home.

More often, however, children are moved from one foster home to another for reasons having to do either with their own behavior, or the combination of their behavior and characteristics of foster families. The most obvious circumstances may have to do with a child who is consistently noncompliant in a foster home, and perhaps even aggressive. Such a child may often end up in numerous different foster homes. The behavior of such a child may be especially difficult to manage in foster homes with several other children (be they other foster children or natural children of the foster parents). The number of children in foster homes tends to be greater than the number of natural siblings that a child has, making adjustment of a child even more difficult. This can be a particular problem in homes where there are a combination of foster children and natural children of the foster parents. The potential for perception of favoritism by the children in the home is particularly pronounced in such a case, and hostilities between the children are more likely.

A natural part of the process of settling into a new home for a youngster is a testing of limits. Skilled foster parents recognize this, and are able to handle it without any major difficulty. However, some foster parents perceive such limit-testing very negatively, and have a difficult time handling anyone but the most docile foster child. Unfortunately the perception that foster parents sometimes have of the children they will receive is that they are neglected children who will show dramatic overnight progress, and bloom into well-mannered and especially grateful individuals. Such youngsters are rare for the foster care system, and foster parents with such expectations are generally disappointed. The major victim of their disappointment is the child, who as a consequence may end up being moved to a new home.

For a child who has already experienced the rejection of an abusive or neglectful parent, or a parent who has totally abandoned him/her, the subsequent rejection by one or more sets of foster parents only further adds to the problem. When this occurs, the system may end up actually doing more harm than good for the youngster. With each successive move to another foster home, the child may get more distrustful of adults, may act out and invite rejection more readily, or may withdraw into him or herself more completely. Often times it makes no difference whether the reason for the move to a new foster home is due to the behavior of the child, or something totally independent of the child, like the illness of a foster parent. Still, the child is likely to perceive the removal from the home as another rejection and the severity of his/her problems may grow.

The best assurance against youngsters bouncing from foster home to foster home is an effective program of recruitment and training of well-qualified foster parents, and an aggressive program of permanency planning that starts as soon as placement is made (if not before). There is a chronic problem in foster care, however, of an insufficient number of foster parents, and particularly an inadequate number to work with special populations, such as older youngsters and children with special problems. If a particular child welfare agency has a severe shortage of such foster parents, then other types of out-of-home placements, such as group homes and group child care facilities should be utilized. If such are not available, then the best precaution against this risk is for the referral agent and the foster care placement worker to try as carefully as possible to match the particular characteristics of a child with foster parents who are well suited for that type of child. The next step then becomes one of providing both the youngster and the foster parents with support and assistance, particularly in the early stages of placement, to increase the likelihood that the placement will succeed. Until, however, agencies receive the financial and staff resources to allow them to recruit and train an adequate number of well-qualified foster parents, this problem is likely to remain a very serious one.

FOSTER CARE MYTHS

The previous section dealt with some of the risks of foster care placement, and in so doing presented information that raises questions about the potential harm/benefit ratio in foster care placement. Such questions need to be raised, particularly since out-of-home placements when not carried out properly carry with them the risk of producing serious harm. The opposite side of this picture, however, is that there has developed a set of misconceptions, or myths, about foster family care that also need to be addressed. These myths present a picture of a system that is grossly ineffective and consistently harmful. One of the reasons for considering these views to be myths is that there not only is an absence of data to support them but often data to support the opposing view. A number of them will be briefly discussed in this section.

Removal Of a Child From His/Her Home Should Be Avoided At All Costs

This statement must begin with an understanding of the conditions under which youngsters end up in foster care. The most frequent single reason is parental neglect while other important factors are parental abuse, severe emotional problems of parents, abandonment by parents, and serious parent-child conflict.[25] In the case of adolescents, this serious parent-child conflict is often accompanied by a refusal by the child to return home or of parents to accept the child home. Further, the accepted practice of child welfare agencies is to explore all other possible placements, such as relatives and family friends, before placement in foster care is made. Therefore, within well-functioning agencies placement of a child in a foster home is only made after it has been determined that the child's own home is a damaging and potentially dangerous environment, and that there are no relatives or friends with whom the child may be placed. Not only is the picture of the social worker swooping down into a family and removing a youngster without just cause largely a myth, but in fact quite the opposite is true—the attempt is made to keep the youngster in his/her home if at all possible through the provision of supportive and supplemental services. As already indicated, it is often the case that there are inadequate supportive and supplemental services available. A demonstration project in Nashville, Tennessee[1] has shown how effective emergency services can help keep families together, for example, but yet such combinations of emergency services as were demonstrated to be effective are most frequently unavailable. Given the distressing statistics and case descriptions showing tremendous and irreversible harm inflicted upon children by their parents[13], however, it is obvious that there are many situations where removal of child from family is necessary for the child's protection.

Removal of Child From Family Produces Serious Damage to the Child

A goal of agencies is that with increased emphasis on permanency planning, removal of a child from his/her home will not produce serious damage. In a well-functioning agency, the child is helped to understand the reasons for placement in foster care, and contact with the natural family is encouraged and supported. Oftentimes, the foster home has a settling, stabilizing influence upon the child, and exposes the child to healthy models of family interaction.

Oftentimes, serious behavior problems of foster children have been attributed to foster home placement, when in fact they had their roots in the natural home. The present state of knowledge of foster care is such that it is difficult to determine the extent to which previously existing problems of youngsters create difficulties in foster care, or the foster home creates serious problems for the youngster. But given the increased findings that a large number of youngsters, particularly older ones, had serious problems upon entry into foster care, and that these problems were one of the very reasons for their entry,[6] the accusation that foster home placement is the cause of all of the problems of foster children is at best a marked exaggeration.

Foster Family Care is Ineffective for Adolescents

This claim is partly based on the observation that adolescents are going through a developmental stage which emphasizes movement towards increased independence, and away from family ties, and therefore placement with foster families is bound to fail. It is also based on the observation, backed up by some data,[7, 9] that placements of adolescents in foster homes are more unstable than placement of younger children in foster homes. While this is the case, treatment of adolescents in general, regardless of the setting, results in more instability than treatment of young children. A recent analysis of this problem has suggested that there is not yet an adequate answer to the question of the effectiveness of foster care for adolescents because foster care programs have not had the resources needed to work with these youngsters.[7] There have been too few homes willing to accept adolescents,[28] and inadequate training provided to the foster parents who are willing.

Special "therapeutic" foster home models have been tested out with adolescents with emotional problems, and appear to be an encouraging option.[12] The success of these programs appears to be related to the fact that they combine financial incentives to attract foster parents, with low casework caseloads, special training for foster parents, and foster parent support systems. All of these features should be present with regular foster care programs, but all too often are missing.

Children With Special Needs Should Be In Residential Treatment Rather Than Foster Care

A recent review of children in a psychiatric residential facility in Florida indicated that given an appropriate selection of foster parents, the children could be treated and maintained in foster home placement (much more economically). The potential therapeutic effects of healthy, well-functioning families is considerable, and the treatment of emotionally disturbed youngsters in families has the advantage of eliminating some of the negative influences that may come from grouping them with other disturbed youngsters in residential facilities. The therapeutic foster home model, already mentioned, appears to have great potential for treatment of emotionally disturbed children.[12] There is a danger that because foster care programs have traditionally been underfinanced, therefore not attracting and retaining enough well-qualified foster parents and staff, that failures will be excessively attributed to foster care as a treatment modality rather than the lack of resources to do the job well.

Being a Foster Parent is a Lucrative Proposition

The board rates paid to foster parents vary considerably from state to state. A recent study found that the rates go down as low as $90 per month in Texas.[21] Another study reported that board rates cover about two-thirds of the actual expenses of raising a foster child.[28] It is only through sophisticated networks of clothes closets and other sharing activities, plus out-of-pocket expenditures by foster parents that adequate care is provided. The demands and responsibility of 24-hour care and supervision of children are so great, and the amount of money paid for board rate is so small as to effectively ensure that few foster parents will continue with this very difficult job for the money. Indeed, at one point in our not so recent history, the claim was made that salaries for teachers should be minimal to ensure that people don't enter the field "just for the money." The same situation seems to apply to foster care. Although the cost to the public for foster family care placement is extremely modest in relation to the cost of institutional placement, the board rates are kept low partly because of the unsupported belief that to raise the payments would result in the wrong types of people becoming foster parents.

REALITIES OF FOSTER CARE

Many of the realities of foster care, both encouraging and discouraging, have already been discussed. These include the facts that placements often end up longer-term than originally intended, return home proves more difficult than expected, and placement in foster homes sometimes ends up continuing a pattern of instability. This section will therefore be restricted to a brief discussion of just two realities of foster care.

Resources for Foster Care Programs are Sharply Limited

Until very recently, the foster care system has had low visibility except for the occasional and inevitable tragic event that gets highlighted in the media. This low visibility stands in marked contrast to a well-publicized field like juvenile delinquency despite the fact that the public sector has 24-hour responsibility for almost ten times as many youngsters in foster care as in juvenile justice. (There were 49,920 children in public juvenile custody facilities in December, 1977.)[22] This low visibility plus the general lack of aggressive child advocacy has culminated in years of inadequate federal/state/local funding for foster care, and minimal public/political support for comprehensive planning and coordination. This lack of support, combined with the rising demands for services, has imposed great constraints on the operation of foster care programs, frequently producing as an unwanted by-product services that contribute to rather than help solve the problems of children. One result is that youngsters who have become more damaged through a series of replacements from home to home and/or "benign neglect" by the system itself often end up being placed in expensive residential placements at greater cost to the public. This is ironic when even small increases in funding for foster family services could end up saving larger amounts of money on institutional care.

There is a Chronic Need for More and Better Trained Foster Parents and Staff

The need for more and better trained foster parents has already been discussed. As foster family care has moved away from being a temporary service in times of special family distress caused by illness and other uncontrollable events to more of a treatment service working with children with special problems, the need for well-trained and qualified foster parents has increased. Yet foster parent recruitment is a very demanding job, often involving much work by agency staff with only very limited return. For example, one study determined that of all people inquiring about becoming foster parents, only 8 percent of the inquirers followed-through with the orientation and application process, and eventually became licensed.[8] Presumably, less than half of this 8 percent would have been willing to accept an adolescent, or a youngster with special emotional problems.[28] As already mentioned, one of the major obstacles to foster-parent recruitment is the inadequate board payments in many areas, and particularly the inadequate payments to work with the more difficult youngsters.

With regard to staffing of foster care agencies, not only are the numbers of staff insufficient, but the training of the staff is also inadequate. Staff typically have bachelor's degrees but these may be in fields irrelevant to the job.[21] High staff turnover, low pay, little opportunity for either preservice or in-service training, high demands for paperwork, exorbitant caseloads, and unavailable management data with which to organize workload demands and priorities contribute further to the staffing problem. One result is that youngsters in foster care are not only confronted with instability in foster home placement, but also frequent turnover of their caseworker.[25] Another result is that the caseworker, feeling undertrained for the job and overwhelmed by demands, often is excessively passive in decision making.

While many human service programs can legitimately make a claim for more resources, such a call seems particularly justifiable with foster care. Despite the difficulty of the job faced by foster parent and caseworker, and despite the importance to the lives of children, both groups receive very little pay and inadequate training. The educational level and pay scale for foster care caseworkers, for example, is typically far below that for counselors in mental health settings although the foster care caseworkers work with very difficult problems, and are placed in a position of important and difficult decision making.

USES AND ABUSES OF FOSTER CARE

Despite the limitations that have been already discussed, foster family care can be a very useful and valuable service if used properly. Proper use requires, first of all, that children are not removed from their own home prematurely. The potential negative effects of out-of-home placements require that communities develop a range of services designed to keep families together. These include the types of supportive and supplemental services already discussed, along with a continuum of mental health services such as intensive individual and family counseling, and day treatment.[10, 11] When families are broken up not because the members were unwilling to seek assistance but because the necessary assistance was not available in the community, then that represents an instance of community neglect. The cost of this community neglect is borne by the youngster, the parents, and the foster care system.

However, even where such services are available they will not always be effective, or parents may elect to bypass them. Also in some cases, parents may elect to voluntarily give up custody of their child. In either case, foster family care is generally the out-of-home treatment of choice, particularly if operated by an agency committed to early planning for a permanent placement. Particularly if the child concerned is of preschool age, and even of preteen years, then the most appropriate out-of-home environment is clearly a family living situation. Within such an environment the child can receive the nurturing and guidance he/she needs while also receiving the type of socialization training needed for optimal growth and development.

With teenagers there is more debate about whether the best out-of-home placement is with a substitute family. It is suggested, however, that if the child shows the capacity to develop attachments to adults, and if there are placements with caring adults available within the foster care program, then such a placement is desirable over residential or group home care for most adolescents. If the behavior of the adolescent is severely troubling and disturbing to adults such that the youngster is likely to experience more rejection in a substitute family, then a group care situation is more desirable.

The ultimate decision of the most desirable placement for a particular youngster, particularly an adolescent, must be made based on an assessment of the child, the strengths and weaknesses of various placement alternatives, and a careful matching of the characteristics of child and placement setting as they interact. To use foster care as the absolute answer for all youngsters because it is the least costly is an abuse of the system, just as the use of group care for all kids under the assumption that adolescents need to grow apart from a family would be improper.

A well-functioning foster care agency will also take into consideration the ultimate objective of placement, e.g., the preparation of the child for adoption, or for independent living if an older adolescent, or to return home, when deciding on the best option for a particular youngster. Such an agency will evaluate the natural parents, if the plan is for the youngster to return to them, and make a determination of the type of placement that will facilitate good follow-through on treatment plans by the parents.

Given the improvements that are being made in foster care, it is expected that the system will become more and more useful. It is also expected that an empirical base will develop to supplement clinical judgment in the decision-making process of what type of placement and youngster match are most suitable.

SUMMARY

This chapter has focused on an overview of foster care with a special look at the risks involved in placement, myths and realities concerning foster care, and uses and abuses of the system. Given the important function of foster care, providing an environment conducive to the healthy development of children who are in need of temporary care, only the highest standard should be applied in evaluating the system. Without question, a look at foster care in 1980 will reveal that the system does not measure up to the standards it should meet in performing such a function. While this is clearly the case when foster care is viewed from the perspective of one point in time, the impression of the system is considerably more optimistic when a longitudinal perspective is gathered. Foster family care has emerged from a number of historical precedents that did very little to take into consideration the individual needs of children, and often ended up enslaving them to adults whose primary interest in them was economic. More recently, foster care has developed from a system serving a relatively small number of youngsters, a low percentage of whom had serious problems, to a system serving about 500,000 youngsters across the country, almost half of whom are eleven years of age or over, and many of whom show emotional and behavioral problems. As these changes in the nature of the population to be served have taken place, foster care has developed a clear mission—that of providing the highest quality care while working towards a permanent and secure placement for a youngster—and has taken large and significant steps towards the achievement of that objective. In that regard, foster care as a program of services in 1980 has made large strides forward from even 1975, and promises to improve even more dramatically in the 1980s. This is critical because as more and more children experience the loss of a parent within their own family through separation or divorce, and as the pressures and loneliness of parenthood continue to build, the need within every community for a strong, therapeutic program of foster family services can be expected to remain high.

REFERENCES

1. Burt, M. R., and Balyeat, R. R. *From Nonsystem to System: Evaluation of the Comprehensive Emergency Services System for Neglected and Abused Children—Nashville and Davidson County, Tennessee.* Bethesda, Md.: Burt Associates, (1975).
2. Chappell, B. Organizing periodic review in foster care: The South Carolina story. *Child Welfare.* **57**:477–486 (1975).
3. Child Welfare League of America. *Standards for Foster Family Service.* New York: Child Welfare League of America (1975).
4. Emlen, A., Lahti, J., Downs, G., McKay, A., and Downs, S. *Overcoming Barriers to Planning for Children in Foster Care.* Portland, Ore.: Regional Research Institute for Human Services, Portland State University (1977).
5. Fanshel, D. Parental visiting of children in foster care: Key to discharge? *Social Service Review.* **49**:493–514 (1975).
6. Friedman, R. M., Ford, G., Lardieri, S., Brienza, D., Murphy, R., and Quick, J. Characteristics of adolescents referred to foster care in 1978 in District VI—Hillsborough County. Tampa, Fl.: Florida Mental Health Institute (1979).
7. Friedman, R. M., Lardieri, S., McNair, D., Quick, J., and Repetosky, C. Foster care for adolescents: Problem or solution? Paper presented at meeting of American Psychological Association, New York (1979).
8. Friedman, R. M., Lardieri, S., Murphy, R., Quick, J., and Wolfe, D. An analysis of foster parent recruitment and licensing procedures: Much work for little return. Tampa, Fla.: Florida Mental Health Institute (1979).
9. Friedman, R. M., Quick, J., Garlock, S., Hernandez, M., and Lardieri, S. Characteristics of adolescents in the child welfare system. Tampa, Fla.: Florida Mental Health Institute (1979).
10. Friedman, R. M., Quick, J., and Palmer, J. Day treatment for dependent adolescents: Procedures and preliminary results. Paper presented at meeting of American Psychological Association, Toronto (1978).
11. Friedman, R. M., and Solomon, E. Day treatment for dependent adolescents: Statistical summary of program participants and outcomes. Tampa, Fla.: Florida Mental Health Institute (1979).

12. Friedman, R. M., and Zeigler, C. Therapeutic foster homes: An alternative residential model for emotionally disturbed children and youth. Paper presented at meeting of Southeastern Psychological Association, Washington, D.C. (1980).

13. Gelles, R. J. Violence toward children in the United States. *American Journal of Orthopsychiatry.* **48**:580–592 (1978).

14. Gilman, D. How to retain jurisdiction over status offenders—Change without reform in Florida. *Crime and Delinquency.* **22**:48–51 (1976).

15. Glickman, E. *Child Placement Through Clinically Oriented Casework.* New York: Columbia University Press (1957).

16. Jeter, H. R. *Children, Problems and Services in Child Welfare Programs.* Washington, D.C.: Children's Bureau, Department of Health, Education, and Welfare (1963).

17. Jones, M. L. Stopping foster care drift: A review of legislation and special programs. *Child Welfare.* **57**:571–580 (1978).

18. Kadushin, A. *Child Welfare Services.* New York: Macmillan, (1974).

19. Kinney, J. M., Madsen, B., Fleming, T., and Haapala, D. A. Homebuilders: Keeping families together. *Journal of Consulting and Clinical Psychology.* **45**:667–673 (1977).

20. Nagi, R. Child abuse and neglect programs: A national overview. *Children Today.* **4**:13–17 (1975).

21. National Commission on Children in Need of Parents. *Who Knows? Who Cares? Forgotten Children in Foster Care.* New York: The National Commission on Children in Need of Parents (1979).

22. National Criminal Justice Information and Statistics Service. *Children in Custody: Advance Report on the 1977 Census of Public Juvenile Facilities.* Washington, D.C.: Department of Justice, Law Enforcement Assistance Administration (1978).

23. Pelton, L. H. Child abuse and neglect: The myth of classlessness. *American Journal of Orthopsychiatry.* **48**:608–617 (1978).

24. Pfohl, S. J. The "discovery" of child abuse. *Social Problems.* **24**:210–232 (1977).

25. Shyne, A. W., and Schroeder, A. G. *National Study of Social Services to Children and Their Families.* Rockville, Md.: Westat, Inc. (1978).

26. Stein, T. J., Gambrill, E. D., and Wiltse, K. T. Foster care: The use of contracts. *Public Welfare* **32**:20–25 (1974).

27. Stein, T. J., Gambrill, E. D., and Wiltse, K. T. Contracts and outcome in foster care. *Social Work.* **22**:148–149 (1977).

28. Thomas, G., Pollane, L., Bransford, R. and Parchure, S. *Supply and Demand for Child Foster Family Care in the Southeast.* Athens, Ga.: Regional Institute of Social Welfare Research, 1977.

29. Wiltse, K. T., and Gambrill, E. Foster care, 1973: A reappraisal. *Public Welfare.* **32**:7–15 (1974).

30. *World Almanac and Book of Facts.* New York: Newspaper Enterprise Association (1979).

Changes in American society are placing considerable pressure on the family as an institution. Within the concern for its survival, especially with escalating divorce rates, is the expressed desire to increase parental autonomy and decrease institutional intrustions. Social policies, formulated with regard to outmoded nuclear family norms, subvert such a desire. Joint custody is seen as one positive and potential policy alternative. After developing a framework for family impact analysis, and clarifying the differences between our families' reality and our perception of social norms and values, joint and sole maternal custody are compared as alternative policy options.

Joint custody is advocated as a positive choice to be carefully considered under specific conditions, rather than as a panacea. Sole custody is found to have many regressive features. Nevertheless, when joint custody is considered within the larger context of shared parenthood, it is found to be severely constrained. While joint custody can be beneficial to the divorcing family, the narrow focus on our legal system and one particular type of family avoids the larger social issues resisting attainment of truly shared parenting. Observations on these issues are presented and an agenda for action suggested.

6

Joint Custody:
As Family and Social Policy

Daniel A. Calvin

I. INTRODUCTION

Recent unprecedented and profound changes have occurred in American families and the laws affecting them. Consequently, with increasing frequency, people are worrying out loud about how the power of government is eroding the institution of the family. Presidential candidate Jimmy Carter proposed (1976) a "conference on families" to provide a forum in which citizens could voice their feelings about the strengths, problems, and needs of the American family. Finally, after considerable delay, the White House Conference on Families was held in 1980 at several sites across the country. Its main purpose "is to examine the strengths of American families, the difficulties they face and the ways in which family life is affected by public policies." Interactions among the world of work, the mass media, the court system, private institutions and American families are being examined.

The key to understanding the significance of the Conference's approach is the special emphasis and priority given to hearing input from citizens, especially parents, along with the "experts." The social policy problems of American families are "wicked"[130] and must be treated as such. Contrary to some expertly formulated prescriptions, we have neither the data nor the tools for solution, and, therefore, the problems of the family must rely upon elusive political judgment for resolution.

As a divorced father sharing the parenting of two young boys, I would like to contribute my perspective to the debate concerning alternative forms of child custody arrangements necessary as part of divorce decisions. By profession, I am neither a psychologist nor a lawyer but a policy analyst, and view sole custody, joint custody, and other options as alternative policies structuring the continuation of parent-child relationships. Similar to the approach of "family impact analysis,"[69, 94, 95] I wish to detail the positive and negative aspects of both sole and joint custody arrangements. Nevertheless, from where I stand, I have a particular perspective and advocate it accordingly.

Therefore, I need to specify two implicit assumptions underlying my presentation. First, also explicit to the White House Conference on Families, too little is expected or required of parents generally and especially during divorce, to direct their own affairs in their family's best interest. In a self-fulfilling prophecy, parents are subverted then held responsible for institutional decisions. Authority must be returned to parents and institutional control to a supporting role. As the Carnegie Council on Children found, "Parents are not abdicating—they are being dethroned, by forces they cannot influence, much less control." They conclude, and it is this paper's guiding principle, that:

> Despite the long-term reduction in familial roles and functions, we believe that parents are still the world's greatest experts about the needs of their own children. Virtually any private or public program that supports parents, effectively supports children. This principle of supporting family vitality seems to us preferable to any policy that would have the State provide children directly with what it thinks they need. (page 76)[74]

Secondly, the "family" created by divorce must be considered as equally legitimate as the one from which it derives. The idea that the nuclear family is "normal" while that of divorce is "pathological" is absurd.

Finally, four criteria govern my policy choice. In line with other significant authors, the most important focus within a custody decision must be that relating to the child: as such, policy must fashion the "least detrimental alternative."[52] However, the standard of comparison cannot be an idealized norm of children from intact, presumably well-functioning nuclear families; the realistic possibilities must be assessed. Third, because each family is different, custody decisions must be individually tailored. Thus, and in line with the first principle, the tailoring, to the greatest extent possible must be done by the parents; government, in this case, the courts, must recognize their limits and provide guiding support rather than coercive direction.[53]

II. THE AMERICAN FAMILY: MYTH VS. REALITY

Social control is maintained by multiple mechanisms. The conceptualization of "norms" as standards is one measure against which acceptable or deviant behavior is determined. Policies guiding decisions are better or worse depending upon the degree to which norms coincide with reality. When they do not, before new or old policies can be analyzed, a closer approximation of reality must be reached.[149] Such a discrepancy now exists between our norm and reality for American families.

A. The Normative American Family

In their social, economic and political functions, families are key units in American and other societies. As socializing environments for the development of children and youth, families are highly determinative of the potential they will realize. Nevertheless, when people say, as they are saying more and more lately, that "the American family" is breaking down, on the verge of death, or conversely that it never has been stronger, someone should ask them to define their terms. The American family? Just which American family do they have in mind? Black or white, large or small, wealthy or poor, or something in between? Do they mean a father-headed, mother-headed, or a childless family? First or second time around? Happy or miserable? Your family or mine?

What is invariably in mind is a white, middle-class, monogamous, father-at-work, mother-and-children-at-home family living in a surburban one-family house. Roles in this stereotypical family are strictly defined—man's as economic provider and woman's as nurturing and supportive. Such a definition now effectively excludes more than half the population.* It is a family type that is increasingly being questioned by the women and young people who come out of it. Yet it remains the standard conception of what the American family is, the model against which all who live differently are judged deviant.

Therefore, while the norm for American public policies is the nuclear family, the first thing to remember about the American family is that it does not exist. Families exist. All kinds of families in all kinds of marital and economic situations. But the idea of the family—what it is supposed to

---

*In 1977, only 6 percent of all American families fit the traditional definition of a working husband, a wife who is a full-time homemaker, and two young children.[113]

be, what a person is supposed to be in his or her role as mother, father, or child—is invariably one of the strongest influences on our lives.

Even though the nuclear family remains the norm but in reality has become a nostalgic dream, many family variations exist for which public policies are inappropriate. Daniel P. Moynihan argued that the black family was "deteriorating" on the grounds that about a fourth of black families did not have a male head. The fact that the mother-headed family, known since the beginning of history, could conceivably be another legitimate family form, was something few considered. And more recently, Richard Nixon, as President, only months before his 1972 re-election bid, took the chance of losing the votes of over eleven million working mothers by vetoing major legislation for child care because its provisions would impede his most important task: "to cement the family in its rightful role as the keystone of our civilization." It is obvious he meant the male-headed nuclear family, because the very next week following the veto, he approved measures to provide child care for welfare mothers, so they could be forced to work, because they did not have a male breadwinner at home.[65] And finally, in 1979, Joseph Califano, as Secretary of HEW, forced the resignation of Patsy Fleming, head of the White House Conference on Families and a black divorced mother, as "an inappropriate leader for a conference on family life."[157]

B. The Reality Of Families

While we see ourselves as living one way, powerful forces are dynamically affecting families to respond in complex and myriad directions. Rather than a singular and static entity operating in a vacuum, families need to be understood as adaptive systems[163] which interact within themselves and with their environment.[3] Family evolution can be viewed from two complementary perspectives—*the* family as a social institution or *a* family over a lifetime.

World wide the dominant family type changes with the level of economic development; throughout currently developed countries the conjugal family predominates while in underdeveloped societies, variations of consanguineal forms prevail.[138] As urbanization/industrialization progress, the nuclear family becomes the major family type.[139] Within the U.S., families have continued to diversify so that there are multiple forms.[48] Four important changes have recently influenced and continue to affect family structure and functioning.

Urie Bronfenbrenner warned several years ago of the increasing stress on the family.[15] Many of the family's traditional functions were being removed and the remaining parental role downgraded. Speaking specifically to psychologists, he has shown that his fears have little effect. Regarding the impact of continual changes, Lamb concludes, "It is our responsibility to determine what consequences these social changes are likely to have, and in this respect the performance of developmental psychologists has been less than inspirational. In the main, they have simply reiterated the assumption that the effects must be harmful. None have heeded Bronfenbrenner's plea for description and assessment of the ways in which demographic trends are translated into individually significant changes in the socialization process." (pages 271–272)[76]

A second important trend is the shift between men and women of traditional family sex roles. Viewing the family as a system of roles, to their dual positions as spouse and parent, traditionally, society has assigned housekeeper and childcare roles as the norm to the wife, with the role of provider assigned to the husband, and child socialization to both.[114]

Oriented differently, while the husband was linked to the world outside the family, the wife was enclosed within it, they were connected via a "family contract" whereby the husband supported the family through his paid work, in return for which the wife took care of him and their children. In so doing, they proved to themselves, their families, and the world that they were man or woman.

The truth of most peoples lives, according to the U.S. Bureau of Labor Statistics, is that it now usually requires a working wife to push family income into middle-class status.[127] Talking about "a woman's place" becomes a moot point when one realizes that the vast majority of women have no choice and work out of economic necessity. Nevertheless, although women have been allowed to enter into formerly male terrain, usually at the lowest levels, men have almost never agreed on any large scale to share responsibility for the home. Invasions of each other's territory are met with resistance and, in the men's case, the effort has been minimal and is still in its infancy. However, this phenomenon is not limited to the U.S. alone; surveys indicate that "men are typically willing to accord women broad political, civil and economic rights; but only if they fulfill their household and family obligations too." (page 143)[8] Sweden appears as the only exception.

Another significant force affecting the changing American Family is reflected in an increasing divorce rate. The divorce rate for 1978 was 5.1 per 1000 population.[104] On the other hand, the marriage rate for 1978 was 10.3 per 1000 population. It, therefore, appears that the (official) American "family" is dissolving at about half the rate it forms. Children were involved in a majority (56 percent in 1976) of divorces. Although couples divorcing in recent years have, on the average, fewer children than couples divorcing earlier, a child today is more at risk of being affected by divorce. The number of children involved in divorce per 1000 children in the total population has grown from 8.7 in 1964 to 17.1 in 1976.[105]

A final major change has occurred in the frame of reference within which child development takes place. Previously focusing on the child's relationship with its mother as the major care-giver, the last decade has incorporated new elements creating a multi-dimensional structure of social objects (persons).[82] The role of the father is now strongly supported as well as those of siblings, peers, and others. No longer is the child thought of as a passive reactor but is known to play an active role in its socialization. The complexity of the world in which childhood socialization occurs has increased but we do not at present have adequate means by which to characterize the total flux of familial interactions as they change over time. Nevertheless, it has been concluded, "that no single element (social object) is either excluded from social development or provides the singular basis on which it ensues." (pages 2–3)[83]

Influenced by these rapid changes, a variety of families exist. The old mythology of a self-sufficient family isolated from the outside world with parents alone responsible for what becomes of their children is no longer viable. (pages 2–23)[74] A new definition of family functions reads:

> The family functions as a facilitating, mediating, adapting, and confronting system for its members who have differing aspirations, capabilities, and potentials. Families both adapt to, and simultaneously influence, the development, structure, and activities of today's complex urban and industrial institutions. But families differ in their adaptive capabilities largely because of variation in form, and they differ in their efforts to mitigate the demands of non-family groups and influence the behavior of outside organizations such as the school, welfare agency, or factory. The primary tasks of families are to develop their capacities to socialize children, to enhance the competence of their members to cope with the demands of other organizations in which they must function, to utilize these organizations, and to provide the satisfactions and a mentally healthy environment intrinsic to the well-being of a family.[36]

These functions now take place in a variety of structures, but it is the interactional dynamics not the form which lead to given outcomes.[91] Work has begun on conceptualizing a "healthy" family[4] and modeling a "normal" family system.[71] Strengths and weaknesses of different family forms have been proposed[148] and preliminary research has reviewed their effects on children.[29, 30, 93] Nevertheless, the overall effort has been too small and needs to be increased, especially regarding families of divorce.

III. DIVORCE: REORGANIZATION OF THE FAMILY

Divorce, as a stressful experience for the family, has occurred at an increasing rate over a long period.[106, 107, 142] It has also been projected that nearly one-half of all children born today will spend a meaningful portion of their lives as children in a single-parent situation before they reach the age of eighteen years.[48] Reflecting the mythical norm, Amitai Etzioni predicts,". . .if (the) increase in divorce and single households continues to accelerate as it did (for) the last ten years, by mid-1990 not one American family will be left."[33]

Nevertheless, as discussed previously, divorce does not mean the death of a family but its redefinition. Viewed in this manner, families are not structurally determined but are social systems operating within many configurations. Therefore, as one variant, divorce means not the dissolution of a family, but its possible reorganization.

> A divorce does not end everything about a marriage. It severs the legal contract between the husband and wife—but leaves a moral emotional "contract" between ex-husband and ex-wife. It shatters the household that was based on the marriage. But it definitely does not break the kinship network that the children of the marriage create merely by their existence.[11]

When divorce occurs, the father's provider role and the mother's nurturing role are extended from the normative "nuclear family" in the forms of child support with visitation and child custodian respectively.* The nuclear family's paradigm of divided paternal and maternal time and responsibility for children is assumed to be the functional process in the "best interest of the child" even though the "family" is undergoing dramatic structural rearrangements. Despite increasing evidence to the contrary, few believe that fathers either can or want to be involved with their children. On the other hand, the wife's wishes as a woman are assumed synonymous with motherhood[6] and she is not effectively given any choice other than to continue the major child-care responsibilities.

Our court system, rather than being independent from cultural values, reflects those norms, sexual stereotypes, and values endemic to society. Public policies, in this case court-ordered child-custody orders, guided by outdated nuclear family norms, treat a mother's and father's parental relationship with their children differently. Alternating throughout history

---

*Alimony is also an extension of the man's provider status but along a different dimension, that of the husband-wife rather than parent-child relationship.

either the father or mother has been given preference in child custody disputes.[37, 38, 39] Under feudalism, the father's rights were paramount. Gradually, with the rise of the Industrial Revolution, a shift took place such that by the early twentieth century, mothers were automatically awarded custody of their children. Operating under the "best interest of the child" doctrine and "tender years" presumption, although nearly all states legally recognize the equal rights of both parents to child custody, courts have declared fathers "unfit" and granted child custody to mothers approximately 90 percent of the time.[99]

Analysis of recent judicial events has suggested that with changes in the decision-making criteria, the pendulum will be moving back toward a more equitable position.* [41] Nevertheless, the current 90:10 bias in favor of the mother demonstrates, as an outcome measure, considerable inequity.

Families undergoing divorce encounter the court system to a greater or lesser extent in a positive or negative manner, but all engage in a process of redefinition having common elements.[119, 140] As the process is currently constituted, it produces predominantly female-headed families. Of all American families, 13 percent are headed by single, separated, divorced, or widowed women. Children living with only one parent rose from 12 percent in 1970 to 17 percent in 1977. One of every six children in the United States is living in a family in which, because of death, separation, divorce, or an out-of-wedlock birth, the father is absent. Moreover, the trend is accelerating, increasing by 81 percent since 1960.[158]

While 19.2 percent of all children under eighteen in 1978 were living with only one parent, only 0.7 percent lived with a divorced father. (Table 6)[142] Although this number represents a 135.6 percent increase since 1970, it cannot be concluded that the distribution between male and female headed families is changing dramatically. Both have increased in number, but "contrary to some speculation, the frequency with which a child in a single-parent family is living with a father has increased no more in proportion to the number living with the mother." (page 6)[141] These data suggest that the bias toward maternal responsibility for child care has remained relatively constant.** Over the last decade, of all family households the ratio of female headed to male headed (no spouse present) households has actually slightly increased the bias toward mothers.[20] Finally, projections to 1995 of the percent distribution of households by type do not estimate any reversal of the current proportions.[21]

However, with high remarriage rates, single-parent families appear to be a transitory phenomenon.[136] For the children, their living arrangement is a

---

*With the "tender years" presumption relegated to a "tie breaker."
**Whether one compares children under eighteen living with mother only to those living with father only or living with a divorced mother to those living with a divorced father, the ratio has remained very nearly 10:1 from 1960 through 1978. (Table H and 142, Table 6)[141]

temporary one, spanning a period of a few years. Only a minority of children under eighteen are likely to spend a major portion of childhood in a one-parent family. Nevertheless, this period represents a psychologically and socially significant part of his or her lifespan. The "blended" family, formed on remarriage, is another structural redefinition of a family over its lifetime.* Needless to say, remarriage does not end all problems, but becomes another stressful time requiring additional support. Research deals extensively with this new system's increased level of complexity.[12, 22, 68, 150, 162]

Whether the divorce experience is positive or negative depends on many conditions. As Wiseman notes, divorce can be treated as "a normal process with specific tasks to be mastered, recognizable stresses to be dealt with, and satisfactions and goals to be sought for. Like any other of life's crises, it is to be avoided when possible; when it occurs, it can be dealt with as a means of achieving growth toward a more satisfying way of life." (page 212)[164] In fact, examining the costs and benefits from a feminist perspective accruing to divorced mothers, Brown suggests that it may be the "chance of a new lifetime."[18] Nevertheless, the key criterion in whether or not to divorce is, "For the sake of the children. . . ?" After review of the psychological effects of divorce, Magrab concludes, "regardless of the short and long-term consequences, divorce or separation at times is the most viable solution to optimizing the potential of that child for sound emotional and personal growth."[90] Social policy and programs must be responsible for these special needs and provide milieu of adequate services to assist in the growth of their own individual human potential. We may choose either to resist growth with mandatory requirements or to support growth allowing alternative choices and support for parental decision-making. Our current policies constrain us to the former, while joint custody appears in line with the latter.

IV. FATHERS VS. MOTHERS AS PARENTS

Even though the father's influence on his child has recently been "found," the mother's relationship is often deemed more important. Before any realistic custody alternatives are possible, we must fully recognize fathers as necessary parental figures. Too often our social values require either that:

- It is traditionally correct, socially fitting, and psychologically necessary that exclusive custody be granted to the mother; or that
- Fathers, by definition, are incapable of being nurturing parents.

These two conclusions are evaluated below.

*In 1977, an estimated 10 percent of children living with two parents were living with a step-parent.[49]

A. The Myth Of Mother's Love[78, 131, 132, 145]

Until the beginning of the twentieth century, "patriarchy" almost exclusively determined the legal status of children. Before the nineteenth century the response was, "the children belong to their father." During the nineteenth century and the early years of the twentieth, customs began to change until, in approximately 1920, the rights of the father ended. From the 1920s on, mothers were virtually assured of the custody of their children even though the mother's paramount claims are not now, nor were they at any time, based on law.

Decisions are based upon a presumption of "mother's love." While Victorian-sounding sentiments are used as justification for custody decisions, there are neither scientific data nor rationale for the presumption in favor of the mother beyond an amorphous but strong conviction that women are by nature, nurturant creatures, and by instinct, filled with love for their children. What is often "instinctive" or "natural" in humans is invariably tied to what a particular culture requires of them.

Industrialization, which split the wage labor of men and the private labor of women, was behind the exaltation of motherhood and the invention of maternal instinct. That is, maternal instinct came along precisely when it was required, making a virtue out of what seemed to be a necessity. Its enshrinement paralleled the development of a new—not God-given—family form which came to be called the "nuclear" family, characterized as a refuge from the world and the social, but not economic, center of personal life. As our culture became both urban and industrialized, the father's activities moved away from the house and thus left, for all practical purposes, the raising of the children in the hands of the mother.

Given that this was the situation (nuclear families in 1920), it was not long before a new ideology about both the family and motherhood arose. Sociologists such as Parsons who speak of the father's instrumental role and the mother's expressive roles in family life fairly ossified the options open to adults. Psychoanalysts, because the child was raised by the mother, assumed her influence was paramount not because anyone could prove it was intrinsically so, but because it was de facto the case. The tendency of other researchers has been to concentrate attention upon the mother as the influential parent and to minimize, as a result, the influence of the father, peers, and the larger social network.

Maternal love must be recognized as a sentiment, a conscious attitude rather than an instinct. The mother's paramount role in the child's life was discovered (and the father's denied) in order to justify the status quo. Ironically, both men and women helped create an ideology that now—with different "families" and economic conditions—victimizes both.

Sentimentalism, in effect, turned sexist and became a new way to keep women in their place. There is a serious fraudulence involved in exalting motherhood. Woman is kept in her place through praise whereas, in earlier times, the same result was achieved by denigrating her. Roman law, which restricted the rights of women, and our current custom of awarding the children to the mother's exclusive care, are not so different. Whether denigrated or exalted, the mother is still just that—a mother and not a full being with motherhood as one of her options.

As Margaret Mead states when acknowledging that both male and female parents are equally able to provide and perform child-rearing functions, the exaltation of "mother":

> . . . is a mere and subtle form of anti-feminism which men—under the guise of exalting the importance of maternity—are tying women more tightly to their children than has been thought necessary since the invention of bottle feeding and baby carriages. (page 480)[96]

The measure of the sexes' equal victimization is that the stereotype provides social and legal barriers to the mother's desire for *economic* parity at the same time that they operate to prevent the father from obtaining *parental* parity.

B. Nonnurturing Fathers

Essentially, the assumption of male inability to be nurturant, caring parents is the converse of the previous issue.[125] Fathers have always been committed to their families but expressed it differently (e.g., dying in wars, earning income); what is being denied is the capability to express it in the same way as women do (e.g., as nurturing parents).[*] Recently, a handful of studies have begun to demonstrate—contrary to stereotypical expectations—that the father's presence can be as deeply felt as the mother's. One summary concludes:

> Evidence from diverse studies suggests. . . that fathers can develop the kinds of strong bonds with infants traditionally reserved for mothers.

---

[*]An essentially similar argument can be applied to the controversial question regarding whether or not women should be drafted and assigned to combat positions. Although there are additional considerations, this stereotype denies women's capability for emotions necessary to combat. Aggressiveness is also a female characteristic but is usually expressed differently. It is really individual choice that is being controlled in both cases.

Contrary to long held assumptions, the 'mother instinct' is not embedded in the bodies and souls of females alone. Instead, maternal behavior can evidently be produced by male and female alike. (page 119)[145]

Still other studies have even begun to postulate a "paternal instinct." But this instinct may prove as useless as the maternal instinct has proven to be. The fact is, it is cultural bias, not biological imperatives, that determines parenting behavior. Studies suggest that the critical aspect of "mothering" is not the providing of food but of warm, comforting physical contact (cuddling, stroking, and soothing). Thus, it is concluded that "the American male is physically endowed with all the really essential equipment to compete with the American female on equal terms in. . . the rearing of infants."[60]

Therefore, while the existence of an important father-child relationship, and the fact that males are potentially capable of nurturant behavior should no longer be questioned, one needs to question how the nature of male and female parenting actually differs. When viewed in a systems perspective, the father's influence becomes more obvious and tantamount to Parsons' instrumental and expressive roles. But this division of labor places the mother in a position of considerable power with respect to the relationship between father and child.* Lynn concludes regarding the role differences:

> The tendency for children to fear the father while viewing the mother as nurturant places the mother in a strategic position to interpret the father to the child. Her expressive role, in which she often mediates between father and child, may allow her either to undermine the father-child relationship or to bolster it. If the father is absent from the home through divorce or death, the mother is in an even stronger position to color the child's image of the father. (page 112)[89]

But these assigned roles depend heavily upon assumption of society's masculine and feminine stereotypes.[16] These differences may be responsible not only for how we view mothers and fathers—mothers as nurturant, fathers as action oriented—but also for how we view men and women in general.[143] As technology gives us the opportunity to transcend our biology, however, these distinctions between mother and father, female and male, are open to change. It is a question of whether policies will support or restrict such an increased freedom of choice. Increasingly, the changing values of our culture prompt more fathers to seek greater involvement with

---

* This position of power for the mother as child custodian is relevant to the "powerless" feelings of a visiting father, discussed later.

their children.[7] But, in the usual divorced household, they are prevented from the chance of doing so.

C. Men And Women As Parents

From the above discussion, it must be concluded that both the mother's and father's relations with their child are important and at a minimum complementary, if not substitutes, to a large degree. Therefore, to focus on the "best interests of the child" criterion from the child's viewpoint alone would miss important actors and relationships. The family as a whole should be the focus.[35] Because of these facts, this analysis requires the utilization of a holistic concept of the child in its family and the recognition that removal of either parent will have a significant impact on the child.

A considerable amount of literature portrays the experience of living in a single-parent family. In line with the majority of such families, most assess female-headed families;[63, 136, 158] a smaller amount deals with male-headed families[5, 45, 62, 72, 75, 98, 117, 118, 144]. Most concentrate on the psychosocial impacts immediately before and after divorce. Recently, Weiss, in *Going It Alone* considers the family life and social situation of the man or woman left to care for children alone.[160] He proposes a theory of the structure and functioning of single-parent households. Summarized:

> The premise of this theory is that the two-parent household maintains a hierarchy—an echelon structure—that the one-parent household can forego. The absence of hierarchy permits the single parent who works full time to share managerial responsibility for the household with the children. The consequences for the children may be a fostering of an early maturity.[161]

Regardless of the sex of the single parent, there are positive and negative aspects associated with this family type. Subsequent sections will evaluate and contrast them to a joint custody situation.

V. POLICY OPITONS: SOLE AND JOINT CUSTODY

It is obvious that there is little understanding that alternatives to sole maternal custody exist. Despite the fact that profound changes in both the family and the ways men and women relate to one another as parents are taking place, these changes are rarely reflected in our institutions. Social change is always swifter than its embodiment in institutional forms. The gap between the world men and women actually inhabit and the one society has been prepared to sanction shows up in painful and difficult ways.

Violent signs of a diasterous public policy are the "kidnappings" that occur between divorced couples, a vengeful musical chairs played with children's lives. Known as "child-snatching," thousands of such cases take place yearly. While hardly a solution to child custody, its increasing incidence is a symptom of the mounting frustration on the part of fathers generally and of despair about the possibility of equity in court.[81]

Today, we are faced with two opposing directions for social policies—sole and joint custody—which at their extremes form the opposite poles between which different combinations of their relative merits exist. In truth, sole custody with liberal visitation approaches but still falls short of joint custody in several respects. On the other hand, joint custody is not a panacea applicable to all situations. However, for the purposes of contrast, they are described as direct opposites. One must keep in mind that this is not entirely correct.

The choice to maximize sole custody follows an adversarial "winner take all" philosophy in line with old nuclear family norms, division of labor, and distinct roles for men and women. While "no-fault" presumptions are increasing between husband and wife, this policy does not extend a similar option to parents and their children. One parent becomes labeled "unfit," and the intrustion of the courts into family life is maximized. One observer concludes:

> When one examines traditional family law philosophy and practices the conclusion reached is that these practices are punitive, that they aggravate an already aggravated situation, that they are not oriented to meeting the critical needs of persons in crisis, that they are paternalistic and condescending, that they are barriers to personal growth because they deny individuals the right to self-determination. Traditional family law is a reflection of another time, another age that no longer exists. A society that allows inappropriate traditions to prevail does a great disservice to itself and its citizens. Traditions should serve the purpose of bringing people closer in a society—not alienating and stigmatizing them as family law continues to do to divorcing persons.[31]

On the other hand, the choice to maximize joint custody follows a "no fault" sharing philosophy in line with newer family norms without required roles for either men or women. Research has shown that under most circumstances, parents are in the best position to work out custody arrangements.[92, 100] They know their children and life styles and are motivated to carry out their own agreements more than those imposed by a court.*

---

*Other authors severely question the capabilities of courts to determine "how or under what conditions the custodian and child are to relate to one another and to others." (Epilogue)[52]

When they are responsible for arranging their own postdivorce relationships with their children, there also is a reduced tendency to shift their responsibilities to others. Additionally, findings have revealed no difference in the ultimate adjustment of children reared by mothers and those reared by fathers; therefore, custody awards should not be made solely on the basis of sex of the parent.[87, 135] This alternative, where feasible, carries on family functions with the least disruption and outside intervention although within a rearranged structure.

Finally, because each case is different, choice of "least detrimental alternatives" must be individually determined on the basis of the "best interest of the child" plus other competing considerations. While we have seen how all members of a family affect the child, additional values may conflict with a child-centered criterion. Basic value conflicts are raised, for example, between concern for the child's welfare and the rights of biologic parents,[52] and between a child's rights and a parent's right to move.[10] These conflicts involve issues greater than child custody, cannot be solved by an expert's bias for child advocacy, and are finally a subject for social decision through political debate.* Thus, the "least detrimental alternative," when other actors are considered, becomes more complicated than just the "best interest of the child" principle, and very difficult to determine. The assessments of sole and joint custody provide information to, hopefully, assist in such determinations.

Conversely, those divorce situations where children become caught in the middle, the subjects of bitter and protracted custody battles, must clearly be considered the "most detrimental alternative," especially for the children, but also for the entire family. Although the data are not available on a national scale, experienced lawyers indicate that close to 90 percent of all cases arrive at the courtroom with the custody question already decided. Some portion of the contested 10 percent represent "bargaining chips" in attempts to apply leverage to points outside the custody issue. Therefore, somewhat less than one-tenth, one article specifying 7 percent,[134] of divorce actions involving custody require courts to make the choice of custodial parent.

This paper is concerned with the implications of norms, values, and social policies applicable to the vast majority of divorcing families, the 90 percent who do not abdicate their parental responsibilities. Goldstein, Freud, and Solnit state that, "by failing to find their own way of resolving

---

*Such value conflicts can be demonstrated in other areas. Regarding the "abortion" issue, some advocates assert that since "life is sacred," there should be no abortions. Nevertheless, while life is highly valued, there are situations—war and capital punishment, for example—where other values supersede some lives' high value. In other words, the prioritization of values is not an expert's prerogative but situational and socially determined.

their disagreements about custody, separating parents voluntarily give up an important part of their autonomy." (page 32)[53] Thus, the state, acting through the courts, is given sufficient cause to modify or terminate a parent-child relationship.* In cases where parents absolutely cannot reach agreement, justification for court actions following those of *Beyond the Best Interests of the Child*[52] *may* apply. However, here we are concerned with parents both of whom are fit and able to reach agreement. Nevertheless, we are still seriously concerned with supports they need to enable them to reach an agreement and implicit social biases which can preclude adequate consideration of less detrimental alternatives.

VI. SOLE CUSTODY AS THE DOMINANT PATTERN

It is the fact that children and their fathers are, in effect, also getting a divorce that leads to many problems of the dominant postdivorce custody arrangement—e.g., sole maternal custody and paternal visitation privileges.** Ironically, current policy works to break the unbreakable. Although few studies conclude as much, all inadvertently document how our current arrangements tend to make ex-parents of fathers, painfully deprived creatures out of the children, and overburdened persons out of mothers. The ways in which the wife is *shut in* with the children and the husband *shut out* are causing many problems. In short, divorce, as now constituted, victimizes everyone involved. Conversely, from what evidence exists, it becomes obvious that in a divorce the needs of the whole family must be considered in order for any one member to thrive.

Beyond the many emotional conflicts, anxieties and pain felt by both parents when they divorce, mothers over and over again reported feeling imprisoned by their children. They felt themselves to be overburdened and experienced great difficulty in reorganizing their lives. For long periods of time, they felt themselves depressed and defeated by the situation.

The divorced mother often is harassed by her children, particularly her sons. But she should not be indicted because of the poor relations between herself and her children. Studies recognize she is overburdened and suggest:

The importance of positive emotional support from other people cannot be overemphasized when children are in a 24-hour responsibility. That is,

---

*The difficult question regarding the advisability of courts mandating joint custody (see *Adler* vs. *Adler, Stamper* vs. *Stamper, Braiman* vs. *Braiman,* and *Dodd* vs. *Dodd,* for examples (Parts II and III)[40] is beyond the scope of this paper. Nevertheless, some research supports the principle that, "when separating parents are hostile to each other, when they do not accept each other as parents, then joint custody is 'advisable.' If they accept each other as parents, any situation (custody arrangement) will work."[2]

**Although this section is written from a father's perspective, as the predominant noncustodial parent, similar conclusions might be reached if trends result in significantly more fathers receiving custody and mothers visitation rights.

children cannot provide emotional support—their love is demanding of the parent rather than supportive. A great, and often overlooked strength of the two-parent family is the presence of two *adult* members, each providing the other with aid in decision-making, psychological support, replacement during illness or absence—someone to take over part of the burden. The solo parent not only has to fulfill all family functions, but has no relief from his or her burden.[153]

While this solo parent is usually the mother, her ex-husband's lot is, in important respects, no easier. The emotional aftermath of divorce that he experiences is very like his ex-wife's, involving feelings of having failed, ambivalence, lingering ties of love and dependence, both grief and relief, mixed fears and expectations about the future, rejection, loneliness, anxiety, hostility, and depression.

Differently from his ex-wife, he also feels the disorienting effects of his new life. Bereft of the continued presence of his children and familiar home setting, his sense of continuity is profoundly shaken. "Fathers," said one study, "complained of not knowing who they were, of being rootless, having no structure or home in their lives."[62] If she is overburdened by children, career and a new, or sought for, personal and social identity, he is, in a sense, underburdened. Quite literally, he has lost not only a wife, but also a home, and most of all his children.

The pain felt at the loss of his children is very strong and can cause previously involved, attached, and affectionate parents to see their children only infrequently as a way to cope with the loss. Under conventional visitation arrangements, the father's experience of loss is so deep and his contact with his children so minimal that he often reacts with what one study calls a "Flight-Followed-by-Fight" pattern.

In contrast to a popular myth that fathers walk away from divorce and their families unscathed and carefree, the evidence here is that a majority of these men experienced stress severe enough to bring on physical problems. There was also considerable evidence of depression, as well as sense of loss. Many fathers seemed to cope with this loss, as well as their feelings of being devalued as a parent, by limiting their involvement with their children.[57]

Father's feeling that he is is being depreciated and devalued—has become in effect disposable—and his sense of helpless rage and depression is the picture that emerges from every study that bothers to even look at the father at all. Fathers have largely been ignored in the research literature and relegated—in a self-fulfilling way—to the status of "theoretical role model."

Children, however, do not view their fathers as theoretical role models. Quite the reverse: just as there is solid evidence that under conventional visitation arrangements, fathers experience a deep and enduring sense of loss with regard to their children, there is equal evidence that children themselves experience the absence of their fathers as extremely painful. One study documents feelings of loss, powerlessness, confusion, and intense longings for their father's return.[152]

Children are not only deeply pained by their father's absence but they interpret it as abandonment; as a consequence, they feel devalued and guilty with few ways to express their anger and confusion. Also, studies suggest, children who are cut off from their fathers are often subject to the erratic behavior, and sometimes anger, of their overburdened mothers. In fact, mothers with sole custody often develop neurotic attachments to their children, putting sons in the role of substitute father or seeing daughters as appendages of themselves.

In sum, all parties are affected by conventional arrangements during divorce. All studies conclude that the positive or negative magnitude of these effects during divorce is correlated with both the extent of conflict between divorced parents and the level of involvement between father and children. Fathers want improved relationships with their children. Only children who saw their fathers very frequently—and for some real length of time—were at all satisfied with the new family arrangement.[135, 152, 153] Even more so than in intact homes, how effective the mother's relations with her children are depends in large part on low conflict with her ex-spouse and how involved he is with the children. In one study's words, when commenting on the need for additional support systems,

. . . none of these support systems were as salient as a continued, positive, mutually supportive relationship of the divorced couple and continued involvement of the father with the child.[62]

Thus, all studies report that with minimal conflict between divorced parents, the frequency of father contact with the child is associated with more positive adjustment of the child. Nevertheless, sole custody arrangements predispose families towards increased conflict and decreased father contact. If the recommendations of Goldstein, Freud, and Solnit that:

a custody decree should be final, that is, not subject to modification, once it is determined who will be the custodial parent, it is that parent, not the court, who must decide under what conditions he or she wishes to raise the child. Thus, the noncustodial parent should have no legally en-

forceable right to visit the child, and the custodial parent should have the
right to decide whether it is desirable for the child to have such visits,
(pages 37 and 38)[52]

were adopted, conflict would be maximized.[*] Thus, the sequential and self-
destructive cycle of events in sole custody is exacerbated. As June and
William Noble state in their book, *The Custody Trap,* "Custody means
control. It means ownership, power, authority."[112] There is no question
that legal responsibility for the child is given to the parent with sole
custody. In major disagreements, the only alternatives open to the noncustodial parent are persuasion or going back to court, a painful, time-
consuming, and often ineffective option.

Fathers, after fighting, may resort to flight. Child support payments for a
minimal relationship add further burdens. Mothers, receiving inadequate
and sporadic support, now represent the single largest subgroup of the
population that lives below the poverty level, more than half depending
upon welfare payments.[61] Each succeeding event carries the family along
into greater stress with no way out. It is a disastrous and too frequent occurrence for children of divorce.

Although those children who fared best after divorce were those who
were free to develop loving and full relationships with both parents,[135] concerned parties (whether judges, lawyers, social workers, psychiatrists and
not least fathers themselves) seem to operate as if there were, in fact, no
alternative to the current arrangement in which the father is radically
severed, literally divorced, from his children. It is possible to affix an
"ex-" to spouse, but no parent can become—at least not without great suffering for all concerned—an "ex-."

VII. JOINT CUSTODY: A VIABLE OPTION

Alternatives to the biased predominance of sole maternal custody need to
be explored. Joint custody is one viable alternative to sole custody with
either parent. While there are other options which might be the best choice
for a particular family's situation, joint custody, where possible, provides a
"least detrimental alternative." Most important, then, is an understanding
of the costs and benefits associated with each and those situations to which
they may be applied. A significant outcome, however, is at least the introduction of choice into the currently deterministic process. Sole custody
may be preferable in some cases, but it does not have to be. People also

---

[*]Also, since sexist social values assign custody to mothers 90 percent of the time, these recommendations, in fact, would lock mothers in and fathers out.

need support in making choices and the remainder of this paper provides information towards those ends.

Today numerous terms are used to identify custody arrangements having various legal, moral, and physical rights and responsibilities for child rearing. "Joint custody," as defined by Roman and Haddad in *The Disposable Parent,* is:

> That post divorce custodial arrangement in which parents agree to equally share the authority for making all decisions that significantly affect the lives of their children. It is also that post divorce arrangement in which child care is split equally between the parents, or, at the most discrepant, child care resolves itself into a two-to-one split. (pages 20–21)[131]

In this quasi-legal form, neither the competence of the parents nor the amounts of time spent with each parent are mentioned. At this level of specificity are other concepts such as "coparenting," "joint parenting," "cocustody," and "shared custody." Although confusing and overlapping, the elemental ingredient to all is a central agreement toward shared parenting. This agreement exists on two levels—the moral and the legal. Mariam Galper explains that, "co-parenting means sharing your children equally," but "this is not necessarily a legal agreement, but can be a moral one." (pages 16–17)[44] Thus, there is an attitude on the part of both parents that both are necessary to their children, that they are intimately connected to one another through their children, and that they respect the other's relationship with their children. In this manner, no fault is attributed or labels of "fitness" or "unfitness" assigned. Likewise, children are not thought of as "property," but as persons, so, therefore, parents do not have "ownership" rights to dispute.

More specifically, at the legal level, these definitions contain two distinct but complementary components—one relates to decision-making and control; the other relates to child care and physical custody. Theoretically, the concept envisions an equal sharing of both elements by each parent. Practically, equally sharing is much more rigidly adhered to in the former than in the latter. In fact, authority and control must remain equal, while child care and physical arrangements should be flexibly determined by the parents as a function of factors such as the child's age, sex, and own wishes and the geographic proximity of their homes. Nevertheless, it can be seen how the first is required for proper operation of the second.

Although several authors have tried to develop a common scheme for categorizing the many different legal interpretations of "joint custody,"[43] no standardization has yet been agreed upon. Continued reference to multiple labels as if they are synonymous is confusing. One authority often cited, Alexander Lindsey, (page 60–61)[86] makes the distinction using "joint custody" and "divided custody." Regarding "joint custody," he states:

> Although the child resides most of the year with one parent, the spouses (or ex-spouses) have joint control of its care, upbringing, and education, and equal voice in decisions pertaining to its health, religious training, vacations, trips, and the choice of schools, summer camps, etc.

On the other hand, "divided custody" means:

> One spouse (or ex-spouse) has the child for a part of the year, the other spouse (or ex-spouse) for the remainder of the year, with reciprocal visitation privileges. Each spouse (or ex-spouse) exercises control over the child while in his or her custody.

Clearly, the major elements revolve around shared control over decisions and alternating arrangements for the physical residence of the children.

Neither of the above definitions is entirely satisfactory, and Freed and Foster, after reviewing cases from several states, found inconsistency in their legal application. However, they do synthesize a nonlegal overview of "joint custody" as, "joint or shared control over the decision-making process plus alternating physical presence of the child according to the circumstances of the individual case." (Part I, page 390)[40]

Thus, contrary to the common custody dispute, there is no "winner" but shared responsibility and decision making. Additionally, while the child's physical residence may remain at one location, more often the residence is changed on a regularly scheduled basis varying from split weeks to split years. While endless combinations are possible, clearly, such arrangements place special demands upon both parents and children.

For the purposes of this paper, I use the term "Joint Custody" to include both complementary parts of the concept. When it becomes necessary to distinguish the two elements from each other, I use joint "legal" custody and joint "physical" custody. The former consists exclusively of the shared decision-making function. Thus, parents are involved in consultation and agreement on all *major* decisions affecting the children. The latter, in addition, refers to the alternating arrangements for the physical residence of the children; in it the timing of changes is variable and day-to-day decisions are made by the parent with whom the children are residing at that time. Thus, the claim that joint legal custody and sole custody with liberal visitation rights are indistinguishable is not true. However, it is true that the differences between divided custody, which can designate a sole custodian, and liberal visitation become blurred. Nevertheless, since joint physical custody is dependent upon joint legal custody, it is considerably different from divided custody.

Criticisms generally fall into two categories which are directed toward the two complementary components of joint custody. First, regarding shared control, it is charged that sharing custody is an impossible alternative because a divorce situation, by its very nature, is not conducive to the kind of cooperation that this type of arrangement demands. Secondly, skeptics argue that children are put in an untenable position, dividing loyalties and physical surroundings which minimizes, as a result, their stability.

There are significant costs to the degree that these arguments are accurate. However, joint custody must be viewed not in comparison to an idealized family, but rather relative to the less than ideal alternatives of sole custody and disposable parents. These costs were previously described. Moreover, additional benefits accure to joint custody, off-setting other potential costs. In the next sections, we will analyze how realistic these anticipated costs actually are.

A. Ex-Spouses' Ability To Cooperate

The adversary nature of our divorce system, especially extended into the issue of child custody, helps to perpetuate a climate of animosity between persons who already have proven they cannot get along as husband and wife. Even with a trend toward no-fault divorce, it is expecting a lot of people under severe stress to be able to share decisionmaking for a child. To the extent that the system casts divorcing parents in the roles of enemies and expects them to be unable to cooperate, a self-fulfilling prophecy is created.

While it is suggested that joint custody can only work for couples with an amicable relationship, the pertinent inquiry should be whether parents are able to isolate their marital conflicts from their roles as parents. Increasing evidence is becoming available from several sources that couples who make commitments to share custody of their children are able to cooperate even though they do not like each other as husband or wife. Summarizing, one study found:

> When couples want to share custody of their children, they are able to isolate out their marital conflicts from their parental responsibilities. In fact, it is not uncommon for joint custody parents to frankly admit their antipathy toward one another but to maintain, at the same time, that they do not intend to harm their children just because they might like to harm one another. (page 19)[132]

In effect, coparents seem to truly consider the best interests of the child. What often begins as a front—an appearance of minimal conflict in the children's presence—becomes in time a reality of self-fulfilling prophecy.

Contrarily, under sole custody, conflict is not minimized. The studies previously cited about sole custody households all pointed out the value of the father's continued and solid involvement with his children and the virtues of low conflict. That is, sole custody seems to work best when, in fact, it is pretty much akin to joint custody. Usually though, sole custody appears to exacerbate parental conflict and it is often used by the mother as a club, forcing the children to be caught in the middle.

Authorities suggest several reasons why parents can cooperate. Some suggest that equal rights eliminate the need for power plays between them. The one-sided power of the sole custodian is neutralized and the powerlessness of the noncustodian reversed, decreasing the possibility of using the children as pawns. Because the arrangement more fully meets *both* parents' needs, rancor diminishes. Also, once the day-to-day pressures of the marriage are eliminated, the reduced tension increases the possibilities of being successful parents. In and of itself, a joint custody award may provide incentive for cooperation, in that, if the relationship breaks down, the award of sole custody would probably go to the parent who did not precipitate the failure. Additionally, it has been suggested:

> If custodial care were to be considered joint responsibility in divorce, as it is in marriage, there would be less opportunity for enmity to replace cooperation. . . . Arguments about child upbringing, financial needs, and the like go on in virtually every marriage, normal or otherwise. These arguments do not have to become more shrill upon separation. In fact, removing the irritating factor of two unloving people living together can probably make them both more responsive to the needs of the children.[112]

When either parent does not feel threatened with the possibility of loss, each is in a healthier position for cooperation.

Another reason joint custody may, in time, minimize parental conflict is because it more fully satisfies the needs of both parents by allowing a combination of "time off" and (if anything) enhanced involvement in child care. It is obvious enough how time off might well suit many mothers and, as for the fathers, studies have overwhelmingly shown that among the divorced, it was the joint-custody fathers who were most satisfied. Those fathers who had more contact with and joint custody of their children were significantly more satisfied than fathers with less contact and no custodial rights of their children. This finding, that it is not just the fact of having children, but the experience of an active ongoing relationship with them that is ego enhancing, supports the work of Erikson, Biller, and others who have noted the importance of such involved parenting for healthy adult development.

Finally, those critics who extrapolate from single experiences condemn the possibility of joint custody for any divorcing family. Horror stories from specific cases are generalized to show that all cases of joint custody are basically unworkable. One such commentary, after making such generalizations, concludes:

> If two adults can interact well enough in relation to their children to really share decision-making, they will exercise custody jointly and meaningfully without court order. If they cannot, an order for joint custody simply subjects the children to trauma, the parents to litigation, and the courts to stress and overwork. (page 202)[80]

While from the narrow experience of a few cases, this may appear true, it ignores the evidence of studies showing parental cooperation, the negative pressures of the system against sharing, and the positive benefits and advantages of a joint-custody decree. When sole *legal* custody has been granted to one of the parents, at that parent's discretion, any one of the agreed upon ways of handling the custody arrangement can be terminated. In the event of a major disagreement about child rearing, the legal power and control clearly rests with the custodial parent. Joint custody vests the legal rights in common to both divorced parents equally. This is significantly different from a moral agreement or understanding between parents. This legal difference is paramount and must not be ignored or undervalued. Furthermore, limited experiential evidence is reported which suggests that litigation and the work of the courts is actually decreased with joint custody rather than increased. (page B60)[35] This decrease appears to be particularly true when based upon a mediated or negotiated settlement. Thus, it appears that inclusion of a mediation or arbitration provision in the initial joint custody agreement, as an alternative way to resolving parental deadlock, has positive effects. It is, therefore, important that such supportive services be expanded beyond their currently limited availability.

B. The Child As "Yo-Yo"

A major objection to joint custody is that the child's loyalties are divided and stability undermined by the continuing parental conflict and by shifting living arrangements respectively. From actual experience with joint custody situations, no such evidence of negative impact has been found. However, the data are limited and further research needs to investigate these important considerations. Nevertheless, authorities condemn joint custody as if there were conclusive evidence, state opinions as facts, and reject testimony that may contradict their preconceptions.

In order to support the impact upon the child of unresolved parental conflict, one must assume that, with respect to the child, parents are unable to cooperate. This objection is contingent upon the previous one, which did not hold up under scrutiny. Joint custody parents do positively value each other as parents, while remaining antagonists as husband and wife. Moreover, one must be realistic about divorcing households and possible alternatives. The pertinent question is not whether there remains any conflict, but which situation creates the least at an acceptable price. Certainly within the highly stressed context of divorce, a joint custody family is no more conflicted than either the predivorce or sole custody family. From the evidence cited previously, one could expect it to be significantly less.

On the other hand, the destruction of the ongoing relationship between the child and one (noncustodial) parent is designed, paradoxically, to protect the no more important psychological relationship between child and custodial parent. The price of such a choice creates hostility and feelings of powerlessness in the parents, guilt and feeling of abandonment in the child, and perpetrates the unequal stereotypical view of parents in the nuclear family norm. Such a price for a mythical reduction in conflict is a high and unnecessary price; a benefit of joint custody occurs because it does not perpetuate these conditions.

Nevertheless, a widely influential book, *Beyond the Best Interests of the Child (BBIC)*—because of the stature of its authors—contradicts these and previously discussed findings.[52] The authors state that "psychoanalytic theory. . . calls into question those custody decisions which split a child's placement between two parents or which provide the non-custodial parent with the right to visit." Further, they advocate that custody be irrevocably awarded to one parent with total authority. In other words, "the non-custodial parent should have no legally enforceable right to visit the child, and the custodial parent should have the right to decide whether it is desirable for the child to have such visits."* *But*—and this can hardly be

---

*In the Epilogue of the second edition of *BBIC*,[52] the authors justify their position after clearly stating they are referring to parents who cannot agree and a child who is severely traumatized by a custody battle its parents cannot resolve. Court intervention is, under these conditions, required to decrease stress and enable the child's continued development. In this case (and the uniquely special example provided), their prescription is necessary, particularly to maintain trust in the custodial parent. "In the child's eyes, the court, by directing him to act against the express wishes of his custodial parent, casts doubt on that parent's authority and capacity to parent." On the other hand, where both parents are fit and capable of agreement (by far the great majority of cases), this reasoning could be detrimental to the child. Rather than protection, from the child's viewpoint, being cut off from a valued parental relationship by court order would be viewed as unwanted and destructive. Additionally, the child could hold the custodial parent responsible for its loss.

overemphasized—there are virtually *no* social science data to support the proposition that a single official parent is preferable to two. In fact, *BBIC* does not contain a single reference to any empirical study in the extensive literature on adoption and foster placement and does not consider data from recent divorce research. It uses but one single citation from non-psychoanalytic literature. Moreover, psychoanalytic data are used in support of their position without acknowledging the major criticisms that have been leveled at the studies from which they derive.

Regarding the desirability of one parent, the authors simply observe:

> Unlike adults, children lack the capacity to maintain positive emotional ties with unrelated or hostile adults. They will freely love more than one adult only if the individuals in question feel positively to one another. Failing this, children may become prey to severe and crippling loyalty conflicts.[52]

In rebuttal, several critics state:

> Yet children *do* have existing relationships with *both* parents and given any chance at all, they show remarkable tenacity about continuing to love them both. Moreover, I know of no studies which show that the legal death of one parent, and the complete subordination of the child to the other's possibly distorted view, is a preferable step for the child's future development. If anything, there is much more evidence—not mere opinion—that it is potentially damaging to the child to be completely subject to one parent's will and that by maintaining close and continuous contact with both parent's, the child is afforded in-depth exposure to two points of view which I believe to be constructive. (page 22)[132]

and, *BBIC* ensures that:

> The court is required to make a decision that increases rather than diminishes the role and responsibility of the courts in child custody cases. Instead of encouraging the example of the numerous cases where parents agree and work out custody arrangements out of court the author's recommendations encourage bitter custody battles. In addition to the social and emotional costs. . . such litigation requires a time-consuming investigation to determine the better custodial parent—procedures that also require specialized personnel and advisors who increase the cost and further complicate the judicial process. (page 23)[132]

From another perspective, one must weigh the advantages of two psychological parents and the decrease in tension from the predivorce family against the difficulties associated with two homes to evaluate the criticism of two homes undermining the child's stability. Technically, from a legal viewpoint, as previously distinguished, "joint custody" does not necessarily include alternating residences. "Joint Physical Custody" (in contrast to "Joint Legal Custody"), includes two homes based upon a schedule worked out to accommodate the particular circumstances of the individual family.* In practice, Grief concludes that the concern over the disruption caused by the two homes is more a concern of others rather than of joint custody families themselves.[57]

One joint custody parent stated:

> What sharing parenthood offers is a new, different kind of stability. . . . I have spent three years helping to make this type of arrangement work and can attest to the fact that two homes have been far better for our sons than one broken one. I think it is certainly more damaging for a child to have only minimal contact with an absent parent than it is to have two sets of clothes, books, and toys.[103]

In another study, Abarbanel found the families benefited from the predictability and stability of their schedules. A joint custody parent concluded:

> Annie doesn't go to a brand new environment one week and a brand new environment another week. It's not like new, new, new. It's like A, B, A, B, A, B. She's got two consistent homes.[1]

Nevertheless, another study reported problems regarding a child's transition between homes.[110] However, the same effects were found if time was equally split between homes or if the child lived primarily with one parent, similar to sole custody. While the problems were not specific to any particular time arrangement, the author concluded with a recommendation for further study rather than a condemnation of joint custody.

C. Joint Custody In Operation

With the increasing number of divorces, joint custody has become more common. Some predict it will be the norm of the 1980s. Whatever the case, the news media currently devote substantial coverage to the divorce prob-

---

*In some circumstances, there is no moving back and forth. In the so-called "bird-nest" arrangement, the parents alternate occupying a common residence in which the children always live. This arrangement may be good for very young children or immediately after separation, but it has usually been temporary. Alternatively, teenagers, who make their own choices, may prefer to stay in only one home.

lem and, especially case studies of joint custody, as a controversial topic. Although each family presents many unique aspects, common themes often run throughout. This section attempts to briefly summarize.

It is very clear that to successfully sustain a joint custody relationship takes energy and commitment. It definitely is not easier than sole custody. While the issues are different, one feels in control of one's family with a sense of power rather than being at the mercy of an impersonal institutional process. In fact, the logistical requirements may be more demanding. Nevertheless, it is felt that the benefits for all members of the family of having relationships with both parents are better and overshadow the difficulties, especially living in two homes.

The key appears to be a mutual trust in the parenting ability of the other parent and, similarly, a belief that its continuation has positive, long-term benefits for all family members. Some mothers, who expected they would be awarded custody, are surprised with a request for joint custody. But as one states, "Initially, I went along with the idea of co-parenting for my husband. And now I wouldn't have done it any other way. Our children didn't have to divorce their parents."[85] For others, joint custody fits naturally; one mother remembers:

There was no elaborate discussion. . . . Both of us were deeply attached to the children, and both of us saw no reason not to continue that attachment on a daily basis. When we decided to separate, I remember thinking, "Richard is a good father. He's not a great husband, but he's a perfectly good father." (page 34)[28]

Still for others, it represents release from a burden they would rather not totally have. Motherhood may be a secondary ambition and while social pressures will not allow them to totally give up custody, their ex-husband assumes the major responsibilities.[134]

Joint custody represents a sense of equality and choice, especially for fathers. There is no "loser." The power games available to sole custodians are avoided. In fact, there may be financial and other positive benefits. As Jay Folberg, executive director of the Family Conciliation Courts, explains:

The real guts of joint custody are that both parents are involved in decisions regarding the child. So, if a father in California with a son in New York is consulted on whether the son should have orthodontics or go to a private school, that father is more likely to make his child-support payments. He is also more likely to make every effort to see the child, despite the distances between them. (page 35)[28]

On the other hand, with joint physical custody, providing two homes with twice as many clothes and toys is certainly more expensive than infrequent and inadequate child support. This represents increased support for the family as a whole but an additional strain on resources already diminished. However, regular contact with the children creates not only an incentive (usually for the father) to provide for their needs, but also realistically brings home to both parents the escalating expenses of child care, promoting more flexible attitudes. Fathers, also, benefit in less tangible ways from the experience of a more independent and close relationship with their children.

After convincing people that divorced parents actually can cooperate, additional problems may complicate the relationship. Some critics suggest that joint custody may be a disguise with which parents perpetuate a remnant of their marriage, thereby not completely finishing their "emotional divorce." However, one study of joint custody concluded that divorced parents were able "to continue a co-parenting relationship while terminating, both legally and emotionally, a spousal relationship." (page B47)[35] Other joint custody parents have felt that cooperation could be carried too far. "We got the feeling that the kids didn't want us to be too friendly. It feeds on their fantasy that Mom and Dad may someday get back together."[85] *

Conversely, the children benefit from the absence of a fantasy endemic to sole custody. Neither do they feel abandonded nor do they feel guilty as the person responsible for causing the divorce, because they never have to "choose" between their parents. Children do have difficulties with the complex logistics of two homes, but appear to accept it as a price for a continuing relationship with both parents.[85] While joint legal custody does not require geographic proximity, the alternating schedule of joint physical custody does require a certain closeness. The degree of "geographic closeness" depends upon factors such as:

- Age and sex of the children;
- School arrangement;
- The child's network of friends and relations;
- Ease and availability of transportation; and
- The family's financial resources.[35]

A particular family's arrangement is usually flexibly determined over time as these factors change. However, a major reevaluation must take place if

*Cooperation is usually limited to major decisions such as medical care, education, and religious training while every day decision are left to whichever parent the children are with at the time.

one parent should want to move beyond a desirable limit of residential difference. Although this parent does not have the right to move to another city and automatically, as in sole custody, expect to take the children along, while that might indeed happen it must be done as a result of a mutually arrived at decision. One writer has criticized court intervention to prevent parents from moving based on a conflict with our society's value for free and easy mobility.[10] Nevertheless, cases have revolved around restricting parental mobility because of the destructive impact it would have on a valued parent-child relationship.* Individual determinations will have to be made between these conflicting values. But as Judith Grief has suggested, "Being a parent means you can't always do what you want to do."[2] Favorable job offers have been available, but were turned down by joint custody parents in favor of staying near their children.

Another special consideration has been the effects of two different sets of rules on the children. As mother and father evolve their respective households, differences in parenting styles will lead to different values and rules. Standards need not be totally consistent as long as they are reasonable. Regarding children's ability to cope, Dr. Spock says, "Children are much better at this than adults. After all, children in intact families adapt to grandparents and teachers, who may have somewhat different requirements from their parents. They can recognize that their parents are two separate individuals, not an institution."[28] Nevertheless, there is an incentive for good communication between joint custody parents in order to avoid being played off against each other by the children.

Pressure may also be placed upon joint custody parents by friends from outside the family. Margaret Mead wrote:

> Among the older generation, there is some feeling that any contact between divorced people somehow smacks of incest; once divorced, they have been declared by law to be sexually inaccessible to each other, and the aura of past sexual relations makes any further relations incriminating. (page 121)[97]

While this applies to both parents, as individuals each is suspected because of their indeterminate sex roles. Fathers who become involved in the daily tasks of child care find their manhood questioned. Women, on the other hand, are criticized for being incomplete mothers and allowing the children's father into their exclusive domain.

---

*See *Entwistel* v. *Entwistel,* 402, N. Y. S. 2d 213 (App. Div. 1978) and *Scheiner* v. *Scheiner,* 336, So., 2d 406 (1976).

Finally, remarriage of either or both divorced parents is probable within a few years, adding new actors and a new level of complexity to the joint custody family. Blended families, even without joint custody, experience a unique set of problems requiring considerable work to resolve. One possible conflict may be between new stepparent and the ex-spouse. The stepparent may wish to close out history by excluding the children's father. On the other hand, the children's father may feel defensive and not wish to share his parental role with someone considered an outsider. This can happen regardless of the custody arrangement, but joint custody has unique pros and cons. If the arrangement includes a half-time sharing of the children, the new "nuclear"* family's parents may try to exclude the children's father, especially one who appears so frequently. This action will represent a threat to the father-child relationship which joint custody tries so hard to protect. At least, with joint custody, the ex-spouse has an equal legal right in the negotiations to rearrange boundaries. On the other hand, joint custody allows the new stepparent time away from his "instant" family and the remarried couple can get to know each other more gradually. Finally, one father, when faced with inclusion of, and competition with, another man in the family, was able to say, "The threat is less than it would be if I were a visiting parent, and the children spent more time with the new man in the house than with me. As a joint custodial parent, new man in the house or not, my sons will always know who their father is."[102]

VIII. AN ACTION STRATEGY FOR JOINT CUSTODY

When at least 90 percent of a population behave in a particular manner, but public policies and the greater attention are focused primarily on the 10 percent minority, one must question, with divorce being so volatile a subject, why there is so little attention paid to the vast majority. It was previously stated, although with limited available data, that the ratio between uncontested and contested child custody cases was assumed to be approximately 90:10.** Also, "It is universally agreed that about 90 percent of all contested custody cases result in awards to the mother. In addition, the mother assumes custody in at least 90 percent of the divorce cases that never reach the court." (page 353)[99] Many authors have justifiably criticized the maternal bias of our court system; considering there were 618,000 divorces involving children in 1976 (Table 2),[142] the universe for which the

---

*The new family unit may wish to appear as a classic nuclear family. But if treated as such, there most certainly will be problems. Completely new issues are generated in the creation and functioning of blended families.
**Although this distribution may be inaccurate to some degree, the argument which follows holds as long as the ratio is not 50:50.

court chose the custodain was approximately 61,800 cases. On the other hand, since the court usually accepts the agreed-upon custodian in an uncontested case, it appears that parents chose an appropriate custodial arrangement in approximately 556,200 cases. To cite only the courts, however accurately, for maternal bias provides a convenient institutional target and scapegoat. Courts are not independent of social values and the stereotypes which we all conform with to some degree. The maternal bias of our entire society appears to be operating, through parental decisions, in a much larger number (494,400) of divorce cases.

This finding does not mean that court reform regarding child custody is less necessary. It means that to adequately consider social policy with respect to joint custody involves much more change than just the court system. Viewed this way, we are confronting a truly "wicked" problem. The next section addresses change aimed at the courts. The final sections begin to address the larger social issues of which joint custody is one part.

A. Joint Custody As A Legislative Presumption*

Most state statutes, like New York's Domestic Relations Law, state: there shall be "no prima facia right to the custody of the child in either parent." The spirit of the law is generally ignored and the presumption is heavily in favor of the mother. This presumption operates in several areas. Although, as Foster and Freed point out, it is a myth that most Amercian courts are dead set against joint custody, per se, and no state by statute specifically forbids such an alternative (Part II),[40] they also conclude,

> Probably, most judges sincerely believe that children, especially infants and daughters, properly and naturally belong with their mothers, and that it would be contrary to their best interests to award sole or joint custody to the father unless the mother is shown to be unfit. (Part I)[40]

Under the guise of the "best interest of the child" and the "tender years" doctrine, judicial prejudice sometimes can rationalize decisions in favor of mothers. While such normative decisions are distinctly out of step with the new realities of American families, they are definitely consistent with a strict conservative philosophy and the preservation of mythical nuclear family norms.

Currently, the trend appears to be diminishing the power of the "tender years" doctrine[41] and interpretations of the child's best interests as follows, are cited with approval:

---

*It is assumed that such a presumption would minimally affect those uncontested cases, unless courts required acceptance of parental choice be contingent upon showing that joint custody had been considered and, if not why. The advisability of courts altering the parent's preference would be questionable.

In determining what is for the best welfare of a child of tender years, the courts must consider not only food, clothing, shelter, care, education, and environment, but also bear in mind that every such child is entitled to the love, nurture, advice, and training of both father and mother, and to deny to the child the opportunity to know, associate with, love, and be loved by either parent, may be a more serious ill than to refuse it in some part those things money can buy.[14]

Nevertheless, this now appears as the exception rather than the rule. Because the outcomes of custody decisions overall show limited perceptible change, rather than merely encouraging joint custody, it is argued that it needs to be the legislated presumption. During divorce proceedings, the presumption, therefore, would be in favor of sharing the children. Instead of the parties trying to prove which parent is more fit, they would have to show why joint custody will not work.

Various state legislatures have instituted or are beginning to consider joint custody statutes. Seven states, Iowa, North Carolina, California, Kansas, Nevada, Oregon, and Wisconsin already have joint custody laws on the books. In Massachusetts, New York, Maryland, New Jersey, and Pennsylvania, joint custody legislation is pending.

The Oregon law, for example, became effective in 1977. It simply provides that the judge may decree joint custody. Joint custody is neither expressly encouraged, nor does it set forth the criteria for when it would be appropriate to decree joint custody.

More to the point is the California law which became effective January 1980:

". . . Custody should be awarded in the following order of preference, according to the best interests of the child: (a) to both parents jointly pursuant to Section 4600.5 or to either parent. In making an award of custody to either parent, the court shall consider which parent is more likely to allow the child or children frequent and continuing contact with the noncustodial parent, and shall not prefer a parent as custodian because of that parent's sex.[23] *

It could be argued that to call for a presumption in favor of joint custody is coercive. But the current bias in favor of the mother is also coercive. Courts must not only reflect prevailing social standards but must also be the arbiters of the justice inherent in those standards.

Equally, by making joint custody, as opposed to sole maternal custody,

*In the second edition of *Beyond the Best Interests of the Child,* Goldstein, Freud, and Solnit also recommend such a criterion, other things being equal, for choosing who should be awarded sole custody. (page 118)[52]

the norm, it will become so for many. Realistically, it simply suggests the capacity for, and importance of, shared parenthood and the powerful social sanction for such an arrangement. When joint custody would not work (where the parents themselves say it will not work), no court in the land will make it happen. This presumption differs from our current bias, which coercively sanctions an arrangement that not only may damage all those involved, but that people are nearly powerless to change. As things now stand, it is very difficult—financially, socially, and emotionally—for men and women to do anything but conform to the irrational bias in favor of the mother. Under joint custody, on the other hand, both parents are equal. If they do not wish to adopt a joint custody arrangement, all they need to do is say so.

Regardless of whether or not joint custody is presumed, its utilization needs to be carefully employed on a case-by-case basis. Several statutes contain and authors have suggested criteria to consider for its application.[99] Where it is presumed, critics charge it provides an avenue for judicial cop-out in lieu of vigorous fact-finding and difficult decisions. For example, in *Braiman* vs. *Braiman,* Judge Breitel states there are cases where the court must "recognize the division in fact of the family" and that "there are no painless solutions. In the rare case joint custody may approximate the former family relationships more closely than other custodial arrangements. It may not, however, be indiscriminately substituted for an award of sole custody to one parent."[13] In other cases, joint custody has been accepted by parents who were not fully aware of what was meant and required, leading to disasterous results.[9] Clearly, where joint custody is not presumed, judges, and other professionals, have been quoted as being convinced of its being unworkable (pages 367–368),[99] which leads one to doubt its being given fair consideration. Even in cases where joint custody could work, lack of knowledge precludes its consideration. "It was clear from testimony given at the Oregon Legislative Hearings on joint custody that knowledge of the possibility of using joint custody is not widespread." as[35] observed even in the book and movie, *Kramer* vs. *Kramer.*[54] Our stereotype of the divorce process apparently prohibits consideration of different alternatives.

B. Cultural And Political Realities

Even if a presumption in favor of joint custody became the uniform law of the land, in and of itself, as the aftermath of the civil rights legislation made clear, the change in the law would not be enough. Without profound changes in the social system and services that both institute and support these changes, no joint custody law can work.

The following recommendations reflect ways to change what was previously identified as the source of our regressive child custody policies. They are conceived of as a package, and a wholesale assault, underlined by change in the law itself, is required. The following is a proposed list: (pages 179–196)[131]

1. Counseling and Mediation Services: Establish a nationwide network of family counseling and mediation services within, but not limited to, the domestic or family court systems. (Such supportive services should be free, or on a sliding-cost scale, and voluntary, unless a custody dispute is involved.)[111]

2. Research: Institute long-term, extensive research on both the impact of divorce on families and the effects of different types of custody arrangements.

3. Work and Day Care: Enforce and strengthen laws that grant the sexes equality in employment and income. Encourage split work shifts. Make day-care facilities available to all who want them at fees that reflect a sliding scale, proportionate to family income.

4. Education I: Incorporate into the school curriculum, nationwide, nonsexist family courses in marriage and parenthood, and courses in alternative lifestyles, at all school levels.

5. Education II: Stress and make mandatory interdisciplinary courses in marriage and divorce for all those engaged in working with families—teachers, psychologists, lawyers, and social workers, among others.

6. Family Law: Remove family law from an adversary climate and redefine the role of the matrimonial lawyer as advocate for the full family and not just one of its members.

7. Expanded Community Programs for the Divorced:
Although this analysis leads to a rational change in public policy and a comprehensive approach for the restructuring of multiple social programs, the political realities and constraints, especially on a more individual and emotional level, are such that there appears to be little chance for full and expeditious implementation. As William O'Neill has observed, "experience has demonstrated that the formal barriers to women's emancipation— votelessness, educational and occupational discriminations, and the like—

are less serious and more susceptible to change than the domestic, institutional, and social customs that keep women in the home." (page 137)[8] He also could have added—"and men out of the home." In crucial ways, what people think about themselves and believe to be their options are the most formidable barriers of all. Thus, our sexist cultural assumptions and their internalization by the majority of men, women, and children present the overwhelming obstacle to change. In this regard, the forces acting against shared parenthood applicable to divorced families are strong, pervasive, and very subtle.

Within two-parent families, a currently significant shift is the increasing employment of women outside the home and the sharing of the male's provider role. However, with regard to their husband's changing contribution to their households, Pleck found, "that husbands' time in family tasks does not vary in response to the changes in wives' family work resulting from wives paid employment." (page 420)[121] Time budget studies confirm that the husbands' contribution to the household did not increase when wives entered the paid labor force in the 1960s and only began showing small increases in the late 1970s.[122] Thus, women, having assumed the new role of provider, still retain almost entirely the older roles of child care and homemaker, giving rise to the newly popular label of "Supermom."[146] Men on the other hand, when work role demands decrease, rather than becoming involved in child care or taking over part of the housework, appear to "increase what they give to overtime, two jobs, or leisure." (page 396)[24]

The Rapoports describe this problem between the slower rate of change in men's family roles compared with the relatively more rapid rate of change in women's roles in paid employment as "psychosocial lag."[126] Rather than viewing this discrepancy as a permanent feature of our society, it can be viewed as reflecting a transitional problem of adjustment. In order to successfully accomplish such a transition, one must overcome the restrictive influences of sex role stereotyping along with the associated power and status conflicts. While the predominant discussion usually focuses on those problems women face in making the transition to employed status, less obviously men also face similar difficulties with changing their parental status. Effective progress requires societal recognition that the "game" involves two capable players rather than, as some would have us believe, an oppressor class and its victims. While "motherhood" has been recognized as a role conferred for purposes of social control, few also view the "provider" role as equally controlling and restrictive.[128]

When women seek employment, pressures are applied from several areas. First, "Motherhood" is the chief sex-typing prescription for women without which a woman often does not feel fully identified.[137] Secondly, women are discriminated against by men in attempts to retain control over traditional power and privilege. Finally, burdened by child care responsibilities and barriers to the best jobs, women participate as "second-class providers" with lower earnings in the lower level of a "dual labor market."

Similarly, men are pressured by family and social forces to maintain traditional standards for the organization of family life. Lein suggests:

> Men's ambivalence to changes in the structure of home life reflects the multiple pressures on them as citizens, workers, and concerned family members. The informal social support systems in which men tend to participate differ in certain respects from those of women—leaving men relatively unsupported to meet heavier demands for involvement in family life. Men's values concerning paid work and their sex-specific relationship to the paid labor force conflict with increased involvement in the day-to-day functioning of the home. Effort expended in home life is often perceived as energy diverted from the primary effort of breadwinning. (page 489)[77]

It is clear that severe limits are placed upon women by forces from outside the family. In a similar way, men face resistance from within the family.[121]

On the one hand, society identifies provider status as preferred and the source of male power; therefore, for a male to engage in child care or homemaking activities is to lose power and status.[32,125] On the other hand, in the home, men often are met with powerful resistance and assume a secondary parenting status playing a dependent "helpful" role.[55] While much research and serious discussion has worried about how maternal employment can be harmful to children,[64] few even consider the question of how paternal employment limits or distorts men's relations with children.

Recently, some authors have begun to detail how conformity with such a stereotype can be hazardous to personal growth and development.[51, 109, 123, 124] If women are "sex objects," men are controlled by being "success objects." From this viewpoint, *both* sexes are victimized by the constraints of sexual stereotyping.

Today, for most adults, parenthood is still parceled out in sex-prescribed roles, and the old cliches prevail: many women still feel that less than full-time devotion to their young brands them as bad mothers, unnatural, selfish, cold, and rejecting; many men do not regard nurturance as their proper sphere. Because child care has traditionally been "women's work," the suspicion lingers that for men to engage in it is unseemly, indeed unmanly. The result is that many women who do combine a career and children feel guilty, and many men are fearful or reluctant to even try. Sharing child care is, in many ways, a threat to both parents: her femininity is threatened and his masculinity undermined. This threat may not be consciously recognized, but it is often at work, making the woman ambivalent about her husband's involvement—experienced at times as an infringement, a loss of her control—and making the man, who is beset with doubts about his capabilities, equally ambivalent and no less fearful of a loss of control, particularly in his career, heretofore a source of his security.

Therefore, even with the rapid changes affecting assumption of new roles in two-parent families, there appears to be a struggle to giving up old, secure basis of power grounded in the stereotypical positions. Nevertheless, the rigidity with which stereotypical roles are held onto by intact families affects the nature of the divorced family.[19] Surprisingly, in attempts to stimulate changes in two-parent families, the women's movement appears in a contradictory position as a source of resistance for divorced families. In analyses of the original[116] and today's[65] feminist movements, the focus on issues outside family life and the failure to achieve changes in domestic life have been pinpointed as reasons why women's lives were not seriously altered. It is striking that feminist literature says not a word about the custody of children after divorce. If child custody is mentioned at all, the tendency is to call for more stringent enforcement of child-support payments, the creation of more and better day-care facilities, and split work shifts for women. This implies that maternal sole custody is taken for granted and, thus, the very conditions feminists decry within the intact household are encouraged in the divorced one.

By sanctioning the entrapment of divorced mothers in the home while advocating the liberation of women (and men) from sex-prescribed roles, the women's movement is caught in a grave contradiction. It is a central tenet of feminism that fathers ought to be more involved with home and child care, mothers less so. But what has not been recognized is that feminist theory is largely restricted to intact families. There is almost complete disregard for the father of the divorced family and the need for his continuing serious participation in the life of his children.

Similar to behavior in other areas, this schizoid response to experience is not wholly unrealistic: there is an understandable reluctance to relinquish the one area of power that women now have. Since women are inadequately prepared for what is in any event a discriminatory job market, many feminists believe that women can ill afford to lose the admittedly problematic status that exclusive parenthood now affords them. This largely unspoken argument is complicated by feminist fears of alienating what it regards as its natural consitituency. These feminists believe that because shared parenthood is seen by many women as a threat, and, therefore, the issue is a political hot potato, it is best dropped so that support from middle America for the women's movement is not lost. Should the movement advocate what many women believe might harm them? A similar paradox plagues ERA proponents.

At the same time, it is surely true that feminists (along with psychiatrists, social scientists, and others) are not themselves free of culture stereotypes.[129] Not only does the most liberated woman often feel guilty about less than full-time child care, she is apt, upon occasion, to exhibit a "reverse sexism" of her own. This sexism takes the form of doubt or negativity about the capacity and commitment of fathers to care for their young. Even in a revolution, rhetoric often outstrips action; it is far easier to talk a good line than to be comfortable living it.

These culturally induced attitudes are strongly resistant to change. When from the very vanguard itself, there is a reluctance to confront the need for the revolution to extend into domestic life, then how much more resistance will be found in the less politically sophisticated, who are, after all, the vast majority? Invasion of the previously exclusive female domain of child care by men has broad implications.[26] The issue of joint custody is only one block in the building of an entire foundation. Truly shared parenthood involves men in a critical situation in a manner which cannot help but have impact. How much impact will depend upon the extent of involvement and how successfully resistance is overcome.

IX. SUMMARY AND CONCLUSION

Throughout this paper, I have tried to present joint custody as a social policy choice different from the usual outcome which predominates today in the great majority of divorce decisions—that of sole maternal child custody. In so doing, I have clearly stated my assumptions and criteria, and, hopefully, successfully described their application. Rather than approach joint custody from either a psychological or a legal perspective focusing narrowly upon the judicial system as the only arena for action, I have tried to take a broader, more systemic viewpoint.

The reality of American families today is much different from the social norms by which they are portrayed and by which we perceive them. Academic paradigms are too narrow and limited to adequately comprehend the scope, diversity, and interrelationships of family reality. Public policies, while impacting heavily on families, are out of date and inconsistent. We need to seriously undertake a concentrated effort to completely overhaul our policies affecting American families. This undertaking cannot be one-sided or rely on the prescriptions of experts. There must be a concerted effort to involve all parts of our society, especially the parents whose input is critical.

Consistent with this idea, I have attempted to analyze joint custody within the context of family reality, but also to determine its interrelationship with larger cultural conditions. As such, joint custody is, from the more narrow view, definitely a positive step forward in line with major trends, but, from the broader perspective, joint custody is seriously constrained and blocked by rigidly held sexual stereotypes. Joint custody will work for divorcing families. Nevertheless, the initiatives and efforts are being generated by the families themselves, with institutions and professions dragging behind. Joint custody is a reality for many families, but whether or not society will accept it as a better alternative is questionable. Shared parenting in America today is being resisted. When one asks if joint custody will work, we must really consider the larger question of what society is willing to do to support real sharing of the family's parental functions. It is not the case that we do not have the capability; to the contrary, the potential exists today like no other time in history, and especially with the conditions available in America. Our question is not, "Can we. . . ?" but "Are we as a society really willing to accept equal and cooperative parenting in a variety of families?" Our dominant values, institutions, and policies are such that the answer, for now, is no.

Nevertheless, we are not alone. No other country, except one, Sweden, has chosen on a national scale to positively address changes which would emancipate men as well as women from the restrictive effects engendered by the traditional sex roles—culturally conditioned expectations imposed on an individual because of their sex. The factual conditions in Sweden today are far from optimal, but there is a general awareness and support for change. We have yet to choose to take supportive action, but this paper is an attempt to raise the level of awareness for such actions.

Swedish Prime Minister, Olof Palme, in an address in this country entitled, "The Emancipation of Man" chronicled his society's struggle toward freedom and equality for both sexes. He chose his title carefully, for in his opening statement he says:

> In your language, man can mean two things—human being and adult male. What I wish to say today is, therefore, embodied in the title I have given my address, 'The Emancipation of Man.' We have talked long enough about the emancipation of women, of the problem of women's role in society. But in order that women shall be emancipated from their antiquated role, the men must also be emancipated. Thus, it is the human beings we shall emancipate." (page 237)[120]

This philosophy is particularly appropriate for this paper. If nothing else, at the minimum, I wanted to advocate that men as people also need liberation from their restrictive roles. Not as guilty oppressors releasing their subjects from constraints, but for themselves. The women's movement is far ahead, and their literature and analyses dominate most discussions of sexual equality, especially with regard to the family. I hope that the male-oriented nature of this paper begins to bring it back into balance.

However, that is not enough. Equality is not an either/or proposition. All of us are in the struggle together and must elevate our analyses towards the greater definition of "Man." Therefore, at the most, I wanted to advocate the position that for joint custody to really work, we must address a far bigger question, and that question concerns and requires the involvement of everyone.

REFERENCES

1. Abarbanel, Alice. Shared parenting after separation and divorce: A study of joint custody. *Amercian Journal of Orthopsychiatry.* **49**(2):320–329 (1979).
2. Weiss, S. M., Joint custody is advisable when separating parents are hostile. *ADAMHA News.* **V**(10):5 (1979).
3. Anderson, Ralph E., and Carter, Irl E. *Human Behavior in the Social Environment.* Chicago: Aldine Publishing Company (1974).
4. Barnhill, Lawrence R. Healthy family systems, *The Family Coordinator.* **28**(1):94–100 (1979).
5. Bartz, Karen W., and Witcher, Wayne C. When father gets custody. *Children Today.* **7**(5):2–6,35 (1978).
6. Bernard, Jessie. *The Future of Motherhood,* New York: Penguin Books, Inc. (1974).
7. Biller, Henry, and Meredith, Dennis. *Father Power.* Garden City, New York: Anchor Books (1975).
8. Blake, Judith. The changing status of women in developed countries. *Scientific American.* **231**(3) 137–147 (Sept. 1974).
9. Blair, Linda. A mother's nightmare of joint custody. *Washington Post.* C1–C2, February 3, 1980.
10. Bodenheimer, Brigitte M. Equal rights, visitation, and the right to move. *Family Advocate.* Summer:18–21 (1978).
11. Bohannan, Paul. The six stations of divorce. *In: Divorce and After,* Pohannan, Paul (Ed.) Garden City, New York: Doubleday, pg. 33–62 (1970).
12. Bohannan, Paul, and Erickson, Rosemary. Stepping in. *Psychology Today.* January (1978).
13. *Braiman* vs. *Braiman,* 378 N. E. 2d 1019, 1020 (1978).
14. *Brock* vs. *Brock,* 212 P. 550 (Washington 1923).
15. Bronfenbrenner, Urie. The origins of alienation. *Scientific American.* **231**(2):53–61 (1974).
16. Broverman, Inge K., et al. Sex-role stereotypes: A current appraisal. *Journal of Social Issues.* **28**(2):59–78 (1972).
17. Brown, Prudence, and Manela, Roger. Changing family roles: Women and divorce. *Journal of Divorce.* **1**(4):315–238 (1978).
18. Brown, Carol, et al. Divorce: Chance of a new lifetime, *Journal of Social Issues.* **32**(1): 119–133 (1976).
19. Bruch, Carol S. Making visitation work: Dual parenting orders. *Family Advocate.* Summer:22–26, 41–42 (1978).
20. Bureau of the Census. Households and families by type: March 1979 (Advance Report). *Current Population Reports,* Series P-20, No. 345 (October 1979).

21. Bureau of the Census. Projections of the number of households and families: 1979 to 1995. *Current Population Reports,* Series P-25, No. 805 (May 1979).
22. Capaldi, Frederick, and McRae, Barbara. *Step-families.* New York: New Viewpoints/ Vision Books (1979).
23. Civil Code of California, Chapter 915, AB 1480, Section 4600(a) as amended.
24. Corfman, E., and Pleck, Joseph. "Married men: Work and family." *Families Today— A Research Sampler on Families and Children,* Corfman, E. (Ed.), NIMH Science Monograph 1, DHEW Publication No. (ADM)79–815. Washington, D.C.: Superintendent of Documents, U.S. Government Printing Office (1979).
25. Cox, Mary J. Joint custody. *Family Advocate.* Summer:10–13, 42–44 (1978).
26. Dinnerstein, Dorothy. *The Mermaid and the Minotaur.* New York: Touchstone Books (1972).
27. Dubbert, Joe L. *A Man's Place: Masculinity in Transition.* Englewood Cliffs, New Jersey: Prentice-Hall (1979).
28. Dullea, Georgia. Is joint custody good for children? *New York Times Magazine.* 33–40, 46 (February 3, 1980).
29. Eiduson, Bernice T., and Alexander, Jannette. The role of children in alternative family styles. *Journal of Social Issues.* **34**(2):149–167 (1978).
30. Eiduson, Bernice T. Child development in emergent family styles. *Children Today.* **7**(2): 24–31 (1978).
31. Elkin, Meyer. Reflections on joint custody and family law. editorial, *Conciliation Courts Review.* **16**(3) (1978).
32. Engels, Friedrick, *The Origins of the Family, Private Property and the State.* Chicago: C. H. Kerr (1902).
33. Etzioni, Amitai. The family: Is it obsolete? *Journal of Current Social Issues.* **14**(1) (1977).
34. Fein, Robert A. Research on fathering: Social policy and an emergent perspective. *Journal of Social Issues.* **34**(1):122–135 (1978).
35. Folberg, Jay, and Graham, Marva. "Joint custody—Myth and reality. *In: Joint Custody: A Handbook for Judges, Lawyers and Counselors,* Milne, Ann L. (Ed.), B45–B66, The Association of Family Conciliation Courts (1979).
36. Forum Fourteen. Changing families in a changing society. *Report to the President: White House Conference on Children* (1970).
37. Foster, Henry, and Freed, Doris. "Child custody: The rise and fall of the feminine mystique, Part I: Introduction." In: *Current Developments in Child Custody,* 5–11. New York: Law Journal Seminars-Press, Inc. (1978).
38. Foster, Henry, and Freed, Doris. "Child custody: The rise and fall of the feminine mystique, Part II: The tender years doctrine." In: *Current Developments in Child Custody,* 5–11, New York: Law Journal Seminars-Press, Inc. (1978).
39. Foster, Henry, and Freed, Doris. Life with father: 1978. *Family Law Quarterly,* **XI**(4): 321–342 (1978).
40. Foster, Henry, and Freed, Doris. "Joint custody: A viable alternative?" Parts I, II, and III. In: *Current Developments in Child Custody,* 381–396; 561–569; and 571–592, New York: Law Journal Seminars-Press, Inc. (1978).
41. Freed, Doris, and Foster, Henry. Divorce in the fifty states: An overview as of 1978. *Family Law Quarterly.* **XIII**(1):105–128 (1979).
42. Friere, Paulo. *Pedagogy of the Oppressed.* New York: Seabury Press (1973).
43. Gaddis, Stephen, and Bentliff. J., Concurrent custody: A means of continuing parental responsibility after dissolution. *Child Custody Litigation: Approach and Avoidance,* A Continuing Legal Education Seminar sponsored by Children's Legal Service and Young Lawyers' Section, Seattle-King County Bar Association, 29–46 (1979).

44. Galper, Marian. *Co-Parenting*. Philadelphia: Running Press (1978).
45. Gasser, Rita, and Taylor, Claribel. Role adjustment of single parent fathers with dependent children. *The Family Coordinator*. 25(4):397–401 (1976).
46. Gersick, K. E. Fathers by Choice: Characteristics of Men Who Do and Do Not Seek Custody of Their Children Following Divorce. Unpublished Doctoral Dissertation, Harvard University (1975).
47. Giele, Janet. Changing sex roles and family structure. *Social Policy,* January/February:32–43 (1979).
48. Glick, Paul C., and Norton, Arthur. Marrying, divorcing, and living together in the U.S. today. *Population Bulletin*. 32(5). Population Reference Bureau Inc., Washington, D.C. (1977).
49. Glick, Paul C., The Future of the American Family. *Current Population Reports,* Series P-23, No. 78 (January 1979).
50. Goldberg, Herb. *The Hazards of Being Male: Surviving the Myth of Masculine Privilege.* New York: The New American Library, Inc. (1976).
51. Goldberg, Herb. *The New Male: From Self-Destruction to Self-Care.* New York: William Morrow and Company, Inc. (1979).
52. Goldstein, Joseph, Freud, Anna, and Solnit, Albert. *Beyond the Best Interests of the Child.* New York: The Free Press (1979).
53. Goldstein, Joseph, Freud, Anna, and Solnit, Albert. *Before the Best Interests of the Child.* New York: The Free Press (1979).
54. Goodman, Ellen. The Kramers: Good drama, bad law. *Washington Post* (January 5, 1980.
55. Goodman, Ellen. Helpful husbands talk back. *The Boston Globe Newpaper Company* (January 1980).
56. Grief, Judith B. Fathers, children, and joint custody. *American Journal of Orthopsychiatry*. 49(2):311–319 (1979).
57. Grief, Judith B. Child absence: Fathers' perceptions of their relationship to their children subsequent to divorce. Unpublished doctoral dissertation, Adelphi University (1977).
58. Grote, Douglas, and Weinstein, Jeffrey. Joint custody: A viable and ideal alternative. *Journal of Divorce*. 1(1):43–53 (1977).
59. Haddad, Richard. Concepts and overview of the men's liberation movement. *American Man.* 1(2):28–35, 64–68 (1980).
60. Harlow, Harry F. The nature of love. *The American Psychologist,* XIII (December 1958).
61. Heclo, Hugh, Rainwater, Lee, Rein, Martin, and Weiss, Robert. Single-parent families: Issues and policies. Office of Child Development, DHEW (1973).
62. Hetherington, E. Mavis, Cox, Martha, and Cox, Roger. Divorced fathers. *The Family Coordinator,* 25(4):417–428 (1976).
63. Hetherington, E. Mavis, Cox, Martha, and Cox, Roger. "The development of children in mother-headed families," In: *The American Family: Dying or Developing.* Reiss, D, and Hoffman, H. (Eds.) New York: Plenum Press, 117–145 (1979).
64. Hoffman, Lois, and Nye, F. Ivan. *Working Mothers.* San Francisco: Jossey-Bass, Inc. (1974).
65. Howe, Louise Kapp (ed.). *The Future of the Family.* New York: Touchstone Books, 1972.
66. Jenkins, Shirley. Children of Divorce. *Children Today.* 7(2):16–20,49 (1978).
67. Johnson, Richard. Visitation: When access becomes excess. *Family Advocate.* Summer: 14–17, 34 (1978).
68. Jones, Shirley. Divorce and remarriage: A new beginning, a new set of problems. *Journal of Divorce.* 2(2):217–227 (1978).

69. Kamerman, Sheila, and Kahn, Alfred. Comparative analysis in family policy: A case study. *Social Work*. 506–512 (November 1979).

70. Kanter, Rosabeth Moss. Jobs and families: Impart of working roles on family life. *Children Today*. 7(2):11–15,45 (1978).

71. Kantor, Daivd, and Lehr, William. *Toward A Theory of Family Process*. San Francisco: Jossey-Bass, Inc. (1975).

72. Katz, Arnold J. Lone fathers: Perspectives and implications for family policy. *The Family Coordinator*. 28(4):521–528 (1979).

73. Kelly, J. B., and Wallerstein, J. S. The effects of parental divorce: Experiences of the child in early latency. *American Journal of Orthopsychiatry*. 46:20–32 (1976).

74. Keniston, Kenneth, and the Carnegie Council on Children. *All Our Children: The American Family Under Pressure*. New York: Harcourt Brace Jovanovich (1977).

75. Keshet, Harry, and Rosenthal, K. M. Single parent fathers: A new study, *Children Today*, May/June, 13–17 (1978).

76. Lamb, Michael, Lindsey, Chase-Lansdale and Owen, Margaret, "The changing american family and its implications for infant social development: The sample case of maternal employment," In: *The Child and Its Family*, Lewis, Michael and Rosenblum (eds.), pp. 267–291, New York: Plenum Press (1979).

77. Lein, Laura. Male participation in homelife: Impact of social supports and breadwinner responsibility on the allocation of tasks. *The Family Coordinator*. 28(4):489–496 (1979).

78. Levine, James A. *Who Will Raise the Children?* New York: Bantam Books (1976).

79. Levinger, George, and Moles, Oliver. *Divorce and Separation*. New York: Basic Books (1976).

80. Levy, Babette A. "Alternatives to adversary procedures." In: *Current Developments in Child Custody*, pp. 183–202, New York: Law Journal Seminars-Press, Inc. (1978).

81. Lewis, Ken. On reducing the snatching syndrome. *Children Today*. November/December, 19–21,35 (1978).

82. Lewis, Michael and Rosenblum, Leonard (Eds.). *The Child and Its Family*. New York: Plenum Press (1979).

83. Lewis, Michael, and Rosenblum, Leonard (Eds.) *Friendship and Peer Relations: The Origins of Behavior*. Vol. IV, New York: Wiley and Sons (1975).

84. Lewis, Michael and Weinraub, Marsha. "The father's role in the child's social network." In: Michael E. Lamb (Ed.) *The Role of the Father in Child Development*. New York: Wiley and Sons (1976).

85. Lewis, Pat. Joint custody: A trend in child sharing. *Washington Star*, C1 and C4 (February 10, 1980).

86. Lindsey, Alexander. *Separation Agreements and Anti-Nuptial Contracts*, Vol. 1, Section 14, (1977).

87. Lowenstein, Joyce S., and Koopman, Elizabeth J. A comparison of the self-esteem between boys living with single-parent mothers and single-parent fathers. *Journal of Divorce*. 2(2):195–208 (1978).

88. Lynn, David B. Fathers and sex-role development. *The Family Coordinator*. 25(4):403–410 (1976).

89. Lynn, David B. *The Father: His Role in Child Development*. Monterey, Calif.: Brooks/Cole Publishing Company (1974).

90. Magrab, Phyllis R. For the sake of the children: A review of the psychological effects of divorce. *Journal of Divorce*. 1(3):233–245 (1978).

91. Marotz-Baden, Ramona, Adams, G., Buecke, N., Munro, B., and Munro, G. Family form or family process? Reconsidering the defect family model approach. *The Family Coordinator*. 28(1):5–14 (1979).

92. Mayo, M. E. Access—child's right or parent's privilege? Should court or custodian decide? *Anglo-American Law Review.* **5**:111–130 (1976).
93. McConville, Brian J. The effect of non-traditional families on children's mental health. *Canada's Mental Health.* **26**(1):5–10 (1978).
94. McDonald, Gerald W. Typology for family policy research. *Social Work.* November: 553–559 (1979).
95. McDonald, Gerald W. Family well-being and quality of life: Humanistic concerns of the family impact analyst. *The Family Coordinator.* **28**(3):313–320 (1979).
96. Mead, Margaret. Some theoretical considerations on the problem of mother-child separation. *American Journal of Orthopsychiatry.* **24**(3):480 (1964).
97. Mead, Margaret. Anomalies in American post-divorce relationships. In: *Divorce and After.* P. Bohannan, (Ed.) Garden City, New York: Doubleday, 107–126 (1971).
98. Mendes, Helen A. Single fathers. *The Family Coordinator.* **25**(4):439–444 (1976).
99. Miller, David J. Joint custody. *Family Law Quarterly.* **XIII**(3):345–412 (1979).
100. Milne, A. Custody of children in a divorce process: A family self-determination model. *Conciliation Courts Review.* **16**:1–6 (1978).
101. Milne, Ann L. (ed.). *Joint Custody: A Handbook for Judges, Lawyers, and Counselors.* Portland, Ore.: The Association of Family Conciliation Courts (1979).
102. Molinoff, Daniel. Days here, days there. *The Single Parent.* **XXII**(3):9–44 (1979).
103. Molinoff, Daniel. Joint custody: Victory for all? *The New York Times* (March 6, 1977).
104. National Center for Health Statistics. Births, marriages, divorces, and deaths for 1978. *Monthly Vital Statistics Report: Provisional Statistics.* DHEW Publication No. (PHS) 79–1120, 27(12) (March 15, 1979).
105. National Center for Health Statistics. Final divorce statistics, 1976. *Monthly Vital Statistics Report: Advance Report,* DHEW Publication No. (PHS) 78–1120, 27(5), Supplement (August 16, 1978).
106. National Center for Health Statistics. *Divorce by Marriage Cohort.* DHEW Publication No. (PHS) 79–1912, 21(34)(August 1979).
107. National Center for Health Statistics. Annual summary for the United States: Births, deaths, marriages, and divorces. *Monthly Vital Statistics Report,* DHEW Publication No. (PHS) 79–1120, 27(13), (August 13, 1979).
108. National Council on Family Relations. Fatherhood. *The Family Coordinator* (Special Issue) **25**(4) (1976).
109. National Council on Family Relations. (Special Issue) Men's roles in the family, *The Family Coordinator* Lewis, Robert, and Pleck, Joseph (Eds.). **28**(4) (1979).
110. Nehls, Nadine. Joint Custody of Children: A Descriptive Study. Unpublished Master's Thesis, School of Nursing, University of Wisconsin, Madison (1979).
111. Nichols, Robert C., and Troester, James D. Custody evaluations: An alternative? *The Family Coordinator.* **28**(3):399–407 (1979).
112. Nobel, June, and Nobel, William. *The Custody Trap.* New York: Hawthorn Books, Inc. (1975).
113. Norwood, Janet L. New approaches to statistics on the family. *Monthly Labor Review.* 100 (July 1977).
114. Nye, F. Ivan. *Role Structure and Analysis of the Family.* Beverly Hills, Calif.: Sage Publications (1976).
115. Nye, F. Ivan. "Choice, exchange, and the family." In: *Contemporary Theories About the Family.* Vol. II, Burr, W., Hill, R., Nye, F. Ivan, and Russ, I. (Eds.), New York: The Free Press (1979).
116. O'Neill, William, L. *Everyone Was Brave: A History of Feminism in America.* New York: Time Books (1972).

117. Orthner, Dennis K., and Lewis, Ken. Evidence of single-father competence in child-rearing. *Family Law Quarterly,* **XIII**(1):27–48 (1979).

118. Orthner, Dennis, Brown, Terry, and Ferguson, Dennis. Single-parent Fatherhood: An emerging lifestyle. *The Family Coordinator.* **25**(4):429–438 (1976)

119. Pais, Jeanne, and White, Priscilla. Family redefinition: A review of the literature toward a model of divorce adjustment. *Journal of Divorce.* **2**(3):271–282 (1979).

120. Palme, Olaf. The emancipation of man. *Journal of Social Issues,* **28**(2):237–246 (1972).

121. Pleck, Jospeh. The work-family role system. *Social Problems.* **24**:417–427 (1977).

122. Pleck, Joseph. Men's family work: Three perspectives and some new data. *The Family Coordinator.* **28**(4):481–488 (1979).

123. Pleck, Joseph, and Sawyer, Jack (eds.). *Men and Masculinity.* Englewood Cliffs, New Jersey: Prentice-Hall (1974).

124. Pleck, Joseph, and Brannon, Robert (Eds.). Male roles and the male experiences. *Journal of Social Issues,* **34**(1) (1978).

125. Polatnick, Margaret. Why men don't rear children: A power analysis. *Berkeley Journal of Sociology.* **18**(45) (1974).

126. Rapoport, R., and Rapoport, R. Working women and the enabling role of the husband. Paper presented at the 12th Family Research Seminar, International Sociological Association (June 1972).

127. Rawlings, Stephen W. *Perspectives on American Husbands and Wives.* Bureau of Census, Series P–23, No. 77, (December 1978).

128. Rehert, Isaac. Men's liberation wants to end illusion about where the power is. *The Baltimore Sun,* Friday, (January 20, 1978).

129. Report to the Task Force on Sex Bias and Sex Role Stereotyping in Psychotherapeutic Practice. *American Psychologist,* December (1975).

130. Rittel, Horst, and Weber, Melvin. Dilemmas in a general theory of planning. *Policy Sciences.* **4**:155–169 (1973).

131. Roman, Melvin, and Haddad, William. *The Disposable Parent.* New York: Holt, Rinehart, and Winston (1978).

132. Roman, Melvin. The disposable parent. Presentation at the Association of Family Conciliation Courts, Minneapolis, Minnesota, May 11–14, 1977.

133. Roman, Melvin, and Haddad, William. The case for joint custody. *Psychology Today,* September:96–105 (1978).

134. Rooney, Rita. When dad is given custody. *Washington Post Parade Magazine,* 4–5 (February 24, 1980).

135. Rose, Rhona. Some crucial issues concerning children of divorce. *Journal of Divorce.* **3**(1):19–26 (1979).

136. Ross, Heather L. and Sawhill, Isabel V. *Time of Transition: The Growth of Families Headed by Women.* Washington, D.C.: The Urban Institute (1975).

137. Russo, Nancy F. The motherhood mandate. *Journal of Social Issues.* **32**(3):143–153 (1976).

138. Ryder, Norman B. The family in developed countries. *Scientific American.* **231**(3) 123–132 (Sept. 1974).

139. Safilios-Rothschild, Constantina. Trends in the family: A cross-cultural perspective. *Children Today.* **7**(2):38–43 (1978).

140. Salts, Connie J. Divorce process: Integration of theory. *Journal of Divorce.* **2**(3):233–240 (1979).

141. Saluter, Arlene F. Marital status and living arrangements: March 1978. *Current Population Reports.* Bureau of Census, Series P–20, No. 338 (1979).

142. Sanders, Ruth. Divorce, child custody, and child support. *Current Population Reports.* Bureau of the Census, Series P–23, No. 84(1979).

143. Sattel, Jack W. "The inexpressive male: Tragedy or sexual politics? *Social Problems.* **23**(4):469–477 (1976).

144. Schlesinger, Benjamin. Single parent fathers: A research review. *Children Today.* May/ June, **12**, 18–19, 37–39 (1978).

145. Segal, Julius, and Yahraes, Herbert. *A Child's Journey.* New York: McGraw-Hill Book Company (1978).

146. Seiden, Matt. "Superdad shares supermom's super burdens. *The Baltimore Sun* (January 1980).

147. Stack, Carol B. Who owns the child? Divorce and child custody in middle-class families. *Social Problems.* **23**(4):505–515 (1976).

148. Sussman, Marvin B. The family today: Is it an endangered species? *Children Today.* **7**(2):32–37,45 (1978).

149. Vickers, Sir Geoffrey. Values, norms and policies. *Policy Sciences.* **4**:103–111 (1973).

150. Walker, Kenneth N., and Messinger, Lillian. Remarriage after divorce: Dissolution and reconstruction of family boundaries. *Family Process.* **18**(2):185–193 (1979).

151. Wallerstein, J. D. and Kelly, J. B. The effects of parental divorce: Experiences of the child in later latency. *American Journal of Orthopsychiatry.* **46**:256–269 (1976).

152. Wallerstein, J. D., and Kelly, J. B. The effects of parental divorce: Experiences of the pre-school child. *Journal of the American Academy of Child Psychiatry.* **14**:600–616 (1975).

153. Wallerstein, J. S. and Kelly, J. B. "The effects of parental divorce: The adolescent experience." In: *The Child in His Family,* Vol. III, Anthony, E. J., and Koupernik, C. (Eds.) New York: Wiley and Sons, pp. 479–505 (1974).

154. Wallerstein, Judity S. Children who cope in spite of divorce. *Family Advocate.* Summer, 2–5, 35–39 (1978).

155. Wallerstein, J. S., and Kelly, J. B. California's children of divorce. *Psychology Today.* 67–76 (January 1980).

156. Wallerstein, J. S., and Kelly, J. B. Children and divorce: A review. *Social Work.* 468–475 (November 1979).

157. *Washington Star.* Family quarrels. A–10 (June 23, 1978).

158. Wattenberg, Esther, and Reinhardt, Hazel, Female headed families: Trends and implications *Social Work* November, 460–467 (1979).

159. Weiss, Robert S. *Marital Separation,* New York: Basic Books (1975).

160. Weiss, Robert S. *Going It Alone: The Family Life and Social Situation of the Single Parent.* New York: Basic Books (1979).

161. Weiss, Robert S. Growing up a little faster: The experience of growing up in a single-parent household. In: Speical Issue, "Children of Divorce," Levitin, Teresa (Ed.) *Journal of Social Issues.* **35**(4):97–111 (1979).

162. Wilson, K., Zurcher, L., McAdams, D., and Curtis, R. Stepfathers and stepchildren: An exploratory analysis from two national surveys. *Journal of Marriage and the Family.* 526–536 (August 1975).

163. Winch, Robert F. "Toward a model of familial organization." In: *Contemporary Theories About the Family,* Vol. I, Burr, W., Hill, R., Nye, F. I., and Reiss, I. (Eds.), pp. 162–179. New York: The Free Press (1979).

164. Wiseman, R. Crisis theory and the process of divorce. *Social Casework.* **56:205–212 (1975).**

165. Woolley, Persia. Shared custody. *Family Advocate.* Summer, 6–9, 33–34 (1978).

"Are you getting the big D?" The daughter of a married patient asked this question as her parents argued. The tenuousness of family life appears to be affecting more children than just those actually experiencing parental separation or divorce. Children are exposed to divorces in their friends' families and relatives' families. All life changes can produce stress, and the stress of parental separation and divorce currently affects an estimated eleven million school children.

But should the school become involved in this personal event in the child's life? The author answers affirmatively, presenting rationale and limits of involvement. Much of the information presented and examples provided come from the author's clinical work with separated families and with school professionals she has trained.

Suggested interventions include direct work in the school with children of divorce. Examples range from counseling groups and lesson units to casual mention of various family styles and available books or resources. Preventive work with all children to teach coping skills in the event of any life change is suggested. Interventions with parents include, among others, presentations at parent-teacher organization meetings and ways to foster more open communication. School personnel can work collaboratively with one another or with professionals from outside agencies. Policies, such as those which affect the relationship of the noncustodial parent with the school, may need to be changed.

Most children in family crisis can be expected to react with some attitudinal or behavioral changes. The knowledge of typical and expected effects for children of various developmental levels will guide school professionals in their interventions and will help them determine whether a child needs help other than what the school can provide.

7

Helping Children Cope With Divorce:
The Role of the School

Ellen A. Drake, Psy. D.

INTRODUCTION

When a child experiences the trauma of parental separation and divorce, the child's school can and should play a major role as a positive supportive influence. Yet, a recent literature search of over 900 journals and books containing hundreds of articles about various aspects of the effects of divorce on a child's life reveals that this chapter will be the first writing of length on the topic. No other chapters or books (and few journal articles) are available on the topic.

Why is so little information available on such an important topic? Perhaps because the area is relatively new—many of the writings originate after 1970. Perhaps the school's influence is minimized as greater emphasis is placed on the home environment. Perhaps some professionals in the mental health field have not yet realized the importance of the school and its potential impact. Also, some school professionals do not agree that helping children through a family crisis should be a function of the school; intervention in the school around divorce issues has been viewed by some school professionals as a personal area out of the domain of the school.[38] Moreover, the schools still feel the impact from the late sixties and early seventies, away from affective areas into the more cognitive, academically oriented areas.[14] It appears unrealistically presumptuous to assume that a child can continue to function academically (with the same degree of concentration, attention span, interest level, and desire to learn) at a time when the family is in crisis or when the child experiences unresolved personal issues resulting in upset, to the degree often encountered when parents separate.

Such avoidance of the affective domain or feelings of intrusion often result from insufficient information or skills regarding when and how to intervene with children in crisis. The reluctance of school professionals to involve themselves in this area has helped create the dearth of literature and, conversely, the lack of forthcoming information has helped create the limited and guarded involvement.

At present, the school is not prepared to make a sufficient social contribution toward ameliorating the unhappy sequelae of divorce.[50] This chapter has been written in an effort to raise the school's "competency level." Provided herein is a rationale for the use of the school as an important resource for children and parents before, during, and after a parental separation; information essential for school professionals who wish to provide these services; methods of intervention with the child, the parents, and more generally, within the school setting; and suggestions for interagency collaboration.

The overall purpose of the chapter is to provide the information necessary to enable school personnel and mental health professionals involved in interactions with school-age children to utilize, more effectively, the powerful potential positive influence of the school in promoting emotional growth and development of children of divorce. Much of the information presented within the chapter has come from professional experiences running workshops and training programs for school personnel and parents, from supervising other mental health professionals who work with school personnel, and through experiences in therapeutic work with families in crisis.

RATIONALE FOR THE SCHOOL'S INVOLVEMENT

What role can the school play when a child's parents are separating or have separated? Children are involved with school and school-related activities approximately one-third of their waking hours each week. During time in school, the child gains exposure to educators' and societal values. The opinions and expectations of persons other than parents help form a self-concept based upon a variety of different attitudes and values. The child experiencing parental separation often has a low self-concept and sometimes feels rejected by one or both parents—but especially by the parent who left. The establishment of a relationship in school to a significant adult, particularly one of the same sex as the absent or noncustodial parent, may be of particular importance in these cases, and self-concept may be raised as a result.

Wallerstein and Kelly recognized the school's importance for children of divorce: ". . . those children who were doing well at the time of the divorce, despite the turmoil in the family, were mature, bright youngsters who were enjoying school and had begun to derive considerable gratification from these out-of-home activities separate from their parents."[50] However, a longitudinal study in California indicated that only 34 percent of school-age children were happy and thriving five years after the divorce while 37 percent were depressed.[48]

Schools are (or can be) constants in this time of swift and traumatic change in other important aspects of the child's life. This is especially possible if the custodial parent and the child do not relocate and, as a result, the child remains in his/her same school with the same teacher, has the same playmates, takes the same bus, etc. "An unfortunate consequence of many separations is that the child and the custodial parents must move to a different school district. This eliminates the possibility of comparison between present and past school behavior since school personnel would not be aware of what the child was like pre-separation."[12] If the teacher works with the child before and after the separation, new problems can be quickly identified and, as a result, support for the child provided, and more intensive help arranged if needed. Teachers can sometimes perceive problems in the school setting that parents may overlook at home due perhaps to preoccupation with their new role and their own feelings: "Parents experiencing the dissolution of their marriage often need to attend to so many aspects of their own lives that need restructuring, that unless the children blatantly express their needs. . . they have to receive their help elsewhere."[10] The teachers can alert the parent(s) to the nature of the problem, and school and home can then work together to help the child.

The school can provide a support system available to the child (and to the family). A variety of single parent organizations and mental health agencies provide either "rap" groups or therapy groups for the separated or divorced adult. These activities and programs help the adult readjust to the role of the single person or single parent. MaGrab[34] suggests that parents who attend to their own personal adjustment are, in turn, fostering better adjustment in their children. While adults can seek out these resources when they are in need, children often cannot or do not express their needs in such a way that the parents would understand and then direct them to available resources. Also, such community programs for children are found in significantly lower numbers than adult programs.

The school is the logical resource for the child, and certainly the most readily available since the child is already present in that setting. Children in schools have access to mental health services involving contact with counselors, psychologists, school social workers, and empathic teachers. When help is provided in the school setting, the child and parents do not have to contend with the possible stigma or labeling associated with the use of outside mental health facilities or practitioners, the expense of such treatment, or child and parental resistance to outside help.[13] In addition, children in schools are grouped by approximate academic level, maturity level, and age level, providing a possible setting for preventive work with classes as a whole. The school also provides a conducive atmosphere for arranging age-appropriate groups for intervention purposes.

Sometimes, it is the parents themselves who interfere with the school's "competency level" in this area. Parents, not uncommonly, keep this relevant information of the significant change in family circumstances from the school. Perhaps many parents may even remain unaware of the degree to which parental separation can affect a child in the school setting. They may fear stereotyping their child or may have great difficulty sharing such personal information with "a stranger," i.e., the teacher. Many parents wait to see if the school "notices a difference" in either the child's academic and behavioral performance, before disclosing any information regarding the family. Negative stereotyping, of course, does occur in some cases. For the most part, however, the child benefits by the teacher's early knowledge of any significant event in a child's life including birth, separation, divorce, remarriage, death, relocation, or serious illness. Gardner finds it unrealistic for a parent to assume that a child's feelings about the separation or divorce will not carry over into the school setting.[20]

Generally, it is unnecessary for the school to be aware of the personal details of the separation. Instead, what the school needs to know is sufficient information to determine the type, degree, and appropriateness of the reactions the child manifests. The school's domain is to educate the child and to help him/her deal with and overcome possible academic or emotional obstacles which may prevent achievement of maximum educational potential. For this purpose, I have devised the following checklist as a device for identifying problems in both academic and emotional areas:

IMPORTANT INFORMATION FOR THE SCHOOL REGARDING CHILDREN OF DIVORCE

CHILD'S NAME: DATE:

WHO IS CUSTODIAL PARENT?

DATE OF SEPARATION:

DATE OF DIVORCE:

WHEN WAS THE SCHOOL INFORMED OF THE SEPARATION? BY WHOM?

WAS CHILD HAVING SCHOOL PROBLEMS BEFORE THE DIVORCE/SEPARATION?

If so, same or different?

Clarify below if different in either degree of problem or type of problem:

WHAT WAS THE CHILD'S INITIAL REACTION TO THE SEPARATION?

Through your observation in the school:

Through child's spontaneous and voluntary report:

Through parent's report:

DOES THE CHILD HAVE CONTACT WITH THE NONCUSTODIAL PARENT? HOW MUCH? WHEN?

WHAT INSTRUCTIONS HAVE BEEN GIVEN THE SCHOOL REGARDING ITS CONTACT WITH (OR INCLUSION OR EXCLUSION) OF THE NONCUSTODIAL PARENT?

HAVE HOUSEHOLD CIRCUMSTANCES CHANGED SIGNIFICANTLY? Ex. move, finances, stepparent, stepsiblings, parent working, etc.

PROBLEM CHECK LIST

DATE: _____

	1 MANY PROBLEMS	2	3 SOME PROBLEMS	4	5 NO PROBLEMS
a. ACADEMIC PERFORMANCE					
b. BEHAVIOR AT SCHOOL					
c. BEHAVIOR AT HOME (IF KNOWN)					
d. EXPRESSION OF FEELINGS					
e. RELATIONSHIP WITH PEERS					
SAME SEX					
OPPOSITE SEX					
f. RELATIONSHIP WITH MOTHER (IF KNOWN)					
g. RELATIONSHIP WITH FATHER (IF KNOWN)					
h. RELATIONSHIP WITH TEACHER(S)					
i. OVERALL ADJUSTMENT					

What can be done in the school to help this child with the *above* problems?

Notes on the Checklist

Teachers, guidance counselors, and school nurses who have used the above checklist in workshops, and afterwards in their classrooms or offices, have found it an important aid for providing basic useful information about the separation. Notice that the checklist does not delve unnecessarily into the personal content areas. A few questions of a more personal nature are included in the checklist (such as any parent-child problems or more specific information about visitation) because of the importance they hold for the child and the possible carry-over effect into the school. Certainly, any information provided by the parent(s) must be given voluntarily, but the checklist also has been used as a device to foster increased parent-school communication which can be of great importance for effective interventions. Also, in order to use check lists such as those suggested above, the schools will need to determine whether such information gathering is permitted by the school superintendent and Board of Education.

INCREASING EFFECTIVENESS OF SCHOOL PERSONNEL

School professionals, whom I have trained, have variously described children of divorce as confused, displaced, hurt, unwanted, unloved, lonely, disappointed, frustrated, anxious, frightened, angry, guilty, bitter, and relieved. These professionals are able to perceive the outward emotional manifestations of the child's feelings. From this starting point, additional training would increase the effectiveness of school personnel in dealing with children of divorce. More specifically, a better understanding of the following areas is desirable: The extent of the problem; the effects on the child as seen within the school setting; methods which aid in identification and assessment of those children in need of either additional or a different type of help; how and when to intervene with the children and their parents as well as suggestions for working with other school personnel; what influence their own values may have; how to intervene in school policy making; and possible ways to work with other agencies for referral and resource purposes.

Extent of the Problem

Fifty percent of all divorces involve children.[41] Each year, over one million children experience parental separation, and currently an estimated eleven million children from single parent families attend school. It is estimated that one out of every six children lives with one parent;[46] this involves six million families. The number or percentage of children who have experienced family disruption in any given school district varies depending upon a number of factors: For example, lower socioeconomic levels have a higher percentage of single-parent families,[52] as well as areas with a higher concentration of apartment dwellings due to the greater mobility of the single-parent family.

It is difficult for accurate data to be gathered in some school districts due to ambiguous data-gathering processes where specific information about the home situation is not requested (such as marital status, custody arrangements, visitation schedules, name differences, and the address of the noncustodial parent). Child study teams, due to the nature of their often explorative work, have greater access to such information. One school district found that one-third of the children referred to the child study team were from nonintact families.[22] A significant number of children in the school are experiencing school problems due to home disruption and multiple changes to which the child must adjust. The realization of the extent of the problem has led to increased interest in how to better handle these children within the school setting.

Effects on the Child as Seen Within the School Setting

Kelly and Wallerstein[29] and Wallerstein and Kelly[49,50,51] have done extensive studies on the typical and expected effects of children experiencing divorce at different developmental stages including preschool, latency, and adolescence. MaGrab[34] summarized the effects from a developmental perspective. Professionals interested in atypical reactions of children either in type, degree, or duration of symptom await additional results of longitudinal studies.

To demonstrate the effects as seen in the school environment, I have extrapolated from existing studies about children generally, and provided examples to substantiate that similar behaviors exist within the school environment. Kelly and Wallerstein, in their five-year longitudinal study of 60 families and 131 children, have found no simple guidelines for recognizing divorce-related behavior and emotional change in the classroom.[27] They have found both in-school and out-of-school responses to depend on the child's developmental level, the child's unique personality, and the degree of conflict between parents during this crisis period. In their interview of teachers, these researchers found that two-thirds of the children showed changes in their school behavior following their parent's separation. The most common problems identified were: lowered academic achievement, anxiety as seen in restless behavior, concentration difficulties, increase in daydreaming, and sadness and depression especially in younger children. More subtle changes were seen in an increase in children seeking out teachers, a need for more attention as seen in an expression of physical proximity. No high correlation was noted between responses seen in school, at home, or in the offices of the researchers.

When a child experiences parental separation, certain behaviors would be considered typical, "normal," or expected. The effects vary from age to age depending on the developmental tasks of that age and the importance of the family for the child at that time of his or her life when the separation occurs. The effects have also been seen as being influenced by gender, relationship with the departing, absent, or noncustodial parent, and relationships between siblings.[25, 32]

Since the average length of marriage has been estimated as six and three-quarter years, many children experiencing parental divorce may be in nursery-school settings or kindergarten programs. The young preschool child in a nursery-school setting is dealing with issues of mastery. This age child commonly exhibits regressive behavior such as relapse in progress of toilet training, and separation anxiety. Neediness, such as reaching out too quickly to strangers, and clinging behavior are commonly seen. The symptoms of regression and clinging will usually last only two or three months if the parent provides continuity of physical care and loving. Sometimes, the working schedule of the custodial parent prevents the continuity and the symptoms persist.

Information about the lasting effects of symptoms or behaviors acquired at a certain developmental age is not yet available, but, through observations of patients in clinical work, it appears that certain symptoms endure through several developmental levels if not attended to. An example is a thirteen-year-old patient, whose parents separated when she was a young preschool child. She clutches onto her mother's boyfriends, calling them Daddy, and tends to stay after school or linger after class to talk to male teachers.

Wallerstein and Kelly found children, ages 4–5, to show increased irritability, temper tantrums, and aggressiveness; these children are angry. Their view of dependability and predictability of relationships has been threatened. Some of these children become encopretic—usually soiling only at home and not in school.[2] Teachers may notice the children experiencing difficulty with change in routines, rejection of teachers who are substituting for the regular teacher to whom the child has become accustomed, and some acting-out behavior, especially on the part of males.[19]

Young school age children, ages 5–6, experience moodiness and longing for the absent parent. A mother seen in therapy had been advised by her attorney to disallow any contact of her five-year-old son with her estranged husband. The teacher, unaware of the family circumstances, commented on the sad expression of the child, describing him as "an unhappy child." The mother said that each day for almost a year, the child asked when he again would see his father.

School-age children, ages 6–7, have difficulty focusing their attention and efforts outside of the family; the frequent result is poor school performance. The child may miss learning some important basic skills and, as a result, school work, in later years, may prove more difficult. Creation of continued achievement problems and feelings of failure contribute to a possible on-going feeling of dissatisfaction with themselves and a generally poor self-concept.

Early latency children, ages 7–8, may appear depressed. Often, they seem sad, vulnerable, and continue to hope for reconciliation. This age group was found to have the most problems adjusting due to inadequate defenses available to them.[29] In a therapy group for children of separated parents, one of the eight-year-old patients drew a picture of a bleeding heart expressing his sad feelings about his inability to get his parents back together again—in spite of his many manipulations as well as more direct attempts.

Later latency children, ages 9–11, typically experience shame and intense anger directed at the parent perceived to have caused the divorce. One eleven-year-old who had read *TA for Kids*[18] told me about her collection of "brown stamps" indicating the anger she had accumulated toward her father. In addition to the conscious, intense anger, half of the children in this age group also noticeably declined in school performance and concomitantly deteriorated in peer relationships. However, in these studies, no correlation has been found between prior school performance and the subsequent drop in school achievement.[49]

Adolescents commonly use distancing and withdrawal from the home in this time of stress. They become increasingly involved in social activities avoiding the home conflict. Some may become pseudo-mature, possibly encountering power struggles with teachers or acting out.

Several studies conducted in school settings focused on teacher identification of problems. Santrock[43] found that teachers rated boys, ages 10–12, without fathers present in their homes, as more masculine, aggressive, disobedient and independent than boys with fathers present. The study concluded that divorce may lead to an increase in the male child's sex-typed behaviors, especially when the separation occurs during pre-adolescence. This was postulated as caused by social deprivation and no father to model self-control or punish deviant behavior. Another study found that young children of separation and divorce, ages 5–10, demonstrated significantly more school maladjustment than their demographically matched controls without crisis histories.[17] The study showed children of separation or divorce had higher scores in acting out, restlessness, obstinance, disruptive behavior in class, and impulsivity. The researchers offered a possible interpretation that the children modeled the parents' predominant behavior during the crisis.

Other researchers studied the effect of father availability on academic performance among third-grade boys. The results indicated that boys whose fathers left were generally underachievers and functioned somewhat below grade level in contrast to those whose fathers were available to them.[4]

Below is a quiz the author has given workshop participants as a means through which they could judge their understanding of the expected behaviors:

QUIZ

Directions:
Below are case examples of children whose parents recently have separated. You, the school professional, are seeing these children go through typical and expected effects for their age. Match the case examples to the appropriate age of the child.

_____ Ages 2½–3½
_____ Ages 3¾–4¾
_____ Ages 5–6
_____ Ages 6–7
_____ Ages 7–8
_____ Ages 9–11
_____ Ages 12–18

Case 1: Cliff stamps his feet when you remind him to take his drawings home with him.

Case 2: Stan has been caught drinking beer and acting "macho" lately.

Case 3: Paul keeps drawing pictures of his mother, father, him and their dog—all together. He seems depressed.

Case 4: Nina almost always looks sad lately and has become moody. Her mother reports to you that she frequently asks about her absent father.

Case 5: Susan suddenly begins to cry whenever you leave the room. When you're close to her, she seems to cling.

Case 6: Ann has never mentioned to you (or to anyone in school) that her parents have separated. She has been keeping to herself lately.

Case 7: Lately, Mark can't seem to catch onto some basic concepts even though he's a bright child.

The correct answers are as follows:
Ages 2½–3½:Case 5; 3¾–4¾:Case 1; 5–6:Case 4; 6–7:Case 7; 7–8:Case 3; 9–11:Case 6; and 12–18:Case 2.

Within a one-to two-year postseparation period, many children no longer exhibit these reactions[35] although the effects tend to persist more in boys than in girls.[52] The probability of children, working through their problems and feelings, increases when school personnel, in addition to the parents, react sensitively and with understanding to the child during this period of transition.

Identifying Children at Risk

Identifying when children need additional help, beyond that which the classroom teacher can provide, constitutes an important and crucial role of the teacher. Separated parents, preoccupied with their own problems, sometimes miss cues their children give which indicate they need help. Other children manifest no problem behaviors at home. An extreme deficit in coping skills may render insufficient the passage of time and the supportive interaction with school personnel or peers.

In order to identify children in need of extra help, school professionals need to be aware of three assessment cues: Type, length, and degree.

Type. When assessing the nature of the problem, the school professional needs to judge whether the child behaves in the way expected for his or her age group. Although the behavior may prove uncomfortable for those with whom the child interacts, the normalcy or deviancy of this behavior needs to be assessed; if the behavior is atypical for that age child undergoing stress, an indice that additional help may be needed has been identified. Atypical reactions include: regression to an earlier developmental stage; delaying with the same behaviors for a long period of time, seemingly unable to move beyond them; or advancing to inappropriate behaviors associated with an older level of development.

The author worked therapeutically with a six-year-old child with unresolved feelings of loss. His father had left when he was four. The child hoarded candy and manipulated the school into providing him with free lunches feigning loss of lunch money which he then used to purchase candy. The child's emotional development was stunted or delayed at the level of insatiable need for nurturance and the retention of belongings. In play therapy, the child played repeatedly, and for long durations, with the cash register and play money. Within a four-month period, the child was no longer hoarding and was using his lunch money to buy lunch.

Length. The second indication for more serious problems is length of time; i.e., has the child continued to manifest these problems for more than a year? (For some children, up to two years has been found necessary for the crisis resolution). The teacher needs to be aware of how long the symptoms exist postseparation. Since most children change teachers as they advance grades, communication will be necessary between teachers as these children advance.

Degree. Teachers can watch for the degree of the problem as the third cue for the need for alternate interventions. Particular awareness for signs of depression and explosiveness are important. One study suggested the hypothesis that parental loss was an important factor in the development of suicidal tendencies—especially for adolescents.[1] Typical signs of depression are: sleeping problems, eating problems (too much or too little), lethargy, accident proneness, irritability, difficulty concentrating, moodiness, tearfulness, sad facial expression, and suicidal thoughts.

Certainly, if a child talks about harming himself/herself or others, an immediate consultation is warranted. If the teacher questions whether a child needs additional help—i.e., whether the type, length, or degree of the problem warrants a consultation—the school psychologist or school social worker could be called in as a resource person.

If further assessment of the problems is needed, several methods may be used. Kelly and Wallerstein,[26] for example, devised a divorce-specific assessment, which I find applicable for use in the schools by child study team members or counseling personnel. The assessment consists of three parts: a history of developmental achievements, an exploration into the child's understanding of the divorce, and a determination of what support systems are available to the child.

History. The brief history includes the gathering of information regarding developmental achievements. Sources for such information are parents, to indicate past academic and behavioral performance, and the assessor's direct observations indicating how the child currently functions. The following questions can then be answered: Is the child different from before? How? Is the child progressing at the same rate? Through use of this information, the child's past and present milestones or levels can be estimated against which to judge the effect of current stresses.

Child's Understanding. I have found the assessment of the child's understanding of the separation to be crucial. I have helped parents to explain and re-explain, as children only process or accept what they are able to at that time. An example of this was in a therapy session with a mother and her two sons ages eight and ten; the younger son had been referred by the school for moodiness and some temper tantrums. When the mother was asked, in the presence of her sons, if she had told her children the reasons for the divorce, she answered affirmatively. I then asked the boys if there were any questions they wanted to ask their mother: In unison, they said, "yea, mom, why did you and daddy divorce?" These children needed to be told again. As the professional explores what the divorce means to a child, it is important to know the child's understanding of the reasons for the divorce, the child's affective responses, and the coping strategies used.

Support System. Of particular significance in this time of family disorganization is the support system available to the child. Support may be forthcoming from the continued parent(s)-child relationship, siblings, extended family, peers, religious advisors, and, of course, school personnel.

An assessment device, called the Family Story Test,[26] is a structured projective which could possibly be used in the school by the school psychologist or by mental health center professionals to provide additional information to the school. The device assesses the child's attitudinal and affective responses. Examples of areas explored are: feelings of self-blame, fear of abandonment, hopes of parents reuniting, placing blame, and fear of ridicule by peers.

Another assessment device, again best used by child study team personnel or those familiar with and trained in the use of projective tests, is a family drawing. I have found the child's projective perception of his/her family as an indice of acceptance of the family circumstances. Common drawings for children of divorce are pictures of an intact family, pictures of them with their custodial parents, or two pictures of them with their "two families." These can be interpreted projectively.

The above projective material, as with all projectives, helps professionals understand the child but needs to be used in conjunction with other sources of information for a comprehensive picture of the child. Once the school identifies type, length, and degree of a child's problems, an educational plan or ways to intervene with this child in the school setting can be formulated.

Influence of Personal Values

Just as all school professionals need to attend to the emotional aspects of the child since they influence the child's educational progress, they need to attend to their own. Since values play a part in guiding interventions, it is imperative that professionals remain aware of their values. School personnel participating in the author's workshops have commented on their values: "I can help the child better if I feel neither parent is to blame";

"I'm a child advocate where the noncustodial parent is concerned"; "I can share what my children went through to show my students that they're not alone"; "How can I be objective when I only know one side of the story"; "How can a mother have left her kids?" "I have problems with the parents living with someone else." Recognition of the values behind these statements—the feelings and opinions about what is right and wrong—and how these values affect their relationships with the child who has experienced parental separation, are important points to consider.

The influence of prejudices and biases when relating to the parents has also caused recent concern. Berry[3] has discussed the impact of negative values toward the male single parents. Kessler, Loxley, and Whiteley developed vignettes of value-laden interactions[31] for training or educational purposes. An education support group developed a questionnaire to secure additional information regarding parental views of school attitudes and values toward children of separation and divorce.[37]

Generally, school personnel with whom the author has worked try to suppress the expression of their values about parental actions and about separation and divorce. Instead, they focus on what the child needs and attempt to handle interactions with parents and children nonjudgmentally and in ways most conducive to the education of the children involved.

INTERVENTIONS

Certainly, understanding children of divorce and assessing the nature and extent of their problems would serve no useful purpose if we then took no positive action. The goals of intervening in schools include the amelioration of the current negative reactions and prevention of chronic effects. More specifically, objectives include: Helping the child to eventually accept the new family situation, adjusting to its changes and necessary school changes as well; increasing the psychological distance between the parents' problems and the child's problems in order to limit the child's concerns to a more manageable level; and providing the child with additional coping strategies in his or her repertoire. Ways to intervene can be divided in several ways: For the purposes of this chapter, they are divided into direct interventions with the child, indirect interventions with the child through the parents or administrative channels, and preventive work with the class as a whole. These interventions will be explained in some detail.

Time and Place For Interventions

Interventions can take place anywhere in the school and at anytime. "An English, math, science, or driver's training classroom seems an unlikely place to teach about divorce and life after divorce, but almost daily the need and the occasion arise."[5] Teachers can be valuable resources to children by just being willing to listen to a child or to a parent then, referring them, when needed, to the school counselor or to a child study team member. Interventions can be spontaneous (during a class lesson, a parent-teacher conference, or even a discussion in the hallway or on the telephone) or they can be planned in the form of a lesson plan or curriculum unit or a speaker at the parent-teacher organization meeting.

Direct Interventions With Children

When a child appears to have problems adjusting to family change, the school can be instrumental in providing support or helping the child learn new or better coping skills. Parental divorce may represent to the child not only a sense of loss, but also failure in interpersonal relationships, and a difficult transition to new life patterns.[34]

School personnel can become effective supports and resources for those children needing a stable figure or a surrogate parent. Being supportive means helping to raise the child's self-esteem and "being there" (as much as possible within the teacher-student role). This support can be accomplished through providing an atmosphere conducive to self-expression, being sensitive to the child's loss (such as on Father's Day or Mother's Day), and including single-parent families in examples of family situations given in class.

If a child with recently separated parents newly enters the school district, teachers need to be sensitive to the child's loss of peer support in addition to the parental loss. The child needs to feel a sense of belonging to the class and to acquire a new support system as quickly as possible. To foster this, the teacher could assign the child a valued responsibility, include the child on committees, have the class members plan a welcoming party or form a "Newcomer's Club," and a unit on the child's previous hometown could be done.

Kelly and Wallerstein found the school supportive in additional ways:

"Many youngsters found some support within the school setting because their attitudes and performance in school provided accustomed gratifications which they were able to sustain in the face of divorce stress. Further, the attention, sympathy, and tolerance demonstrated by numerous teachers, who had been informed about the divorce, was sustaining to a number of children feeling emotionally undernourished at home. . . Teachers became a central stable figure in the lives of several children in the months following the separation, in some cases, the only stable figure in these children's environment."[28]

The school professional needs to keep in mind the expected effects on children (discussed earlier) and intervene accordingly. For example, younger children experiencing anger may need additional opportunities to play, the primary method through which they resolve their emotional conflicts. The teacher can encourage play around the family changes merely through providing "dress-up" adult-like clothes, doll houses and furniture, people and animal puppets, finger puppets, a toy car, and household items such as a toy refrigerator and stove, sweeper, and tool-like items in order that common household scenes can be played out.

Moody children could have access to an inflated plastic clown for punching, or toy percussion musical instruments such as drums and banging tools such as hammers as constructive and acceptable ways to sublimate the feelings. Involvement in sports such as tag, dodge ball, races, or basketball, all help relieve the intensity of a child's feelings through a societally appropriate outlet. Creative experiences such as using modeling clay, pasting and cutting, or finger painting could also be used for this same purpose.

Children of young school age need to remove their thoughts from the home situation and, instead, become involved in their own activities—and especially refocus back onto school. Teachers can provide creative and industrious activities and possibly even a tutor when needed to assure the child's continued school progress. Teachers might suggest a camp experience for part of the summer or encourage the child's involvement in after-school or Saturday clubs, organizations, events, activities and groups. Through such out-of-home experiences, the child would increasingly focus on successes, abilities to cope and master experiences. Teachers, child study team personnel, and guidance counselors can provide a liaison relationship with information about the availability of such activities.

Children need to learn to communicate their feelings. Such communication may help release depression that some school children may experience. One may assume that if a child has acquired the skills to communicate with teachers and peers, communication of feelings with parents and siblings would also be easier for these children. Teachers, to help their students communicate feelings, can encourage this level of communication around any subject as a means to facilitate growth through practice. They can review with the children a list of possible feelings or have them choose "possible feelings a person might have in a situation like this" from the list below:[14]

happy	sad	patient
joyful	depressed	guilty
fearful	disappointed	amused

comfortable	relaxed	uncomfortable
angry	anxious	eager
nervous	calm	lonely
silly	frustrated	impatient
bored	enjoy	confused
contented	discontented	upset
pleased	disgusted	interested
uninterested	satisfied	dissatisfied
loved	unloved	liked
disliked	wanted	unwanted
annoyed	scared	afraid
glad	courageous	proud
restless	hopeful	

Many other techniques are possible and some other examples are provided: Children can draw pictures of feelings; choose possible situations from a box, then express feelings about these situations. Children develop additional communication skills when taught empathic assertion[30]—a three-step process of empathizing with another's feelings, expressing their own feeling(s), and assertively expressing their opinion regarding what action should be taken. The teacher (or other school professional) can also use empathic assertion to model an effective method of communication. Children generally enjoy role-playing or what this author calls "practicing" when conducted in a school setting.

Children experiencing shame can be paired with other children whose family has experienced separation and possible spontaneous conversation regarding their similarities (and differences) may occur. Pairing children of divorce, who do not mention or allude to their family situation, with children open and willing to communicate can lead to a natural "opening-up" to a peer, should the child want to do so. With this age child, a school social worker, psychologist or counselor could run a group[6, 53] and thereby diminish the feelings of "differentness" and shame and directly help them learn new coping skills through discussion, feedback, and role playing. The classroom teacher could initiate a class discussion or even a class unit about various types of family lifestyles giving the message that all families are alike in some ways and different in other ways and all are acceptable family styles. Having books written for children about divorce available in the classroom as typical reading books along with other children's books as well as the teacher's periodic casual mention of separated parents generally, single parent homes, stepparents, etc., could also help decrease shame.

Interventions with adolescents are similar to those for the young school age child: Help the teenager distance from the family problems. Involvement in school activities and peer relationships, team sports, and group projects will help the adolescent keep perspective on: What are my problems and what are their problems. The adolescent can understand, more than the younger age groups, that all people have faults, and a greater awareness of parental and their own strengths and weaknesses may ensue.

Indirect Interventions

Indirect interventions benefit the child, but the method involves working with those who have direct contact with the child—such as parents or school personnel, rather than with the child. Some children are not receptive to direct interventions; some schools will not allow group counseling or classroom discussions on an affective level; and some parents disallow their children from disclosing any family information. When working indirectly, other methods become available for helping parents and school personnel to work more effectively with the children. Such educational contacts or programs may result in increased knowledge, or behavioral and attitudinal changes which, in turn, positively affect the children. Coddington[8] saw parental separation as the most potentially stressful life event a child can undergo. The need for parental and professional intervention, indirectly, if not directly, becomes important to help the child understand and express feelings and to cope more effectively.

Indirect Interventions with Parents

Some indirect intervention programs for parents include: speaking to separated and divorced parents at parent-teacher meetings, presenting a program in cooperation with the adult school, and running special programs and workshops for parents in the township library, community mental health center, and school building. At these educationally oriented programs, the parents need reassurance about the confidentiality and use of the content information they provide the school and about the attitudes of school personnel toward children experiencing parental separation. Information crucial for parents to understand involves the importance for the child of continued on-going contact with the noncustodial parent[25] (whenever possible), guidelines for parents working cooperatively in spite of personal difficulties as estranged or former husband and wife,[7] the expected effects of the separation on the children, the importance of cooperating and communicating with the school, and the availability of child study and community resources. A list of books useful for parents and for children experiencing separation with its resulting difficulties could be provided. (Books in the local community library and school library could be perused to determine availability of such resources).

When parents separate, professionals can help inquiring parents understand what basic information their children need to have: That their parents still love them; they (the children) did not cause the separation; they cannot change the situation; and there will be some changes in their lives as a result. The parents can also receive help in expecting transitional stress on their child's part. The parents could be guided regarding the additional patience, support and attention the child might require at this time. The teacher, or other school professional, could also help the parent understand the importance for the child of sharing feelings (not necessarily information) with friends, the importance of continued access to extended family and to the noncustodial parent (if possible), and the importance of not triangling the child.

School personnel disseminating this information can decide the format through which this process is accomplished—whether within the school setting or, in cooperation with a mental health agency or professional. All interventions with parents should be voluntary with the parent having the option to refuse school involvement.

School personnel, also, indirectly can help children through encouraging parental communication with schools—around any issue. This openness sets a pattern, increasing the likelihood of parents to share with the school that a separation has occurred or is imminent. If teacher, child study team members, nurses, guidance personnel, or administrators demonstrate sensitivity to the special needs and circumstances of the single parent, the likelihood of parent-school communication will increase.

The difference between educating parents and providing therapy to parents (or to children) needs to be clarified. Therapy is out of the province of the school unless administrators approve of either child study team or guidance intervention on this level. Teachers can stay out of the therapeutic realm and in the educational realm by refraining from giving specific advice in areas unrelated to the child's school functioning. The teacher also can provide the parent with some generally known educational guidelines with the parents then determining the suitability of these guidelines to their situation. Examples of guidelines follow:

1. By specifically including the school in the child custody papers or separation agreement, some future parental conflict may be avoided. The parents can agree and inform the school about the noncustodial parent's

accessibility to the child in school, to the child's records, to the child's teacher, and involvement in the child's school activities and events.

2. Parental expectations for themselves and for the child can be re-evaluated. Is the parent trying to run the household in the same way that was possible when two parents were available and, as a result, overinvolving themselves and their children in chores and activities, leaving insufficient time to enjoy one another.

If the school professional encounters a situation with either parent or child in which he or she feels uncomfortable, referral could be made, with approval of the principal, to the school psychologist or social worker or to an outside professional or agency. The model of empathic assertion, discussed earlier as a technique useful for children, could be used by the teacher for diplomatically disengaging from a parent who perhaps seeks therapy rather than education. An example of how to phrase this might be: "You seem to want more information about your child, but I don't have this kind of information to give you. Perhaps you would find it useful to talk to someone who could help you more than I could such as _____."

Indirect Interventions With Other School Personnel

Mental health professionals with affiliations outside the school can train various school professionals interested in acquiring additional knowledge and skills for working with children of divorce. In turn, trained school personnel then can become resource people themselves. The acquisition of such knowledge and skills may foster increased sensitivity or additional programs and revised policies.

When planning cooperative training programs with another agency or institution, differing policies between the two institutions regarding confidentiality of records must be kept in mind with procedures altered accordingly. Community mental health centers are often willing to run programs in the school—training parents or school personnel. In this capacity, this author trained guidance counselors to run groups.[16] Such agencies can also be available with on-going therapeutic groups, for example, as a referral source.

For policy changes in the schools which affect all children, administrative cooperation and approval is needed. One possible policy change involves demographic information-gathering procedures. When only one line is provided for parents' names, Mr. and Mrs. is presumed. The school may need to change the nature of its forms in order to determine whereabouts and accessibility of a noncustodial parent, or to encourage parental disclosure of such information.

Administrative policies regarding the noncustodial parent should be formulated. (This will probably involve the superintendent's consulting with the Board Attorney). According to the Federal Educational Rights and Privacy Act (FERPA),[47] noncustodial parents have access to their child's school records unless an opposing court ruling indicates otherwise. New York City schools have adopted a policy that when a noncustodial parent requests record review, the custodial parent is informed, and if no opposing court document is provided, the school grants accessibility of the noncustodial parent to the child's school records.[40] Owing to the legal sensitivity of this issue, schools are advised to seek clarification and formulate policy.

Preventive Work

When using a preventive model, the child is not yet known to have problems, or the parents have not experienced a separation. Coping skills are taught which help the child through all life changes and crises—perhaps a separation from a loved one through divorce, a relocation, birth of a sibling, a remarriage, a death of a pet.

McDermott[36] stressed the importance of school personnel identifying and working with children of separation and divorce through a preventive modality: ". . . the school has an obligation to intervene at this time in order to prevent reactions from going underground and thus to prevent future disorder. . . . " The number of preventive programs in schools increases as schools become increasingly aware of the many children experiencing parental separation and the possible long-term effects on the children.

The programs can be a whole-class method which includes all children. The purpose, as with direct intervention programs with children in crisis, is to increase coping skills. The widespread occurrence of divorce affects children even from intact homes. A school principal (with an intact family) related a story where his young son worried he would not return from an administrator's convention. Likewise, as a married patient and her husband argued, their nine-year-old daughter inquired whether they were "getting the big D," as she called it. Children worry about the tenuousness of their own families as they watch their friends, classmates, and perhaps cousins go through parental separation.

Several examples of preventive school programs can be found in the literature. Teachers can design programs unique for their classrooms or model their program after those found workable. One program detailed in the literature helps elementary children learn to cope with change, specifically family change.[24] The program teaches coping skills through role playing and discussion. Gardner suggests Family Living courses in the high schools.[19] Other programs designed for use with children are detailed elsewhere in the literature.[11, 23, 30, 37, 39] A comprehensive review of programs formulated or led by school psychologists can be found in an article by Drake.[9]

Other possible suggestions for preventive interventions which teachers have found helpful are: Including various family types, e.g., intact, single parent, reconstituted, in classroom reading material and in conversation or lesson presentation; supports available within the school, i.e., the guidance counselor as "someone to talk to" may need to be periodically clarified; encouraging the expression of feelings and a problem-solving approach may prove useful; teachers or the school librarian can have books available in the classroom or in the school library on the topic for children to read. Some of the more popular books help the children identify feelings and acquire coping skills. *The Journal of Clinical Child Psychology*[44] provides an annotated bibliography of books available. Three of the author's favorites for different age level children are *Divorce Is a Grown-Up Problem*[45] for preschool children, *The Boys and Girls Book About Divorce*[21] for elementary children, and *How to Get It Together When Your Parents Are Coming Apart*[42] for preadolescents and adolescents. (It is recommended that teachers read these books themselves prior to recommending them for use.) A problem of most books available is that school is seldom mentioned. The book by Richards and Willis[42] is an exception.

CONCLUSION

The schools, by virtue of the population they serve and the extent to which they, of necessity, must become involved in children's lives, need to be aware of the problems children have which affect their academic growth and emotional development. However, awareness is insufficient. School professionals need to know how to help children through life crises such as a parental separation and divorce and schools can be an additional resource to the parents as well.

The school can have a profound and lasting effect on the child's coping abilities. It is through increased sensitivity, continued growth in knowledge, additional training, and skill building on the part of school personnel, that the school and home can join together working cooperatively to lessen or prevent any negative long-term effects of divorce.

REFERENCES

1. Adam, K. S., Lohrenz, J. G., and Harper, D. Suicidal ideation and parental loss. *Canada Psychiatric Association Journal.* **18**(2):95–99 (1973).
2. Bemporad, J. R., Pfeifer, C. M., Gibbs, L., Cortner, R. H., and Bloom, W. Characteristics of encopretic patients and their families. *Journal of the American Academy of Child Psychiatry.* **10**(2):272– 292 (1971).
3. Berry, K. K. The male single parent: The experiences and prejudices. Presentation at American Psychological Association Convention New York (1979).
4. Blanchard, R. W., and Biller, H. B. Father availability and academic performance among third grade boys. *Developmental Psychology.* **4**(3):301–305 (1971).
5. Bledsoe, E. Divorce and values teaching. *Journal of Divorce.* **1**(4):371–379 (1978).
6. Cantor, D. W. School-based groups for children of divorce. *Journal of Divorce.* **1**(2):183–187 (1977).
7. Cantor, D. W., and Drake, E. A. *The Divorced Parent: A Professional's Approach to Divorcing Families.* New York: Springer Publications, in press.
8. Coddington, R. D. The significance of life events as etiologic factors in the diseases of children—II. A study of normal population. *Journal of Psychosomatic Medicine Research.* **16**:205–213 (1972).
9. Drake, E. A. Children of divorce: Review of programs in the schools. *School Psychology Review.* **10**(1): In press.
10. Drake, E. A. The school: A major source of support and help for children of divorce. *Marriage and Divorce Today: The Professionals' Newsletter* Prescod, S. (Ed). **5**(22):1 (1980).
11. Drake, E. A. Helping the school cope with children of divorce. *Journal of Divorce.* **3**(1):69–75 (1979).
12. Drake, E. A. Helping children cope with stress of divorce. Presentation at American Psychological Association Convention. New York (1979).
13. Drake, E. A. Collaboration between community mental health center and school psychological services. Presentation at American Psychological Association Convention. Toronto (1978).
14. Drake, E. A. Skill development in communication of affect: A psychoeducational program for sixth-grade students. *Dissertation Abstracts International* (1977).
15. Drake, E. A., and Bardon, J. I. Confidentiality and interagency communication: Effect of the Buckley Amendment. *Hospital and Community Psychiatry.* **29**(5):312–315 (1978).
16. Drake, E. A., Klein, A., and Mintz, M. Training school guidance counselors to lead groups: A preventive program. In press.
17. Felner, R. D., Stolberg, A., and Cowen, E. L. Crisis events and school mental health referral patterns of young children. *Journal of Consulting and Clinical Psychology.* **43**(3):305–310 (1975).
18. Freed, A. M. *TA For Kids (and grown-ups, too).* California: (1973).
19. Gardner, R. A. Social, legal, and therapeutic changes that should lessen the traumatic effects of divorce on children. *Journal of the American Academy of Psychoanalysis.* **6**(2):231–247 (1978).
20. Gardner, R. A. *Psychotherapy With Children of Divorce.* New York: Jason Aronson (1976).
21. Gardner, R. A. *The Boys and Girls Book About Divorce.* Pennsylvania: Haddon Craftsmen, Inc. (1970).
22. Gross, R., Dibbell, J. F., and Petti, M. Family composition of students referred to child study teams. *School Psychology in New Jersey.* **19**(1):13–14 (1977).

23. Guerney, L. and Jordon, L. Children of divorce—a community support group. *Journal of Divorce.* **2**(3):283–294 (1979).

24. Holdahl, S., and Caspersen, P. Children of family change: Who's helping them now? *The Family Coordinator.* October (1977).

25. Jacobson, D. S. The impact of marital separation/divorce on children: Parent-child separation and child adjustment. *Journal of Divorce.* **1**(4):341–360 (1978).

26. Kelly, R., and Berg, B. Measuring children's reactions to divorce. *Journal of Clinical Psychology.* **34**(1):215–221 (1978).

27. Kelly, J. B., and Wallerstein, J. S. Children of divorce. *The National Elementary Principal.* October:51–58 (1979).

28. Kelly, J. B., and Wallerstein, J. S. Brief interventions with children in divorcing families. *American Journal of Orthopsychiatry.* **47**(1):23–36 (1977).

29. Kelly, J. B., and Wallerstein, J. S. The effects of parental divorce: Experiences of the child in early latency. *American Journal of Orthopsychiatry.* **46**(1):20–32 (1976).

30. Kessler, S., and Bostwick, S. *Beyond Divorce: Coping Skills For Minors.* Atlanta: National Institute for Professional Training in Divorce Counseling (1977).

31. Kessler, S., Loxley, J., and Whiteley, J. M. Divorce Part II: The Divorcing Family. (Film Strip). Washington, D.C.: American Personnel and Guidance.

32. Lamb, M. E. The effects of divorce on children's personality development. *Journal of Divorce.* **1**(2):163–174 (1977).

33. *Los Angeles Times.* Schools fail the single-parent family. 5 March 6, 1979.

34. MaGrab, P. R. For the sake of the children: A review of the psychological effects of divorce. *Journal of Divorce.* **1**(3):233–245 (1978).

35. McDermott, J. F. Divorce and its psychiatric sequelae in children. *Archives of General Psychiatry.* **23**:421–427 (1970).

36. McDermott, J. F. Parental divorce in early childhood. *American Journal of Psychiatry.* **124**(10):1424–1432 (1968).

37. *Network: The Paper for Parents.* Md: National Committee for Citizens in Education. March, May, November, 1978; May, 1979.

38. *New York Times.* Programs aid the children of divorce: C1, C4 February 19, 1980.

39. *New York Times.* Single parents face special problems with the schools (January 7, 1979).

40. *New York Times.* Matter of fighting for one's rights. (January 7, 1979).

41. Norton, A. J. A portrait of the one-parent family. *The National Elementary Principal.* October:32–39 (1979).

42. Richards, A. and Willis, I. *How to Get It Together When Your Parents Are Coming Apart.* New York: David McKay (1976).

43. Santrock, J. Effects of father absence on sex-typed behaviors in male children: Reason for the absence and age of onset of the absence. *The Journal of Genetic Psychology.* **130**:3–10 (1977).

44. Separation and divorce—Selected readings for children and adolescents. *Journal of Clinical Child Psychology.* **6**(2):63–67 (1977).

45. Sinberg, J. *Divorce is a Grown-Up Problem.* New York: Avon Books (1978).

46. U.S. Bureau of the Census. *Marital Status and Living Arrangements:* March 1974 (Current Population Reports, Series P-20, No. 271). Washington, D.C.: U.S. Government Printing Office.

47. U.S. Department of Health, Education and Welfare. *Custody and Parent Rights Under the FERPA.* Communication re Section 438, 1974.

48. Wallerstein, J. S., and Kelly, J. B. California's children of divorce. *Psychology Today,* January:67–76 (1980).

49. Wallerstein, J., and Kelly, J. B. The effects of parental divorce: Experiences of the child in later latency. *American Journal of Orthopsychiatry.* **46**(2): (1976).
50. Wallerstein, J. S., and Kelly, J. B. The effects of parental divorce: Experiences of the preschool child. *Journal of the American Academy of Child Psychiatry.* **14**(4):600–616 (1975).
51. Wallerstein, J., and Kelly, J. B. The effects of parental divorce: The adolescent experience. In: *The Child in His Family,* Vol. 3. Anthony, E. J., and Koupernik, C. (Eds.) New York: Wiley and Sons (1974).
52. Weingarten, H., and Kulka, R. Parental divorce in childhood and adult adjustment: A two-generational view. Presentation at American Psychological Association Convention. New York (1979).
53. Wilkinson, G. S., and Bleck, R. T. Children's divorce groups. *Elementary School Guidance and Counseling.* **11**:205–213 (1977).

Very little is known about the children of gay parents and particularly about how they handle changes in their families. The present discussion draws primarily from clinical experience and a survey conducted of eighty-two gay parents regarding their 164 children. Comments are of necessity suggestive rather than authoritative.

All of the children represented in the sample had lived through separation from a heterosexual parent and 24 percent had also lived through separation from the same-sex lover of a gay parent. Approximately 30 percent of these children were currently living in gay families, and 50 percent viewed the gay parent's same-sex lover as either another parent or as a member of the family. Of those living with their heterosexual parent, 15 percent were not allowed to see their gay parent.

The majority of these children received negative input from peers and relatives regarding gay lifestyles; a quarter of them also received such input from their heterosexual parent and from teachers. In fact, very few received exclusively positive input from their heterosexual parent regarding their gay parent's lifestyle.

Issues of concern to these children include dealing with homophobic input, the isolation stemming from secrecy, and implications for their own sexual identity. Supportive networks are helpful, as are discussion groups where ambivalent feelings about the gay parent and the same-sex lover can be aired. The two key issues reported by gay parents were dealing with guilt about their children's potential stigmatization and knowing when and how best to come out to their children.

8

Children of Gay Parents: Homophobia's Victims

Dorothy I. Riddle, Ph. D.
Maria de Lourdes Arguelles, Ph. D.

"Children of gay parents"—for many this means a contradiction in terms. In the collective unconscious, the twin acts of having and keeping children are still zealously reserved for the heterosexual couple. Single heterosexual parents are just becoming acceptable. Homosexuals who have children in an attempt to become "normal" are perhaps understandable. But gay persons who choose to be parents are a wholly different matter—unacceptable and what is perhaps worse, inconceivable. In an ambience of increasing conservatism (Lasch, 1979), this unthinkability more often than not becomes an attitudinal set of censure and outrage.

In actuality, at least a third of all lesbians and a tenth of all gay men have children (Bell and Weinberg, 1978). An additional 19 percent of all gays are involved in active parenting. However, very little is known about children of gay parents and, more specifically, about how they handle the dynamics of their households. Certainly one can speculate that the elements of secrecy and societal unacceptability make it more difficult for these children to deal with household disruption in general and separation from important parental figures in particular. Indeed, professional workers with children in gay families are often unaware of the key elements in the child's grieving and readjustment.

The literature on gay parents is still scanty and is in large part anecdotal. The primary focus to date has been on child custody issues (e.g., Armano, 1973; Basile, 1974; Blackman, 1977; Boggan, et al., 1975; Hunter and Polikoff, 1976; Martin, 1979; Riley, 1975). A few studies have attempted to describe the particular issues faced by gay parents (e.g., Bryant, 1975; Clark, 1977; Goodman, 1973; Martin and Lyon, 1972; Pagelow, 1975; Voeller and Walters, 1978).

The literature on children of gays is virtually nonexistent. Riddle (1978) has presented a theoretical analysis and literature summary regarding gays as role models for children. Lewis (1980) and Miller (1979) have written about therapeutic work with children of lesbians. The single longitudinal study to date of children of lesbian mothers found these children to be as well-adjusted as children of heterosexual divorced women, with the problems reported being those usually seen when children have lived through divorce (Kirkpatrick, Roy, and Smith, 1976).

Because so little is known about children of gays, any data reported in this article is by nature preliminary and suggestive rather than authoritative. The issues discussed are based on clinical experience gained with children and parents, prior literature on gay families, and survey data collected from eighty-two gay parents. The gay parents sampled (see Appendix A for questionnaire) were sixty lesbian mothers and twenty-two gay fathers, from thirty towns and cities across the United States. Since gay parents were reached through network distribution, all of these parents were known to someone other than themselves as gay. Totally closeted gay parents could not be included by nature of the sampling technique. The sampling technique and nature of the questions focused on parents who had children under eighteen years of age. The findings reported are intended to stimulate further research as well as more helpful therapeutic interventions with children of gay parents.

WHO ARE THESE CHILDREN?

Information about the 164 children obtained through the present survey was of necessity indirect. Some gay parents indicated that their children helped complete the survey; for most, that was not the case.

The Children's Parents

The average respondent to the survey was Anglo (88%), between the ages of thirty-five and fifty (63%), with nontraditional religious affiliations (45%), graduate education (51%), and in a white collar or professional occupation (73%). Since minorities tend to be more closeted, the 12 percent represented in the sample were more than had been hoped for. The high level of education among the gay parents represented is underscored by the fact that only 5 percent of the sample had no college education.

The majority of respondents were from the southwest (35%), metropolitan areas in California (20%), or metropolitan areas in the northeast (11%). Most of the parents (79%) worked outside the home. Over half (60%), of the parents surveyed were supporting two to three persons on their income. While the median income for the sample was $15,000, 64% of the lesbian mothers had a median income of under $20,000.

A significantly greater proportion of the lesbians (82%) than of the gay men (50%) had legal custody of their children, $\chi^2 = 9.54$, df $= 3$, p $= .023$. Sixty-eight percent of the lesbian mothers had their children living exclusively with them, while only 41 percent of the gay fathers had their children living with them. An equal proportion of lesbian mothers (15%) and gay fathers (14%) shared joint custody of their children with the heterosexual parent. Only 19 percent of the lesbian mothers, but 46 percent of the gay fathers, never had their children living with them.

It is interesting to note that the general societal belief that children belong with their mothers seems to hold irrespective of lifestyle. There is a growing trend, however, to place children with the most appropriate parent, regardless of sex. Such a generally positive trend could result in more lesbian mothers being divested of their children, especially given the growing conservatism regarding gays.

The Children Themselves

Of the 164 children referred to in this survey, 77 were female and 87 were male. Family size ranged from 1–6 children. Females ranged in age from four to twenty-eight years, while males ranged from two to thirty-three years. Children under eighteen years of age totaled 160, or virtually the entire sample.

Most of the children (87%) were born in the context of heterosexual marriage; in 68 percent of the cases, the birth was planned. Even though many of the gay parents were in heterosexual marriages, 43 percent of the parents were aware of being gay at the time of the child's birth. Not only were many of the children planned for, but they were planned for by a gay parent. Thus, parenting in this sample was not the exclusive prerogative of those identifying as heterosexual.

Seventy-nine percent of these children lived with their gay parent; most commonly, that parent was a lesbian mother. Based on this sample, if the child had a lesbian mother, the chances were 58 percent of living with that mother; if the gay parent was male, the child's chances were 21 percent.

Sixty-eight percent of the children were in the legal custody of their gay parent, while 17 percent had the right to visit with that gay parent. Fifteen percent had no right to see their gay parent.

Children and Separation

The vast majority (88%) of these children had lived in heterosexual families at one time, all of which had stayed together for at least a year and most (85%) for over five years. Most of these children (85%) had lived through the total dissolution (separation and divorce) of this heterosexual family unit, while the remainder had lived through at least the separation stage. For 41 percent of the children, the dissolution of the heterosexual family had occurred at least five years prior, while for 85 percent it had occurred at least one year prior. In only 3 percent of the instances was the separation as recent as six months ago.

For children living in gay families, most (59%) had been together for one to five years, with 25 percent having been together for over five years and the remainder for less than one year. Gay families with two parental figures of the same sex present constituted 30 percent of the living units surveyed. Of the children who had experienced such a family constellation, 38 percent had lived through a separation from an adult who had been their gay parent's same-sex lover. Thus, 24 percent of the entire children's sample had had to deal with separation from a parent's same-sex lover. In 40 percent of the cases, the separation had occurred within the past six months; for an additional 40 percent, the separation had occurred at least one year prior.

Not too surprisingly, the most recent separation experiences of the children surveyed were from their parent's same-sex lover. This phenomenon is important to note since no work has been done to date on helping children lament such separations. It is also important to note that, though the dissolution of the heterosexual family was less recent, children's feelings about that dissolution may not be resolved, especially if they have had to deal immediately with their gay parent's newly disclosed identity (Lewis, 1980).

GENERAL STRESS FACTORS FOR THE CHILDREN

In addition to the general stress issues of separation and divorce for all children, there are several factors unique to the children of gay parents. One important factor is the nature of the separation and its consequences. Children's experiences of separation appear to be different depending upon whether the parent's partner had been same-sex or opposite-sex.

Dissolution of Heterosexual Families

When the separation was from an opposite-sex partner, the child's gay parent initiated the separation 73 percent of the time. The vast majority (82%) of the children continued to have a parental relationship with the heterosexual parent after the separation. The remainder were either friends (5%) or had no relationship. Of the children who had experienced separation from a heterosexual parent, 32 percent showed school or behavioral problems, 30 percent were withdrawn and sad, and 21 percent were observably anxious. Of this same group, 44 percent were also more relaxed, 34 percent were happier after the separation, and 19 percent showed no effect.

While in some ways separation from a heterosexual parent was more difficult than from a parent's same-sex lover, it carried with it the comfort of familiarity. Many of the children had peers with heterosexual parents that were divorced, and so this event could be readily discussed with peers. This sharing with peers provided a support that was unavailable when gay families dissolved.

A confounding variable was that of how child custody was handled between the biological parents. Since custody is often lost by skilled parents simply because of lifestyle, it was not surprising that 15 percent of parents sampled voluntarily gave up primary custody in order to avoid an incriminating court battle which they felt would only harm the children. For children who were given to the heterosexual parent for these reasons, but who would have preferred to stay with the gay parent, making sense of the occurrence was difficult. The T.V. documentary, "A Question of Love," has vividly portrayed the hurt and bewilderment of a nine-year-old boy taken from his lesbian mother against his wishes and simply because of her lifestyle.

Dissolution of Gay Families

In the families surveyed, separation from a same-sex lover was not as clearly initiated by the child's parent. In fact, the parent initiated separation only 51 percent of the time, while the lover initiated separation 31 percent of the time and mutual consent was involved 14 percent of the time. Thus, in the dissolution of same-sex relationships there were more possibilities for the parent and the child to feel abandoned.

Only 6 percent of the children separating from a parent's same-sex lover continued to have a parental relationship with that adult. More typically, the children either maintained a friendship (41%) or had no continuing relationship (53%). By contrast, the child's parent was just as likely to retain a familial (16%) or friendship (37%) relationship with a same-sex lover as with a heterosexual spouse after separation. The children themselves were as likely as in heterosexual divorce to feel better after the separation—47 percent were more relaxed and 40 percent were happier. However, a higher percentage (27%) showed no effect, and fewer had any noticeable problems: 13 percent had school or behavioral problems, 10 percent were withdrawn and sad, and 13 percent were anxious.

One potentially traumatic aspect of separation from a parent's gay lover, however, is that the role relationship is not societally defined and thus cannot be easily understood and processed with peers. Yet the children appeared to be handling such separations relatively well. Although parental relationships did not tend to continue, the vast majority of the children who continued to relate to the lover did so as friends. In all instances, the children experienced less stress if they had the option of a continuing relationship with the adult who was leaving.

Economic Implications

The economic impact of the separation upon the child's family differed by the nature of the separation and the sex of the parent. If separation was from a heterosexual parent, the economic situation worsened for 49 percent of the families, got better for 35 percent of the families, and remained the same for 17 percent of the families. When the separation had been from a gay lover, the economic situation got worse 29 percent of the time, better 35 percent, and stayed the same 35 percent of the time.

Economic impact differed, though, by sex of the gay parent. The only group of gay fathers whose economic situation worsened after separation was that of fathers with custody of their children who separated from an opposite-sex spouse. In general, the economic condition of gay men improved after separation. Lesbian mothers, however, were noticeably worse off after the dissolution of a heterosexual marriage whether or not they retained custody of their children. Since lesbian mothers were earning less on the average than gay fathers and were likely to be supporting more persons on that income, leaving a heterosexual marriage definitely affected the child's standard of living.

HOMOPHOBIC• MESSAGES TO THE CHILDREN

One major problem of children of gay parents is their sense of invisibility. The lifestyle of the parent forces them to deal with being different, rather than "normal." Unfortunately, this feeling is often directly reinforced by

•Homophobia refers to the fear of homosexuality or the fear of same-sex intimacy.

those around them. For example, a young kindergarten boy produced a drawing of his family (his mother, her woman lover, his sister and himself) and was told that he had made his "father" look like a woman and so should draw the picture over again. During a period of separation, the child naturally wants to feel acceptable and "normal."

Knowledge About Parent's Lifestyle

In the vast majority of instances (89%), these children had been told of the parent's gay identity by the gay parent. Parents clearly felt it best that children hear it first from them. The majority of the parents felt that by the time a child was six, they were old enough to understand what being gay meant. The median age of the children in this study was twelve years, and 95 percent of the parents agreed that by twelve years a child was old enough to understand about being gay. Many of the children of this study were aware that their parent believed that it was all right to love someone of the same sex. In 70 percent of the families, the children knew that one of their parents *did* love someone of the same sex; in 24 percent of these cases, the children had been privy to the fact that the parent was in a committed relationship with a person of the same sex. An additional 7 percent knew that their parent was in a same-sex lover relationship, commitment unspecified.

Input from Others

In 63 percent of these families, children received negative input regarding gay lifestyles. The majority of this input came from peers (79%), relatives (52%), and the heterosexual parent (27%). Unfortunately, given the amount of time children spend in school, in 27 percent of these cases the negative input came from teachers. Some parents (23%) were unaware of whether or not their children had received any negative information.

Fifty-eight percent of the parents felt their children received positive input about a gay lifestyle. Twenty-five percent of the time such input came from relatives, 22 percent from peers, 23 percent from their heterosexual parent, and 16 percent from teachers. Thus, heterosexual parents were as likely to be negative as positive about gay lifestyles. Teachers were more likely to be negative than positive, relatives were twice as likely to be negative, and peers were overwhelmingly more likely to be negative.

The strong negative input from peers was especially difficult for older children to handle. A number of parents, both in the survey and in clinical interviews, reported that as children entered junior high school, they became much more homophobic. Although the children had felt quite comfortable with and supportive of their gay parent's lifestyle up until then, at eleven or twelve they suddenly became adamant about wanting to be in a "normal" family. They found the "queer" jokes of classmates increasingly difficult to ignore.

There are several adjustments a child may be making regarding their sense of family during a separation. If a same-sex lover has entered the picture for the first time, they may hold that person responsible for the disappearance of their heterosexual parent, believing that if that person were to leave their biological parents would get back together. Or they may be struggling with how to define the role of that new lover: "You're a member of our family now, right? So are you like a godmother that lives with us?" In the meantime, relatives, especially grandparents, may be expressing disapproval over the form that the family is taking, leaving the children bewildered.

If the separation is from the same-sex lover, children may be getting little support for their grieving. For most children in gay families, the parent's same-sex lover does play a significant role. For example, in the forty-eight families surveyed where the gay parent currently had a same-sex lover, 21 percent viewed that lover as another parent, 44 percent as a friend, and 29 percent as a family member. However, the child's relatives may be delighted when the gay family dissolves, bewildering the child who was very attached to that person. Messages such as, "Well, she was never really family," are difficult for children to interpret when that person had indeed functioned as family.

Even more difficult are messages to the children about the gay parent. Heterosexual parents may earnestly explain that the gay parent is "sinful," that the new relationship is "an abomination." "Queer" jokes at school suddenly take on new meaning in reference to the gay parent. Some children simply get confused and upset; others attack the gay parent in rage. If the children don't live with the gay parent, then the homophobic messages may begin to outweigh the reality of the parent-child relationship.

Of the children in the sample, 32 percent were currently living in heterosexual families. Half of these children could not visit with their gay parent at all. The children who did live with gay parents still had to deal with the homophobia of the heterosexual parent. Only 20 percent of the children had heterosexual parents who did not say negative things about their gay parent's lifestyle.

Impact of Messages on Children

The impact of a parent's gay lifestyle on the children under eighteen was perceived very differently in the different families. On the whole, the experiences were seen as positive by 49 percent of the parents; they reported that their children had become more tolerant and accepting of others. Thirty-one percent of the parents reported no impact. However, 27 percent felt that their children felt different from their peers and 10 percent reported that their children got actively harassed.

Parents' perceptions of the children's attitudes were that 50 percent would not care about the sex of their next partner, 28 percent would want the next lover to be of the same sex, and 22 percent would want the lover to be of the opposite sex.

Since there is so little general understanding of homosexuality, inevitably children begin to wonder about implications for themselves. Is it catching? Should they let a gay parent be affectionate with them? Do they have to grow up gay in order to please that parent? Children living in more metropolitan areas had much more accurate information about gay lifestyles, $\chi^2 = 250.22$, df = 195, p = .004. However, even these well-informed children and many parents are unaware that researchers have documented that children of gay parents are no more likely than the children in heterosexual families to become gay themselves (Green, 1978; Miller, 1979). In fact, Bryant (1975) has pointed out that lesbian mothers are more likely than heterosexual mothers to support their children in whatever lifestyle they choose. A major difficulty for children of gay parents is the lack of a forum for open discussion of such issues.

SECRETS AND THE CLOSETED PARENT

Of the parents responding, 70 percent had known that they were gay for over five years, an additional 17 percent for over three years but less than five years, 12 percent for one to three years, and 1 percent for under a year. The vast majority (86%) of gay fathers had known that they were gay for over five years. However, 17 percent of the lesbians had known for less than three years, 20 percent had known for three to five years, while 63 percent had known for over five years. Thus, gay men had known for a significantly longer time, $\chi^2 = 8.74$, df = 3, p = .03.

The majority (73%) of the parents responding felt that their gay identity was something of which to be proud, 5 percent were indifferent, and 22 percent were unsure as yet. None of the sample felt that being gay was something of which to be ashamed. No gay parents had received counseling primarily dealing with their parenting role as a gay parent. However, some parents interviewed worried that their lifestyle would somehow be harmful for the child. Other parents, during the process of divorce, were struggling not only with grieving the loss of a primary relationship but also with a newly admitted gay identity and how or whether to share this with their children.

The Impact of Secrecy

Because of the nonacceptance of gay lifestyles in our society, sooner or later gay parents are in the position of trying to explain to their children that their lifestyle should not be generally discussed. With younger children, this can be handled relatively matter-of-factly. However, as children approach adolescence, they quickly begin to understand that the parent's lifestyle provides them with some leverage. The following scenario is not uncommon: "If you don't let me use the car (buy me new clothes, let me stay out late. . . .), I'll tell dad, (grandfather, neighbors. . .) that you're queer." Since the gay parent usually fears a custody battle which could be precipitated by such a revelation, the parent often feels pretty powerless.

For children who do not abuse the information, it is quite stressful to feel that there is something about their family which they mustn't tell. Jones (1978) comments that he has never been approached by the child of a gay parent for counseling. By and large, children in gay families learn to be guarded about their home life until they know that they can trust the other person (Hall, 1978).

Coming Out to Children

How and when to come out to a child are some of the most frequently asked questions by gay parents. Berzon (1978) has an excellent discussion of both the process and the importance of coming out to one's children. Several writers (e.g., Martin & Lyon, 1972; Miller, 1979) have documented the fact that honesty and candor with children pave the way for a stronger and closer relationship. However, our clinical experience indicates that a gradual introduction to gay persons and gay lifestyles is more successful than a sudden revelation.

If a parent does not come out to the child, often that parent relinquishes custody without a court battle in order to avoid disclosure. The children in this instance are often bewildered by why the parent "let them go," and the gay parent finds it difficult to explain without revealing lifestyle information. Miller (1979) points out that closeted gay fathers (especially if they are still in a heterosexual marriage) often overindulge their children out of guilt, while also spending relatively little time with them. Coming out to the child usually results in increased, better quality time together as well as a modeling of honesty and self-acceptance.

WHAT HELPS THESE CHILDREN?

When asked what made separation/divorce easiest for their children, the two most common explanations given by parents were relief at being out of a stressful situation (19%) and cooperation from the ex-spouse (25%). The parents reported that what made separation/divorce most difficult were having one parent gone (47%) or the child's feelings of upset and sadness (25%).

Parents reported that the majority of the children (77%) had never received any counseling because they had a gay parent. Twenty-one percent had received counseling which had been helpful, while 2 percent had received counseling which the parent perceived as detrimental. The majority of children (65%) receiving counseling had been counseled by private therapists; of the remainder, 20 percent had received help from a mental health agency, 10 percent from a gay counseling service, and 5 percent at school.

Supportive Services for Children

From the survey, it is obvious that gay parents have given considerable thought to what counseling or supportive programs would be helpful for themselves and their children. Of these parents, less than 1 percent felt that counseling for gays and their children should be the same as for the heterosexual parent and his/her children or had in fact given no thought to it. A small number of the parents surveyed felt that only gays should counsel them and/or their children. An equally small minority felt that it was essential for the therapist to be a parent. Being gay and having parented (as distinct from being a biological parent), however, does give unique insight into the stressed world of the child of a gay parent.

Overwhelmingly, parents reported that what helped their children was being able to talk about what was going on to someone other than the parent. The children needed to be reassured that their parent and family was acceptable, needed to process how to handle "queer" jokes and their own homophobia (especially as they entered junior high), and needed support in issues with stepparents who were their parents' same sex.

Children of gay parents need information about the nature of homosexuality within the context of general sex education (44%). In particular, counselors need to allay fears that a gay parent has no use for an opposite-sex child. An effective counselor would be one who could deal with the most common myths and stereotypes surrounding homosexual behavior and lifestyles.

In designing counseling services for children of gays, many parents (59%) felt that it was essential the children be provided with the tools to deal with antagonizing peers and to a lesser degree with heterosexual relatives. Specific skills and resources need to be supplied so that the child can deal effectively with overwhelming societal prejudice (existing and/or anticipated). Role-playing typical situations can be very helpful.

The need for building support systems among children of gays was mentioned by 26 percent of the parents, especially to help assuage feelings of being "different". Such support groups can help the children work through mixed feelings which they may be unable to share constructively with their gay parent. Lewis (1980) found, for example, that children's initial reaction to finding out that their mother was a lesbian was verbal acceptance because of love and respect for the parent. Feelings of pain and anger were denied and, if expressed at all, tended to be expressed towards the same-sex lover. How the parent disclosed the information was strongly related to how free the child felt to express ambivalence. All children living in gay families need help working through day-to-day relationships with the live-in "stepparent," especially as that person is not acknowledged as a parental person by peers (and often relatives as well).

For younger children, the primary issues center around the isolation caused by the need for secrecy about the parent's lifestyle. For older children, concerns are more related to the implications, if any, for their own sexual identity. Counselors with these children need to support the gay parent's concerns regarding tolerance of different lifestyles. Parents repeatedly argued that their children must feel free to choose their own lifestyle. In a society where the limits of tolerance are too rapidly narrowing, gay parents and, in particular, gay families seem a bastion of openness and self-choice.

Parents also noted a need to address issues of sexuality and routine separation/divorce stresses. Children of gay parents need factual information about sexual identity and development, and time to discuss their own fantasies and fears. Children of gay parents also need support in dealing with feelings of loss, lifestyle change, and other common issues related to the separation/divorce process.

An often overlooked group of children are those living with the heterosexual parent. In our sample these children represented 32 percent of the children. Since heterosexual parents are unlikely to be supportive of the gay parent's lifestyle, such children need help being able to maintain good feelings about the gay parent despite homophobic input.

Supportive Services for Gay Parents

Children can also be helped through providing help and support to the adults involved. Gay parents repeated needing reassurance that they were not *a priori* harming their children, which could include information about how children's personal identity develops (see Riddle, 1978) and how to help children deal with societal intolerance. Also, the lovers of gay parents need support in stepparenting, a usually invisible role, and how best to help the children through the separation and divorce.

A key issue in counseling for gay parents was that of how to and when to share gay identity (26%). Practice in the process of coming out and some assessment as to when to come out (in terms of children's age and social circumstances) were seen as essential services in a gay parents' group.

One issue to keep in mind in working with gay parents is the generally high level of education among such parents (which we have found to be true also in clinical settings). These parents are usually aware and concerned about the difficulties their children experience because of their lifestyle choice. In fact, Goodman (1973) reports that the parent's guilt over possibly harming the child through stigmatization was the single most difficult issue for lesbian mothers. Once the guilt had been worked through, other parenting problems rapidly receded.

General Observations

Because of the intense homophobia in our society, Hall (1978) stresses that validating gay lifestyles is the single most important intervention which a counselor can make. Such validation is crucial for both the children and the parents. The children need to feel that they are part of a larger group of a particular kind of families, rather than the only "queer" family. The parents need reassurance that they are not being bad parents by subjecting their children to ridicule. Analogies to other minority families are helpful, as is information on how few families actually fit the stereotyped T.V.-image heterosexual nuclear family.

Supportive services for gay parents and their children are essential, especially in the smaller cities and towns. Ideally, such service can be offered in the context of groups like Divorce Recovery rather than within a therapeutic setting with its implication of maladjustment. Any such services must take into account the need for secrecy because of the very real potential loss of child custody, employment, housing, etc. It is unrealistic, for example, to expect that gay family members would participate openly in a predominantly heterosexual support group or that children in heterosexual families would discuss an absent gay parent in such a setting.

Services for gay parents and their children need to be offered, whenever possible, by counselors who are either gay or who have worked through their own homophobia and who have some parenting experience. It can be very helpful for children of gay parents to know that persons other than gays are supportive of their parents' lifestyle; however, heterosexual counselors need to be as aware as possible of the realities of gay families, both their joys and stresses. Until such time as supportive services become available, accessible, and acceptable to gay families, the impact of parental loss compounded by homophobia on children of gays will continue unabated.

APPENDIX A: SURVEY OF GAY PARENTS AND THEIR CHILDREN

As part of an article on children of gay parents, we are gathering information on how gay lifestyles may affect children, especially during times of parental divorce and separation. We are interested in separation from both same-sex and opposite-sex partners. We need all the data we can get, so please pass copies on to friends who are parents. Please answer the following questions (placing a check mark on the appropriate line) and return the survey to:

> Dr. Dorothy Riddle
> Psychology Department
> University of Arizona
> Tucson, Arizona 85721

Additional comments may be made on the back page. All answers will be anonymous; please do not include your name. If you want to receive a copy of our article, please send a separate letter to Dr. Riddle requesting one. Thank you very much for your cooperation.

NOTE: To simplify sentence structure, we have used the plural "children" to refer to one or more children.

Survey

Demographic Information

1. Sex

    _____ (1) Female
    _____ (2) Male

2. Age

    _____ (1) under 18
    _____ (2) 18–24
    _____ (3) 25–34
    _____ (4) 35–50
    _____ (5) over 50

3. Religious affiliation

    _____ (1) Jewish
    _____ (2) Catholic
    _____ (3) Protestant
    _____ (4) Mormon
    _____ (5) Other _____

4. Ethnicity

    _____ (1) Anglo
    _____ (2) Mexican-American
    _____ (3) Black
    _____ (4) Native American
    _____ (5) Oriental
    _____ (6) Other _____

5. Primary source of income

    _____ (1) Employment
    _____ (2) Family
    _____ (3) Alimony/Child support
    _____ (4) Public Assistance or Welfare
    _____ (5) Social Security or Pension
    _____ (6) Other _____

6. Annual gross family income

    _____ (1) less than $5,000
    _____ (2) $5,000–$9,999
    _____ (3) $10,000–$14,999
    _____ (4) $15,000–$19,999
    _____ (5) over $20,000

7. Persons supported by family income:

    _____ (1) one
    _____ (2) 2–3
    _____ (3) 4–5
    _____ (4) more than 5

8. Educational level completed

    _____ (1) grade school

    _____ (2) high school

    _____ (3) some college

    _____ (4) college degree

    _____ (5) graduate degree

Information About Children

11–12. Ages of children:

    Male Children

    (1) _____

    (2) _____

    (3) _____

13. Context of children's birth

    _____ (1) heterosexual marriage

    _____ (2) single parent, other parent known

    _____ (3) single parent, other parent unknown

    _____ (4) children were adopted

    _____ (5) other _____

15. Were you aware of being gay when you were having children?

    _____ (1) yes

    _____ (2) no

9. Occupation: _____

10. Town/city where you live

    _____

    Female Children

    (1) _____

    (2) _____

    (3) _____

14. Were the births planned?

    _____ (1) yes

    _____ (2) no

Information About Children (continued)

16. Would you have children again, given the chance?
    _____ (1) yes, because _____
    _____ (2) no, because _____
    _____ (3) don't know, because _____

17. Are your children living with you?
    _____ (1) yes
    _____ (2) no, because _____

18. Do you have legal custody of your children?
    _____ (1) yes
    _____ (2) no, but visitation rights
    _____ (3) no, and no visitation rights

19. What do your children know about your gay lifestyle?
    _____ (1) nothing
    _____ (2) that I believe it is all right to love someone of the same sex
    _____ (3) that I love a particular person of the same sex
    _____ (4) that I have a committed relationship with someone of the same sex
    _____ (5) other _____

20. Who told your children about your lifestyle?
    _____ (1) I did
    _____ (2) their heterosexual parent
    _____ (3) my same-sex lover

_____ (4) their relatives

_____ (5) their peers

_____ (6) other _____

21–23. What kind of input do your children get about gay lifestyles from:

	Negative Input	Positive Input
(1) their heterosexual parent	_____	_____
(2) their peers	_____	_____
(3) their relatives	_____	_____
(4) their teachers	_____	_____
(5) other _____		

24. How do your children view your present same-sex lover?

_____ (1) as another parent

_____ (2) as a friend

_____ (3) as a family member

_____ (4) other _____

_____ (5) I don't currently have a same-sex lover

25. How old do you feel a child needs to be in order to understand what being gay means?

_____ years old

26. What impact does your gay lifestyle have on your children?

_____ (1) no impact

_____ (2) they get harassed

_____ (3) they feel different from their peers

_____ (4) they are more tolerant and accepting of others

_____ (5) other _____

191

Information About Separation & Divorce

27. Present relational status

    ———(1) single
    ———(2) married (heterosexually)
    ———(3) divorced
    ———(4) widowed

    ———(5) living with same-sex partner
    ———(6) living with opposite-sex partner
    ———(7) separated from same-sex partner
    ———(8) separated from opposite-sex partner

28–29. *In addition to* your response to Item #27, have you ever been (check more than one if appropriate):

	Same-sex Partner	*Opposite-sex Partner*
(1) married to	———	———
(2) divorced from	———	———
(3) widowed from	———	———
(4) separated from	———	———
(5) living with	———	———

If you have ever been separated or divorced, please answer Items #30–47. Otherwise, please skip to Item #48.

30–31. How long have you been separated/divorced from:

	Same-sex Partner	*Opposite-sex Partner*
(1) less than 6 months	———	———
(2) 6 months–1 year	———	———
(3) 1–3 years	———	———
(4) 3–5 years	———	———
(5) over 5 years	———	———

32-33. Who initiated separation/divorce from:

	Same-sex Partner	Opposite-sex Partner
(1) I did	_____	_____
(2) my partner did	_____	_____
(3) mutual agreement	_____	_____
(4) other _____	_____	_____

34. Reason(s) for separation or divorce: _____

35-36. In your opinion, is your economic situation since your separation or divorce from:

	Same-sex Partner	Opposite-sex Partner
(1) better	_____	_____
(money less tight)		
(2) worse	_____	_____
(money more tight)		
(3) about the same	_____	_____

37-38. How long had you been with your:

	Same-sex Partner	Opposite-sex Partner
(1) less than 1 year	_____	_____
(2) 1-3 years	_____	_____
(3) 3-5 years	_____	_____
(4) over 5 years	_____	_____

Information About Separation & Divorce (continued)

39–40. How have your children been affected by your separation/divorce from your:

	Same-sex Partner	*Opposite-sex Partner*
(1) no effect	___	___
(2) happier	___	___
(3) more relaxed	___	___
(4) more anxious	___	___
(5) withdrawn and sad	___	___
(6) behavior problems	___	___
(7) school problems	___	___
(8) other ___		

41–42. What kind of relationship do your children now have with your ex-:

	Same-sex Partner	*Opposite-sex Partner*
(1) parental relationship	___	___
(2) good friends	___	___
(3) casual friends	___	___
(4) no relationship	___	___
(5) other ___		

43–44. What kind of relationship do you now have with your ex-:

	Same-sex Partner	*Opposite-sex Partner*
(1) "family"	___	___
(2) good friends	___	___
(3) casual friends		

(4) no relationship _____ ||

(5) other _____ ||

45. In your opinion, do your children hope that your next partner will be:

_____ (1) a same-sex partner because _____

_____ (2) an opposite-sex partner because _____

_____ (3) do not care

_____ (4) do not know

46. What made your separation/divorce most difficult for your children?

_____

47. What made your separation/divorce easiest for your children to accept?

_____

48. How long have you known you were gay?

_____ (1) less than 1 year

_____ (2) 1–3 years

_____ (3) 3–5 years

_____ (4) over 5 years

49. For you, your gay identity is:

_____ (1) something to be proud of

_____ (2) something to be ashamed of

_____ (3) a matter of indifference

_____ (4) don't know yet

Use of Counseling Services

50. Have your children ever received counseling because they had a gay parent?

_____ (1) no (please skip #51)

_____ (2) yes, and it was helpful

_____ (3) yes, and it was detrimental

Use of Counseling Services (continued)

51. Where did your children receive such counseling?

    _____ (1) in school
    _____ (2) in a mental health agency
    _____ (3) in a gay counseling service
    _____ (4) other _____

52. If counseling services for children of gay parents were offered, what major issues should be covered?

    1. _____
    2. _____
    3. _____
    4. _____

53. Have you ever received counseling primarily dealing with your parenting role as a gay parent?

    _____ (1) no
    _____ (2) yes, and it was helpful
    _____ (3) yes, and it was detrimental

54. If counseling services for gay parents were offered, what major issues should be covered?

    1. _____
    2. _____
    3. _____
    4. _____

Thank You.

REFERENCES

Armano, B. F. The lesbian mother: Her right to child custody. *Golden Gate Law Review.* **4**(1), 1–18 (1973).

Basile, R. A. Lesbian mothers I. *Women's Rights Law Reporter.* **2**, 3–18 (1974).

Bell, A., and Weinberg, M. *Homosexualities: A Study of Diversity Among Men and Women.* New York: Simon and Schuster (1978).

Berzon, B. Sharing your lesbian identity with your children. *In:* Vida, G. (Ed.). *Our Right to Love: A Lesbian Resource Book.* Englewood Cliffs, New Jersey: Prentice-Hall (1978).

Blackman, M. K. *In the Best Interests of the Children: A Resource Pamphlet for Lesbian Mothers.* Los Angeles: Center Press of the Alcoholism Center for Women, 1977. (Available from Iris Feminist Collective, Box 26463, Los Angeles, California 90026.)

Boggan, E. C., Haft, M. G., Lister, C., and Rupp, J. P. *The Rights of Gay People: The Basic American Civil Liberties Union Guide to a Gay Person's Rights.* New York: Avon Books (1975).

Bryant, B. Lesbian mothers. Unpublished master's thesis, School of Social Work, California State University, Sacramento (1975).

Clark, D. *Loving Someone Gay.* Millbrae, California: Celestial Arts (1977).

Goodman, B. The lesbian mother. *American Journal of Orthopsychiatry,* **43**(2), 283–284 (1973).

Green, R. Sexual identity of 37 children raised by homosexual or transsexual parents. *American Journal of Psychiatry.* **135**(6), 692–697 (1978).

Hall, M. Lesbian families: Cultural and clinical issues. *Social Work.* **23**, 380–385 (1978).

Hunter, N. D., and Polikoff, N. D. Custody rights of lesbian mothers: Legal theory and litigation strategy. *Buffalo Law Review.* **25**(3), 691–733 (1976).

Jones, C. R. *Understanding Gay Relatives and Friends.* New York: Seabury Press (1978).

Kirkpatrick, M., Roy, R., and Smith, K. A new look at lesbian mothers. *Human Behavior.* August: 60–61 (1976).

Lasch, C. *The Culture of Narcissism: American Life in an Age of Diminishing Expectations.* New York: W. W. Norton (1979).

Lewis, K. G. Children of lesbians: Their point of view. *Social Work.* **25**, 198–203 (1980).

Martin, D. Psychological implications in lesbian mother custody cases. Paper presented at the annual meeting of the American Psychiatric Association, Chicago, May (1979).

Martin, D., and Lyon, P. *Lesbian/Woman.* New York: Bantam Books (1972).

Miller, B. Gay fathers and their children. Paper presented at the annual meeting of the American Psychiatric Association, Chicago, May (1979).

Pagelow, M. D. Lesbian mothers. Unpublished paper, Sociology Department, University of California, Riverside (1975).

Riddle, D. I. Relating to children: Gays as role models. *Journal of Social Issues.* **34**(3), 38–58 (1978).

Riley, M. The avowed lesbian mother and her right to child custody: A constitutional challenge that can no longer be denied. *San Diego Law Review.* July: 799–864 (1975).

Voeller, B., and Walters, J. Gay fathers. *Family Coordinator.* **27**, 149–157 (1978).

Wolf, D. G. *The Lesbian Community.* Berkeley, California: University of California Press (1979).

At the present time, nearly a half-million men and women are incarcerated in American prisons and jails. Many of them are married and have dependents, including children. It is estimated that as many as 200,000 children experience what it means to have a parent in prison for a longer or shorter time.

The chapter by Dr. Enid Gamer and Ms. Ann K. Schrader examines the problems that such families encounter and the types of intervention possible in helping them. Their contribution is particularly valuable because there is very little previously published information in this area.

9

Children of Incarcerated Parents: Problems and Interventions

Enid Gamer, PH. D.
Ann K. Schrader, A.C.S.W.

INTRODUCTION

When we send an adult to prison we are often removing a parent from some child's life. Although there are no reliable statistics on the number of children who are affected by a parent's incarceration we can estimate that the figure is probably in the hundreds of thousands.

In 1978, on any given day there were more than 460,000 adult men and women serving time in prison and jails.[16] Many of these individuals were married with dependents. Data from 1974 indicates that 52 percent of the male and female inmates in state prisons had been married, with relatively few divorces prior to or during incarceration. Combining married and single inmates, 60 percent reported one or more dependents; 15 percent had four or more.[18] Data on female inmates alone indicate that 70 percent of the 15,000 women in jails and prisons in 1970 were mothers, with an average of two children each.[14] Thus, conservatively estimating one child for every two inmates gives us a figure of over 200,000 children who, first hand, are experiencing what it means to have a parent in prison.

Most of these children are young. A national study of children of incarcerated mothers found that over 60 percent were under ten years of age;

22 percent were under four.[14] (Unfortunately, comparable data is not available for children of incarcerated men.)

Their parents for the most part are young as well. U.S. census data on female inmates shows that 70 percent are under twenty-five;[14] the majority of male inmates are under thirty.[28]

Contrary to public expectation most men and women are serving relatively short sentences for victimless or nonviolent crimes. On the average a woman will stay in prison for eighteen months, a man for between two and three years.[11] State prisons, which primarily house male inmates report that just under half of their population is incarcerated for nonviolent crimes.[29] A survey of sixty-three women, detained at Riker's Island in New York, indicated that 79 percent were charged with or convicted of victimless crimes or crimes against property.[14]

Thus, over 200,000 children belong to incarcerated parents. Their parents tend to be young, for the most part are not violent and can expect to be reunited with their families before the children are old enough to leave home. Yet in spite of their numbers remarkably little attention has been paid to the children themselves and to the inmate's role as a parent. We are especially pleased that the editors of a book dealing with children of separation and divorce have thought to include this neglected population. We welcome the opportunity to call attention to their situation and their needs in an effort to encourage social service agencies to consider these children and their families when planning outreach and intervention programs.

Over the next several pages we will review several common experiences faced by children of prisoners. We will discuss how imprisonment is described to the youngsters; the nature of their caretaking arrangements; the type of mothering or fathering received from the incarcerated parent; visiting conditions; the nature of their social relationships, and their behavioral and emotional reactions to the incarceration.

The final section of this chapter will review various intervention strategies and programs. Some address the children's needs directly. Others describe programs which offer support and assistance to the parents themselves.

EXPERIENCES AFFECTING CHILDREN OF PRISONERS

Learning About the Incarceration

Results of several studies suggest that in general, children are not offered satisfactory explanations regarding the imprisonment. They are either deceived outright, told partial truths, or straightforwardly given a full recounting of the events with little attention paid to their level of understanding.

Studies describing how children find out about incarceration suggest that between one-third to a half of the families deceive the children as to their parent's status. They may be told instead that their father or mother is away working, is in school, or has joined the Army. Some children may even be taken to prison and then told that this is where their father works or where mother goes to school.[1, 24, 26] In most families, whether or not she is the prisoner, the mother explains incarceration to the children. Thus, many fathers remain uncertain as to what their children have been told.

It is easy to understand why parents conceal the facts. They are fearful of losing their child's respect and want to save themselves and their children from embarrassment and upset. Other factors influencing how much of a secret will be kept include the nature of the crime (e.g., crimes of a sexual nature are more likely to be concealed) as well as the family's social status. There is likely to be more pressure to keep things quiet when a spouse is the only one on the block to have gone to jail.

Some of this deception occurs against the wishes of the incarcerated parent. Several would like the chance to tell the children their side of things but are dependent upon having the children brought to them. They are helpless to force a visit when the spouse or caretaker chooses to prevent a reunion. It is particularly painful for such parents to be ignorant of what the children know or think about them.

We can anticipate that concealment and deception serve to increase the child's anxiety. A youngster who is uncertain about what has happened to his parent is more likely to be preoccupied, worried, and fearful.

Children who are not given an accurate account are probably also discouraged from talking about the absent parent. Thus, in many cases the children may be forced to come to terms with the event by themselves. Under these circumstances misunderstandings and distortions are free to grow and can affect relationships with their caretakers, parents, and peers. We will return to a discussion of these issues in sections to follow.

Caretaking Arrangements

Although there have been no systematic studies of caretaking arrangements for children of incarcerated men, those studies which have looked at other dimensions of the problem suggest that by and large the children remain with their mother.[19, 24] If, however, family finances are tight, the mother may have to work and board younger children with relatives. We remember quite clearly one incident at Walpole Prison. A mother came for a weekday afternoon visit accompanied by two attractive, well-mannered and well-cared-for girls, about seven and nine years old. She was weeping on and off throughout the afternoon, often burying her head in her husband's lap. We learned at the end of the visit that she had just, that morning, put her two other children, ages twelve months and three years, on a plane for Virginia. This mother felt she had to work and decided to send her youngest two children to live with their grandmother in the South.

Although in most cases the mother continues to care for her children, chances are good that the quality of care will be negatively influenced by a variety of factors. There is likely to be a drop in family income, rejection by family and friends, perhaps one or more forced moves, and loneliness.[1, 19, 35] Given all these stresses, her temper and patience are likely to be short, she will be subject to depression, and generally be less available to her children.

What happens to caretaking arrangements when it is the mother who is sent to prison? Generally the children are cared for by extended family. A national survey of incarcerated mothers showed that only one child in eight was placed in foster care with strangers; the great majority, over 75 percent, lived with relatives, friends, and neighbors.[14] In many instances, the children did not have to move into a new home since they were already living with extended family at the time of their mother's arrest.[2, 12, 14] In spite of this apparent stability it is important not to underestimate the shock of separation and the continuing loss. Between 50–75 percent of the children lived with their mother at the time of her arrest and for many this was their first separation.[2, 12, 14]

Role of the Imprisoned Parent

How does prison affect a mother or father's capacity to parent? Generally incarceration makes them feel helpless and powerless. Circumstances of the marital and parental relations have drastically changed. No longer does the parent have the freedom, authority, or opportunity to act on behalf of his/her child. It is difficult for parents to appreciate their importance to their youngsters when they are unable to support them, discipline them, or share in various activities. Some parents report feeling particularly unable to "tell their children what to do" since they have "done wrong" themselves.[12] We, ourselves, have seen fathers discourage family contact for a host of reasons including concern that the prison environment may be too frightening, humiliation about their current circumstances, or avoidance of the inevitably painful leave-taking at the end of the visits.

Mothers in prison frequently report feeling responsible for their children, and remain concerned about whether their children are adequately fed and clothed.[14] However, in spite of this wish to remain connected, researchers report a sense of futility. As one woman emphatically stated, "You can't be a mother and be in prison."[2]

There is, of course, a group of parents in prison who lack parenting skills altogether, even though motivation may be present. We mentioned earlier that inmates are young. One study of women in a Maryland institution found that most were between fifteen and nineteen years of age when their first child was born. Given their extreme youthfulness and their continued dependence upon their own parents, they were unable to assume a parental role vis à vis their own offspring. About half the sample showed several instances of role confusion or role reversal. Mothers treated their children as peers or siblings; often the children behaved as parents, warning mothers about being "bad" and promising to care for them upon release.[12]

We have emphasized difficulties in parenting from within prison. To give some flavor of the kind of interaction that can be maintained despite almost insurmountable odds we offer the following vignette:

Peter was a twenty-eight-year-old illiterate laborer from a rural community, father of three children, with no criminal record until he shot and killed his wife. His young children were put in foster care and he was sentenced to life in prison. He learned to read and write and doggedly followed the progress of his children. Though the children originally rejected him because of their mother's death, this man persisted in his efforts to contact them and to advocate for their well being in the foster care system. He formed a relationship with the foster parents and after two years was able to exchange visits with the children. He treasured their letters and swelled with pride when the eldest insisted, despite family pressure, on retaining his name. The children have made a good adjustment to their foster home and are doing well in school. Clearly they have benefited from his interest in their welfare and his obvious love for them. It is our expectation that many inmates, with adequate encouragement and information, would, like Peter, be capable of maintaining an essential parenting role in their children's lives.

The Experience of Visiting in Prison

Important factors influencing an incarcerated parent's interaction with his/her children are the ease of visiting and the conditions under which visits occur. Perhaps the most potent obstacle is simple separation. State prisons are usually located far away from the urban centers where most prison families live. Making a visit entails a good deal of travel time with attendant expense. These factors alone tend to discourage visiting.

Prisons are carefully designed to prevent violence and escape. They are not designed to support self-esteem or to permit dignified human interaction. They are frequently surrounded by high walls, often with gun towers. Entry into the prison is preceded by security checks which can include searches of adults and children alike for concealed drugs, weapons, money, and other forbidden articles. Many prisons have metal detectors. In order to clear them, visitors are required to remove all jewelry, glasses, belt buckles, sometimes even shoes. In high security facilities no personal articles or gifts such as pictures, books, flowers, or special foods can be brought inside. Visitors may be asked to submit to body searches or face the consequence of refusal to submit, which is being turned away; others may be interrogated by guards.

Once inside, the amount of contact allowed between inmates and their visitors can vary. In the most structured settings, all visiting is done from behind a glass or screen with communication via telephone. Other facilities permit the inmate to sit next to, or hold onto a spouse or lover; the inmate and his visitors may even be allowed to walk around an outdoor yard. Of course, all visits, at all times, are supervised by guards from central surveillance points.

In spite of these conditions, children are not strangers to prison. There are no age restrictions so infants just several weeks old, as well as toddlers, preschoolers, and school-aged children can be admitted. Figures suggest that between 44–55 percent of inmate parents have at least monthly visits with their youngsters.[2, 26]

Over a seventeen-week period, the Washington State Prison Pre-School Program operating one day a week counted service to 224 children.[34] In our own Walpole Prison Play Program, we counted attendance by 354 children over fifty-three weekday sessions. Ages of the participants ranged from eight months to thirteen years. Figures on the number of weekend visits by children are not available but they are estimated to be several times the numbers just cited since Saturday and Sunday are the busiest visiting days.

Although prisons permit children to enter, they make no accommodation for them. Children are expected to sit quietly, without toys or materials to occupy them, for anywhere from one to several hours. At Walpole Prison, the only acknowledgment of their presence before the playgroup was allowed to begin were signs directing parents to "take responsibility" for their children. In essence that meant "do not let them run around or in any way disturb officers and other inmates." It is easy to see how visiting under these circumstances can turn into an ordeal for children and their parents. No matter how anxious a parent may be to see his/her three-year-old, there is little to say after the first five minutes, and a visit often deteriorates into a series of commands to sit still, stop crying, or any one of a number of variations on this theme. One little boy was observed after many reproaches for attempts to amuse himself, quietly watching a slow drip of water through the leaky roof form a puddle on the prison floor.

Social Interaction

Having an incarcerated parent tends to isolate youngsters and their families from the larger social world. Women and children are both rejected and rejecting. Wives report coolness from former friends and associates as well as increased pressure to move out of their community.[2] The stigma placed on their husbands generalizes to close family members. One woman expressed it by saying that others think "where there's smoke, there's fire, I had no one to talk to at all."[19] Even relatives who may be helpful at the time of arrest and trial tend to withdraw their support once the crisis is over and the situation becomes stable.[17]

In defense, wives and children isolate themselves, deceive and lie to neighbors and friends. We know little about the comparable social situation of men who are close to incarcerated women. However we do know that children of incarcerated mothers try to keep her whereabouts secret.[31]

There is some suggestion that the children's self-imposed isolation does not diminish with time. Sack[25] reported interviews with twenty-two children who regularly visited their father at the Oregon State Penitentiary. He found that the children could rarely name more than one or two friends while some appeared friendless. Several left school quickly after class to go directly home in a clear effort to avoid other children. Others indicated that schoolmates could not come to their homes because their father was in jail.

Children are especially vulnerable to taunts and teases by peers. McGowen and Blumenthal[14] describe a twelve-year-old girl whose mother was in prison. Her schoolwork deteriorated and assaultive, aggressive behavior increased when a classmate began to taunt her, calling her mother a "jailbird." The result was a short stay at a detention center. Upon her return to class the authors report that the students left her alone but there seems to have been no real acceptance of this youngster by her peers.

We can only speculate on the effects of this isolation. Developmental theory suggests that good peer interaction teaches one about the perspectives of others and helps to diminish one's own egocentricity.[20] Sullivan[32] suggests that close friendships during the school year offer the opportunity to share feelings and thoughts, allowing one to validate one's sense of self worth. It is through these interactions that a child learns he is not alone with worries and concerns but that similar ideas are shared by others. Above all he learns that he is acceptable to others. Children of imprisoned parents do not have the same chance to develop these close trusting relationships. By keeping their worries and feelings a secret, they limit opportunities to put their problems into perspective. They lack the solace of a sympathetic friend. The chance to resolve serious issues through intimate, empathetic discussion, is lost to them.

We have briefly reviewed some of the experiences common to all children who have a parent removed to prison. They suffer confusion, intimidations, and disruption. They are often isolated within their communities and schools. What are the children's reactions to these circumstances? In an effort to describe common behavioral and emotional reactions to a parental incarceration we will review the limited research on this population and add to it our own experience with children from Walpole Prison.

THE CHILDREN'S REACTIONS

Studies suggest that the children face adjustment difficulties at home and at school, with family and friends. Outbreaks of delinquent or antisocial behavior can be expected in a small segment of this population. Although many of the adjustment problems seem to be mild and transitory, when combined with other factors, parental incarceration can lead to serious problems.

We acknowledge that in some cases, removal of a disruptive, unstable, and abusive parent comes as a relief to the child. However, these are not the majority of instances and for the purposes of this discussion we will assume a positive attachment to the parent on the part of the child.

Prevalent Behaviors

One set of behaviors observed after the incarceration is difficulty with caretakers. Children were often described by their mothers as "fighting over little things." Verbal rejection of the mother was likely when the father was imprisoned. Comments such as "I don't want you I want my daddy" were frequent.[26] In a sample of six Boston families, all with incarcerated fathers, preadolescent boys were described as "rebellious," "bossy," and "openly disobedient" toward their caretakers.[24] There is some suggestion that this behavior is exacerbated when a nonrelative cares for the child.[2]

This hostile and aggressive behavior reflects a pervasive sense of stress and uncertainty shared by all family members at the time of incarceration. It can also reflect anger at the ineffectiveness and inability of significant and seemingly powerful adults to save the imprisoned parent. In still other instances, the caretaker may be the recipient of displaced unconscious anger toward the incarcerated parent. For all these reasons the adult having primary responsibility for the child will stand a good chance of bearing the brunt of that child's negative feelings, the motivations of which may be but dimly recognized and acknowledged.

School adjustment and performance often decline after a parents's incarceration. Freedman and Esselstyn[7] studied over 200 children in kindergarten through seventh grade, all with fathers in prison. Teachers were asked to compare these children to randomly selected controls. Children of inmates were rated below average more often and above average less often on a variety of social and psychological measures including achievement, schoolwork, participation, self-concept, companions, and family interest. In Sack's[26] Oregon sample half of the seventy-three parents studied reported a drop in their children's grades and an increase in aggression during the school day. Younger children were especially prone to school phobias. Similar results are reported for a small urban sample[24] and for children of incarcerated mothers.[2]

The most conspicuious and troubling behavior is that which harms people or damages property. Children who demonstrate such behavior are often dismissed as having "bad blood" or as "likely to wind up like their parents." This undifferentiated and simplistic analysis masks the underlying dynamics and is of particular concern to the authors because it discourages helpful interventions. The reader may recall the case illustration introduced earlier of the twelve-year-old girl who was sent to a detention center for fighting in school. She was considered, by the professionals responsible for her care, as starting to behave like her mother and in need of "learning some limits." It was only upon return to her classroom that it became clear that she was provoked to assault by classmates who taunted her about her "jailbird" mother.

Studies tend to discourage the notion that children of prisoners are necessarily destined to repeat their parents' crimes. Delinquency, when it occurs, is often a transient problem appearing soon after the time of incarceration. Persistent imitation of a parent's criminal behavior seems to occur only under special circumstances.

Sack[26] in his sample of seventy-three children found only six preadolescent and adolescent youngsters, who demonstrated antisocial behaviors. For three, the behavior was short lived and relatively mild consisting of brief episodes of stealing or temporary truancy. In his second study[24] three out of twenty-three children (13%) showed rather severe antisocial behavior within two months of their fathers' incarceration. Again all were young adolescents, and most were male. Of the nine children just described, seven were boys.

One can understand some antisocial behavior as an active attempt to identify with the parent and to regain closeness. One eight-year-old boy was difficult to control after he discovered the whereabouts of his father. When a policeman discovered him tampering with locks the boy said he wanted to join his father in prison. Another boy who started to steal after his father was jailed for larceny said outright "I'm just like my father was."[24]

Nevertheless, to view the more serious and sustained antisocial behavior simply as identification with a parent's incarceration would be misleading. Sack and his colleagues[26] make the crucial point that such extreme behavior occurs only within the context of chronic family turmoil characterized by marital discord, physical abuse, and divorce.

A recent review by Rutter[23] fully supports this interpretation. It seems clear that no single, chronic stress carries psychiatric risk. However, multiple stresses greatly increase the probability of disturbance. Clearly incarceration is a stress but alone it would probably not cause long-standing, psychosocial damage. However, when combined with family disruption, economic hardship, and other serious difficulties, chances are far greater that the child will show antisocial and aggressive behavior.

It is tempting to speculate on how these dynamics operating together at the time of incarceration can result in a negative antisocial self-image in any particular child. A youngster who acts out in response to family stress after a parent's incarceration runs the risk of being identified with the prisoner, e.g., "You're just like your father, you're gonna wind up like him if you don't watch your step." Once labeled as "being like a lawbreaker" the child may absorb and internalize the comparison, especially if such an identification reinforces his own need to be like the absent parent. Such an identification encourages continued negative or delinquent activities which in turn reinforce the developing sense of an antisocial or criminal self.

The following vignette offers an example of identification in the context of family instability and without interaction with the incarcerated parent. Tom never knew his parents as a small child. Before his birth Tom's father was incarcerated for life for a murder which occurred during a robbery. When he was six months old, Tom was left in the care of an aunt. At age seven Tom began a series of foster home placements punctuated by visits to reform schools. His placement between the ages of 12–19 was especially difficult. The foster parents showed him no real interest and indeed, were often abusive. During these years he learned of his mother's whereabouts and when he sought her out she responded with rejection. Tom remained loyal to his own parents whom he was sure were innocent victims of corrupt police. By his early twenties Tom was married with one small child. He was arrested soon after the baby's birth for murder committed during the course of robbery. Tom's case is remarkable for the almost slavish repetition of his father's behavior. Both left their first small children, both committed murder during robbery, and both were sentenced to life in prison.

Emotional Reactions

What feelings underlie the school problems, hostility at home, and episodes of delinquency? So far as we can determine, children experience heightened sadness, anxiety, anger and guilt.

Sack et al.[26] noted that wives of prisoners almost always comment that the children miss their fathers. The women report that the youngsters often talk about the absent parent and the good things they used to do together. It is interesting that this reaction was reported even for children whose mothers did not consider them to be "that close to their fathers."

When a child has just lost one parent, what is to prevent him from fearing the loss of another adult close to him? Some of this fear accounts for nightmares and separation anxiety demonstrated by younger children. Anxiety can also be generated by ideas about the prison itself and what may be happening inside its walls. Sack et al.[24] reports on the behavioral improvement of two boys after their first prison visit. Both seemed calmer after directly questioning their father about prison. However, if children are younger and unable to verbalize their concern, there is a good chance their anxieties will not be recognized.

One of the authors (E.G.) was familiar with a five-year-old boy who was regularly taken by his mother to Walpole Prison to visit with her friend. He was fairly active, but aside from silly, immature behavior appeared to have no major difficulties. He interacted easily with his mother and her friend as well as with the teachers and children of a play group within the prison itself. We then had the chance to meet and talk with the boy and his mother one evening outside of prison. As soon as the topic of imprisonment and visits were raised, the youngster stopped what he was doing and put his hand over his mother's mouth. The topic was clearly unpleasant for him although he could not verablize his discomfort. Instead he offered his "silly" laugh and tried to disrupt the conversation. Seeing his active and immature behavior so clearly in the context of discussion about the prison itself made us realize for the very first time the strain he frequently experienced during the visits.

Children may also fear that they themselves will have to go to jail. One young boy showed aggressive behavior, biting and attacking schoolmates two weeks after his father was imprisoned for armed robbery. During an interview he said that this father was in jail because he was bad and boasted that he was bad too. Shortly thereafter, he suddenly stopped and said, "I'm not going to jail, am I?"[24]

Feelings of anger and guilt are frequent. These emotions can stem from childrens' immature thought and egocentricity which encourages them to interpret their parents' actions solely from their own perspective. For example, they may become angry that their parent is unavailable to do the kinds of things most parents can do with and for their children, e.g., attend a birthday party, or take them to a ball game. It is difficult for them to realize that their mother or father may want to be with them but simply can't arrange for that to happen. Also there is anger toward the parent for leaving. The child may feel that "if he or she really cared about me, how could they leave me in this mess."

Children's egocentricity also encourages self-blame and guilt for a parent's imprisonment. Children may secretly reason that their own behavior contributed to the events leading to confinement and thus seek punishment through provocative or antisocial behavior.[25] It is particularly easy to see how these feelings could be generated if a crime is explained in terms of family need, e.g., "We needed the money for clothes and food and so daddy took what didn't belong to him."

Children can be subject to humiliation and a sense of shame. They look to their parents as role models for what can be accomplished in this world. Having a parent who goes to prison makes that a likelihood for themselves as well. Both the humiliation and the sense of prison as a future reality is expressed in the words of a fourteen-year-old girl anticipating her mother's release after a two-year incarceration.

"Sometimes you don't know what to feel about a mother like the one I have. First you hate her, then you love her. . .I was ashamed to be her daughter, like I said. Some kids say their mother does this or that but I have to say my mother's a convict. I couldn't even use the excuse that she was innocent, 'cause she told me she wasn't. . .We'll be together and see how it goes. If it works out, fine. If it doesn't we'll split up. . .Maybe someday we'll be having our regular weekly meetings at a restaurant somewhere. . .Or maybe she'll end up back in jail. Or maybe I'll end up in jail. . ."[14]

Finally, one last emotion should be discussed; the child's sense of loyalty. Inmates at Walpole Prison have described the need they felt as young children and adolescents to defend one or another incarcerated relative against family gossip. One man described how he communicated daily with his father who was in jail, not far from his school yard. Every lunch hour he would go to the jail and his father would let down a string from his window. The young man would carefully tie something on, it could be a chicken leg or whatever else he happened to have. His memory of his father reeling in the line to see what was on the other end remains vivid and pleasurable to this day.

Thus, many of the children have strong attachments to their parents and want to remain loyal and loving. We also know it is particularly difficult for young children to integrate the conflicting aspects of a parent's personality: the loving, caring side with the angry, acting out, impulsive side that landed him or her in prison. It is not until age nine or ten that children begin to think in terms of internal motivations,[6] and not until adolescence that personality is understood to be composed of several different, perhaps conflicting traits.[27] Thus youngsters, (and it will be recalled that most incarcerated parents are young and have children who are under ten years old) will tend to focus on the positive aspects of their parents and deny their other qualities. They may insist that the parent was misunderstood, or framed; or vacilate between intense feelings of acceptance and rejection. Either of these situations can cause intense emotional upheavals for the child, his caretaker, and the incarcerated parent.

INTERVENTIONS

We have seen that the consequences of incarceration for families left behind include loneliness, social isolation, financial problems, and depression. We know these circumstances do not have a uniform effect upon children and that some react with far more sadness, confusion, and anger than others. Although we are not able to predict the effects of a parent's incarceration on any one child, we can say with some certainty that problems will be more severe for those whose families are less able to cope with the disruption that accompanies arrest and imprisonment.

In the material to follow we will describe several different forms of intervention. Some are addressed to marital or family needs and do not directly involve the children. However, since the parents have primary responsibility for and influence upon the child, programs or services which increase their sense of security and acceptance are bound to have a positive influence on the way they interact with their youngsters.

Before we proceed, one caution is in order. Many social service and mental health professionals run the risk of presuming that families who choose to maintain close ties with prisoners are exhibiting mental disorder. Though mental illness surely exists among families of prisoners, it is not a precondition for being close to an adult in prison. This tendency to misinterpret the family's continuing interest as an indication of underlying pathology may be one reason why mental health clinics are rarely utilized by these families.

Three areas of intervention have particular relevance for children and will be discussed. They include explanations, visiting conditions, and community-based family support systems.

Explanations

From the children's point of view a clear explanation, offered at their level of understanding, helps to clarify confusion and egocentric interpretations of the event. Children should understand that they were not responsible for their parents having been sent away. They should be told, with sensitivity, the circumstances of the situation, the reason for the incarceration, the parents' current circumstances, and future plans as far as they are known. Without such clarification, children are left preoccupied and worried. Perry[19] gives the example of a young adolescent sitting forlornly in front of his house. When asked what was the matter he said, "I wonder what really happened to Daddy."

It is quite likely that children can come to terms with jail and punishment more easily than we anticipate. We know that children expect to be punished for bad acts. Further, the form of punishment they choose tends to be far more severe than what most grown-ups would agree is a fair retaliatory measure.[20] What generates difficulty in the child's mind therefore, is not the necessity of punishment, but having to deal with secrecy and half truths.

We have talked about the child's need to identify with parental role models. A parent sent to jail and described as "bad" "worthless," or "incapable of amounting to anything" leaves the child alone with positive feelings felt toward him or her. As we have seen the child may also feel anger. Taunts by peers become especially painful since the child is torn between feelings of loyalty to the parent and the wish to reject him. Thus, in addition to providing explanations, significant persons should acknowledge, with the child, the positive qualities in the absent parent. The child is then given both the opportunity and the permission to identify with these positive aspects of the parent. We understand that this is a difficult and delicate task, especially for family members who may have little distance on the situation and a good deal of anger towards the inmate and the system.

If the inmate parent can be helped to discuss the incarceration with his or her child, it can allow for more relaxed and successful visits. One inmate with a four-year-old daughter described how painful it was when she asked "Daddy, when you coming home?" He was at a loss to answer the question, fully understanding all of its inherent implications. Similarly, other inmates have said that the most difficult part of a visit with their young children is saying goodbye. It is at that time that the inevitable question, "Aren't you coming home with us?" is raised.

Explaining incarceration must be an ongoing process; one which allows the inmate and child to talk with each another about what it means for them and which allows the child to express his anger, sadness, and love. It is just this kind of communication that will help the child define himself in relation to the inmate and enable him to deal more successfully with his larger community of family and peers.

Visiting Conditions

Visiting helps maintain family relationships. Several programs have been developed which strengthen parental and marital ties and which make the experience of visiting a positive one.

Typically visits take place under crowded and noisy conditions with virtually no accommodation made to the children's presence. Over the past few years some programs designed specifically for children have been instituted. "Sesame Street in Prison" a nation-wide program supported by the Children's Television Workshop offers to train inmates in child care and provides materials and equipment for use by the visiting youngsters. Individual institutions such as the Washington State Reformatory[33] and Purdy Treatment Center[3] have set up their own play programs. Our own play group at Walpole Prison meets two afternoons a week. Fathers and mothers are encouraged to use the time to teach their children how to use the materials and how to play with others.

It is our conviction that special programs which focus upon youngsters and their capabilities help transform the class of "children" into a group comprised of individual personalities and talents. Special materials, as well as thoughtful, sensitive treatment by play group leaders give a visible acknowledgement of the children's right to visit and the parents' right to have them visit. In addition these programs clearly say that youngsters have different needs than do adults which should in some measure be accomodated by the institution.

In addition to meeting the child's needs directly, a word should be said about visiting programs which help foster positive relationships between husbands and wives. Supportive feelings between marital partners can only help to have a positive influence upon how their child is cared for.

With many visits limited to an hour, a couple may just be getting to an important concern when they are forced to leave it and one another. Limited time puts pressure on couples not to argue or express dissatisfactions; no one wants to leave in the middle of a fight. Sometimes a man and wife need at least a couple of days over which they can return to a troublesome issue and reach some resolution. Conjugal visits are one answer to this need for privacy and time and are permitted by several institutions. Purdy Treatment Center for Women in Washington State has separate apartments that can be used for overnight family visits.[3] Officials of Attica prison in New York State have hoisted trailers over the walls for private marital visits. In Mississippi conjugal visits have been permitted for years.[22] Telochape, a minimum security prison in California maintains two apartments on the grounds. Forty-six hour family visits are permitted for inmates who are within three months of a release date. The California program was described by one inmate as motivation for him to work to get out of prison and to stay out.[13]

Family Support Systems: Prison Based

In addition to extending visits and improving the conditions under which they occur, other prison-based programs could be developed which would support the family unit and strengthen the inmates' role as parents.

Courses which cover aspects of family life education and interpersonal communication can be valuable. They might include information about child development, communication techniques, and conflict resolution. Some institutions for women have instituted weekly discussion groups and/or courses on child development. (Readers who are interested in learning more about these programs are referred to McGowen and Blumenthal).[14] Purdy Treatment Center for Women operates a nursery school for community children employing resident inmates as aides.[3]

Similar programs are not typically run for men since there is far less attention paid to their roles as fathers. However, our experience running a child development seminar for men at Walpole prison suggests there is sincere interest on their part to learn how to have a strong and positive influence on their children.

There should also be orientation for families to the prison and correctional system. As we will see, some community self-help groups provide this service. However, many families do not have access to these organizations or may not be aware of them. The authors[8] have outlined a comprehensive orientation program which could be run at prison, attended by both inmates and family members. Matters to be addressed would include information regarding the network of state-wide institutions; rules and regulations concerning visits and other aspects of communication, e.g., telephone calls, letters and gifts; and information about family resources available in their own communities.

Family Support Systems: Community Based

The most effective helpers to families of prisoners thus far have been the families themselves. Many wives are reluctant to seek help from professionals for several reasons: The stigma that families experience makes them pessimistic about being understood when presenting their difficulties. They view authorities as hostile to them and their husbands. In addition, many may view the acceptance of aid as a sign of weakness.

Indeed, many professional counselors might have difficulty providing wholehearted support to a wife whose chief complaint is her loneliness for a husband who is serving time for a series of serious crimes. For understanding and advice she can more comfortably turn to other women who have experienced the same difficulty.

Several self-help groups exist and, though none are exactly alike, all place a high priority on the support of family ties during incarceration.

In Massachusetts, Family and Friends of Prisoners has been in operation for six years despite considerable financial difficulty. The group was organized by wives and friends of Massachusetts residents who are incarcerated here or in other states. They maintain an office in an urban Boston neighborhood and will attempt to help, twenty-four hours a day, with any problem presented to them. The group's standard services include owning and operating a van for transportation to major institutions at visiting time, clothing drives, and a children's Christmas party. They have begun to sponsor rap groups and offer individual counseling upon request. In addition to these activities they publish a monthly newspaper which contains contributions from families, inmates, and citizens concerned about the correctional process. Members have openly criticized correctional policies. The publicity they have received for their advocacy work has caused some difficulty for the group in gaining access to the prison itself.

Prison Families Anonymous (PFA) is based in Hempstead, New York. The group philosophy states, ''. . . Through the understanding we have for each other, we try to find the strength to deal with our problems. By helping ourselves first, we learn that we are better able to help our loved ones. . . ''[21] Rap groups for children of inmates as well as for adult relatives are sponsored by this organization. In addition, PFA works closely with the New York Correctional System. Staff are present each week in a Nassau County Correctional Center lobby to provide support to visitors. Staff also maintain a desk in an arraignment court lobby to help families cope with court procedures.

Nationally based groups such as Friends Outside, Volunteers of America, and Seventh Step offer similar practical services to families and inmates.[1] They help meet the recurring needs for emergency services (clothing, food, and money); transportation; and counseling to assist man's adjustment to prerelease or parole.

CONCLUSION

It has been our intention to alert the reader to problems faced by children of inmates, a surprisingly large, yet hidden population. We have discussed interventions which have direct bearing on the youngsters involved such as the communication of clear and appropriate information about the imprisonment and the provision of adequate visiting conditions. We have also emphasized the importance of support services to the family unit. If some of the very real social, economic, and marital pressures can be relieved, parents will be freer to attend to the needs of their children.

In addition, the prison experience itself can become a time to learn about and focus upon a child's development and necessary parenting skills. Parenting and incarceration become less incongruous when we recall that roughly half of all inmates are parents and most will be released in time to resume care of their children.

Families themselves have long recognized their need for support and have turned to one another. This chapter has been written in the hope that further supports to children and families will be developed. If we have accomplished nothing else we hope to have stimulated the reader's imagination and interest in developing relevant services within their own communities.

BIBLIOGRAPHY

1. Bakker, J., Janus, L., and Morris, B. Hidden victims of crime. *Social Work*. March: 143–148 (1978).
2. Baunach, J. The families of inmate mothers: Perceptions of the separation from their children. Paper presented at the Conference on Incarcerated Parents and their Children. National Institutes of Health, Bethesda, Maryland, October (1979).
3. Buckles, D. *Intervention programs for mothers and children at Purdy Treatment Center for Women.* Paper presented at the Conference on Incarcerated Parents and their Children. National Institutes of Health, October (1979).
4. Family and friends of prisoners. *Visiting at Walpole Prison,* Boston (1979).
5. *Family Support Project, Final Report.* Commonwealth of Massachusetts, publication no. 6605 + (105–50–1–73–CR) (1973).
6. Flapan, D. *Children's Understanding of Social Interaction.* New York: Teacher's College Press (1968).
7. Friedman, S., and Esselstyn, T. The adjustment of children of jail inmates. *Federal Probation.* December:55–59 (1965).
8. Gamer, E., and Schrader, A. *Correctional Family Coordinator,* unpublished manuscript. Massachusetts Department of Mental Health, Medfield, Massachusetts (1978).
9. Goldfarb, R. L., and Singer, L. R. *After Conviction.* New York: Simon and Schuster (1973).
10. Goleman, D. Bleeding heart. *Psychology Today.* June (1978).
11. Kwartler, Richard (ed.). *Behind Bars: Prisons in America.* New York, Toronto: Random House (1977).
12. LaPoint, V., Radke-Yarrow, M., Sekris, S. L., Strope, B., and Fairley, B. *Imprisoned mothers and their children: Behavioral and affective dimensions of their relationships.* Paper presented at the Conference on Incarcerated Parents and their Children. National Institutes of Health, Bethesda, Maryland, October 1979.
13. Lloyd, G. P. A family visiting programme for offenders in custody. *Med. Bio. Ill.* **19**: 146–149 (1969).

14. McGowan, B. G. and Blumenthal, K. L. *Why Punish the Children?* Hackensack, New Jersey: National Council on Crime and Delinquency (1978).

15. Metzler, Charles. *A Statistical Description of Residents of the Massachusetts Correctional Institutions.* Boston, Mass.: Department of Corrections (1979).

16. National Council on Crime and Delinquency. Memorandam. Hackensack, New Jersey: December (1979).

17. Owens, C. *Families of black offenders: Relationships with their extended family.* Paper presented at the Conference on Incarcerated Parents and their Children. National Institutes of Health, Bethesda, Maryland, October (1979).

18. *Profile of Prison Inmates.* Special Report SD-NPS-SR-4. National Council on Crime and Delinquency: Hackensack, New Jersey. August (1979).

19. Perry, P. The forgotten victim: An exclusive report on the families of prisoners. *Mental Hygiene.* **57:**11-14 (1973).

20. Piaget, Jean *The Moral Judgment of the Child,* New York: The Free Press (1965).

21. Prison Families Anonymous. *Prison Families Anonymous,* Mimeo. flyer Hempstead, N. Y. (1979).

22. Reiger, W. A proposal for a trial of family therapy and conjugal visits in prison. *American Journal of Orthospychiatry.* **43**(1):117-122 (1973).

23. Rutter, M. Maternal deprivation, 1972-1978: New findings, new concepts, new approaches. *Child Development.* **50:**283-305 (1979).

24. Sack, W. H. Children of imprisoned fathers. *Psychiatry.* **40**(2) 163-173 (1977).

25. ———, *Reactions of children, ages 5-15, to the incarceration of a parent.* Paper presented at the Conference on Incarcerated Parents and their Children. National Institutes of Health, Bethesda, Maryland, October (1979).

26. Sack, W. H., Seidler, J., and Thomas, S. The children of imprisoned parents: A psychosocial exploration. *American Journal of Orthopsychiatry.* **46**(4):617-627 (1976).

27. Selman, R. S. *Interpersonal thought in childhood, conception of peer roles, preadolescence, and adolescence: A structural analysis of developing conceptions of peer relationships.* Paper presented at the meetings of the American Psychological Association (1975).

28. *Sourcebook of Criminal Justice Statistics.* U.S. Department of Justice, Law Enforcement Assistance Administration, National Criminal Justice Information and Statistics Service, June (1979).

29. *Sourcebook on Criminal Justice.* Washington: D.C.: U.S. Government Printing Office (1976).

30. Spiro, B. E. The future course of corrections. *Social Work,* July:315-320 (1978).

31. Stanton, A. *Female offenders and their children: The effects of maternal incarceration on children.* Paper presented at the Conference on Incarcerated Parents and their Children. National Institutes of Health, Bethesda, Maryland (1979).

32. Sullivan, Harry S. *The Interpersonal Theory of Psychiatry.* New York: W. W. Norton (1953).

33. Taylor, H. and Durr, B. Preschool in prison. *Young Children.* September:27-32 (1977).

34. ———. A Family Education Center at the Washington State Reformatory. Mimeo. Booklet, copyright (1976).

35. Williams, E. Y., Elder, Z. B., and Williams, S. Y. The psychological aspects of the crimes of imprisoned husbands on their families *Journal of the National Medical Association.* pp. 208-212 (1970).

Dr. Joanne Greer's chapter addresses a problem of increasing social significance in American life—that of adolescent pregnancy, and more particularly as an occurrence in disrupted families.

It is clear from her contribution that girls and young women from disrupted families are at considerably greater risk with respect to possible pregnancy than similar young women from intact families. In her material she surveys very effectively and fully the larger developmental and social issues involved, and she charts out clear roles for professionals to fill in meeting the special needs of pregnant young women from families no longer intact.

10

Adolescent Pregnancy in the Disrupted Family

Joanne G. Greer, Ph. D.

INTRODUCTION

Adolescence is a difficult period for most American girls, even under the best of circumstances. The peer culture, the school, the church, and the family seldom "sing out of the same hymnbook." Conflicting signals about the meaning of approaching womanhood abound. Is a woman all heart, or should she have brains too? Is a woman sexy, or nurturing, or both, and, if so, when should she be which? It is well known that youngsters go through a period when they find it hard to believe that their married parents even indulge in sex. Thus mother doesn't seem much of an authority on the subject. During this period the lucky girl finds a dependable sounding board in a teacher or an older sister, or perhaps an adult friend, counselor, youth worker, or school nurse. Many more learn about sexuality from undependable sources, or from experience, and over 10 percent end up pregnant every year.

If this is the situation of the girl with the "normal" family life, what can we say about the daughter of the disrupted marriage? She knows for a fact that mother, whom she may love deeply, no longer wishes to have sex with father, whom she may also love deeply. The reverse may also be true, and it is also possible that mother and father are mutually disenchanted with each other. Most likely she is in the custody of mother at a time when she longs for father's admiring confirmation of her growing maturity as a female. One or both parents may be dating when she starts dating, and her social life and theirs may be in conflict. Her impending approach to adulthood may be a source of pain as well as pleasure to the parents, because it is a reminder that they are growing older. This is particularly true if either parent has not found a new love interest. And if they have, there is the competition of a new stepmother or stepfather, or perhaps new ready-made siblings. At a time of her life when she longs to be at the center of the family stage, she may in fact be an ignored, taken for granted, or forgotten player.

Many of these hurts are unavoidable in the family which is experiencing separation or divorce. And the separation or divorce may have been the best, most realistic option for all, both parents and children. But the family structure has been altered in ways which will present unique developmental tasks to the young adolescent girl. It is well for the school, the church, the community service workers, and particularly the parents, to be aware of this. Just as we speak of a "frame" in which the psychotherapist does therapy or analysis, in the same sense we speak of a "frame" in which a parent does parenting. Alteration of the frame in either case also alters the capacity of the nurturing person to hold and sustain the dependent person. In divorce or separation this alteration occurs of necessity, based on environmental circumstances, and certainly does not constitute an indictment of the parent. Nevertheless, some parents, particularly the more guilt-ridden ones, may deny that the parenting frame has been altered with such comments as "John and I remain the best of friends," or "I always consult John and we try to agree on all matters to do with the children." The therapist or other family helper must not collude in this ignoring of reality, or reality-based solutions to problems will become relatively inaccessible to the family. And, with their deep idealism and sensitivity to hypocrisy, adolescents will be the first in the family to decline to participate in such game-playing.

THE HELPING PERSON

Statistically, approximately 10 percent of females under age 18 become pregnant at least once. This figure includes the daughters of both intact and separated couples. Thus, we may safely assume that, in a work situation which encompasses contacts with divorced or separated couples and their children, a teen pregnancy in a client family will not be a rare occurrence.

Girls and parents alike may contact a nonmedical person first, because of a current or previous helping relationship. The first human services resource person that a thirteen-year-old notifies of a pregnancy may be the youngster's favorite teacher. The mother may first contact a former marriage counselor or therapist, or a church pastor. Most likely, the first professional contact will *not* be at a specialized adolescent pregnancy clinic. It is unprofessional for teachers or youth workers to take the point of view that teen pregnancy is a problem which they are not competent to deal with. Of course certain referrals are in order, but the appeal for *emotional* support has been made, presumably, to an *emotionally significant* person, who must respond to the implied trust. In choosing a career path which involves one with youngsters or families, one also assumes responsibility to be adequately prepared and knowledgeable about community resources and referrals those clients may need. Teen pregnancy is such a common occurrence that it is puzzling to find that some human services personnel are, by and large, unprepared to receive such a confidence. For example, in a recent study done by the author of family planning clinics in seven different states, *none* of the local high schools maintained formal linkages with the clinics for referrals for contraceptive education, contraceptive services, pregnancy testing, abortion, or prenatal care.

In traditional churches with only male clergy, a male celibate clergyman may become a devout family's first focal point for help. The cognitive and emotional tasks involved in preparing for and accepting such a pastoral role are impressive, but not impossible. And, no matter what the official view of a specific church on premarital sex, if the girl seeks out the help of her clergyman it is essential that he not fail her. In passing it should also be noted that the girl's own selection of a male confidant may have major psychological antecedents related to the absence of her divorced father. These must be handled with understanding and, if possible, clarified for her.

Notification of pregnancy frequently occurs late, especially from younger girls who may have more difficulty grasping the realistic implications of missed menstrual periods. As a consequence, thirteen- and fourteen-year-olds may be forced into the multiple risks of a term pregnancy because it is too late to safely or legally offer the option of abortion. Awareness of the general noncoping performance of the young adolescent in managing her pregnancy makes it imperative that the family helper be well organized, in order to maximize the time available for careful decision making. Often the helper may have to make referrals for, or actually make, health care delivery arrangements. But even more important, the helper must make careful provisions for both current and future psychological assimilation of the personal and family meaning of the pregnancy.

PSYCHOLOGICAL DIMENSIONS OF ADOLESCENT PREGNANCY CRISES

In public health, as in every other field, styles change. At one time it was fashionable to place deep interpretations on cases of sexual acting out by adolescents. During recent years the pendulum seems to have swung to the opposite extreme, and it seems an article of faith to many public health policy makers that if we could just distribute contraceptives efficiently enough the problem of untimely pregnancies would be solved. As in many problems, the optimal solution probably lies in approaches somewhere between the two poles. It is an indisputable fact that some pregnancies, particularly among the very young, occur because of sheer ignorance. But there is a substantial residual of puzzling cases. What is the explanation of the high repeat pregnancy rate of some teens after their first live birth or abortion? Surely they now know the facts of life, particularly since it is customary to instruct them and supply them with contraceptives after abortion or delivery. New York researchers Irving R. Stuart, Ph. D. and Carl F. Wells, Ph. D. gathered data on repeat abortions of teens at one medical school affiliated clinic, and identified clients who had had up to twelve abortions during their teen years. Educational efforts were unsuccessful with these clients. Why? The sequence of twelve abortions is not a psychologically meaningless, random occurrence. The failure of the clinic education and service program with such a client contains information about her which can be examined to serve her better. Insufficient study has been given to the interaction of *being pregnant* and *being adolescent*. A few possibly relevant theories are sketched out below, but the phenomenon is not well understood. However, simply because there is no general, well understood conceptualization of the psychodynamics of adolescent pregnancy the helper must be even more alert to and perceptive of esoteric meanings for an individual client.

The Developmental Tasks of the Primipara and the Adolescent

The Primipara. It appears clear from the literature that there are identifiable female developmental tasks associated with the first pregnancy, similar in scope to the tasks of puberty and menopause. Psychoanalytic developmental research confirms and amplifies the folk wisdom of women in this regard. Grete Bibring notes that all three of these events are points of no return for a female: once an adolescent you cannot become a child again, once menopausal you cannot bear children again, and once a mother you cannot be a single unit again in the same way as before. The developmental process of pregnancy involves relationships to the sex partner, to the self, and to the child. The event of impregnation causes a representation of the sex partner to become a part of the self. The first task of pregnancy is to accept this intrusion, to psychologically integrate and merge with this foreign body which becomes part of the self. The second stage begins when quickening is felt, and the body of the child is first acknowledged as a new, separate object within the self. At this point the woman begins to prepare for delivery and separation. At delivery, the mother will have reached a point of freely changing fusion with the child which will vary with his needs and growth. But for all time the child will remain a part of the outside world, yet a part of herself, and also a part of her sexual mate.[2] Obviously the success of the primipara in attaining and sustaining such orientations to herself and her child as Bibring describes, will depend on her level of maturity, the supportiveness of the infant's father, and the availability of her mother or a mother substitute to assist her in this final initiation into womanhood.

Brazelton and Als,[5] in a research setting, noted that prenatal psychoanalytic interviews with normal adult primiparas uncovered anxiety of almost pathological proportions. Bibring and her coworkers confirmed by clinical interview and diagnostic psychological tests a regressive shift in their subject primiparas after quickening occurred, with a marked prevalence of oral, anal, ambivalent, or hostile material. This occurred regardless of the personality profile at the beginning of pregnancy. Both research groups concluded that such disruptions were normal, and were a necessary prelude to the reorganization necessary to assume the role of nurturer to the infant.

If analogous changes occur in the much less mature young adolescent primipara one wonders about the girl's capacity to make rational decisions about anything. Certainly it is not logical to assume that, when the adult married primipara regresses, the unwed adolescent primipara does not. The author noted, in informal observations and staff interviews at a rural public health clinic for mothers and infants, certain indications that this is a problem of underestimated dimensions. Staff noted difficulty in verifying that some girls understood what, in fact, had happened to their bodies, even after patient attempts at explanation, and questions handed in at rap sessions showed either a touching level of sexual ignorance or a substantial loss of prepregnancy maturity. One prenatal care class at this clinic utilized coloring books to teach self-care and infant care, and a class of pregnant thirteen- to fifteen-year-old teens was observed diligently and happily coloring pictures entitled "My Baby."

The Developmental Tasks of the Female Adolescent. The developmental tasks of adolescent girls fall into two categories: moving gradually *away from* certain psychological stances and love objects of childhood, and moving gradually *towards* new psychological stances and love objects of adulthood. The ties with the parents must be loosened, in order that the bonds with the peers and the lover/husband of adulthood may become possible. The opinions and values of the parents must be examined, and the automatic acceptance of these opinions and values must cease, so that the teen may learn to think and act in an autonomous fashion. Childhood games, fantasies, and real assignments concerned with "taking care of mommy or daddy" become less emotionally significant, while career training and/or marriage with a home of one's own become eagerly anticipated goals. Realistic preparations for these goals gradually draw the young person out of the home nest, both geographically and psychologically. In the current U.S. culture, depending on individual differences, social class, and career aspirations, this process may be drawn out until the early thirties, and in no case could it be conceived of as concluding before age eighteen.

Recent research on adult development has served to highlight the unavoidability of these tasks of adolescence, demonstrating that they resurface, sometimes traumatically, for later resolution if avoided in the teens. Students of family systems theory have also illustrated with compelling case data the impossibility of the adolescent's graceful maturation if her parents are themselves suffering from severe conflicts or developmental arrests, thus forcing *her* to mother *them*. Such a family structure leaves the girl little emotional energy, time, or psychological freedom to attack age-appropriate developmental tasks in an efficient way. Instead, her mental confusion and unmet emotional needs may well lead to relationships which are both precociously intimate and unprotected by contraception.

The once held view that all sexual activity and every pregnancy in a teen were forms of delinquency currently seems simplistic. Family theory has made a major contribution to understanding the dynamics of such behavior. It appears that in the case of girls with certain types of hopelessly chaotic home situations, these behaviors can be a relatively intelligent although usually unconscious strategy to escape from a diversity of threatening intrafamily pressures such as incestuous attractions or pathological interdependence. If the result is the establishment of a household of her own, either on welfare or with her sex partner, she may have made the best of a bad situation and got a fresh start in life. Each individual is different, of course, but it is always well to question whether some circumstance within the home itself has led to early sexual activity.

Developmental Compromises. If a divorced mother is perceived as helpless or abandoned, a girl may find it impossible to acknowledge and undertake the "heartless" task of absorbing career training or serious marital plans. An out-of-wedlock pregnancy effectively short-circuits development, making both career and marriage unlikely. The infant also provides a compromise of sorts between the maturing daughter's womanly needs and her continuing childish attachment to her mother. Max Sugar hypothesizes that, among a large group of adolescent mothers he observed, some even seemed to be making an unconscious ambivalent gift to the maternal grandmother in the form of an infant for the maternal grandmother to mother. He also hypothesized that, particularly in one-parent matriarchal families, the infants sometimes served as a ransom for the young mothers who were attempting painfully to separate from their mothers, noting that some of the girls actually deserted their infants and gave them to the grandmother.[17]

The adolescent may hesitate to move freely out of the parental sphere of influence because of the parent's emotional need for the daughter, but she may also hesitate because her own childhood need to be mothered has not yet been met. In such a case she is torn between her developing sexuality pulling her toward adult pursuits, and her reluctance to leave the nursery supper table without first being properly fed. Out-of-wedlock pregnancy represents a compromise between becoming an adult woman by bearing a child, and remaining a dependent little girl by remaining in mother's household and under her supervision. She then carries her conflict about mothering, as an adult, and being mothered, as a child, into her relations with the infant. In some cases the highly ambivalent relationship between mother and daughter and the intensity of the unmet needs of the daughter create an unconscious expectation of fulfillment, in that the grandmother will mother the infant, a part of her daughter, as she has been unable to mother her daughter. Thus the daughter expects to obtain vicariously what she could not obtain directly. As a practical, everyday living arrangement, such a household has a balance of power which effectively blocks the daughter's progress toward independent living. Instead, she may become biologically a grown-up, but psychologically remains in a state of developmental arrest which perpetuates her pathological dependency and self-defeating behavior. Both abortion and adoption will be unattractive options to such families, because keeping the baby serves to facilitate certain unconscious goals of the adolescent girl, and perhaps of her mother as well. Obviously the infant of such a primipara has an esoteric significance to her which is quite different from that in a normative mother-infant relationship. For the normally mature new mother serves the needs of her infant, and only secondarily does he serve hers. Sugar[17] hypothesized that such unconscious processes as these were operative in the formation of multigenerational matriarchal households among the New Orleans population of public clinic patients he studied. He also noted that the young primipara was hostile to the infant's father, whether present or absent. Her primary emotional and practical resource was her own mother.*

Other Possibly Relevant Theories. Balint,[1] in seeking to explain repetitive thrill-seeking behavior, speaks of the need to verify that one's body is capable of certain feats. This explanation has a certain appeal in conceptualizing a theory to explain the behavior of teen girls who become pregnant and abort repeatedly. Pregnancy advanced enough to show or to skip several menstrual periods may serve to verify feminine potency. Laufer[14] indicated that some adolescent suicides are related to a feeling on the youngster's part that her body belongs to the parent and not to her, and thus it is a possession of the *parent* which is damaged. Following this same line of thinking, the testing and verifying of the daughter's ownership of her body as an adult person may be a second function of adolescent pregnancy. Additional evidence of this possibility appears in the work of Bibring[3] and her coworkers. They noted even with their adult married primiparas, that the first pregnancy seemed to release the young woman from her infantile bondage to her own mother, and changed their relationship to that of coequals. This realignment appeared to be simultaneous with the partial shift of the grandmother's libidinal investment from the daughter to the daughter's baby.

Standard Explanations. The ideas touched upon above, do not, of course, exhaust the possibilities in explaining why a young girl happens to become pregnant. In addition, the factors of romanticism, peer pressure, socialization of females to be overly compliant to the wishes of males, sexual ignorance, and lack of contraceptive sophistication are all relevant in at least some cases. Rape, seduction, and the continuum of coercion in between certainly do occur. In addition, the level of pure sex drive in the adolescent girl is really not known. Adolescent pregnancy in present-day society is a complex phenomenon, and it has not yet been adequately studied. However, in a family which has been emotionally torn by divorce or separation, unconscious factors are probably of even greater significance than in the average family. Because of this probability, such factors should be considered carefully in trying to understand and help such a family through an adolescent pregnancy crisis.

*The reader is cautioned that the New Orleans culture is atypical of the U.S. as a whole for both black and white populations.

PREGNANCY DECISION MAKING: ABORTION, ADOPTION, OR MOTHERHOOD?

When an underage daughter becomes pregnant, parents tend to focus first on the external issues: the girl's changing figure and their attendant embarrassment, or economic or school problems. The counselor or therapist must provide balance, and attempt to also elucidate the psychological significance of the pregnancy for all concerned. Only in this way can an optimal plan be made to deal with the pregnancy.

The Twelve- to Fifteen-Year-Old Client

The very young daughter of divorced parents is probably at greater risk of pregnancy than the girl in an intact family. Sexual exploitation by a stepfather or the mother's boyfriend is unfortunately a potential problem for the young adolescent daughter of a divorcée. In addition, she may be less supervised with boys of her own age than the girl with two parents in the home. Her mother may be preoccupied with her own social and work life, give little guidance, or even little sex education. If the divorce was recent and painful, the mother may be too depressed to even notice her daughter much. The very young girl who is pregnant because she was partially ignorant of sexual facts, or was forced or taken advantage of, may suffer intense feelings of anger toward her sex partner and her inadequate parents who did not inform or protect her. For her the unborn child is an intruder and perhaps a symbol of parental neglect.

To the extent that the pregnancy is imposed on her without her full sexual knowledge or free consent, her developing autonomy and sense of personhood may be lastingly damaged. It seems that an abortion would be the removal of an unwelcome burden, and a restoration of some semblance of the status quo. In her case the best course of action seems obvious. However, the counselor has a further, not so obvious task. The youngster who is not accorded full control of her body in becoming pregnant should not repeat that unfortunate experience in being relieved of the pregnancy. Time must be taken to instruct her thoroughly in the physiological facts so she herself can decide whether to abort. If this personal decision takes on for her the symbolic meaning of reclaiming her own bodily integrity, it can ameliorate any previous sense of helplessness and passivity.

When parents disagree, the mental health counselor or social worker who feels that abortion is the best solution for a very young girl must be very sure that either this solution is acceptable in the girl's current social milieu, or the girl has alternative support systems available, such as a shift of custody to the parent who condones abortion. For a pregnant girl in the early teens, solutions must be family systems oriented, since a permanent removal from a reasonably adequate family support system is not in her best interest. If the girl's family has been religiously educated to believe abortion of a developing fetus is murder, a full-term pregnancy may be less psychologically traumatizing than an abortion. This is particularly so if her family's cultural concept of the deity is punitive and vengeful. In such families, unfortunately, there is a tendency to see God's punishing hand forever after, in every untoward event the girl encounters. When the girl's parents are divorced, one parent may maintain past religious beliefs and cultural values while the other rejects them, and the question of a daughter's abortion will precipitate bitter arguments. In such a case it is even more important to try to clarify what the girl herself believes and what she herself wishes to do. When she is ambivalent, it is best to take a conservative position and avoid advice which violates the family's past traditional beliefs in any way. If it is clear that there is no attachment to the unborn baby, and only personal morality prevents its abortion, then the girl's ultimate freedom from the infant can be secured through adoptive placement. Such an arrangement is also clearly in the newborn infant's psychological best interests.

The Older Adolescent

The case of the older adolescent, perhaps ages sixteen and up, has different complexities. Here, also, the pregnancy may result from partial ignorance, an accident or an exploitative sexual encounter, and there may be little emotional attachment to the fetus. But in this age range there is more possibility that the baby was fathered by a male to whom there is intense, long-lasting attachment, and the baby is loved specifically as his child. Medical considerations aside, an adolescent pregnancy presents a good psychological prognosis for motherhood to the extent that, as in a normal adult pregnancy, it represents the unborn child of a regular sex partner with whom there is a significant love relationship. It may even be that the conception was deliberate or semideliberate. The emotionally involved older teen may have very tender feelings toward even an accidentally conceived child, and she may wish to bear and keep the infant, with or without the psychological or financial support of the father. Unfortunately, these feelings may be based in dubious romanticism which will not stand up to the strains of premature motherhood. Clearly an older teen is more capable of surviving on her own, given standard welfare support services, and has more options for independent action. However, for the sake of all concerned, she must be encouraged to look in a balanced way at all three of her options: abortion, adoption, or motherhood. Further, she should be coached to make her decisions in two stages: (1) abortion versus gestation, and (2) "keeping" versus adoptive placement. At the first stage she need only consider the personal meaning of continuing the pregnancy. If she does choose to continue to term and carries the baby successfully, she then has several months to consider options for herself and for the infant. The counselor must help her compare these options to her own values, ambitions, resources, and current competencies in a realistic way. Abortion or adoption must not appear unnatural, cowardly, selfish, or unfeminine to the counselor, or such attitudes will be communicated to the client, presenting her with only a pseudo-choice if she is to retain her self-esteem. It may be helpful to arrange visits with young women who kept their infants, as well as others who aborted or placed for adoption. Visits with families that have adopted children can also be arranged, and can be very helpful in understanding this option.

When Abortion is not an Option

The options available for any individual pregnancy are severely constrained by a time frame of no more than eight months and perhaps as little as two months for a pregnancy which has been concealed or which concludes with a premature birth. Abortion is completely safe only in the first trimester, and is illegal after the second trimester. Strict legal considerations aside, late second trimester abortions are less likely to be ethically acceptable to the available medical personnel, or even to the client family, because the fetal body is so much more developed. Obviously for the advanced accidental pregnancy the choices are motherhood or adoption.

In the author's opinion it is extremely regrettable that adoption has become so unfashionable, both with human services workers and with adolescents. The "might as well" philosophy is an unjustice to both the adolescent and to her infant. By this is meant the attitude that, since this pregnancy has in some sense catapulted her to instant adulthood, she "might as well" have a living doll to play with instead of an education, a career, and a later marriage. When this mentality is encountered with reference to lower-class girls or minority girls, the author feels that it implies subtly that they have little personal potential for achievement or upward mobility. However, the same attitude underlies the current "baby chic" in the public high schools of some affluent suburbs. An optimal arrangement must be found for the young girl who still needs time to grow up and to be educated to her full intellectual potential before undertaking the tasks of mothering. She should be encouraged to have faith that there will be more babies in the future when she feels ready for them, and to consider her own interests without guilt. The statement is often made that the girl who has a baby at age sixteen has 90 percent of her life script written for her, and none of it is good. Need this be, with adoptive parents of impeccable credentials languishing on waiting lists for as long as five years?

Psychological Considerations in Adoption

Adoption can, of course, be delayed for a period of time after delivery, allowing for leisurely decision making by the natural mother. But no ethical human services professional should advise undue delay, given current knowledge about the importance of one permanent caregiver for an infant in the first year of life. Optimally, an adopted infant should enter the care of his adoptive mother as soon as possible after birth. In some states placement can be accomplished within a week of birth, if the adoption has been planned for. Legal paperwork proceeds more slowly but, again, should be accomplished as rapidly as possible to facilitate the permanent bonding of adoptive mother and adoptive infant.

If adoption is chosen, the birth mother (natural mother) should be encouraged to think of herself and to act as a significant planner for her infant's future. Her wishes about adoptive placement, such as religion or ethnic group of the adoptive parents, must be respected. Obviously the girl who chooses adoption requires sophisticated social and psychotherapeutic services to handle crisislike emotional tasks on such a rapid time schedule. She will also require supportive psychotherapy to deal with themes of loss in the months following the baby's adoptive placement. These may be somewhat softened by the hope of a reunion when the child is grown, but will still be significant for many girls. Legislation on mechanisms and consent procedures for such reunion is currently in a state of flux, and the client must be given the best current information without raising unfounded hopes or fears.

It has been hypothesized that only women of very high or very low ego development relinquish their offspring without major trauma. This statement might be well borne in mind by the counselor, along with the related, well-documented fact that very young mothers of low ego development have comparatively high rates of child abuse. Currently 90 percent of teen mothers keep their babies, often with very few supportive social services. There is no assessment of their fitness to have custody of an infant, unless the reporting systems for suspected child abuse pick up the case. These reporting systems and their related social service systems have a rather poor track record for rapid and successful intervention. In one study of fifty infants, eight died while still in the custody of their abusing mothers, most at less than five months of age.[7] There is a pressing need to assess the availability of a stable member of the family system (not necessarily a female) who is willing and able to function as what Freud and Goldstein term the "psychological parent" of the infant.[10] If the pregnancy is advanced, and the girl and her family system appear to be extremely poor risks, an attempt should be made to influence her toward adoptive placement, followed by a leisurely completion of her own childhood. Clearly human services personnel have some ethical obligation to influence the infant's survival and his quality of life, even if they have no legal mandate to do so.

THE CLIENT WHO KEEPS HER INFANT

Statistically speaking, the future is rather grim for the girl who keeps her infant. Eight out of ten women who first assume a mother's role at age seventeen or younger never complete high school. Seventy percent will be pregnant again within the next two years. Women whose first birth was in the teen years are much less likely to ever work and much more likely to be on welfare than women who had their first child in their twenties. In a recent U.S. study one-third of the mothers who had had their first child between ages thirteen and fifteen were living below the Federal poverty level. The counselor or social worker who subscribes to the principles of sexual equality should consider long and hard whether he or she can recommend such a future for a female client. Realistically speaking, however, the infant may meet strong emotional needs in the client for "someone to love *now*" or, regrettably, "someone to love *me, now*," even when all the evidence for delaying motherhood has been made quite clear. Since legally the decision to bear and keep the child is entirely the mother's, even if she is as young as age twelve, all interested adults are essentially relegated to an advisory role. If she does choose to keep the infant, helping persons should try to arrange for the multitude of supportive services needed to improve the chances of a good outcome for her and her baby.

The following section will describe an ideal service package, including social and psychological services as well as medical. Depending on community characteristics, urban or rural, geographic area, and socioeconomic factors, some or even many of these services may be missing. The potential helper should search for what the community can offer and establish contacts. National health planners sometimes point to the success of costly model programs for teen parents, while neglecting to acknowledge that very, very few teen mothers actually have access to these programs, and funding to make them available in every community is extremely unlikely.

SERVICE DELIVERY SYSTEMS FOR PREGNANT ADOLESCENTS

Providing proper care for adolescents who plan a term pregnancy requires special approaches not usually necessary with mature pregnant women. Adolescents of all social classes are infrequent users of all health services and especially are sporadic users of prenatal care, because of ignorance, fear, or negligence originating in depression. They must be motivated and guided to seek and fully utilize necessary care or they will present themselves at the time of labor with little or no prenatal care, physically and emotionally unprepared for childbirth, for parenting, or for the separation losses of adoption. Because of the teen primipara's special needs, a private practice general practitioner for prenatal care is not the best choice, although in a rural community there may be no other option. Pregnancy under age sixteen is by definition a high risk pregnancy. The danger of death for the teen mother and death or disability for her baby is 2.5 times that in a pregnancy of a twenty- to twenty-four-year-old. When available, publicly funded maternal and infant clinics or university hospital-based adolescent pregnancy programs are to be preferred because they provide prearranged, prepackaged access to the whole spectrum of medical, social, and psychological services which are necessary to optimize the pregnancy outcomes.

Comprehensive service needs do not apply only to daughters of poor families. Suprisingly, the author found, in recent analysis of birth data for a very large Southern city, that white, upper-class girls under sixteen were the most likely of all age-race-social-class combinations to have received little or no prenatal care of any kind and to bear an infant of low birth weight. The broad range of health, education, and supportive social services required by pregnant teens of all social classes are best delivered through comprehensive, single-site programs or closely linked, cooperating programs. This is true many times over for the girl of any social class without a stable, intact family to provide emotional support and find services for her.

Comprehensive care can be based in a number of different settings: hospital, public agency, private agency, school, or church. The ideal program will always include the following services:

1. *Medical Care.* It has repeatedly demonstrated that adequate prenatal care for adolescents reduces their complication rates drastically. Programs which have reduced adolescent complication rates to levels equal or better than those of mature pregnant women are ongoing at various demonstration sites. A few of these model programs are the University of Michigan Women's Hospital at Ann Arbor, the Comprehensive High School Clinic of

St. Paul, Minnesota, the Delaware Adolescent Program, and the Johns Hopkins Center for School-Aged Mothers and Their Infants in Baltimore. These centers try to get the pregnant girl under care during the first trimester. This is the least dangerous period for abortion, and the proper time for commencement of prenatal care for a term pregnancy.

Many therapists, counselors, teachers, and even mothers of girls are not aware of the health dangers of pregnancy at a very young age, and the corresponding need for prompt medical attention as soon as pregnancy is suspected. Yet the pregnant girl will be dependent on one or more of these information sources to learn the proper way to care for herself. A girl who wishes to carry her baby to term with no pressure for abortion sometimes conceals the pregnancy from her parents, even after she has shared the information with a teacher or counselor. In this case, she should be directed to free public sources of care, such as health department clinics. She can use these clinics securely and wait until she feels ready to inform her parents, without being deprived of proper medical care.

2. *Psychosocial Services.* Several studies have demonstrated that socioeconomic and psychological factors may be more important than simply the age of the young mother in creation or prevention of medical pregnancy complications. The physicians who direct the adolescent pregnancy clinic at the University of Michigan hypothesize that it is their program's attention to the teen psychosocial problems which explains their success in reducing the complications of pregnancy. Much of this success is credited to the female psychiatric social workers and nurse clinicians who "mother" the girls in small peer groups of six to eight which meet regularly, creating a situation similar to an extended family. Most pregnant adolescents are in need of such support, and this is even more true of the daughter of a divorce or separation, who may have little emotional access to one or even both of her parents. Even adolescents who put up a good front, and appear reasonably conflict-free on the surface, may be in significant trouble intrapsychically. Most of them are having difficulties related to the pregnancy in their interpersonal and family relationships, and have significant anxieties related to economic and educational issues. A formalized, close-knit support system can reduce psychic strain by providing other significant adults and peers, and sometimes assist in repairing damaged relationships with loved ones.

3. *Nutrition Education and Counseling.* The proper diet of an expectant mother and the diet of the typical teenager have little in common. The girl must follow proper eating habits if she plans to carry the baby to term, both for the sake of her own still developing body and for the sake of the infant's optimal start in life. Eating a balanced diet, in the face of psychological upset, pregnancy-associated nausea, and a history of im-

proper eating habits is a difficult assignment for a young girl, and she needs instruction and encouragement. The person who is primarily in the role of a counselor, therapist, or teacher may not recognize this a personal responsibility, but the support of medical advice by these psychologically significant adults will mean that the advice is more likely to be followed. The proper care of one's health is always one good sign of acceptance of one's self and one's situation, and reflects an appropriate self-love. it is also one of the few marks of love of the unborn baby that the expectant mother can show. Refusal to eat, or to eat properly, is not only a serious physical health problem, but can be a symptom of a serious psychological problem, and deserves the attention of all potential helpers, not just the doctor or public health nurse responsible for prenatal visits. Refusal to eat may reflect a subconscious desire to destroy the baby or oneself, and raises the questions of whether the pregnancy should be continued, or whether custody of the baby should be retained after birth. In such a case, very carefully nondirective counseling should be used to elucidate whether intentions to continue the pregnancy or to keep custody of the baby are based on family, boy-friend, or peer opinions, cultural stereotypes of the female role, or a desire for self-punishment, rather than a true desire to become a mother at this point in life. The decision to terminate a pregnancy or to place her infant for adoption may be particularly agonizing to a girl who has lost daily access to her father, and perhaps her male siblings, in custody proceedings. If her prepregnancy plans and personal ambitions are infeasible for a teen-aged mother, the conflict engendered may be too severe to face directly without special help, and may be manifested only through psychosomatic symptoms such as lack of appetite.

4. *Education.* The pregnant girl who does not abort has unique educational needs during and even after the pregnancy. These educational needs fall into two categories:

- *Continuation of Academic Career.* Provision must be made for continuation of studies. Public school systems are no longer permitted by law to exclude or segregate pregnant schoolgirls. However, if the teaching staff is punitive or rejecting in attitude, the girl herself may avoid attending, using her condition as an excuse. Private schools can, and often do, exclude pregnant students, and transfers to the public system must be arranged. Someone, a school pupil personnel worker, a mental health worker, a school nurse, or a parent, must take responsibility for making explanations and arrangements. Teachers must be informed and the girl herself must be helped to deal with both peer group and staff reactions. Peer reactions may range from admiring envy to disapproval, depending on the subculture and the region of the country. Girls who are embarrassed by this attention may prefer the greater privacy of a separate facility, either a maternity home or a day school program. It has been demonstrated that the school dropout rate after delivery is much lower when the girl has been enrolled in a special pregnancy-oriented program, whether a maternity home, a special day school, or a health facility-based comprehensive care program. This is probably due to both the social and emotional support and to the superior planning services available from specialists.

● *Pregnancy-related Education.* Pregnant teens require instruction in self-care and preparation for labor. This instruction is best communicated in a special teen comprehensive program but may also come from the same sources an adult woman uses: the attending physician or a public health nurse.

5. *Pregnancy Aftercare.* Underage mothers require supportive services after the pregnancy, whether they retain custody or place the infant for adoption. They will need postpartum medical supervision longer than an adult woman. Most of these girls continue to be sexually active, and an appalling number are pregnant again within eighteen months of delivery. For this reason they should be routinely provided contraceptive instruction, an ongoing source of contraceptive supplies, and ongoing gynocological health care, including regular venereal disease screening.

The young mother who retains custody of her infant will require special supportive services for many years. Some of the standard services are parenting classes, day care, education program, job training, medical care, food stamps, and Aid for Dependent Children payments. Follow-up studies of mother-child dyads under supervision of comprehensive care programs is being carried out, but final conclusions will have to wait until the infants themselves reach maturity. Follow-up of dyads outside formal service programs is almost impossible, but probably they will fare more poorly. As noted above, only a small percentage of teen mothers and babies have access to comprehensive care programs.

DIRECTIONS FOR FUTURE PSYCHOLOGICAL GROWTH

The "crisis" nature of an adolescent pregnancy essentially precludes the leisurely, in-depth approach to insight and decision making found in psychoanalytic psychotherapy. However, a mechanical approach to the managing of the pregnancy which ignores its possibly obscure psychological dimensions, and the uniqueness of each client and her family, is doomed to long-range failure. Such an approach has a high potential to exacerbate intergenerational conflict and self-defeating behavior on the part of the client. Moreover, it is statistically probable that the stage will be reset for repeat pregnancies, embodying repeated attempts to master the unidentified underlying conflicts.

At least two potential uses exist for an insight oriented approach in serving the family experiencing an adolescent pregnancy crisis:

1. Depending on the family's receptivity and the counselor's skill, it may be possible to communicate in simple terms some currently useful understanding of the family's unconscious processes which are relevant to the situation.

2. In family or client interviews, the helping person can try to identify the possibly obscure personal determinants of the present situation which are specifically relevant to decisions about continuation or termination of the pregnancy, and adoption or retention of the infant. It may be possible to determine what the optimal strategy is to minimize the internal conflict and future trauma of the young client, and steer the management of the situation so that the way is prepared, or at least not blocked, for in-depth therapeutic efforts in the future. The therapist can then comment to the parents, "After the abortion (or after the baby is born) Jane may want to work with a therapist to understand herself better, and get better control of her life". Or one may say to the girl herself, "It's hard for you to think through the meaning of what has happened right now, but it will be important for you to do so when you are ready to, because this is a very important event in your life." The nature of such a communication will, of course, differ with the individual girl, her family, and her circumstances. Very few youngsters will think of such a learning and assimilation strategy on their own, and yet for some it may be vital to their future emotional survival. Such comments create an open door for a return to the servicing agency or another agency in the future, whenever the desire exists to thoroughly understand the past and use it for adult growth. Such advice may be remembered for many years, and may be recalled when significant events in later life, such as an adult pregnancy, revive memories of and feelings about the first pregnancy.

CITED AND RECOMMENDED READINGS

1. Balint, Michael. *Thrills and Regression.* New York: International Universities Press. pp. 23-26 (1978).
2. Bibring, Grete. "Some considerations of the psychological processes in pregnancy." *In: The Psychoanalytic Study of the Child,* Volume XIV. New York: International Universities Press. pp. 113-121 (1959).
3. Bibring, Grete, Thomas F. Dwyer, Dorothy S. Huntington, and Arthur F. Valenstein. "A study of the psychological processes in pregnancy and of the earliest mother-child rela-

tionships." *In: The Psychoanalytic Study of the Child,* Volume XVI. New York: International Universities Press. pp. 9–72 (1961).

4. Blos, Peter. "Preoedipal factors in female delinquency." and "Postscript 1976." *In: The Adolescent Passage.* New York: International Universities Press. pp. 221–253 (1979).

5. Brazelton, T. Berry, and Heidelise Als. "Four early stages in the development of mother-infant interaction." *In: The Psychoanalytic Study of the Child,* Volume XXXIV. New Haven: Yale University Press. pp. 349–370 (1979).

6. Chilman, Catherine S. *Adolescent Sexuality in a Changing American Society.* Washington: U.S. Government Printing Office #017-046-00050-1 (1979).

7. Elmer, Elizabeth. "Studies of Child Abuse and Infant Accidents." *In: Mental Health Program Reports—5,* Segal, J. (Ed.). Washington D.C.: Department of Health, Education, and Welfare # HSM 72-902 pp. 58–85 (1971).

8. *Fertility and Contraception in America: Adolescent And PreAdolescent Pregnancy:* Hearings Before the Select Committee on Population, Ninety-fifth Congress, Feb. 28–Mar. 2, 1978, Volume II. Washington D.C.: U.S. Government Printing Office (1978).

9. Friedman, Alfred S. et al. *Therapy with Families of Sexually Acting-Out Girls.* New York: The Springer Publishing Company (1971).

10. Goldstein, Joseph, Anna Freud, and Albert Solnit. *Beyond the Best Interests of the Child.* New York: The Free Press (1979).

11. Gorovitz, Samuel, et al. "Moral Problems Concerning Life and Death." *In: Moral Problems in Medicine.* Englewood Cliffs, New Jersey: Prentice-Hall. pp. 290–335 (1976).

12. Greer, Joanne G. "Community linkages and outreach services in adolescent contraception clinic programs." *Public Health Reports.* 94(5):415–419. Washington: U.S. Public Health Service (1979).

13. Kestenberg, Judith S. "Regression and reintegration in pregnancy." *In: Female Psychology.* Blum H. (Ed.). New York: International Universities Press. pp. 213–250 (1977)

14. Laufer, Moses. "The body image, the function of masturbation, and adolescence: Problems of ownership of the body." *In: Psychoanalytic Study of the Child,* Volume XXIII. New York: International Universities Press. pp. 114–137 (1968).

15. Meeks, John. "Illegitimate Pregnancy." *In: The Fragile Alliance.* pp. 242–257 Baltimore: Williams and Wilkins Company (1971).

16. Stierlin, Helm. *Psychoanalysis and Family Therapy.* New York: Jason Aronson (1977).

17. Sugar, Max. "Developmental Issues in Adolescent Motherhood" *In: Female Adolescent Development,* Sugar, M. (Ed.) New York: Brunner-Mazel. pp. 330–344 (1979).

Part IV

Treatment Within the Family Unit

The five chapters of Part IV are concerned with treatment within the context of the family. Their approach is both broad and deep in scope, and they provide an opportunity to become aware of current thinking and practice in working with children whose problems, in part, are traceable to their being members of families rent by separation and divorce.

In Chapter 11 Dr. Marla Isaacs offers a systems model for the possibilities of prevention of problems that arise under the special conditions with which the book deals. Her chapter takes the reader through an examination of family strategies as these may impede or further the process of divorce to the ways in which professionals can mount effective counterstrategies and families can learn to work more effectively together.

Care-giver infant-interactions are the subject of Chapter 12, prepared by Dr. Judith Harris, Dr. Nancy Haslett, and Ms. Dorothy Bolding. The authors define the syndrome and indicate the settings in which it occurs. Finally, after a careful review of the pertinent literature, the contributors suggest a format for prevention and, when necessary, crisis intervention in terms of early warning systems.

Chapter 13 is from the Remarried Consultation Service of the Jewish Board of Family and Children's Services in New York City, and its authors set forth the wide variety of problems in relationships that children face when one parent, or sometimes both, remarry. Such problems are often of traumatic intensity, and professionals must be fully aware of them and prepared to deal effectively with their many aspects.

In Chapter 14 Dr. Mary Whiteside offers a family systems approach to understanding the special problems and characteristics of families of remarriage. She concerns herself not only with assessment but also with treatment strategies that take fully into account the complexity of each family situation.

The final chapter, by Dr. Joan Kelly, considers the effects of large numbers of divorces each year on an ever-increasing number of children, now running literally in the millions. The break-up of traditional family units poses unique problems with respect to visitations of children from such divorces with their noncustodial parents. Her research and clinical experience, both of which speak clearly in her presentation, increase the reader's appreciation of the complexity of the issues—and of the possibilities for rational and satisfying outcomes.

This chapter examines the concept of "prevention" and its application to families of separation and divorce. Children who appear very adjusted at the beginning of the divorcing process may become very unhappy, symptomatic, or seriously disturbed at the end. Parents and children enter the divorcing process with often unconscious strategies, needs, and desires. Such strategies form the framework for the divorcing process and may interact in a fashion that stalemates the process itself. The therapist in a preventive service must: (1) Examine and determine the strategies, not always conscious, of the different family members; (2) determine the ways in which these strategies when woven together may stalemate the divorcing process; (3) devise a therapeutic "counter-strategy" so that family members can get "unstuck" and construct a more appropriate future. The paper expands these concepts by examining three cases which demonstrate typical ways in which parents stalemate the divorcing process. With each family, the mode of failure or the likely mode of failure is examined, the therapeutic interventions are constructed and their effects are discussed. The cases are presented within a systems framework. It is proposed that such a framework can integrate within one perspective the responses of the children and the behaviors of the parents.

11

Treatment for Families of Divorce: A Systems Model of Prevention*

Marla B. Isaacs, Ph. D.

INTRODUCTION

The Concept of Prevention

This chapter examines the concept of "prevention" and its application to families of separation and divorce. Children who are not seriously disturbed and are not even symptomatic will nonetheless undergo a great deal of stress when their parents separate. Throughout the divorcing process, mothers and fathers parent their children with less intensity, attention, and care. Custodial mothers are overwhelmed with the task of raising their children; one parent is often guilty for initiating the separation and therefore stops setting limits for the children; the child suddenly sees much less of one parent or sees that visiting parent in a very new situation; and all the family members may experience intense feelings of anger, depression, fear, loneliness or even elation. In this unstable and intense emotional climate, parents nonetheless must make long-lasting decisions about the care of their children. They need to decide custody and visitation pro-

*Work on this chapter was supported with a grant to the Families of Divorce Project from the Pew Memorial Trust. The author would like to thank Braulio Montalvo and Larry Hirschhorn for their helpful comments on the manuscript.

cedures, they must establish a way of relating to their ex-spouse, who despite the divorce, remains the child's parent, and they must alter and then consolidate their relationships with their extended families. They are in the process of re-establishing themselves as single parents or as visiting parents. Such decisions must be made with the greatest of care and forethought, yet the emotional climate within which the divorcing process takes place can lead instead to impulsive, self-defeating or punishing decisions. Thus children who appear very adjusted at the beginning of the divorcing process may become very unhappy, symptomatic or seriously disturbed at the end. A preventive divorce counseling service provides a setting within which parents and children can make thoughtful decisions, explore their reasons and motives for acting in the way they do and limit their tendencies to "act out" in a way that damages their own and their children's long-term interests.

Getting "Stuck"

Parents and children enter the divorcing process with often unconscious strategies, needs, and desires. An abandoned father may wish for reconciliation; a mother who left the marriage may feel that she deserves to be punished for ruining her children's lives; a ten-year-old may decide to protect and nurture her abandoned father. Such strategies form the framework for the divorcing process and they may interact in a fashion that stalemates the process itself. The family member may get "stuck" so that one, two, or all the family members may be caught between the experience of their old family now dissolved and the as yet underdeveloped new arrangements and life-patterns they must construct. They live in a no-man's-land between their "phantom family" of the past and the still to emerge life-patterns of their now more differentiated futures. Thus, the therapist in a preventive service must: (1) Examine and determine the strategies, not always conscious, of the different family members; (2) determine the ways in which these strategies when woven together may stalemate the divorcing process; (3) devise a therapeutic "counter-strategy" so that family members can get "unstuck" and construct a more appropriate future. In this way children who may suffer, perhaps permanently, as the result of an incomplete divorcing process will emerge capable of proceeding with their age-appropriate developmental tasks.

A Brief Example

Let me present a brief example in which the parents are using the child by establishing a pseudo-mutual system of cooperation. Workable in the short run, it may in the end damage the child by stalemating the entire divorcing process. Mother and father are dealing with the problems of custody with minimal conflict; the seven-year-old daughter is not symptomatic in any way and apparently is coping with the separation with considerable comfort. The lack of parental conflict and the child's response auger well for the divorcing process. It looks as if this family requires no counseling. Yet if we examine the actual strategies of each parent, we arrive at a very different conclusion. Mother left the marriage, but because she had no money or job, she left her seven-year-old daughter with her husband. During the marriage she dealt in drugs and now worries that the court would not award her custody of her daughter. Thus, with the help of a very good psychiatrist, she is able to move out, she stops dealing in drugs, enrolls in school and gets a part-time job. Looked at in strategic terms, it is clear that she is unconsciously "buying time," hoping to postpone a custody battle until the time that she looks like a "fit" parent. Thus, she cooperates fully with her husband in arranging her visitation with her daughter and sometimes flirts with him when they meet. The husband loves his wife, is devastated by her leaving, and wants her back. He interprets her cooperative and sometimes flirtatious behavior as a sign that she may wish to return to the marriage. Thus, he is very conciliatory, hoping in this way to win her back. Mother and father thus produce a joint "strategy system" in which a low level of conflict masks unrealistic expectations and unconsciously duplicitous behavior. We can predict that when the wife gets a lover or sues for legal divorce, the cooperative agreement between mother and father will fall apart. The husband will feel duped, believing that his wife did not live up to her part of their unspoken agreement. He may stop cooperating with her since he will feel doubly hurt. He was first abandoned and then fooled. The wife will feel surprised that her husband has suddenly stopped cooperating when things had been going so well and may be angry that the husband is now angry after she had been so conciliatory, even though he had been such a "poor" spouse in their marriage. A severe conflict full of anger and disappointment may ensue. In such a case, the therapist should work with the husband so that he cooperates with his wife, not to get her back, but to protect his child. In this way he is prepared to face the possibility that his wife may not return. The therapist should work with the wife so that she does not give flirtatious messages to her husband but still cooperates with him to protect her child. She must see that her decision to become more mature and responsible establishes her as a fit parent (whatever the courts ultimately decide) and that she need not protect her "flank" in a duplicitous manner to establish her claims for custody. The therapist thus attacks the parents' pseudo-mutual system of cooperation.

When people get stuck in the divorce process, they create sequences that may serve their needs—each parent's cooperation in the above case—but stalemate the entire process in the end. Without counseling, the husband would continue to misinterpret his wife's behavior, believing that if he cooperated with her, he would win her back. The wife would in turn interpret his behavior as a sign that though she left him, he would willingly give her custody of their child. Thus, even if the child is not symptomatic, preventive counseling can predict how the divorcing process may be stalemated, and how the child may be affected.

Outline of the Chapter

This chapter will expand these concepts by examining three cases that came for treatment at different points in the divorcing process. These cases were chosen for three reasons. First, they demonstrate typical ways in which parents stalemate the divorcing process. Second, they demonstrate that even when parents are ostensibly cooperating with each other, the strategies they construct can create dysfunctional sequences through which all family members get stuck. Third, while the children in all three families were clearly suffering, only one family had a child who was symptomatic. In the first case, in which mother had waited three years since the separation to come for treatment, Kimberly had begun to act out and was regressed. Here we can speculate about continued and escalated symptomatology had the family not come for treatment. In the second two families, all the children were functioning well in all areas of their lives and none had traditional psychiatric symptoms. Yet their responses to the separation, their sadness, increased neediness, fighting with sister, protecting a parent, were all responses that needed attention, so that the children would not develop pathological behaviors at a later date.

With each family I will examine the mode of failure or the likely mode of failure, and will then examine the therapeutic interventions constructed for each case. I will start by reviewing the presenting problems of the children and will describe the parent's relationship. I will examine the "strategy" of mothers and fathers as well as the situation and response of the child or children. I will then look at the effects of the therapeutic interventions.

The first family with one child, Kimberly D., comes to treatment three years after the parental separation, clearly "stuck" in a pathological system which has promoted general regression in this eight-and-one-half-year-old girl. We will see how the child's symptom maintains the phantom family of the preseparation period, and recreates a preexisting pattern for the child and her parents. I will show how the therapist developed a "counter strategy" that takes account of the separate strategies employed by each parent in dealing with each other and the child, and how this prevented the development of further problems for Kimberly.

The second family, with eight- and ten-year-old daughters, comes thirteen months after separation. Father and daughter are becoming stuck in dysfunctional sequences during visitation that recreates a preseparation conflict for the family. With mother and the girls, a central issue involves mother's ability and willingness to modulate the pacing and timing of her own life so that it falls more in synchrony with the needs of her daughters. We will see how her request for counseling fit into her strategy for dealing with her children and her ex-spouse.

Our third family, also with eight- and ten-year-old daughters, is a father custody case in which father brought his family to treatment only five months following the permanent separation. The children feel stuck in a situation in which they see little of mother and miss her but cannot tell her, in which father feels overwhelmed by the job of being a single parent but cannot ask for help, and in which mother feels she cannot see more of her children but is depressed because of the truncated role she now plays in their lives. We will see how all family members are victims of parental strategies which have resulted in stalemating the divorcing process for all concerned.

THE CASES

CASE 1—PRESENTING PROBLEMS—HELPING MOM FAIL

In our first case, Kimberly, an eight-year-old only child, was throwing screaming tantrums and mother was unable to control her. Kimberly was five when her parents separated three years ago. In the last year or so of the marriage, father had been involved with other women, had traveled a good deal, and was away from home much of the time. In the year following the separation, mother reported that Kimberly actually saw her father more frequently since he visited on a regular basis. After the first year, mother moved away from father, to a nearby city to be close to her own mother. Kimberly, who missed her father's regular visits constantly complained to mother about the move. At the time of the first session, Kimberly visited father about once a month in their old house, and would spend much time during the visits with her best friend who lived next door to dad. The visits were easy for father, because Kimberly had this friend. Kimberly's parents had not yet divorced, and were on "friendly" terms.

Kimberly's acting out was extreme. She felt that she could not always control herself after her tantrums began. The tantrums which occurred every three weeks were "screaming bouts" in which Kimberly, who lived with mother in an apartment house, would scream at the top of her lungs for an hour at a time while mother would stand helplessly by. After the screaming session that occurred before treatment began, a neighbor called the police because she feared that mother was abusing the child. When the tantrum ended, mother would call father to complain and ask for advice and father would become angry that mother could not control Kimberly. Finally, mother and daughter would make up and get into bed with each other and go to sleep.

Kimberly presents herself as a highly intelligent but developmentally regressed eight-year-old. She was regressed in all areas of her life except school where she performed excellently. She had only one friend, whom she saw infrequently when she visited father. She had made no new friends in the city in which she had lived for two years, and was involved in a regressive, dependent, and manipulative relationship with mother.

We have then an only child who was five when her parents separated. Kimberly stayed with mother, Mrs. D., a lonely and isolated woman, who withdrew from adult social life and became entangled and enmeshed with her daughter. Mrs. D. did not learn to set limits for her daughter after the separation. Instead, she grew afraid of Kimberly's explosiveness, anger and seemingly uncontrollable tantrums, and relied on her husband when Kimberly proved uncontrollable. At the same time, mother lived side-by-side with her daughter more as a sister than as a parent. To fill her loneliness, mother allowed and implicitly invited her little girl to share her bed with her. Kimberly felt that mother needed her and always joined mother in bed. Prior to the separation, Kimberly had been a girl with friends. But to be a sister to her mother, she gave up her friends, except for the one in the city where dad lived.

Had this family come to treatment in the first year, this entangled and stalemated relationship could have been prevented. The therapist would have seen that the child was giving up her social life and her own bed and could have prevented this before these routines became stabilized. The therapist could have early helped mother become a parent who did not require her ex-spouse to discipline her child. In addition, the therapist could have helped mother to move ahead with her own life so that mother would rely on neither her husband for support nor her daughter for friendship.

Parental Strategies

Mother's helplessness served several functions. By being incompetent with her daughter and calling father, mother ensured that father remained involved with the family. In this way, she maintained the phantom family of the past. Mother knew that father was pulling away from the family, and offered Kimberly's behavior as a way of pulling him back. By staying helpless she induced grandmother to criticize her parenting. In this way she could fight with grandmother, acting very much as an adolescent daughter who rebels against a restrictive mother. In turn the fight enabled her to be reengaged with her mother, paradoxically bringing the two closer together. This strategy helped mother to both ward off her loneliness and ignore the fact that, as a woman in her forties, life might be passing her by.

Mother similarly tolerated Kimberly's tantrums to get close to her. The fights result in greater closeness. They slept together at night, much like a husband and wife who fight and then make love. Yet to keep the child close, mother had to keep the child regressed, so that Kimberly did not make friends. Instead, mother offered an "adult relationship" in place of peer relationships. Mother became Kimberly's sister and offered Kimberly comfort in bed. In addition, mother overtly feared that Kimberly loved grandmother more than mother, and may have also feared that her daughter preferred her ex-husband. By having Kimberly sleep in bed with mother, mother reassured herself that her daughter loved her as well.

Father's strategy was much simpler. He wanted to be much less involved in the family. However, since he had left the marriage he felt guilty. He colluded in sustaining his ex-wife's incompetence, since in that way he could "save the child" from an incompetent mother. This relieved his guilt since, even though he had left his daughter, he was able to periodically save her. Finally, Kimberly who was a victim of this process also had her own strategy. Kimberly recreated her family of the past when she had her tantrums because that made mother call father. The girl, as did mother, sensed father's withdrawal and her screaming helped to get father back. Since the tantrums ended when mother and daughter slept together in bed, they enabled daughter to get closer to mother.

In sum, mother, father, daughter and grandmother together produced a dysfunctional sequence in which mother became incompetent to pull father back, to keep her daughter close to home, to become the adolescent daughter of her own mother, and to postpone facing the realities of her own life situation. Father colluded to relieve his guilt, daughter colluded to get father back and help mother, and grandmother colluded to gain two children—her daughter and granddaughter.

Therapeutic Interventions

The therapeutic interventions had two foci: helping mother to set limits on Kimberly and helping mother and daughter differentiate so that each could find age-appropriate activities and friends, Kimberly with other children her age and her mother with adults. The problem of differentiation was attacked in two ways. The therapist addressed the issues of Kimberly sleeping in mother's bed and mother's plans for herself. The therapist had to proceed cautiously. Timing and pacing were important, and mother needed to feel as little pushed as possible. The therapist approached the bed-sharing problem by telling mother that eventually she would need to get Kimberly out of her bed, but concurring that getting her out was not easy. It was important that mother go slowly and not remove Kimberly until *mother* was ready. The support could not be removed too soon.

The therapist of course spent a great deal of time helping mother control Kimberly's screaming tantrums. The therapist instructed mother not to call father at the end of a tantrum and the two discussed whom else she might call. They planned a different ending in which mother could call father only *after* she had dealt effectively with the screaming, and not while she felt incompetent. The therapist also rewrote the other ending—of mom and Kimberly in bed together—and told mother that they could not be in bed after such an incident. But more importantly mother was encouraged by the therapist to prepare herself for a fight that she could win and was helped to take an active part. They discussed fighting suggestions and the therapist had mother practice in the office how she might hold Kimberly during a fight at home. This allowed mother and daughter to laugh about the fights, but it also showed Kimberly that mother would not allow Kimberly to take over. Mother's agreement to not call father now was a way for her to decrease her dependence on father and face the end of her marriage. Since she agreed to give up calling him after she had proven to be an incompetent parent, she also had less reason to remain incompetent.

Mother was also helped to help Kimberly to make friends once again. The therapist gave mother the task of planning overnights for Kimberly, helping Kimberly plan ways to invite friends to the house. Mother and daughter were thus engaged together in a task that would help the daughter to differentiate. In addition, Kimberly saw that mother had the therapist for support and thus no longer relied solely on Kimberly.

The therapist worked individually, as well, with Kimberly to give her control over the tantrums and to help her to differentiate. She had mother buy Kimberly a diary with a key, and defined the diary with mother's permission, as off limits to everyone. The therapist asked Kimberly to record the screaming incidents in the diary, and to take particular note about what occurred right before one of the tantrums. This helped Kimberly gain some control over the screaming incidents, and allowed her to think of herself as an active participant within, rather than a victim of, the tantrums. It also provided a way for Kimberly to feel that she was solving the problem of the tantrums since she had said that she did not want them to continue, but did not feel she could stop once she got started.

Midway through the therapy, after the tantrums had stopped, the therapist asked Kimberly to pick two times during the week to have the tantrums, one time when it was in Kimberly's control, and one time when it was not. In this way, the therapist further increased Kimberly's control over her tantrum behavior. The therapist also asked Kimberly to use a tape recorder at that time, and to turn it on when the tantrum started and off when it ended, representing in a concrete way the control that Kimberly could have over them. Kimberly, however, refused to participate. She insisted that she no longer needed to have tantrums.

The therapist used the diary to further help mother and daughter differentiate. The key and diary thus became metaphors for Kimberly's right to and need for privacy. The therapist helped Kimberly prepare for her return to her own bedroom by having Kimberly describe her bedroom in detail and talk about how she would like it to look. This helped Kimberly see that she could get something very nice when she left her mother's bed.

The treatment brought changes. After nine sessions, mother described how at the beginning of a screaming incident, she immediately took control. Mother began to talk about returning to graduate school and joining a community orchestra. She began to leave the house. Kimberly also made changes. She now had friends who were coming to her home and had been writing in her diary which she showed to no one. Bedsharing proved to be the most unyielding problem because while mother had begun to move out, she had not assembled any companionship for herself. Bedsharing thus waxed and waned in frequency, revealing the bottom line to be mother's loneliness.

Case 2—Presenting Problems—Mother is Rushing

Our second case is that of Katy and Sarah F., eight- and ten-year-olds, brought to the Divorce Counseling Service by their mother. There were no presenting problems, rather mother stated that she wanted to make sure that she was doing the right things for her children. She hoped that counseling would prevent divorce-related problems from emerging later. At the time of the initial session, the parents had been separated for a little over a year. The children were with the mother during the week, and with father each weekend. The girls had gone through many changes—changes in household, neighborhood, school and friends. The presenting problems did not show children with classic psychiatric symptoms and pathology. However, the girls were seen in a state of distress manifesting diffuse anxiety, feeling torn between their wish to like mother's boyfriend and love their father, and feeling guilty about their wish to be with their friends while visiting father whom they also wanted to see.

Two key areas of difficulty emerged—one with mother and one with father. Mother's problems with timing, pacing, and boundaries created great discomfort for her daughters. Mother, who left the marriage after twelve years, was becoming more and more serious with her boyfriend, Tom. The girls actually liked him, but were torn between their wish to like him and their love for their father. Mother, however, did not make this conflict any easier for them. She did not respect the boundaries that needed to be maintained between her boyfriend and her children, so that her children might feel that as they grew closer to Tom, their relationship with father was safeguarded nonetheless. The mother violated boundaries of both time and space. Soon after she introduced her boyfriend to her children, she gave him a backrub on the living room couch. The children found this difficult to watch and Katy quickly said "Don't get personal on the couch." Mother brought this up in one of the sessions. The therapist discussed this incident with the children and Sarah who had been silent during the incident, but was most upset by it, explained her difficulty by saying, "that's what you used to do with daddy." Mother conceded that backrubs had been a special sign of affection between her and her husband. She was clearly pushing too fast, unrealistically hoping that her children would accept her boyfriend as their father as quickly as she had accepted him as a potential new husband. Mother displayed similar timing problems right before termination. After having protected the children for some time, mother decided that she was being "dishonest" and had her boyfriend sleep over on a weekend when the girls were at home. She did not discuss this decision with the therapist, and felt that she could prepare the girls for the occasion by talking to them about it before it happened. After the weekend, mother told the therapist that the daughters had not in fact experienced any problems. She was reporting the event simply to "catch the therapist up" on what had been going on. The therapist, however, felt that it could have been disturbing to the girls and spoke with them without mother present. Sarah, in particular, had been very upset about it. She thought that her mother was behaving immorally. She said in addition that her mother makes them feel that they have to love Tom, since she is always talking about how much she loves Tom and that makes them feel that they need to love him too. Sarah added that they liked him, but that they didn't see him every weekend the way mother did, and that they had their father. Thus clearly problems of timing, pacing, and boundaries remained central to the mother's impact on the divorcing process. She was rushing and pushing her daughters.

Father and the girls had problems with visitation. The girls were upset because father would "pick on" them, and particularly on Katy, during dinnertime. Father felt that Katy had terrible table manners, and would criticize her incessantly. Invariably, within two hours of the start of the weekend, father and children were fighting. In addition, the girls had no friends where dad lived and had nothing to do there. The only time Sarah could see her best friend was on weekends, but since she visited father then she could not see her at all. Sarah felt that visits to father precluded her going to parties and movies with friends. Yet, Sarah could not tell her father how she felt. She wanted to see him but wished also to protect him. She did not want him to think that she preferred to be elsewhere. She said it made her feel guilty even when she thought about it. Father was depressed and passive. Prior to counseling, he seemed content to maintain a conflicted relationship with his daughters until such time that he "became less depressed." He did not know how to spend time with his daughters and did not have the energy to learn. He told the therapist how each Friday he rushed out of the office to pick up his children. He anticipated seeing them with excitement. Yet the closer he got to their house, the more anxious he became, and the more he felt that he had had no time to make the transition from his workweek to the weekend. He needed to go have a drink and unwind, but was not doing so. Finally, father did not let the girls know that he had a social life. When a woman called, he took the phone in the other room. The girls then felt that their visits stopped father from going out. They imagined that this was one reason why father was so critical of them. Thus the girls were overwhelmed by their father's needs and their own wishes. They wished to see him but felt that he had other interests. They knew, however, that he was sad because he "remembers how nice it was for us as a family together." Finally, they often wished to visit their friends rather than their father. Father, in turn, did not know how to be with his daughters. He was depressed and passive because his wife had left him and he did not know how, or perhaps did not wish, to help his children adjust to his new social life.

Parental Strategies

Mother was happy to be out of her marriage, but was left with a great deal of guilt. She came to therapy to reduce her guilt for leaving as well as her guilt for continuing to develop in her own life. She understood that her husband was depressed and angry and she feared that she might be sucked back into an entangling involvement with him to relieve her guilt and satisfy her children. Thus she believed that her relationship with Tom would stand as the "final nail in the coffin" of her dead marriage and that father and children would see that the old family could not be reconstructed, but she faced problems of pacing. If she went too fast the children might become upset, they might in turn upset their father (by letting him know about the seriousness of mother's relationship) and his anger might in turn disturb her children, drawing mother into an entangling fight with father. Yet she didn't want to move too slowly either. She wished to bring the divorcing process to an end so that she could start her life anew. She unconsciously understood that she might go too fast. Like someone nearing the end of a long trip who sees the goal and consequently picks up speed, she was tempted to rush the last few miles of her journey. Thus she came to therapy for good reasons. To close the book on her marriage without excessively upsetting her children or her ex-husband, she needed protection from her own impulse to rush, she wanted support for her children, and strength to cope with her husband's responses. Her decision to sleep with Tom toward the end of treatment reflected I believe a "test" of how fast she could move and how the therapist might slow her down and help the children.

Father's strategy was to keep his marriage alive. To do this he had to keep his wife angry at him for if they fought he could still feel close to her. He was threatened by the prospect that she might totally disengage from him. To do this he chose to recreate an old family struggle. Throughout the marriage mother complained that father was a "neat fanatic" and that he unfairly and excessively criticized Katy for her table manners. Thus father simply reproduced this conflict when his children visited to both re-engage his wife in a fight and communicate to both his wife and children that he was unhappy.

In addition, I suspect that father wanted mother to feel sorry for him. He kept his social life secret from his children in part so that they would report to mother that father was all alone. Father thus used both anger and guilt to re-entangle his wife in their now defunct relationship. Finally, though father hoped to become a successful single parent, his passivity (reflecting his sense of failure), his anger at his wife, and perhaps his guilt over finding some satisfaction in his own separate life prevented him from finding some balance between his requirements and his children's needs.

Therapeutic Interventions

The therapist helped mother to control her pacing and timing in both individual and family sessions. When alone with the therapist, mother often discussed how she might pace her developing relationship with Tom. Mother was careful to report any comments her daughters made which suggested that they were uncomfortable with what she was doing. Together they discussed these incidents, and mother grappled with her conflict between being "open and honest" while not further upsetting Katy and Sarah. The therapist told mother that she needed to slow down in front of the girls, and then helped her fashion a plan of action with which she was comfortable. The girls then joined mother in a session, and the therapist helped them talk to mother about their discomfort. Since mother was prepared to listen, she was able to understand why her daughters were uncomfortable when she kissed Tom and gave him backrubs in front of them. Since the therapist had told her that she needed to slow down, so that she could *gradually* reveal the full dimensions of her relationship with Tom to the girls, mother did not fear she would have to hide the nature of her relationship with Tom indefinitely.

After mother invited Tom to spend the night with her at their house, the therapist again first worked with mother, and then with mother and the daughters together. Alone with mother, the therapist told mother that she might again be going too fast for the girls. Mother admitted that she had told them that she loved Tom very much and that she might marry him, but wasn't sure. The therapist helped mother to see that by presenting the relationship as such a serious one, she was inviting the girls to become very involved with someone who might not remain in her life. Mother admitted that even if she were to marry, she would not even consider moving in with him for another two years. The therapist helped mother to see that she was not acting in her daughters' best interests by her protestations of love. If the girls grew close to Tom and the relationship did not work out, the girls would suffer another great loss. Mother was told to control her excitement when around the girls, and not let them know how much Tom meant to her. Mother understood the importance of what the therapist told her but still believed the girls had been comfortable with Tom sleeping overnight. The therapist then saw the girls and it became immediately clear that they had been quite uncomfortable that night. The therapist got permission to invite mother back into the session, and Sarah told mother directly how she felt. This intervention proved decisive. Mother turned to the therapist and said that she needed to hear this directly from her children. With these interventions, the therapist becomes the pacemaker and mother cannot continue to use the girls in that function—to modulate her entry into the new relationship.

The therapist helped father develop himself as an effective single parent, by shaking him out of his complacency and passive stance, by letting him know how upset his children were. Father was able to build more flexibility into visitation, so that his girls could sometimes stay overnight with friends, and begin the visits the next day. This helped the girls see that their father was not entirely dependent on them, and that he also understood their need to be with friends and was not hurt by this. Father also agreed that his daughters could bring a friend along with them once a month. Similarly, father agreed to let his children know that he did have a social life with other women but that this in no way limited his interest in them and his desire to fully be their father.

The Impact of Preventive Counseling. Counseling helped the parents and children avoid an emerging vicious cycle of behavior which may have trapped all of them. Mother may have moved too fast and significantly upset her children who were already unhappy with the many changes in their lives. The children would have carried their unhappiness to their visits with father, exacerbating the dinner conflicts. Father in turn might have intensified the conflicts to prove to mother that she could not start a new life without great cost to the children and to re-entangle her in a fighting relationship with him. In turn if these fights escalated, father would have continued to organize the visits without care and effort, and would have neglected his own needs out of guilt. The resulting tensions would have increased his passive stance—his feeling that he was a victim, and would have further encouraged him to hide his social life from his children so that his former wife might feel sorry for him.

Finally, the children would have felt rejected by both parents. They would have been pushed too fast by their mother and would have felt that their father experienced them as burdens in his life. While they were without symptoms one year after the separation, they could have become symptomatic had this dysfunctional sequence emerged.

Case 3—Presenting Problems—The Children Fight More

Father, who had custody of two daughters, Susan, age ten, and Emily, age eight, came to our service five months after his separation. He had noticed that his daughters were fighting much more with each other, and he thought these fights were signs that his daughters were troubled. He felt overwhelmed with the new task of raising his children alone. The girls saw their mother for dinner one night a week, and spent Saturday night at her house. Dad remained in their home, and mom moved one mile away, to a very small one-bedroom apartment, where the girls had no space for themselves and no beds.

The two girls were intelligent, asymptomatic youngsters who were nonetheless very sad. They protected their parents, and were not sure that their parents could deal with them. They missed their mother very much, but had not been able to let her or let their father know this. They were afraid she was too busy for them. They told the therapist that they wished they could speak to mother on the phone nightly, but thought she wouldn't be home or would otherwise be unable to call them. They did not find it easy to express their needs or feelings to either parent, and worried on the one hand that mother might abandon them and that father might succumb to his grief. Thus they said nothing, and protected both parents. Their arguments with each other had, in fact, escalated, but the therapist was not concerned. Since they could not express their needs, the fighting was a way for them to not feel alone in a vacuum, to feel together in their sadness.

The marriage had lasted for eleven years, and ended precipitously when mother no longer wanted to remain with her husband. They had married when she became pregnant at twenty-one and was forced to give up college and a career to become a full-time mother. At separation, mother was yearning for a life of her own, wanted to finish her undergraduate education and get a graduate degree. Father was in love with his wife and did not want the marriage to end. When she talked of separation and asked him to move out, he found the thought of living alone without the children simply staggering. He felt desperate about it. He suggested instead that she move out. He told his wife that she frequently said that she wished she could be free of the children for some period of time in order to develop her own interests and skills. He argued that she could be relieved of the everyday care of the children. Mother paid attention to this argument and to her husband's refusal to leave and agreed to move out. She agreed that it wasn't "fair" to make him move out, since after losing his wife he would now lose his children.

Shortly after the separation father took up with mother's best friend. Emily and Susan began spending time with the best friend's children. Mother felt angry at father for robbing her of much needed support and she began to believe that her children enjoyed being with their new-found family. While at first she enjoyed being alone she soon began to feel isolated. She did not call the children regularly, feeling on the one side that she would be intruding on father's territory and believing that her children, happy with their new substitute mother and siblings, did not need her.

Finally, father while overburdened by his new single parenting role, did not call mother for help, feeling that he should not intrude on her newly won privacy. Thus father, mother and children were rapidly and inappropriately disengaging from one another.

Parental Strategies

Mother gave up her children out of guilt over leaving her husband and because she wished to progress with her own development. She wanted to be free, but her feelings of guilt led her to create the self-punishing formula that to be free she had to be unneeded by her children. But as she felt and believed herself to be an appendage in her daughters' lives, she became very depressed. Thus she fatally compromised her new sense of freedom. In addition, she probably unconsciously believed that if she responded to her own mothering needs and her daughters' need for help, she would be pulled back into the role of primary caretaker. She thus constructed an "all or nothing" stance, in which to be free was to be unneeded and isolated and to be needed was to be engulfed and trapped.

Father had been protective of his wife during the marriage. She was young and pregnant when they first married. His strategy was to continue to protect his wife after the separation. He needed her help with the girls but did not ask for it. Father sensed that his wife wanted to be out on her own, and he protected her when they separated by insisting that he be the one to take the children. She then was able to fight him for them without admitting to herself or to her children that she wanted to be free of them. He did not call her for help because he was protecting her from the burdens of child rearing. However, he was also angry at her and got back at her by taking up with her best friend. He could rationalize his anger because she was not helping with the burden of child rearing. When away for a weekend, he left the children with the best friend rather than asking mother first if she would be willing to take them or even telling mother where they were. Thus as he disengaged from his wife, he simultaneously protected and got back at her. This made it difficult for her to respond since if she accepted his protection she had to pay the price of bearing the consequences of his anger.

Therapeutic Interventions

The therapist focused the treatment in three ways. The therapist helped mother re-engage with her children. She helped father become a more effective single parent, and she helped the children openly express their needs to their parents. Early in the treatment, the therapist helped mother see that she was giving up her children and how sad and depressed this made her, but the therapist did not push her to take the children back. Mother was relieved to find out how needed and missed she was by her children, and was equally relieved that the therapist did not push her to become the children's primary caretaker. When mother saw that she could have a more fulfilling relationship with her daughters without being pulled back in as primary caretaker, she could abandon her "all or nothing" self-defeating stance. She began calling her daughters once a day and initiating more contact with them.

The therapist helped mother and the girls to arrange how and when they would contact each other. Mother arranged, for example, to call the girls every evening to say goodnight to them. This helped the girls to feel that they were not being abandoned, and helped mother to feel connected to her daughters' every day life. Thus when she saw them on the weekend, she did not have to "catch up" on their lives, a process which left her feeling very distant from her children. She was also encouraged to spend more natural time with her children and advised by the therapist that she need not spend all the time alone with them, but could invite over their friends and hers. The visits at last became enjoyable.

In joint sessions with mother and father, the therapist helped them establish a working relationship around the children. The therapist helped the parents to see that father was protecting mother, and father realized that he was persisting in behavior that had been a basis in their failed marriage. Mother was able to assert herself, telling him that she did not need his protection, and then they worked out the logistics of how mother could help father with the girls while feeling that she was not intruding in his life. In one session father talked about the kind of help that he would like from mother. He wanted to call her if he thought the girls particularly missed her; he wanted help from her in planning their wardrobe, etc. Mother said that she would like to be in charge of their clothing but had very little money and did not want continually to call her husband for money. Father suggested that he keep an account open from which mother would draw money to buy clothing for the girls. Mother also mentioned how it upset her to see her girls' hair too long and not properly kept. Father was happy to put mother back in charge of this area, as well as overall grooming. Mother understood that she could be a part of major decisions as well about her children, and father understood that he would not have the sole responsibility in planning such things for them as schooling, summer camp, etc. Finally, mother let father know that if he were to leave town again, she wanted to be the first person he asked to take the children. He did not have to protect her by worrying about whether she was busy or not.

The therapist helped father become a more effective single parent by working with him alone and jointly with the children. The therapist helped him develop compromise solutions to problems that had irritated him such as getting the girls to clean their rooms, sort their dirty laundry, etc. The therapist also helped him help his children to express their sadness both verbally and physically. He learned to give them extra hugs at particularly difficult times.

The therapist worked with the children together, individually, and with each parent. The therapist told them that they needed to learn to ask for something when they needed it. They were helped to understand their own responses to their parents' separation and the therapist assured them that other children also had a hard time when their parents divorced. The therapist told them they may feel sad on any particular day and that they needed to learn to ask for an extra hug from their dad when they felt that way. The children found that father was responsive. When his older daughter asked for an extra hug the first time, he gave it happily and let her know how pleased he was that she had asked him. The children were helped to state very specifically what they wanted from mother, and they became comfortable with mother's calling every night. In addition, they were able to tell her if they were watching a television program or were busy with homework and were unable to talk. When mother reassured them in a session that she would never be too busy to hear from them, they felt comfortable calling her when they wanted to hear her voice. The children became less protective of their parents when they saw that their parents were better able to deal with them and with each other, and when they felt certain that mother would not abandon them.

Counseling thus prevented a highly dysfunctional sequence from emerging. Had the family not come, father, mother, and children might have dangerously disengaged from one another. Mother would have withdrawn because she felt unneeded; father would not have called mother because of his twin desire to both protect his wife and strike out at her; the children would not have called for mother for fear that she wished to be alone, and they could not ask help from father because of his visible grief. Guilt, protection, and anger created a set of strategies that when woven together placed the family members in a pathogenic sequence. It is likely that without counseling, after two or three years the children would have entered treatment, depressed, symptomatic, and mourning for what was once a very close mother-child relationship.

SUMMARY

This article has been based on a family systems perspective. We have seen the way in which parental behavior and children's responses form the context within which all the family members respond to and experience the divorcing process. I examined the three cases by analyzing mother's and father's stragegy and describing the ways in which those strategies mesh to create actual or potential dysfunctional sequences. These sequences stalemate the divorcing process so that some or all of the family members get "stuck" within it. Ultimately, such sequences emerge because one, some, or all family members cannot make the necessary transition from the phantom family of the past to the new life arrangement they must construct for the future. Counseling, when effective, breaks these dysfunctional sequences, and allows the parents and children to proceed with their appropriate developmental tasks.

The following diagram summarizes the three cases:

Case 1

Presenting Problem	Mother's Strategy	Father's Strategy	Children's Situation	Therapeutic Interventions
screaming tantrums	1. Stay helpless to keep father in and maintain the phantom family. 2. Keep child young so child does not leave mother. Mother then does not have to face her own loneliness and her own developmental tasks. 3. Tolerate tantrums to stay helpless and to get close to daughter. 4. Become an adolescent daughter to her own mother so that she need not face the possibility that life is passing her by.	1. Wants limited involvement. 2. Is pulled in out of guilt for leaving, and desires to "save his child" to reduce his guilt.	1. Regressed; no peers. 2. Wishes to be closer to dad. 3. Senses father's withdrawal so screams to get father back. 4. Tantrums way of getting close to mother.	1. Limit setting. 2. Create time for mother alone while helping her to get child out of bed. 3. Change dysfunctional sequence so father is not called after incompetence and mother does not allow child in bed after tantrum. 4. Support separation and differentiation between mother and daughter. 5. Help mother to plan her future.

Case 2

Presenting Problem	Mother's Strategy	Father's Strategy	Children's Situation	Therapeutic Interventions
Nothing—make sure children remain OK	1. Wants to feel less guilt about leaving. 2. Wants to proceed with own life and new relationship without harming children. 3. Wants to communicate to father and children that marriage is definitely over.	1. Wants to keep marriage alive. 2. Wants mother to feel sorry for him.	1. Problem with mother's pacing and timing around boyfriend. 2. Torn between desire to like boyfriend but love of father. 3. Not free to express needs forcefully because protecting both parents.	1. Help mother with pacing and timing. 2. Help father and children with visitation—get it "unstuck".

Case 3

Presenting Problem	Mother's Strategy	Father's Strategy	Children's Situation	Therapeutic Interventions
Father overwhelmed Children fighting more	1. Guilty for leaving but wants to be free to develop, go to graduate school, etc.	1. He did not want the divorce and remains protective of his wife. He senses her desire to be free of full-time caretaking and insists that he won't leave the children. He protects her from guilt over abandoning them.	1. Miss mother.	1. Get mother involved with children.

Case 3 (*cont.*)

Presenting Problem	Mother's Strategy	Father's Strategy	Children's Situation	Therapeutic Interventions
	2. Allows herself to feel unneeded by children so that her freedom from them is not threatened.	2. Also hostile to wife for leaving him and gets back by taking up with wife's best friend.	2. Can't express needs because fears that mom might abandon them or father would succumb to his grief.	2. Help parents to have more balanced roles in caretaking with children.
	3. This creates conflict and being unneeded makes her feel depressed and miss the children.			

Prior research has emphasized either the age-determined responses of children to divorce, or actions and feelings of the parents. My contribution and the contribution of the Families of Divorce Project rests in a systems framework in defining behaviors as strategies and showing how these strategies together produce sequences which may be dysfunctional. Such a framework can integrate within one perspective the responses of the children and the behaviors of the parents.

Infant and child "failure to thrive" is still considered by the medical profession at large as being due solely to organic causes. The authors, Drs. Harris and Haslett, and Ms. Bolding, not only review the extensive literature on the subject but clinically support their contention that distortion of caregiver-infant interactions underlie many of these cases. They illustrate their discussion with appropriate case histories and provide an interesting conceptual framework for practical use in detecting, preventing, and treating nonorganic failures to thrive. It should be of practical value to medical and nonmedical practitioners in the field.

12

Nonorganic Failure to Thrive: A Distortion of Caregiver-Infant Interaction

Judith A. Harris, M.D., F.A.A.P., F.C.C.P.,
Nancy R. Haslett, M.D.
and Dorothy D. Bolding, M.S.W., A.C.S.W.

INTRODUCTION

This chapter is designed to enable the mental health and allied health professional to recognize nonorganic failure to thrive and to provide appropriate intervention to families who have such an infant or child. This goal will be accomplished by provision of a framework within which the professional can understand and manage such families. Relevant aspects of the literature that provide helpful concepts and innovative approaches will be reviewed. The primarily medical conceptualization of failure to thrive will be integrated with the psychological and psychiatric aspects of diagnosis and management. The concept and utility of the interdisciplinary team as an approach to diagnosis and management will be explored. The essential components of an inpatient management program will be outlined and the procedures necessary to plan out-patient and follow-up services will be delineated.

Central to the understanding of nonorganic failure to thrive is the concept that it represents a distortion, disruption, interruption, cessation, or failure of development of the caretaker/infant interaction, attachment and/or bond. If this is clearly understood, it becomes simpler to identify those situations in which failure to thrive is prone to develop and to initiate effective crisis intervention or, through anticipatory guidance, to undertake primary prevention.

Finally, for those who become as intrigued with this medical/emotional/psychological syndrome as are the authors, there is a reference list of articles that cover in greater detail many aspects that this chapter will be able only to highlight.

Definition of the Syndrome and Historical Perspective From the Literature

More than thirty years ago, Anna Freud (1946) documented in the psychiatric literature that transitory emotional upsets can be reflected by feeding disturbances in normal infants. In more extreme cases of maternal deprivation, neglect, or abuse, a spectrum of gastrointestinal syndromes has been reported. These include failure to thrive, psychogenic vomiting, food refusal, and rumination (Kempe and Helfer, 1972).

Definition

Failure to thrive has been defined by Barbero and McKay as a term used for "infants and children who, without superficially evident cause, fail to gain and often lose weight." (in Nelson, 1979, pg. 311). Failure to thrive can be divided on the basis of etiology into organic and nonorganic categories. Organic failure to thrive is caused by the presence of some definable medical disease or condition. To establish that an organic condition is present or even to indentify the organ system(s) involved could be as simple as child's play or so difficult that it would challenge the most astute diagnostician. Nonorganic failure to thrive, on the other hand, is failure to gain weight or loss of weight in the absence of any physical illness, disease, or condition. It results from a wide variety of psychosocial circumstances that will be elaborated in more detail in subsequent sections. The common theme in all nonorganic failure to thrive is the presence of a problem or problems in the area of the relationship between the infant or child and his caregiver. A third category of failure to thrive is that in which both organic and psychosocial factors are operant. These may be among the most perplexing cases because of the difficulties with separation of those organic factors from the psychosocial ones and further with the determination of which of the two is the more critical etiologic agent.

The bias of physicians is that failure to thrive is an organic problem. If nothing is found, it becomes of less interest and may not even be considered a medical problem. A new area of interest called infant psychiatry may help to change this bias. Diagnosis of infant depression (Bowlby, 1953), withdrawal and apathetic conditions which are the bases for nonorganic failure to thrive may provide a new challenge and evoke more interest. When these more specific diagnoses are made, the less specific label "failure to thrive" should be replaced by the more specific and appropriate diagnosis.

Historical Perspective

In the thirteenth century Salimbene, a medical historian, described an experiment ordered by Emperor Frederick II who "wanted to find out what kind of speech and what manner of speech children would have when they grew up, if they spoke to no one beforehand" (Rose and McLaughlin, 1949). He, therefore, instructed their foster mothers and wet nurses to provide for their physical needs but not to speak to them. Salimbene goes on to record that "he labored in vain, because the children all died. For they could not live without the petting and the joyful faces and loving words of their foster mothers" (Rose and McLaughlin, 1949).

Although this phenomenon continued to be commented upon by popular novelists like Charlotte Brontë (1847) who were the social critics of their time, it failed to make its appearance in the medical literature until 1915 when Dr. Henry Chapin, at a meeting of the American Pediatric Society, discussed the high mortality of institutionalized infants. Despite his early work, little more was done on the subject until the late thirties and early forties when a dual appreciation again dawned. Bakwin (1949) writing in the pediatric literature presented an arresting profile of infants less than six months of age who had been in an institution for some period of time. Around this same time, Spitz (1945, 1946) and Spitz and Wolf (1946) gave the psychiatric community the terms "hospitalism," "marasmus," and "anaclitic depression" to describe these infants and their behavior.

These descriptions were followed in the fifties by the work of Bowlby (1953, 1956) and Bender (1941) who concerned themselves with the late effects of such extreme deprivation. They were able to document frequent later appearances of severe and extreme personality problems and delinquent behaviors. Their work was further elaborated by Ainsworth (1962) and others. Ainsworth concerned herself with the effects of maternal deprivation.

The sixties saw the emergence of the "environmentalists" who like Caldwell (1975) went beyond the effect of the mother or primary caregiver to assess the total environment that surrounded the infant. Not only did this conform to the prevailing attitude of the time to let mothers "off the hook" but also provided valuable insights with respect to a host of other variables that play a role in normal development. During this same period Thomas, et al. (1968) turned attention directly back to the infant with their observations on the individual differences of infants. Much of their work dealt with the issue of infant temperament and its manifestations. Particularly notable were their observations of the effect on adults of cuddly infants versus fussy infants versus irritable or inconsolable infants.

These aforementioned researchers and their observations were the building blocks upon which were established the work of pediatricians like Klaus and Kennell (1976) who began to look critically at the factors that contribute to the formation of an attachment or bond between mother and infant and those factors that retarded or disrupted that bond. At the present time, research in infant development is in a most exciting phase. The infant is now looked upon as an "active" participant in the development of bonding and attachment. He is no longer considered the "blank slate" upon which all things must be written, or the "empty vessel" that must be filled. He is now considered coequally with his caregivers in the formation and development of his emotional life and personality.

PRESENTATIONS, SETTINGS AND SITUATIONS

It would seem apparent that a syndrome measured so easily by the simple parameters of weight and height would be recognized immediately any time it occurred. Yet, this is not always the case, particularly with nonorganic failure to thrive.

Institutions and Hospitals

In many places in which young children are institutionalized away from the observation and custody of their parents, conditions continue to prevail that contribute to failure to thrive. Overcrowding with personnel of insufficient numbers to provide an adequate caregiver/infant ratio may lead to environmental and maternal deprivation with subsequent physical and developmental failure (Spitz, 1945, 1946). Often the caregivers are ill-trained and underpaid. Job dissatisfaction leads to a high personnel turnover with additional loss of continuity for these babies. Depression and despair lead to failure to grow normally. It is also highly likely that a child in an institution may have a handicapping condition or a sensory impairment that masks the nonorganic component. Investigations may be deferred because it is assumed that the failure to thrive results from the disability.

Most good private pediatric practices and services provide opportunities for contact with parents of infants and small children (Klaus and Kennell, 1976). However, chronic care units, large understaffed public hospitals, and intensive care units may not be so fortunate. Damaging separation of parent and child may occur for prolonged periods. It is now well established that premature infants and their parents have real bonding problems which may contribute to a failure-to-thrive state. Since these infants are small already, the failure to gain may go unnoted.

Families Who Have Lost a Member Through Death

In a recent case, known to the authors, a five-month-old baby cared for primarily by her maternal grandmother was admitted to the hospital with severe failure to thrive that included vomiting and occasional rumination. Careful elucidation of the family and social history revealed that the biological mother who worked full-time had never learned to feed the baby. When the maternal grandmother's brother became terminally ill and subsequently died, no one appreciated how much the grandmother's emotional distress and withdrawal affected the baby's weight gain.

The grieving process, although not pathological if not prolonged, nevertheless has significant depression associated with it (Kübler-Ross, 1978). When this grieving occurs in a parent, particularly the feeding parent, it is very likely transmitted to the child. If it is one of the parents, especially the mother, who dies, there is no doubt that adequate parental substitution must be found immediately or nonorganic failure to thrive and even death can ensue. Small infants and children can be easily overlooked and passed from hand to hand as families attempt to cope with "larger" problems.

Maternal Depression

Postpartum depression can range from the so-called "baby blues" to serious depression in the context of major mental illness such as the manic-depressive disorders or the schizophrenias. The more serious and prolonged depression may lead to major disruption of family life, separation, or divorce. (Anthony and McGinnis, 1978) At the very least, hospitalization of the mother results in mother-infant separation and possible maternal deprivation.

In the more minor mood disturbances that do not result in such dire circumstances or necessitate hospitalization, the impact on the child may still be appreciable. In fact, it is the more subtle, chronic, and masked depressions in which one might confidently expect to find a high proportion of nonorganic failure to thrive cases (Prugh and Harlow, 1962).

Families in which Parents are Separating and/or Divorcing

There are many known ways that a child might be affected by either the early marital difficulties or the actual separation (Gardner, 1978). If it occurs while the child is in utero and continues into the first year of life, failure to thrive might well ensue. Neglect, maternal depression, maternal-infant separations, or even child abuse can result. In one review, 33 percent of forty-two abused children had failure to thrive on admission (Kempe and Helfer, 1972).

Although divorce rates are extremely high, there has been little systematic effort to seek out potential or actual problems in the children and arrange preventive therapeutic counseling. In divorce, one should start with the notion that the children always suffer. Therefore, one is always doing the next best thing under less than ideal circumstances. Recently the authors encountered a seven-year-old girl unable to keep anything on her stomach from the evening her father left her mother until she had been hospitalized for ten days. In this case, paranoid delusions in both parents had been transmitted to the child who felt that she had had "a curse" laid upon her.

Another example of failure to thrive in an older child occurred in a four-year-old boy whose parents were involved in an extremely hostile-dependent relationship from which they could not free themselves. The father would be gone for months at a time leaving the mother bereft of financial or emotional support. The child suffered from a particularly severe form of growth failure known to be related to psychosocial factors, i.e., psychosocial dwarfism (Powell, et al. 1967). In this syndrome no growth hormone is elaborated. No matter how many calories are ingested, growth does not occur. Characteristically, the child resumes growth only after the parents are treated or the child is removed from the disruptive environment. There were multiple etiologic factors in this case, however parental discord not only negated a therapeutic plan but ultimately sabotaged all treatment efforts and resulted in early psychiatric institutionalization for the child. Literature on the incidence of the various forms of growth retardation manifested by infants and older children whose parents divorce and separate is sparse. The authors' experience in both a large public and a small private hospital suggest that the incidence is high.

A final case vignette highlights another causal factor in the life-cycle spectrum of failure to thrive. This patient is a now thirteen-year-old girl whose parents had finally divorced when she was four-years-old. She began life with an operation that necessitated removal of enough of her digestive tract to leave her vulnerable to malabsorption. If she eats fatty foods, she enhances her failure to thrive because of her malabsorption problem. She represents an example of a child with both organic and nonorganic factors.

Her father, who raised her, controlled her diet, forced her to eat, and sat with her for hours to insist that she eat. As she approached puberty, he engaged in sexual activity with her. Her lowest recently recorded weight was forty-five pounds at age eleven years but at the present time at thirteen years of age after removal from her home and initiation of psychiatric treatment she now weighs sixty-two pounds.

Families Developmentally Lacking Parenting Skills

When parents are themselves teenagers, immaturity may compound relative deficiencies in knowledge and skills for child care. The traditional extended family available to instruct young parents is becoming increasingly unavailable. With smaller families, fewer children have experience with the care of their sibs. They bring to the task of parenthood critical gaps in knowledge, sensitivity, and skills to nurture and teach babies. Special groups vulnerable to these deficiencies are teenage parents (LeBow, 1978), the young parent, the isolated parent, the handicapped parent, and the simply inexperienced parent.

Another group in need of additional parent training are the parents of handicapped children (Barnebay and Ruppert, 1978). They have additional need for expertise, patience, and developmental information. The child's need for stimulation is greater for longer periods of time than that of normal children. These parents need to be provided with more insight about themselves, a greater capacity for tolerance, and for patience. The reasonably successful parent of normal children may find that he or she does not have sufficient information to parent a handicapped child without difficulty or distress. It is also well known that many marriages are disrupted and even terminated under the stresses of caring for a handicapped child.

The handicapped child is especially prone to failure to thrive. Caloric needs may be higher because of involuntary movement or muscle spasticity. Eating functions may be impaired, e.g., chewing, sucking and/or swallowing, so that food ingestion is slow and difficult. Self-feeding may not be possible and resistance to eating can easily develop.

Just as child abuse occurs in all social strata, deficiencies in parenting skills occur at every socioeconomic level. In fact, there may very well be a correlation between lack of parenting skills and the incidence of abuse (Fontana and Schneider, 1978). It can no longer be assumed that all parents either want to or can parent successfully. Certainly, it cannot be assumed that all parents have the knowledge and skills necessary to parent a child successfully.

Single Parent Families

The single parent who attempts to raise a child alone may have no difficulty at all. It depends on the resources available to him or her, the individual's basic personality strength, previous experience with children, and any disabilities, vulnerabilities, and predispositions in the child. Because it is the quality of the interaction with the parent that is critical, the presence of single parenthood or any of a variety of unusual parenting styles does not in and of itself lead to a child who fails to thrive.

Intact but Chaotic Families

In chaotic, multiproblem families children may be subjected to as much isolation as if the family were not intact. There can be overstimulation in emotional or sexual spheres leading to a variety of types of behavioral reactions. Such families are at very high risk for infants with failure to thrive. Individual family members' needs are not adequately met. Children may be cared for by many different persons, with or without an adequate relationship to the child or skills appropriate to his management.

Children may be seen as vehicles to meet parental needs and expectations, not vice versa. Children who do not meet these needs may be rejected, neglected, or even abused. A particularly demanding or difficult child is therefore quite vulnerable to the syndrome.

When mental illness is also present, the same problems arise as were discussed in the section on maternal depression. The environmental problems simply compound the difficulties of problem resolution or therapeutic program establishment.

In summary, this section has highlighted various settings and situations in which nonorganic failure to thrive is likely to be manifested. Pursuit of investigations of children of high-risk persons who are themselves parents will yield discovery of many child victims. Even in settings in which children are not usually seen, thought of the possibility of the problem will lead the examiner to pursue relevant questions regarding the welfare of that parent's children.

ASSESSMENT AND EVALUATION

Exclusion of Organic Causes

Although Barbero and McKay (in Nelson, 1979) state that most instances of failure to thrive have psychosocial origins, the authors of this chapter remain convinced that nonorganic failure to thrive is a diagnosis made by the *exclusion* of organic causes. There is no simple laboratory or x-ray examination to determine that failure to thrive is of psychosocial origin, therefore, appropriate x-ray and laboratory determinations to exclude physical illness and conditions need to be performed. This workup need not be exhaustive or costly but should be directed at screening each of the major organ systems.

Much can be done to exclude organic causes by a thorough history that is directed toward the elucidation of symptoms related to each of the organ systems and by the performance of a careful physical examination. These are supplemented by screening laboratory and x-ray studies as outlined in Table 12-1. In the absence of suspicious or positive results from any of these tests, one can safely conclude that no organic cause exists and begin to address the psychosocial aspects. Such a workup should involve only a few days of hospitalization. Indeed, it could even be done on an outpatient basis. However, the virtue of hospitalization to allow direct behavioral observation cannot be over emphasized.

The authors do not propose that mental health and/or allied health professionals should order or direct such a medical evaluation. The medical evaluation is described here because we feel it incumbent upon any health

TABLE 12-1. Causes for Organic Failure to Thrive and Screening Tests for Them.

Organ System	Screening Test(s)
Central nervous system	Developmental assessment Neurologic exam
Gastrointestinal tract	Number and characteristics of stools Stool fat, parasites
Respiratory system	Chest x-ray, arterial blood gases, pulmonary function studies
Cardiovascular system	Chest x-ray, arterial blood gases, electrocardiogram
Genitourinary system	Urinalysis, blood urea nitrogen, serum creatinine
Endocrine system	Growth chart, thyroid studies, blood sugar, serum calcium and phosphorus, x-rays for bone age
Other causes: cystic fibrosis	sweat test
chronic infection	Tuberculin test, chest x-ray, white blood cell count, immunoglobulin level
collagen vascular	physical examination, bone x-rays, specific blood tests, e.g., lupus prep
malignancies	chest and abdominal x-rays, white blood cell count for immature cells, urinalysis
partial cleft palate	physical exam, observation of feeding
chronic liver disease	liver function studies

professional who would embark upon a treatment program for nonorganic failure to thrive, to *assure* that such a workup has been performed. This can be accomplished simply by a phone call to the child's physician or by review of the medical records.

Psychosocial Assessment

Family Study. The process of completion of a study of the failure-to-thrive child's family provides the setting in which to initiate and develop a therapeutic relationship with the parent or other adult who will remain the child's caregiver and a participant in the treatment process. It is crucial that the team member who will be the parent/caregiver's therapist initiate the study and develop it within the framework of the dynamics of the situation (i.e., crisis *vs.* noncrisis) and within the dynamics of the establishment of a treatment relationship. If the situation is a crisis one, e.g., the child's life is in danger or charges of abuse/neglect are being brought; then the parent's therapist should be introduced as a member of the team concerned both with the survival of the child and the care of the parent during the crisis. Exposure of the parent/caregiver to an "intake" person and then transfer to a "treatment" staff person cannot be justified, whether the situation is a crisis or not.

The therapist for the parent/caregiver should identify immediately and clearly his role as concern for the parents' welfare, participation in the study and treatment of the child, and follow-up with an open invitation to the parent/caregiver to express his most pressing concerns. The parent/caregiver therapist must convey empathy, availability, and a willingness to share in the knowledge of the terribly frightening or angry feelings evoked by the child's study. In addition, the parent/caregiver's therapist should be prepared to take a stand for the protection of the child but not be manipulated into taking "sides". The parent/caregiver therapist must be prepared to invest heavily in the child and family, in terms of time and timing and in terms of the intensity of the feelings aroused in all family members and all staff.

It should be clear at this point that the family study process is the first step in the family treatment process. The study process has a therapeutic goal as well as an information goal, and must be paced according to the stresses of the situation and the coping abilities of the parent/caregiver and any other significant persons. Also, the family study should include information derived from observation of parent/caregiver and child interaction.

From an information perspective, the completed family study should cover the material contained in the Family Study Outline that is found in Table 12-2. It should be noted that this outline refers to the way informa-

TABLE 12-2. Family Study Outline.

I. Description of the parent/caregiver's most felt stresses or concerns and preferences for help at the time of initiation of the study. Note the setting of the first contact.

II. Description of the support system(s) currently available to the parent/caregiver and the response made to the child's hospitalization or other definition of the problem. Adequacy of means to meet caregiver's needs for rest, meals, companionship (Garbarino and Crouter, 1978).

III. Development of the child from birth to present age, with particular emphasis on early feeding history, the "fit" between parent/caregiver style and infant temperament, detailed account of child care arrangement from birth to present (Moore, 1975), and account of efforts to solve the growth problem.

IV. Description of mother/caregiver strengths and weaknesses as interactive partner reflected in course of attachment and separation/individuation that has evolved. Included in this section would be references to the following:

    A. Parent/caregiver's own childhood (Frommer and O'Shea, 1973; Fraiberg, et al., 1975; Adelson and Fraiberg, 1977).

    B. Marital history (Anthony and McGinnis, 1978; Brown, 1978).

    C. Maternal mental and physical health (Anthony and McGinnis, 1978; Basch, 1975).

    D. Report of observation of infant/mother/caretaker interaction (Bakeman and Brown, 1977; Caldwell, et al, 1963).

V. Description of history of attachments to figures other than mother, and current status of these relationships (Lamb, 1977).

VI. Analysis of other independent variables influencing mother or other primary caregiver/infant interaction. Included in this section would be:

    A. Socioeconomic and demographic variables such as poverty of material and social resources (Garbarino and Crouter, 1978; Adams, 1975; Bradley and Caldwell, 1978).

    B. Mother's out of home work during the infancy and early years of their children's lives (Moore, 1975; Murray, 1975; Moulton, 1979).

    C. Number of other children/relatives dependent on mother for emotional support (Moulton, 1979).

    D. Child-rearing practices (Wortis, et al, 1963).

VII. Current coping strategies of primary caretaker. Reference should be made to family alliances, friend alliances and the therapeutic alliance with parent therapist and other members of the team and staff.

VIII. Identification of the stage at which the family unit is functioning as it relates to the treatment process and the immediate function of the treatment team. Specification of the next steps.

tion is to be organized in writing. It is *not* a guide for the conduct of interviews with the family beyond the information is sections I and II.

Parent/Child Observation. Introduction. In the past, a failure-to-thrive workup was considered complete when all of the laboratory tests returned within normal limits, and the numerous physiological/organic/medical consultants declared the child free of major organ system disease. The other criterion used to confirm the impression of nonorganic failure to thrive was evidence of weight gain and/or developmental progress during hospitalization.

Finally, consultation with a psychiatrist, behavioral pediatrician, ward psychologist, or social worker would result in a study of the family's state of function. If problems were identified in that study; when a reasonable weight gain was established, the diagnosis confirmed, and the family confidently referred for further intervention; the child would be discharged to home follow-up and quite likely to an unchanged environment and/or unchanged parental conditions. The author's experience with such cases in a large public hospital has been that the medical/organic evaluation is usually obtained quite methodically and quickly. Within ten days to two weeks the child could be discharged with an established weight gain and both parent and professional satisfied that the cause was found and that the child had no "serious" disease.

Clearly, the above description of an evaluation process reveals gross deficiencies in the diagnostic process that lead almost inevitably to grave errors and omissions in the ultimate treatment program planned for the child and his caregivers. There is no substitute for direct observation of the caregiver/child interaction. In fact, evaluation should not be considered complete *until* the parent/child interaction has been studied thoroughly, hypotheses concerning it tested and confirmed or rejected, objectives for intervention determined and tried and at least the beginning of a change in the parent/child interaction established.

Suggested Observation Schemes. In hospital or home the richest possibilities for observation center primarily around direct caregiving activities, such as feeding; but also include diapering, bathing, toileting, and dressing. The next richest area is the spontaneous interaction between caregiver and child with emphasis on the quality and quantity of emotional interaction including spontaneous play, face-to-face encounters; exchange of affection, and the mother's sensitivity to the child's cries. All of these observations can be performed by an examiner who has an established nonjudgmental, warmly supportive relationship with the caregiver. Observations should be made serially although deficiencies in the interaction may be quite noticeable in the earliest conversation.

Competencies Required of Caregiver/Child Observer. The N-CAST Project under Dr. Kathryn Barnard at the University of Washington School of Nursing in Seattle has developed feeding, home, and parent assessment scales for nurses to use in direct observation of parent/child interaction. Their model includes a "trainer" who has been instructed in their model, video tapes, and training manual. In nine two-hour sessions the nurses develop reliability with the three checklists. Dr. Barnard's group also has utilized their assessment scales to predict mothers at high risk for child abuse and neglect (Summers, 1979).

Individuals from other disciplines who have been trained in interviewing, child development, and clinical observation should be able, with some supervised practice, to master the process of clinical appraisal by observation of caregiver/child interaction. The primary skill required is the ability to assess the quality of interaction and sensitivity to affective communication between the caregiver and the child.

The observer should have a basic knowledge of early childhood development including normal and pathological patterns of physical and mental growth. Some problems with swallowing, vomiting, absorption, and regurgitation can appear to be psychological when actually they are physical. One must also keep in mind that failure to thrive may develop from a dual or plural etiology that involves both physical and emotional factors.

Categories of Problems Discovered. The categories of deficiencies observed may occur in the parent, the child, or the home environment. The parent may have obvious lack of basic parenting skills, inadequate knowledge of child development and related information. There may be failure of satisfactory bonding or attachment on the part of the parent toward the child. There may be signs of symptoms of a severe mental disorder in the parent which interferes with adequate handling of the child. There could be evidence of unusually harsh or punitive management of the child that would cause suspicion of covert child abuse.

The child may show signs of depression or apathy. There may be lack of energy, motivation, or activity. There may be signs of failure of attachment of the child to the parent. The child may appear to be disturbed or to behave in a bizarre manner. The child may show rejection of the caregiver or undue compliance that suggests long standing problems and/or abuse. Finally, the child may demonstrate overt physical problems which are obvious only during caregiving activities.

It is now a generally accepted assumption that environmental factors (the family and neighborhood) account for a substantial portion of all developmental and cognitive difference among infants and young children. The correlation between environmental factors and varying outcomes in children was first described in social structural terms, such as social class of the family.

A small number of investigators have pursued the analysis of "environment'' as the independent variable and have focused on the processes that occur in the daily lives of children. As Caldwell and her associates (1975) and White and associates (1979) have stated, it is more pertinent to examine what environmental events parents/caretakers *actually provide each day* for infants and young children than it is to record *what they might be able to do,* as reflected by demographic indices, i.e., income earned, years of school of father, mother, etc.

Caldwell and her associates have produced an instrument, the *Home Inventory,* that permits assessment of certain selected environmental events which occur frequently in the lives of infants and preschool children. This instrument correlates very well with the intellectual abilities of infants and young children at three and six years of age and is best known and most often used for this purpose. Less appreciated is its usefulness as a predictor of clinical malnutrition at four years of age, based on data gathered from administration during the first year of life (Cravioto and DeLicardie, 1972). Its usefulness to assess events which taken together constitute ''emotional climate'' avoidance of restriction and minimal use of punishment in a predictable, manageable way has been pursued only in initial and pilot studies.

Infants and young children become an ''at risk'' population when a biological handicap restricts interaction and communication with their caregivers and/or when their ''environment'' fails to understand, sustain, or promote the interactions and communication necessary for health, growth, and development. The quality of the ''environment'' will determine to a large extent the actual manifestations that at risk children will develop. Separation and divorce can so disturb the environment of infants and very young children that threats to physical and mental health may occur because these situations may force too many changes and disruptions in the daily lives of the children. An evaluation of the child's home can identify the processes sustained for the benefit of the child and those that are disturbed or even destroyed for the child. Such an evaluation provides baseline data, predictive information, and suggests areas in which intervention is currently needed. It is a standardized evaluation of the home and family environment of children up to six years of age that can be a very useful supplement to the traditional clinical study of the family.

INTERVENTION MODEL

The intervention model proposed by the authors includes four components: (1) Hospitalization of all children suspected of failure to thrive who are less than eighteen months of age and hospitalization of selected children ages eighteen to thirty-six months or older for a minimum of three to four weeks for diagnosis and initiation of child and parent treatment; (2) interdisciplinary team assessment and treatment planning; (3) three to nine months' treatment of the caregiver/infant interaction system; and (4) continuation of the usual health care system for the child and developmental guidance for the parent.*

Infants and children less than eighteen months of age who fail to thrive have very little body weight reserve and may present a life-threatening situation. If their parents or legal guardian cannot agree to the hospitalization then the assistance of the appropriate child protection service should be sought. Older infants and children should be hospitalized if the failure to thrive is thought to be a result of abuse or neglect or if there is concern that abuse or neglect might occur. The primary care physician should be willing to admit the child to a hospital with adequate diagnostic facilities and be willing and able to allow a parent to be in constant attendance for as long as needed. The primary physician should also be familiar with the concept of interdisciplinary treatment and be willing and able to help establish working relationships between the team, the hospital nursing staff, and the hospital administration.

The interdisciplinary assessment and treatment planning team proposed in this model includes pediatrics, nutrition, child psychiatry, social work, pediatric neurology, infant and parent education, occupational therapy, and developmental child psychology. Such a team has the capacity to assess the multiple biological, medical, nutritional, cognitive, behavioral, emotional, and social aspects of the distorted caregiver/infant interactions; to develop intervention goals and strategies, and to be of assistance with problem-solving and consultation.

The three- to nine-month treatment period may be a continuation of hospitalization for very young infants and for those older infants whose weight gain reflects a very slow resumption of normal metabolic processes. Two or three team members continue to implement the team designed treatment plan. The pediatrician continues daily supervision of the health status of the infant and is the liaison with the nursing service, the hospital administration, and medical consultants involved with the child and parent. The educator continues teaching activities with the parent. The social worker continues parent support and ego mastery work. Formal psychological evaluation of the infant may be undertaken during this stage of treatment in order to obtain baseline values. Formal psychological assessment of the parent is not included in this model.

The fourth component in this model is a culturally normative approach

---

*The word "parent" is meant to indicate one or both parents whenever it is used in this chapter. In two-parent families, the relationship of each to the other, as well as to the child is addressed. The singular form is used for ease in writing and in reading.

to child health and development. A primary care physician again assumes responsibility for health supervision of the child, and the parent receives developmental and anticipatory guidance from a single professional. In our model the social worker from the team continues to see the parent on an as-needed basis, as determined by the parent. Formal psychological evaluation continues to be available from the team developmental psychologist upon parent request and in accordance with acceptable professional standards.

INTERVENTION STAGES

The authors' experience has been that treatment of child and parent progresses through four stages: (1) An initial stage of *crisis* which may require hospitalization and life-saving support measures for the infant, psychological support for the parent, creation of an expectancy of change by the parent, and the initiation of new parenting behaviors; (2) a stage of *stabilization and consolidation* of new behaviors in child and parent; (3) a *transitional stage* of preparation for resumption of family life in the community; (4) a *normalization* and phasing down stage. The issues of each stage, the goals and the decisions to be made about the issues structure the tasks and roles of the team in this model.

Crisis Stage

In the first stage the issues are: (1) Decision to hospitalize or proceed out-patient; (2) assessment of parent's nurturing skills, play skills, emotional status, and child response; (3) success or failure of the initial behavioral change program for parent; and (4) success or failure of parent in the utilization of the support and education efforts being made. Shaping the *initial crisis* stage is influenced by the primary decision to commence treatment as an in-patient or out-patient, by whether the parent gives voluntary or coerced consent to the decision, and by the urgent need to establish a therapeutic milieu for the child. The later portion of this initial crisis stage is shaped by the success or failure of the infant feeding program and by the success or failure of the parent support and education program. In a successful initial stage the parent develops trust in the team members and accepts the required modifications in the extent and type of parenting he/she is to provide under supervision. External forces which would dilute trust of the team are resisted. Team members follow usual disciplinary paradigms in their treatment of the crisis aspects of the care of the child and parent and introduce the parent to work with a team.

Various team members conduct their assessment of the strengths and deficits in the caregiver-infant interaction and design an integrated plan for intervention. As initial acute medical and nutritional problems are addressed, parent attention and energy become more available for investment in a change of nuturing and play interaction.

The therapeutic milieu and feeding program for a child is more easily created and maintained in a hospital than in the child's home, and daily medical evaluation of the infant's status is possible. For older infants and for young children, home milieus can be created and maintained; but team members must visit frequently and regularly during the initial stage.

Stabilization and Consolidation Stage

The issues of *the second stage* are: (1) The maintenance of the therapeutic milieu and feeding program for the infant; (2) the cognitive and emotional demands over time made on the parent by the intervention plan. In-patient maintenance of the therapeutic milieu and feeding program has several critical aspects. These include: (1) Justification of continued room occupancy on a pediatric medical and/or surgical floor; (2) adequate information delivery to nursing and administration personnel so that they remain comfortable with the amount of time nonmedical personnel spend on the floor; and (3) coping with the major challenge of providing the same "feeding" nurses for the infant as long as needed despite weekends, holidays and the customary rotation of nursing duty schedules. Attention has to be directed toward making the milieu therapeutic for the parent also. This entails: (1) Prevention of isolation (particularly when the admission has been coerced); (2) conferences with nurses about the novel role they have with the parent; and (3) the approvals necessary to permit the parent to violate some customary hospital regulations with respect to patient and visitor behavior.

Maintenance of an out-patient therapeutic milieu and feeding program entails the creation of an extensive and dependable support *block* that includes a surrogate mother to feed the infant, if indicated; the provision of regular medical and nutritional monitoring (on a weekly basis); very frequent education and social work home visits and ready access to the team for consultation. To keep the milieu therapeutic for the parent requires support of basic needs, planned respite, adequate information on the child's program, and reduced parental responsibility for total care of any other siblings. It may require that a family member or friend room-in to help with the infant, provide companionship to the parent, and help with the care of the other children. If the therapeutic milieu and feeding program are stable the parent will usually invest in the educational and play intervention program quite willingly. As the months go by, however, the cognitive and emotional demands on the parent remain heavy, and continued emotional support and pacing of demands for parental change become critically important. The child's weight gain must be established and become steady if there is to be a successful passage through this stage and readiness for the next one.

Transitional Stage

The issues of *the third stage*: (1) Team demand that the parent decide and signal his/her readiness to undertake independent child care; (2) the development of a plan, mutually acceptable to parent and team, for trial periods of independent care; and (3) mutual decision making regarding a definite date to terminate team responsibility for regular supervision of the infant and parent.

The issues of this stage precipitate fears and anxieties in the parent characteristic of the termination phase of many treatment approaches and are resolved in work with the parent therapist. Trial "separations" from hospital and/or team provide occasions that permit the parent to experience the stability of the child's improvement, his/her own new competencies, and evoke issues related to resumption of usual home schedules and child health supervision.

Normalization Stage

The issues of *the fourth stage*: (1) Again, the physical, cognitive and emotional demands on the parent for continuation of his/her new behaviors in addition to his/her usual family and household routines without frequent team support; (2) the impact of emergent development tasks with all children in the family on the caregiver/infant system; (3) maintenance of a system response to the growing and developing infant; and (4) adoption of an appropriate, increasingly normalized plan for contacts with professionals who can advise on child health and development.

It is to be expected that the parent will initially, in this stage, continue to be anxious about his/her ability to continue to interact appropriately with the child who is now thriving and at the same time adequately responding to other family members. Clear statements of the possibility of meeting needs in a family and practical assistance in division of responsibilities will be needed for some time. Follow-up appointments should be spaced so that the parent is both supported and allowed to experience his/her own new abilities. The promise of accessibility to the team through the parent therapist in case of an emergency facilitates return to the normative pattern of health supervision. Anticipatory guidance during the phasing-down process can include formal psychological re-evaluation, particularly if school placement will be necessary. Additional community parent education opportunities can be suggested. Depending upon the parent's particular strengths and weaknesses a plan for final termination can be developed.

PITFALLS AND BARRIERS TO SUCCESSFUL TREATMENT

There are a number of barriers to be overcome before one can conclude that treatment has been successful. One common mistake is to hospitalize only during the diagnostic period and to discharge too soon. A second common pitfall that creates a major obstacle to successful outcome is reliance on a traditional, single discipline treatment model, such as traditional psychiatric or social casework treatment. An example of an expectable outcome where one discipline alone attempts to treat is the case of S. S. was the product of a full-term, planned pregnancy. Birth weight was 7 pounds 12½ ounces. He was begun on Isomil® formula because his older sibling had been a "problem feeder," and was discharged from the hospital at three days of age with his mother.

At his six-and-a-half-week checkup, he weighed 10 pounds and 11 ounces; he appeared well although his mother complained that he vomited. He was seen again at seven-and-a-half weeks of age and had lost approximately 4 ounces. X-rays of the gastrointestinal tract were obtained and reported to be normal although the radiologist nòted the incidental findings of multiple fractures of the fourth, fifth, and sixth ribs on both the right and left sides of the chest. These were in various stages of healing. Skull x-rays were obtained which showed a right parietal skull fracture. He was hospitalized.

After thirteen days he was discharged to his parents with follow-up arranged through the local child protection service and family pediatrician. By six-and-a-half months of age S. weighed only 11 pounds 12 ounces and was again hospitalized. Figure 12–1 shows his growth curve. There is a strong likelihood that after age seven weeks, no overt physical abuse occurred. However, a deficit in parenting and nurturing skills was left unexamined and untreated until the child was admitted at six-and-a-half months of age in a moribund state.

Follow-up has continued now for five-and-a-half years and his physical growth and development are normal although he still exhibits some problems on projective psychological testing. A team assessment and treatment approach is practically always necessary because both child and family have multiple needs the treatment of each of which is a vital link in the treatment chain. The child needs a physician, a nutritionist, a behavioral specialist, one or more varieties of special therapist, a nurse, perhaps a temporary parent surrogate, a child psychiatrist and/or psychologist. The parents need a person for support who behaves in a nonthreatening,

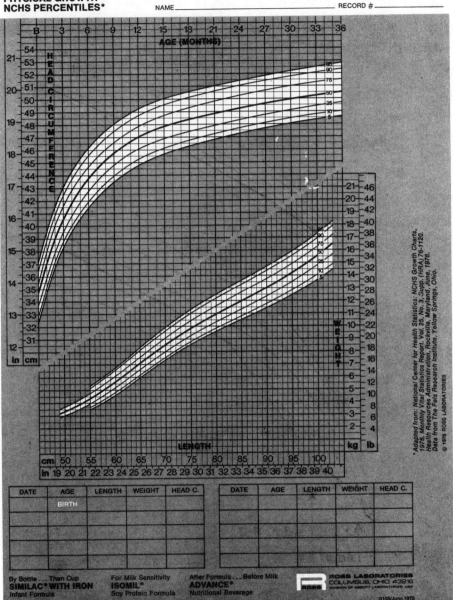

Figure 12-1. This growth chart, provided free of charge by Ross Laboratories, shows serial length and weight measurements for S. from birth to three years of age.

helpful manner. They also need specific educational instructions and techniques. It would be very difficult for any individual to successfully treat a serious case of failure to thrive alone or without help of several consultants.

The following case of T.R. illustrates a more complete team assessment and treatment plan.

T.R., a white female, was referred by her private pediatrician at the age of three months for severe failure to thrive. She was hospitalized in an inpatient facility at which her mother could be present continuously. The child had been vomiting since two weeks of age. Her birth weight was 4 pounds 8 ounces. (See Figure 12-2.) "The baby would not accept her milk." The mother was depressed throughout the pregnancy because of serious marital problems. In fact, T.R. was three months old when the parents ended a seven-month separation. One week prior to admission the mother had struck her husband for wasting money on drinking. She described her husband as "an immature child" who cared for her and their children but who displayed poor judgment. At the time of admission the mother was having suicidal thoughts, problems with sleep, and much cognitive depression.

She had a prior history of a suicide attempt at age sixteen and of one commitment to a mental institution. She perceived her relationship with her own very controlling and critical mother as one factor in her depression. T.R. was lethargic, appeared chronically ill, was thin, cried frequently, and exhibited constant rumination. She seldom smiled but could be interested easily in her mother, strangers, or a mobile over her bed. She was even tempered, placid, regular and rhythmical in her food, sleep and care demands. She readily accepted new people and adjusted well to room changes. Direct observations of the parent and child confirmed that except during actual feeding, when the child was cradled in mother's left arm, the mother commonly held T.R. either so that her back touched the mother's stomach or cradled her high in the left arm so that baby's shoulders, neck and head lacked any firm contact with mother's body. When moving the baby mother held her clasped around her abdomen. In this position, the child wildly waved her arms and legs and twisted her head about. She was placed in her crib "head first" after which her body and legs were "dumped in."

The feeding situation was extremely frustrating to the baby for several reasons: (1) The large hole in the nipple allowed her huge amounts of formula and banana flakes in only four or five sucks after which; (2) mother removed the bottle, placed baby on her shoulder to burp which; (3) led baby to protest actively (kicking, vocalizing, waving arms, turning head

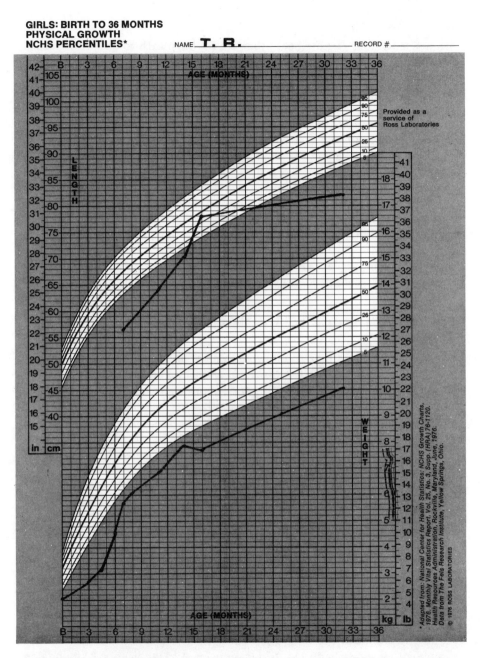

GIRLS: BIRTH TO 36 MONTHS
PHYSICAL GROWTH
NCHS PERCENTILES*

NAME **T. R.**   RECORD #

Figure 12–2 T.R.'s serial length and weight measurements do not show the dramatic move into
the normal range exhibited in Figure 12–1. Both her low birth weight and continuing stress and
turmoil in her family and environment could be contributory factors.

285

from side to side, arching back) then to; (4) burp with some spitting afterwards; and (5) the entire bottle was finished in only ten to eleven sucks during which the above sequence recurred twice. Mother was genuinely concerned with producing a burp and did not seem aware that baby finished feeding in a heightened state of tension rather than in a semisomnolent or quiet inactive state. Baby would finally fuss herself to sleep in mother's arms and be put into her crib. Mother expressed concern that spitting was so messy saying "little girls are supposed to be dainty but maybe she's going to be a tomboy like I was." No eye contact was observed during these feeding sequences. It was quite obvious that the baby was exquisitely sensitive to maternal tension and manifested this sensitivity by vomiting. Contributing factors included: maternal skill deficits, significant financial problems, and marital problems of a severe nature.

Hospitalization for a period of four to six weeks with the parent in residence was recommended as necessary to interrupt this cycle.

PREVENTION AND CRISIS INTERVENTION, EARLY WARNING SYSTEMS

Systems are in place that could detect almost all who fail to thrive if they were used adequately. (1) The Maternal and Child Health (MCH) Program of the U.S. Department of Health and Human Services (DHHS) supports public well-child clinics in each state. Another MCH program that has been in operation since the 1934 Social Security Act is Crippled Children Services (CCS). CCS programs have been implemented by almost all states. Most CCS services generally have income eligibility guidelines and are more directed, therefore, to the medically indigent or needy sector of the child population. (2) There is an Early and Periodic Screening, Diagnosis and Treatment (EPSDT) program to which all Medicaid-eligible children are entitled. The EPSDT program is in place in all but a few states. (3) There are various financial assistance plans such as Supplemental Security Income (SSI), and Aid to Families with Dependent Children (AFDC). (4) There are various public child welfare programs such as foster care and adoption and day care licensing bureaus. (5) The Civilian Health Assessment Management Program for Uniformed Services (CHAMPUS) for the families of servicemen and women is another service. (6) There are also Child Protection Centers (CPC); (7) juvenile court systems; and (8) community mental health centers. (See Table 12-3.)

Public Law 94–142 entitled "Education for All Handicapped" mandates a free appropriate education at public expense for all handicapped children ages three through twenty-one years. Its Child Search component is char-

TABLE 12-3 EARLY WARNING SYSTEMS.

Public Sector

MCH ⟨ Well-child Clinics / CCS

Medicaid ⟨ Health Services / EPSDT

CHAMPUS

Child Protection Centers

Child Welfare Services

Bureau of Education for Handicapped ⟨ Child Search / Special Ed. Services / Related Support Services

Private Sector

Physicians

Dentists

Nurses

Therapists ⟨ OT——MT——AT / PT——RT——DT / RT——AUSP

ged to identify all health impaired children and others to enroll them in special education classes and to provide those support services required to assure an optimal opportunity for them to learn. Besides this public sector, there is a large and varied private sector that offers health care, as shown in Table 12-3. Since Medicaid legislation extends the right to the welfare recipient to seek private care, many of these private services are available to them.

Given that the standards for physical growth and development are well studied and that free physical growth charts are available from several pharmaceutical firms, this plethora of public and private providers should reach almost every child and identify those who fail to thrive.

It would be ideal if families in trouble, with significant marital problems, separation, and divorce that affect the health and minds of their children could be identified early on in their neighborhood health or mental health centers, by private practitioners and efficient, appropriate referral and early and effective treatment begun. Even more effective would be the widespread availability of anticipatory guidance.

Neighborhood Mental Health Center Network

Community mental health centers should be in a central and logical place to be of help in recognition and prevention before borderline or mild problems become major problems. In order to fulfill this role staff will need some retraining, a greater emphasis on understanding normal and abnormal growth and development, and closer communication with their colleagues in Family Practice and Pediatrics. A mental health center should have small and larger scales and some growth charts available at a minimum. Growth charts are generally available at no cost from pharmaceutical firms. They should insist on consultation on all underweight children and should develop innovative preschool and infant intervention programs.

Anticipatory Guidance

This chapter has discussed a number of presentations of the failure to thrive syndrome which should make it possible to identify cases earlier, and to find cases in other than traditional medical centers.

Factors in the history of the parents should alert one to the possibility of having a child with a failure to thrive problem. Anticipatory guidance would then be possible to administer and might be given by professionals or paraprofessionals either within or out of the health field. (Benedek and Benedek, 1978).

The components of an adequate guidance program would have to be individualized but a few essentials would have to be achieved in each case: (1) Exact knowledge of the particular child's caloric and other nutritional needs; (2) Demonstrate competence in the parent's ability to relate affectionately to the child; (3) Demonstrate competence in the parent to carry out routine caretaking procedures in a playful, gentle manner, comfortable and enjoyable to the child; (4) Demonstrate competence of the parent to feed the child appropriately for age in pleasant surroundings without force, an adequate, attractive diet; (5) Demonstrate competence by the parent to play playfully with the child with available toys, suitable for the age of the child.

Prompt Treatment

Where nonorganic failure to thrive has already developed, treatment should be instituted as soon as it is recognized and the etiological factors accurately identified. During the first two years of life the brain is in a period of rapid growth and some of the reduction in number of brain cells, and size of the brain may not be reversible (the behavioral effects of malnutrition can include later alterations in learning, memory, perception, intelligence, and perhaps even patterns of behavior).

Untreated cases can have as outcomes chronic growth failure, increased susceptibility to infections, short stature, mental deficiency, and even death from intercurrent infections (Spitz, 1946).

The long-term effect of inadequate or incomplete parent-child bonding on the personality of children is also potentially devastating. Much psychopathology, sociopathy, chronic impairment of self-esteem mechanisms with resultant personality disorder, psychosomatic and psychotic disorders can be traced to parent-child problems in the first three years of life.

To obtain prompt treatment a collaborative relationship is necessary with the parent. Because he/she is included in the treatment process it is often easier to involve him/her initially. It is suggested that he/she, if at all possible, be allowed to room in with the child; or at least spend most waking moments in the treatment setting for as long as it takes.

In summary the authors have presented, through a review of recent literature and an analysis of their experience, a conceptual framework for mental health professionals to use to detect, prevent and treat nonorganic failure to thrive in infants and young children. The model for intervention presented integrates clinical and research findings relevant to the treatment of the distorted caregiver/infant interaction characteristic of this syndrome.

REFERENCES

Adams, Paul L. Children and paraservices of the community mental health centers. *Journal of the American Academy of Child Psychiatry.* **14**:18–31 (1975).

Adelson, Edna, and Fraiberg, Selma. An abandoned mother, an abandoned baby. *Bulletin of the Meninger Clinic.* **41**:162–181 (1977).

Ainsworth, Mary D. "The effects of maternal deprivation: A review of findings and controversy in the context of research strategy." In: *Deprivation of Maternal Care: A Reassessment of Its Effects.* Contributors: Ainsworth, M.D.; Andry, R.G.; Harlow, R.G.; Lebovici, S.; Mead, M.; Prugh, D.G.; Woolton, B. World Health Organization Public Health Papers #14, W.H.O.: Geneva Switzerland (1962).

Anthony, E. James, and McGinnis, Manon. "Counseling very disturbed parents." *In: Helping Parents Help Their Children.* Arnold, L. E. (Ed.) p. 337 New York: Brunner/Mazel (1978).

Bakeman, R., and Brown, Josephine V. Behavioral dialogues: An approach to the assessment of mother-infant interaction. *Child Development.* **48**:195–203 (1977).

Bakwin, H. Emotional deprivation in infants. *Journal of Pediatrics* **35**:512–521 (1949).

Barbero, G. J., and McKay, R. James. "Failure to Thrive"; *In: Nelson Textbook of Pediatrics.* Nelson, Waldo E. (Senior Editor) Philadelphia: W.B. Saunders Co. (1979).

Barnebey, Norma and Ruppert, Elizabeth. "Parents of chronically ill or physically handicapped children." *In: Helping Parents Help Their Children.* Arnold, L. E. (Ed.) pp. 174–182 New York: Brunner/Mazel, (1978).

Basch, Michael F. "Toward a theory that encompasses depression: A revision of existing causal hypotheses in psychoanalysis." *In: Depression and Human Existence.* Anthony, E. J., and Benedek, T. (Eds.) pp. 485–534, Boston: Little, Brown and Company (1975).

Bender, L., and Yarnell, H. An observation nursery. *American Journal Psychiatry* **97**:1158 (1941).

Benedek, Richard S., and Benedek, Elissa P. "Parents and the divorce court worker". *In: Helping Parents Help Their Children.* Arnold, L. E. (Ed.) pp. 391–403 New York: Brunner/Mazel (1978).

Bowlby, John. Some pathological processes set in train by early mother-child separation. *Journal Mental Sciences* **99**:265 (1953).

Bowlby, John, Ainsworth, Mary D., Boston, M., and Rosenbluth, D. The effects of mother-child separation: A follow-up study. *British Journal of Medical Psychology* **29**:211 (1956).

Bradley, Robert, and Caldwell, Bettye, M. Home observation for measurement of the environment: A revision of the preschool scale. *American Journal of Mental Deficiency.* **84**:235–244 (1979).

Bradley, Robert, and Caldwell, Bettye. Screening the environment. *American Journal of Orthopsychiatry.* **48**(1):114–130 (1978).

Brontë, Charlotte. *Jane Eyre.* London: Smith & Elder (1847).

Brown, Saul L. "Functions, tasks and stresses of parenting: Implications for guidance." *In: Helping Parents Help Their Children.* Arnold, L. E. (Ed.) pp New York: Brunner/Mazel, pp. 22–34. (1978).

Caldwell, Bettye M. et al. Mother-infant interaction in monomatric and polymatric families. *American Journal Of Orthopsychiatry.* **33**:653–664 (1963).

Caldwell, Bettye, Bradley, Robert, and Elardo, H. "Early stimulation." *In: Mental Retardation and Developmental Disabilities: An Annual Review,* Vol. VII. Wortis, J. (Ed.) New York: Brunner/Mazel, (1975).

Chapin, Henry D. A plea for accurate statistics in infants' institutions. *Tr. Am. Pediat. Soc.* **27**:180 (1915).

Cravioto, J., and DeLicardie. "Environmental correlates of severe clinical malnutrition and language development in survivors from kwashiorkor or marasmus". *In: Nutrition: The Nervous System and Behavior.* Scientific Pub. No. 251. Washington, D.C.: Pan American Health Organization. (1972).

Fontana, Vincent J., and Schneider, Cecilia. "Help for Abusing Parents". *In: Helping Parents Help Their Children.* Arnold, L. E. (Ed.) pp. 259–269, New York: Brunner/Mazel (1978).

Fraiberg, Selma, Adelson, E., and Shapiro, V. Ghosts in the nursery: A psychoanalytic approach to the problems of impaired infant-mother relationships. *Journal of the American Academy of Child Psychiatry.* **14**:387–421 (1975).

Freud, Anna. The psychoanalytic study of infantile feeding disturbances. *The Psychoanalytic study of the child.* **2**:119–124 (1946).

Frommer, E. A. and O'Shea, G. Antenatal identification of women liable to have problems in managing their infants. *British Journal Psychiatry.* **123**:45–63 (1973).

Garbarino, James, and Crouter, Ann. Defining the community context for parent-child relationships: The correlates of child maltreatment. *Child Development.* **49**:604–616 (1978).

Gardner, Richard A. "Guidance for separated and divorced parents." *In: Helping Parents Help Their Children.* Arnold, L. E. (Ed.) pp. 279–291, New York: Brunner/Mazel (1978).

Kempe, Henry, and Helfer, Ray E. (Eds.) *Helping the Battered Child and His Family.* Philadelphia: J. B. Lippincott Co. (1972).

Klaus, Marshall, and Kennell, John H. *Maternal-Infant Bonding*. Saint Louis: C. V. Mosby Co. (1976).

Kübler-Ross, Elizabeth, "Helping parents teach their children about death and life." *In: Helping Parents Help Their Children*. Arnold, L.E. (Ed.) pp. 270–278, New York: Brunner/Mazel (1978).

Lamb, Michael, E. Father-infant and mother-infant interaction in the first year of life. *Child Development* **48**:167–181 (1977).

LeBow, Myrtle, L. "Helping teenage mothers." *In: Helping Parents Help Their Children*. Arnold, L. E. (Ed.) pp. 304–314 New York: Brunner/Mazel, (1978).

Moore, Terrence W. Exclusive early mothering and its alternatives: The outcome to adolescence. *Scandinavian Journal of Psychology*. **16**. 255–272 (1975).

Moulton, Ruth. Ambivalence about motherhood in career women. *Journal of the American Academy of Psychoanalysis*. **7**:241–257 (1979).

Murray, A. D. Maternal employment reconsidered: Effects on infants. *American Journal Orthopsychiat*. **45**:773–790 (1975).

Powell, G. Brasel, J., and Raiti, S., et al. Emotional deprivation and growth retardation stimulating idiopathic hypopituitarism: II Endocrinologic evaluation of the syndrome. *New England Journal of Medicine*. **276**:1279–1283 (1967).

Prugh, Danna G., and Harlow, Robert G. "Masked deprivation in infants and young children." *In: Deprivation of Maternal Care: A Reassessment of Its Effects*. Contributors: Ainsworth, M.D., Andry, R.G., Harlow, R.G., Lebovici, S., Mead, M., Prugh, D.G., and Woolton, B. World Health Organization Public Health Papers #14, W.H.O.: Geneva, Switzerland (1962).

Rose, J. B., and McLaughlin, M. M. *A Portable Medieval Reader*. New York: Viking Press (1949).

Spitz, Rene A. Hospitalism. *The Psychoanalytic Study of the Child*. **1**:53 (1945).

Spitz, Rene A. Hosptialism: A follow-up report. *Psychoanalytic Study of the Child*. **2**:313 (1946).

Summers, G. Personal communication from G. Summers, NCAST staff, (1979).

Thomas, A. et al. *Temperament and Behavior Disorders in Children*. New York: New York University Press (1968).

White, Burton L., Kaban, Barbara, and Attanucci, Jane. *The Origins of Human Competence*. The Final Report of the Harvard Preschool Project. Lexington Mass.: Lexington Books (1979).

Wortis, H., et al. Child-rearing practices of a low socioeconomic group. *Pediatrics*, **32**:298–307 (1963).

In the chapter that follows, Helen Crohn and her collaborators offer us a panoramic view of the issues and problems that children and adults have to deal with in families of remarriage. It is clear from their presentation that children confronting the remarriage of one or both parents may well face traumatic life changes that professionals have a responsibility for understanding and relieving, where the latter is possible.

Using a systems approach that seeks to involve all the persons in both the old and the new marriage that have a significant relationship with the child, the authors set forth clearly and systematically their approach to the therapeutic issues and challenges—and tell us about some of the positive outcomes that may develop and may serve to enrich the lives of children caught in such new kinds of relationships.

13

Understanding and Treating the Child in the Remarried Family

Helen Crohn, M.S.W., Clifford J. Sager, M.D., Evelyn Rodstein, M.S.W.
Holly Steer Brown, R.N., Libby Walker, M.S.W., Joan Beir, M.S.W.*

We define the remarried (Rem) family as one in which one or both marital partners have been divorced, abandoned, or widowed by a previous mate and are now either married or living together in a committed relationship with a different partner. Children from one or both previous relationships may be living in the household, visiting, or both. The couple may also have children together. Other terms commonly used for the Rem family are blended, reconstituted, step or second families.

Remarriage is not a new phenomenon but its incidence, rather than the rare instance, has now become commonplace. This is a direct result of our high divorce rate and the urge to end singlehood and recouple in a committed relationship. It has been estimated that about thirty million adults are connected to remarried family situations and that currently thirteen million children under the age of eighteen are living in stepfamilies. These facts mean that a significant number of children are living this alternative family form, with all its strengths and shortcomings.

*From the Remarried Consultation Service of the Jewish Board of Family and Children's Services, Inc. New York City.

Professional literature based on clinical work and mythology has emphasized the problems and difficulties encountered in Rem families. However, a successful Rem family often has a great deal to offer a child. It provides exposure to a variety of values, lifestyles, opinions, feelings and relationships which can be greatly enriching. In this mèlange of a form of extended family the child can learn to appreciate and respect differences in people and ways of living. He has a chance to receive and reciprocate affection and support from his extended family. He faces the challenge of being able to forge a workable relationship with people who have been strangers to him and with whom he didn't choose to live. He can observe one if not both natural parents in a good marital relationship, and use this as a model for his own future love relationships. If he was an only child, he may gain the experience of cooperation that a subsystem of children offers.

For a child to be in a Rem family, he has to have experienced a series of stresses and major changes, initiated by the disruption in his nuclear family, followed by the physical separation of his parents, to experience another major change when one of his parents remarries. When a child successfully weathers these many shifts, his development is likely to proceed and be enriched. The traumatic nature of these changes, however, as well as the complexity of Rem families and the conflicts that may be produced by the two-household system often contribute to different types and severities of symptom formation in the child.

Our point of view for evaluation and treatment of the child is to conceptualize the problem in terms of how it arises and is maintained by the extended family system. We see the Rem family as a new, significant variation of family life, and a structural variation in the sense that the nuclear family model is not applicable. In its practical application, this means that we include in the treatment parts of the extended family that are involved with the child, including the noncustodial parent, the stepparent, stepsiblings and possibly others.

Our present focus will be the child under twelve years of age, who has two living biological parents, at least one of whom is remarried. We will briefly outline the major stress points and changes in the child's life which foreshadow Rem and proceed to discuss which variables we have found significant for the child to flourish in Rem and what the child may typically experience emotionally and relationally in the Rem family.* Finally, we will deal with the treatment aspects when the Rem system goes awry and what is significant in terms of therapy techniques, processes, goals, and countertransferential reactions.

---

*For purposes of clarity, we are excluding families in which one natural parent is deceased and also the special problems of adolescence. Both areas will be discussed in a forthcoming book.

PRE-REM STAGES

Discord in the Nuclear Household.

Prior to separation, the child is a witness to covert or open conflict between his parents. He may be excluded from their difficulties or drawn in as one who is blamed or used in the struggle of one against the other. He may have been expected to "cure" a failing marriage and have failed, or his normal developmental needs may "cause" the pressure between the parents. One or both parents may inappropriately use him as a confidant and advisor, or the parents' difficulty may have been kept a "secret." In himself, the child feels the push and pull to each parent, he may blame himself as the cause of their problems and experience the impending threat to security. He fears abandonment which then becomes a reality when one parent leaves. (See Figure 13-1). In sum, the child loses his "holding environment" (Winnicott, 1965; Sandler, 1960), the place in which he was growing up and the only place he ever knew, never to get it back again. In response to this loss, he may become pseudo-mature and suddenly old, a child who has had to grow up too quickly.

DOUBLE SINGLEHOOD

Both parents establish "single-parent" homes. The child is most often in his mother's custody with visits to his father. His immediate reaction may be one of relief that the hostility of the marriage has ended. Typically, the mother may return to work and there may be a radical shift downward in the standard of living. Children may reside with the maternal grandparents who become surrogate parents to them. Simultaneously, their mother is once again a child in her parents' household and a peer to her own child. (See Figure 13-2). There can be a marital-like bonding between the custodial parent and the child and intensification of Oedipal wishes and fears. The child may become extremely enmeshed or hostilely defensive against inappropriate close bonding. He may parent the parent and be overly concerned with the parent's well-being.

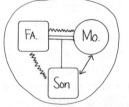

Figure 13-1. The child witnesses conflict between his parents. He is drawn into an alliance with mother which carries over into relationship with father which is conflictual.

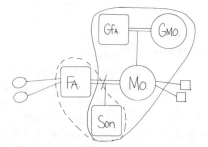

Figure 13-2. The parents separate and child and mother live with maternal grandparents who act as surrogate parents. The child visits father. Both parents start to date others.

When the custodial parent begins to date and be increasingly involved with the new partner, the child is in danger of being expelled, and there is the threat of another loss. He may become symptomatic, withdraw, compete with his parent for or against the new mate, display hostility, align with the grandparents against the parent, or leave the field in favor of the other parent's household.

OCCURRENCE OF REMARRIAGE

The child's fantasy of reuniting his biological parents ends when one remarries and is further reinforced if a "joint child" of the remarriage is born. The first child may experience the remarriage as a "second divorce," particularly if there has been intense bonding during the "single parent" stage, and if it is his custodial parent who remarries for whom he had been a surrogate mate. His role is now usurped by the new spouse; if there are stepsiblings, his ordinal position as oldest or youngest or as only boy or only girl may be changed.

Although to the parent remarriage means the anticipation of greater stability, to the child it means changes in role, living arrangement, standard of living, possibly school and peers. He once more has to deal with two "parents" and compete with siblings who are strangers. He visits his noncustodial parent and his maternal grandparents who may not have yet relinquished the role of surrogate parents. His live-in household may also change as children from the "other family" visit with their noncustodial parent on weekends. (See Figure 13-3). The child has involuntarily become a part of an extremely complicated Rem system with incomplete knowledge of its structure and function. His expectations were based on the experience in his nuclear family, on popular ideas about families, upon his fantasies of a "new life," and on folklore about the stepfamily. He brings with him all the baggage of his previous life changes whose issues often remain unresolved as the new family tries to consolidate into a viable unit.

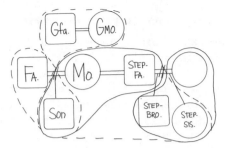

Figure 13-3. The mother remarries a man who has two children from a previous marriage who visit weekends and summer. The child lives with mother and stepfather, visits his biofather and grandparents.

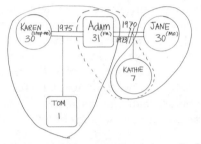

Figure 13-4. The Thomas family at time of referral.

Variables Affecting the Child's Successful Adaptation to Rem.

There are many variables that facilitate or impede the child's adaptation to Rem. These include constitutional, intrapsychic, historical, relational, and environmental factors. Our findings relevant to these parameters concur with those of several other authors (Tessman, 1978; Gardner, 1976; Ransom, 1979; Messinger, 1976; Duberman, 1973; Bernard, 1971).

Constitutional and Intrapsychic

These are primary variables for the child's healthy adaptation to Rem. The child meets life situations with his own intrapsychic structure and personality strengths, with the ways he has at hand to cope with change and stress, and to deal with the conflicts within himself and with others. All of these affect how he manages his Rem situation.

Physical factors play a part too: whether, for example, he is in good physical health or his life is disrupted further by medical needs. Age is another variable which is influential in the sense that it is the very young child and the young adult who tend to assimilate into a new Rem family most easily, with the middle groups being most problematic.

Mourning and Cutting Loose Old Relationships

The way in which the natural parents dealt with the loss of their first mates is meaningful for the child and affects his ability to adjust to Rem. If the parents were unable to mourn, and did not provide pathways for the child to mourn the former root family, then it is likely that the child will remain emotionally connected to the old system and make a peripheral attachment to the Rem family. If the child has not worked through his loss, he resists the acceptance of a stepparent.

If there was intense bonding between the child and his custodial parent during the single parent stage, both parent and child may find it difficult to relinquish this exclusivity and allow room for the stepparent. The time span between marriages is an important variable here: both too long and too short seem to have an adverse affect on the adjustment to Rem. If double singlehood lasts too long, the parent-child roles are that much more rigidified and resistant to change; if singlehood is too short, it is likely that mourning processes have not been completed for child and parent. Based on our clinical observation, but without adequate research with nonclinical families, we suggest not less than one year and preferably under three years to be the optimal period of time for singlehood.

Which Parent Remarries

With our clinical population, our impression has been that the adjustment of the child is more problematical if it is the custodial parent who remarries rather than the parent the child visits. This follows from the fact that there is less disruption in the primary household of the child. However, it is not uncommon that the remarriage of a noncustodial parent will reverberate in the other household to the extent that the custodial parent may make a major shift at the same time. (i.e., begin to date, move, change jobs, begin living with someone).

The Relationship Between the Ex-spouses

If there is ongoing hostility between the bioparents, the child's adaptation to Rem is more difficult. The hostility is often played out by using the child as a messenger between households; having him inform on one parent's life to the other or negatively identifying him with the ex-spouse ("You're just like your father—no good.") Conversely, a civil relationship between the bioparents in which the child's needs are addressed facilitates the child's adaptation to Rem.

The Child's Relationship with His/Her Bioparents

There are several combinations of Rem possibilities which can affect the child differently: (1) The custodial parent has remarried, the noncustodial parent remains single; (2) the custodial parent is single, the noncustodial parent has remarried; (3) both the custodial parent and noncustodial parent have remarried. In all three configurations, the child needs permission of both bioparents to become a real member of Rem. If he perceives in configuration (1) and (2) that his unmarried bioparent is unhappy, he may feel too guilty to attach himself to the stepparent.

In (1), where the custodial parent has remarried, that parent may be freed from the burdens of single parenthood and may become much more accessible to the child; for example, in the case of a woman who no longer has to work. On the other hand, in any of the three cases, the remarried parent may withdraw from the child, because of his/her involvement with the new spouse and/or stepchildren. In these instances, the remarriage is a loss for the child and may affect his development adversely.

Contractual Expectations

Rather than a written contract, the children and adults enter the Rem situation with a variety of expectations, both conscious and unconscious, stated and unstated (Sager, 1976). For the child, these expectations relate to what he expects to receive from his parent, stepparent, and stepsibs, and what he expects to give in return; they also relate to what he expects the family as a whole to be, the amount of closeness and distance there will be, who will have authority over whom, how responsibilities will be divided, and so forth. What is crucial is to what extent the child's contract melds or conflicts with those of the other family members. For example, the child may want to depend on his stepparent as a parent, while the stepparent may expect a peerlike relationship with the child in which the child displays a great deal of autonomy. Often the custodial parent expects his/her new spouse to take over rearing and/or discipline of the child while the child expects that the bioparent will continue to be the primary one. It's common that a childless stepparent will see the child as the chance to have reciprocal parent-child love fulfilled, while the child sees this demand as disloyal to his other unmarried bioparent. Or, the child may see the remarriage as a chance to reexperience a more complete parental home with structure and stability, while the parent's and stepparent's contracts are to be mates in love first and parents second. All the possible contractual conflicts between child and family and the degree of conflict contribute to a more problematic adjustment for the child.

Ordinal Position and Sibling Constellation

The child's integration into the Rem family may be inhibited if his ordinal position in that family is changed. If he is accustomed to being the responsible eldest child, and then acquires older stepsiblings, he may no longer be relied on for leadership or comfort. The resultant displacement will affect his self-esteem and sense of belongingness. Conversely, an only child, who may have been "babyfied," might suddenly find himself with several smaller stepsiblings and the expectation that he should be the more grown-up responsible one. In another instance, his bioparent may continue to "babyfy" him while his stepparent sets expectations of more mature behavior.

The sibling constellation is also important for the adjustment of the child to Rem in the sense that it can be facilitative ("We're all in this together") or maladaptive where there is a great deal of competition for the adults, where there are striking differences in school achievement, in friendships, in amounts of clothes, possessions, and money available.

Cultural, Religious, Socioeconomic Factors

The Rem family will often be a combination of divergent cultural, religious, and socioeconomic backgrounds. Often the home household and the visited household are divergent too. These differences are problematic in terms of how they are dealt with rather than simply troublesome for the children. If differences are respected both between households and intrahousehold, a more favorable situation for the child will be established than if there is an intense pressure to change or conform or a pretense of pseudo-mutuality (Peck, 1974) or pseudo-wholeness (Duberman 1973).

Grandparents, the Extended Family, the Community

The grandparents and extended family, such as aunts and uncles, can be highly significant for the adaptation of the child to Rem, particularly if they were highly involved with the child during the single parent stage. Their approval is needed for the child to feel free to form new attachments. Unfortunately, the extended family may hang on to the child and/or interpret the remarriage as a disloyalty to the "old" family. The community is also positively influential, to the extent that Rem is commonplace and blends in with the social environment. With other children available who have stepparents, the child can find peer support and learn ways of coping with his situation.

Change of Residence, School, Peer Group

The integration of the child with Rem is more difficult if in addition to a new family, he is uprooted and moved to a new community, a new school and therefore needs to make new friends. It is preferable, although not always possible, if something in the child's outside life can remain continuous rather than subjecting him to total upheaval.

THE EXPERIENCE OF REM FROM A CHILD'S PERSPECTIVE

Multiplicity of Relationships

In order to understand how the child experiences Rem, one should be aware of the multidimensional system of interaction. The young child, perhaps depleted by the events leading to Rem, has to rally his forces and begin to understand and deal with a system where the number of members has increased and the rules have become increasingly unclear. Every move he makes reverberates in at least two households. When a child asks for help with his homework from his stepfather, there are implications for his natural father living on the other side of town and for his stepsiblings who see their new brother take their father's time. A holiday or a birthday are not just days to be enjoyed anymore, but a time of tension to make sure everyone in the family is satisfied and no parent or stepparent feels slighted by where and how the child chooses to spend his time.

If the Rem household is a destructive one, the child is able to leave the field by spending weekends in the household of the other bioparent:

> John, age eight, lives with his mother and stepfather in a tense home where he is not allowed to assert himself or be angry, but he is constantly castigated for being passive and stupid. When he spends weekends with his father and stepmother, he is able to speak up and get positive encouragement for his point of view. Although this is confusing to John, without his weekends he may grow up believing that being himself is a dangerous and impossible idea.

For the child, changing back and forth between households may not have a positive effect, but may make the child experience himself emotionally as an orphan. One must keep in mind that, vertically, the child has already had several household changes, and now, horizontally, he has to relate to at least two households, both of which may also not be constant. For instance:

A ten-year-old girl residing with her mother and stepfather is an only child during the week, but an oldest child on the weekends when her stepfather's toddler children come to visit. When she visits her biofather who has a young teenage stepdaughter, the former girl then becomes the younger child.

The systems and roles in each household may be quite different, and the re-entry from one to another is typically difficult for the child in that a sense of loss adjustment reoccurs each time.

Positive Potential

There are many positive aspects of the multiplicity of Rem for the child. After seeing a destructive marital relationship between his bioparents, he can gain positive models and a feeling of stability from the loving interaction of the Rem couple. He gets care and attention from his stepparents, sibs, and grandparents that adds to the bounty from his natural parents. The multiplicity of personalities, styles of living and values may give the child the rich mosaic of life of an extended family without its structural certitude and monolithicity. If the child has experienced limitations in his relationship with a bioparent, he may be able to compensate for this lack with the stepparent. A child whose mother is a stern, distant person may look to the warmth and gentleness of his stepmother as a way of getting some other needs gratified. His father may love him but have a limited education; the child may find intellectual stimulation from a brighter, more educated stepfather. His breadth of choice of a future mate is broadened insofar as he is influenced by parental introjects and projections (Dicks, 1967; Sager, 1976).

Divided Loyalties

If the households of the ex-spouses are hostile, the child may be used as a mediator between them and divided loyalties between his feelings for the two bioparents and between the bioparents and the stepparents. The child may be forced into feeling as if he has to choose between parents and the consequent anxiety engendered by this may cause him to withdraw or pull back into a pseudo-independent stance. The child may also experience divided loyalties between his natural siblings and stepsiblings, particularly where a stepsibling is close in age and becomes a buddy to the child, thereby usurping the exclusive role his biosibling may formerly have had.

Divided loyalties may extend to grandparents where a child may like his new, acquired stepgrandparents, but feels the resentment of this by his biograndparent.

Pseudo-Independence

The pseudo-independent stance of a child will often have originated during the stage of double singlehood in which the child was left to his own devices in the midst of postdivorce chaos. This stance is the direct result in such cases of the loss of the child's "holding environment." This pseudo-independence may become reinforced or heightened by the remarriage. For example:

Annie, in the custody of her mother, was eleven when her father remarried a woman with two children of her own. Prior to this, Annie had been responsible for herself while her busy professional mother worked. Her visits to her father, who was very attentive, had been times when she could be a "child" again. After the remarriage and with her father's increasing involvement with his new wife, stepchildren and then a new baby, Annie became increasingly involved with her peer group and then exclusively with one boy, to the extent that she formed a premature couple bond with him. With this pseudo-independent stance, she opposed all parental dictates, became sexually involved and made the demands of an older adolescent. When these were denied, she and the boyfriend would disappear for days and engage in minor delinquent activities.

Often the child will repress any hostility he feels toward his bioparent for fear of another abandonment and will project his hostility onto the stepparent. If even this expression of conflict is too dangerous, the child may withdraw into a depression that is synergized by unresolved mourning. Unfortunately a parent who has also repressed mourning may feel threatened by the child's grief and attempt to cut it off. The child may withdraw further into depressive mourning or act it out in rebelliousness and antisocial behavior.

Incest Fears

The incidence of incest between stepparent and child and among stepsiblings is higher than among their biological counterparts. The tragedy of Phaedra is not unique. The weakened incest taboos in the Rem family may hinder the child from reaching out to the stepparent for normal parenting. Often the Rem couple is at the start of a new marriage and a honeymoon air of sensuality pervades the household. A child's Oedipal-like attachment to a stepparent is not so safe where blood ties don't exist to raise the acting-out threshold for stepchild or stepparent. For mother to watch her five-year-old flirt with her daddy can be a threatening experience. But if "daddy" is a stepfather, all three family members may experience anxiety which may be defended against by withdrawal and distancing that is maintained by a constant series of hostile acts.

EVALUATION AND TREATMENT

A systems approach is essential in working with children in Rem families in order to conceptualize and explore the presenting problems on multiple levels and to develop a flexible program for intervention with individuals, the couple, the Rem family, the extended family—including both bio-and all stepparents, grandparents, and the network as a whole. Although the treatment process may involve one or more parts of the family, it is important to keep in mind how the "treated part" fits into the entire system of interrelated persons. The ex-spouse must often be our concern on equal terms with the new adult couple and all the children. Similarly, the therapist is a member of a professional system. He/she can call on colleagues to work with a subsystem and has the advantage of colleagal conferences to get technical support as well as help with his/her emotional reactions. The fact that the client's therapist is part of a team is introduced at the initial contact when the client telephones and is first referred to a staff member of the Remarried Consultation Service.

Incidence of Behavioral Problems

In our agency practice, the major complaint most often presented by the Rem couple concerns problems with a child: parent-child relations, impulse control, school problems and depression are cited most often. Often the child is seen as the singular cause of all the discord in the Rem family; disgruntled parents and stepparents often wish that the child would just vanish so that they could proceed with their marriage.

In our assessment and treatment of 213 Rem families between May 1, 1977 and May 31, 1979, a total of 367 children were involved. Of this group of children the following percent of the total number of children manifested behavioral disturbances (any child might have revealed one or more of these forms of behavior):

	%
1. Impulse control problems (including substance abuse)	38
2. School problems	36
3. Pseudo-independence/maturity	23
4. Dysfunctional relationship with parent(s) total	83
a. with custodial parent	37
b. with noncustodial parent	30
c. with stepparent	34

5. Disturbance in peer relationships   21
6. Psychosomatic complaints   12
7. Extruded child (psychologically and/or physically,
   including battered child)   23
8. Depressed state   29
9. Satisfactory adaptation (including relatively
   free of problems in above categories)   9

Only 9 percent of the 367 children were considered to be free of behavioral problems. The 91 percent described as having problems did not necessarily have difficulties that were severe enough, or were of an etiological nature that indicated a need for therapeutic intervention. Many of these could be dealt with in an educational or guidance program. We did not compare this group—who were seen in a clinical setting—to Rem families who were not seekers of help or to the children of intact, nuclear families.

In some instances marital complaints were the presenting problems. At times the major issue between the adults would be seen by them as a child's behavior, or the bioparent's overconcern for a child or a stepparent's criticism of a child's behavior.

It is also common that a child will be referred who is in the custody of his still-single parent and visits with the remarried parent. In a more traditional model the child and the custodial parent would have been seen in therapy, with perhaps a token contact with the noncustodial parent. The approach we suggest here includes this "other" parent from the outset.

INITIAL STAGES

At the first telephone contact, the therapist is not allied with any part of the system. The client is introduced to the idea of the system by inviting in for the first sessions the members of both households. The therapist is more likely at this point to have the greatest leverage in bringing in many members of the Rem system, thereby avoiding a feeling of exclusion and alienation which may occur after the initial session or sessions have been held without some members. An example of this exclusion is the disloyalty a child experiences when one bioparent is not only not invited to participate but is not informed. Perhaps the child may even have been coerced into secrecy about the therapy session.

It is our preference for the therapist during the first telephone contact to establish in a sensitive, caring manner with "firmth"* that the index-

---

*"firmth," firmness and warmth.

patient-child has or had at one time *two* bioparents. This is a basic tenet in working with such children, as both parents are needed for and are part of their emotional identifications. We will back away when feelings are so strong that the caller prefers not to come at all. We avoid presenting our position as "do it or else." In the initial phone call the therapist will establish the following:

1. WHO: The relationship of the caller to the child; If a nonbioparent, how is the caller involved with the child and for how long?
2. WHY: Why are they calling? (Presenting complaints, symptoms).
3. WHAT: What is their partner's reaction to calling us for therapy?
4. WHO: Who is the family?
    (a) Living-in-household: adults and children-names, ages; frequency of out-of-house visits and with whom do they visit; who are the members of the visited residence; geographical proximity of visited residence.
    (b) Out-of-house: children; names, ages where each resides, who resides with other members of out-of-house, frequency of visits in.
5. Are there others living away from parents? college, married, institutions, other residences.
6. How long have the above arrangements been in effect?
7. Have there been other residential combinations? If so, what contributed to changes and when?
8. What is the other bioparent's reaction to the request for treatment?

The caller is then urged to speak with other involved parental figures to enlist their availability during the evaluation sessions which may take from one to four visits, one-and-a-half, to two hours each. Frequently, clients verbalize anxiety about meeting or having the therapist meet with an ex-spouse, out of fear that the child will fantasize the bioparents reuniting or because someone "will get killed," owing to ex-spouse hostilities. The therapist gently reminds the adult that the child lives in both parents' worlds and that it is in the best interest of their child for the adults to work together. It is most important to emphasize that it is the parenting and step-parenting issues, which are on their and our common agenda, not the ex-marital issues, such as alimony. It is then up to the therapist to be directive and maintain the limits of the agenda during the sessions. Whom to include, when to include them and how to set up a session are matters of artful timing and sensitivity on the part of the therapist. There are no hard and fast rules, although we try to include the primary parental figures from the outset. Other members of the extended family, such as grandparents and aunts and uncles, may be brought in, particularly if they played major roles with the child during the single parent stage and may still have strong bonds with the child. To exclude them would again be to put the child in a loyalty bind.

To ignore persons who may have significant input to the presenting problems and their exacerbation and/or continuance often later produces sabotage by those who were excluded. It is most important for the therapist to be flexible. For example, it is often necessary to see each bioparent separately to facilitate trust in the therapist or to promote comfort in the joint sessions. The clinician may have to enlist a cotherapist for another person in the system, who may be in an isolated role position and in need of support. For example, a noncustodial parent, after a bitter divorce and custodial fight, may feel that the Rem family's therapist must be allied with his/her former spouse and antagonist. To be included in the treatment program, he may need his own therapist to meet with individually for one session and then act as a support/interpreter for him in conjoint sessions. We utilize a model for this that is adapted from McGregor's (1964) multiple impact family therapy. Often a therapist may be assigned for the children, the Rem couple and for the former spouse if only for a brief period. They may meet separately with their subsection as well as when the entire group meets together.

The Genogram. The therapist's acceptance of "differences" of the two households as demonstrated by having two sets of toy family figures in the office and by his respect for the various surnames in the family, is further facilitated by collaboration with the family in drawing a genogram at some point during the evaluation stage. Our experience has shown this to be a nonthreatening anamnesic tool in which very young children are able to participate with the adults in a creative process.* Unresolved mourning, feuds, family skeletons, patterns of physical illness, divorce and remarriage are effectively demonstrated in this task. The adults frequently gain a heightened awareness of the complexity of their child's worlds. For the child, the genogram makes the absent parent "real" and gives him permission to discuss this parent. For the therapist, it is a way to quickly ascertain who is in the family, where they live, and how the family changes as children move in and out for visitation. It is also a vehicle to obtain a thorough history of the child and family, including former significant relationships. There is often a tendency to overlook the history when a family presents itself in crisis. However, we find history invaluable for dealing with the crisis effectively. The genogram is out on the table during each ses-

*For a thorough explanation of the genogram, see Guerin (1976).

sion so that it is a live instrument to be added to, helping to elucidate roles and relationships.

Goal Setting. "Treatment" has actually begun with the first phone call. In the way the initial call and the evaluation are done, often sufficient clarification of the problem takes place to make work toward additional goals unnecessary. The therapist's acceptance that "you can't go home again" and that the Rem family will never be the same as the "original" family (nor should it be) promotes realistic goals of individuation and differentiation of system members. Goals are set for both the family as a whole and for the individual needs of members. It is important to consider the noncustodial bioparent as well as the needs of the in-household Rem family. Clear contracting with the family as far as its goals is part of our treatment approach. The therapist's knowledge of family and child development as well as his special knowledge of Rem comes into play in setting goals as well as throughout the entire treatment process.

For the child, it is also appropriate not to lose sight of his individual needs which may predate or be largely independent of Rem. For example, with learning difficulties one must be able to distinguish between what is functional and what is true organic deficit. Educational-psychological assessments are utilized as needed. There are times when individual sessions for the child are indicated; when and how and why are based on the assessment skills, training and biases of the clinician.

TREATMENT TECHNIQUES

Starting with his skill and knowledge of family therapy, the clinician approaches Rem, keeping in mind what special issues are applicable as well as the emotional and interactional issues which are universal rather than unique to Rem. He will involve the family in clear contracting and goal setting and be able to assign tasks as indicated to facilitate goal attainment. He should be able to move in and out of different levels of understanding and intervention as needed, from dealing with both observable behavior and conscious motivation to preconscious and dynamic factors if indicated.

We employ a multimodal technique in the sense that we include individual, couple and conjoint family therapy as well as groups, multiple family therapy and network, in various combinations when and as needed. The timing of the various modalities and who shall be included or what subsystems worked with at any time are essential to developing a workable approach to a particular family. Seeing a child alone too early in the course of treatment frequently precludes involvement of the adults in therapy. Child treatment later on is, however, usually more acceptable to the child and less likely to be unconsciously sabotaged by the adults, who no longer need the scapegoat and who are prepared to offer the child a healthier and more nutritious environment.

Different issues and techniques may necessarily be involved for the variations of Rem that are seen by the clinician. However, there are some common Rem family issues which are often addressed during therapy in some form and which have direct bearing on the child's functioning: unresolved mourning, the special use of history, clarification of expectations of roles and relationships for the child and all adults, exposing myths, helping the family understand the whole system to which they belong and delineating and respecting differences among individuals and households.

Unresolved mourning can be a major blockage to integration occurring among the members of Rem; here mourning is referred to in the larger sense of the failure to grieve for the dead or absent parent, for the "old family" and way of life. The therapist may find the expression of this in the child's inability to adjust to a new school or neighborhood, longing for the former place of residence or through indirect expression such as complaints about food. The therapist will then involve the family in a delayed mourning process, with the recognition that "you can't go home again." This can be done with family as a whole, or it may be more relevant in many cases to break the family into the bio-units, so the child is seen with his biological parent and sibs.

A primary difference in Rem family therapy as compared to treatment of the intact family is the *special use and meaning of history*. While many family therapists approach work with the nuclear family with a deemphasis on history and concentration on the here and now interaction, in the Rem family *history is most vital*. First, it determines cross-generational alliances which are reinforced by blood ties. To try to shift alliances so that they are more appropriate for the family's development is to contend with the bonds and events of the past.

History is also used to create a *ritual* in which the family members are acquainted with or are introduced to each other. This often has not occurred as a pre-Rem process but is vital for the family to be able to appreciate and deal with one another. Ritualizing is done by the therapist eliciting material (with everyone present) about each family member and how he or she developed prior to Rem and by making connections for the family in terms of similarities and differences.

While *exposing myths* is also a part of work with nuclear families, there are some myths that are unique to Rem. Among these are the wicked stepmother, instant love, the perfect mate, the idealized absent parent, the perfect family (Schulman, 1972; Visher, 1978, 1979). Another way to conceptualize "myths" is in terms of the conscious and preconscious "contracts" of the adults and children in Rem, to the extent that these are influenced by social expectations. Part of therapy is to dispel the myths but the therapist must be sufficiently aware of his own attitudes and expectations to carry this out. A renegotiation process takes place in which Rem members begin to form realistic expectations of their family roles and relationships. Sager (1976) has set forth a method of working with these "contracts" that is applicable for child-parent relationships as well as between adults.

A primary therapeutic process deals with helping the Rem family refocus the problem, much as is done with the nuclear family. In other words, this is to help the family redefine the child's problem in terms of the whole. The therapist helps the family *understand the expanded system,* including nonhousehold members, how they affect one another and the child or children. This process facilitates descapegoating the child who has often been blamed for the Rem family troubles.

Peck (1974) points out that it is the Rem family's press for members to be the same and intolerance of variation which promote pseudo-mutuality in the family and precipitate further disruption and crises. The therapist will stress or exaggerate the variety of feelings, attitudes, values, and behavior to illustrate that differences are not only there, but are to be expected and that difference is all right. Paradoxically, stressing difference rather than pushing for harmony can facilitate the growth of Rem in a more genuine way.

ROLE AND PROBLEMS OF THE THERAPIST

Because of the complexity of Rem families, the sense of loss, and the chaos and crisis that are often presented, we have found that therapists are likely to develop both counter-transferential-like reactions and therapeutic burnout, both of which are likely to hinder the treatment process. These reactions on the part of therapists can best be dealt with through heightened awareness of the clinician, through peer consultation, and through cotherapy.

Unrealistic Expectations

Many Rem couples marry with the hope that the new marriage will right all previous disappointments and wrongs and that this time *their* marriage contract and expectations will be fulfilled. Often family members also expect that all their unmet needs will now be fulfilled. These idealistic and unrealistic expectations are enhanced by having the nuclear family or the "Brady Bunch" as a model of Rem. If the therapist buys into these unrealistic expectations, he may become dragged into feelings of hopelessness that so often characterize these Rem families. To accept the fantasy is to get caught up in the disappointment.

Denial. If family members deny their conflicts and disappointments and focus their troubles on the child, the therapist may sense that certain material is forbidden, join the denial, focus on the child and/or encourage pseudo-mutuality. Therapists also tend to collude with families in their denial of history as important or relevant to the present problem. Family members may be ashamed of their pasts, and therapists may make judgments about "two-time losers." Because of the confusion and complexity of dealing therapeutically with noncustodial parents, grandparents, and out-of-household children who are not easily accessible, therapists may collude with the family in denying the relevance of these members of the system and exclude them.

Splitting Parents. We have found that therapists have not been careful enough to help children in Rem families preserve the positive parts of their images of both bioparents. We need to counter the tendency for the custodial parent to be all-good, the noncustodial parent and/or stepparent to be all-bad. This kind of splitting may produce devastating results in a child's sense of himself and of his parents. The therapist may also play out this reaction in sessions, by allying with the child against the "bad" parent or competing with the parent for the child's affection.

Abandonment Fears

Loss and abandonment are prime issues for children and adults in Rem and may trigger the therapist's own abandonment anxieties. Often a child has been abandoned by one parent, and the therapist may be drawn into becoming the good parent to the child, the one who doesn't leave. Children often use abandonment as a threat—"If I can't have my way, I'll go live with Daddy." These threats and fears can affect the therapist to the extent that he becomes anxious and immobilized, thus contributing to more chaos.

Control Issues

As the therapist is faced with the chaos, ambiguity, and disequilibrium of Rem, he may attempt to ally his anxiety by becoming overcontrolling (as harried stepparents do) and by taking impulsive therapeutic steps. He may rush too soon in an overinvolved manner to create order and then push the family out in despair when the chaotic system doesn't right itself quickly. A greater tolerance for ambiguity and chaos is needed.

Cotherapy. Cotherapy is one way to deal with the therapists's nonproductive responses to Rem; it also provides the family with the experience of witnessing cooperative collaboration, as well as decreasing abandonment anxieties. Cotherapy reduces the possibility of triangulation with a child against one of the adults. It allows for multiple transferences where one therapist can act as the absent parent, or a missing member who is important. For the therapist, cotherapy provides much needed nourishment and support and the refueling necessary to deal with the complexity, chaos, and sense of hoplessness of Rem. When cotherapists are not available or possible, a colleague group for the sharing of experiences, successes, and frustrations can serve the therapist in providing support and needed distance from his work.

CASE REPORT: THE THOMAS FAMILY

The initial telephone call came from Karen, age thirty, the stepmother to Kathie, age seven. The presenting complaint from Karen concerned Kathie's behavior when she visited Karen and her natural father, Adam, age thirty-one. The stepmother stated that Kathie monopolized all of Adam's time, that she ignored her and the new baby, Tom, and that she often was angry and hard to control. Kathie lived with her mother, Jane, age thirty, and her visits to father and stepmother were erratic. Since she presented so many difficulties, the visits had been terminated altogether and Kathie saw her father occasionally outside the house. The stepmother stated that Kathie was breaking up her marriage with Adam. (See Figure 13-4).

The therapist set up the initial session to include Kathie, both bioparents, her stepmother and her half-brother Tom who was eleven months old at the time. This was done by having Karen and Adam speak to Jane about coming in. The initial session was tense; Kathie, a cute, precocious seven-year-old sat between her father and mother, with her stepmother, Karen, off to the side holding the baby. Karen complained about Kathie's being greedy and taking too much of her father's time and affection. Kathie complained about not seeing her father more, saying that it was Karen's fault. She felt everything would be okay if she and daddy were alone, because Karen was too strict. Karen was critical of Kathie on this point, and since Adam remained silent, her criticism escalated. Adam finally stated he felt his wife expected too much from Kathie, which was understandable since she had never been around girls Kathie's age before. He was content with the situation, but came to the session only because Karen wanted him to and she was threatening to leave. Jane, Kathie's biomother, felt that Adam should see Kathie more often and talk to her more about her problems. She also stated she had trouble getting Kathie to listen, but understood that Kathie was still very upset about the new baby.

A genogram was drawn and the history was explored more fully with all the family members present.

Background Information

Jane and Adam had been married in 1968. She was an accomplished advertising copy writer; he had dabbled in many jobs, including the arts and in business. In essence, Jane supported the family, while Adam tried to find his way career-wise. Their relationship, which had been fairly good at the beginning of the marriage, began to disintegrate when it became more and more clear that Adam was not able to "find" himself. When Jane became pregnant with Kathie, Adam made himself unavailable to her, and after the child's birth was unable to relate to the baby. Many arguments ensued; finally Jane left when the baby was one year old, feeling that she may as well free herself of Adam who couldn't support her anyway. Thereafter, she had several live-in boyfriends, perhaps hoping to provide a father for Kathie. In her attempt to be a "good mother," she never returned to work. She lived on welfare and child support, and therefore continued to be angry at Adam when he didn't provide financially.

As Kathie grew up, Adam made half-hearted attempts to relate to her but with difficulty since he himself had had meager models for parenting in his experience and was still involved with "finding myself." He often would promise to visit but failed to appear or made the visits with Kathie painfully brief. Still, Jane encouraged him to father Kathie, and would idealize Adam to the girl, no matter what happened in reality.

Two years after the separation, when Kathie was three, Adam began to date Karen who, with her less critical style and ability to support him, was able to encourage him to the point where he set up a fairly successful business of his own. She also related well to his child, which compensated Kathie for her father's lack of parenting skills. The relationship between Kathie and Karen began to wear down when daddy remarried, and became even worse when Karen got pregnant. After the birth of Tom, Kathie's fantasy of her bioparents reuniting ended and she dealt with this by ignoring Karen and the new baby, relating exclusively to her father when she visited. In his turn, Adam became overly indulgent of Kathie and unable to set limits, creating a parenting vacuum. Karen filled this vacuum by gradually fitting into the role of critical stepmother because Adam did not support her more benign efforts, and she became increasingly frustrated and isolated. Karen was also beginning to recognize that Adam's ability to be a father was limited, and she projected her anger at him onto Kathie. In addition, she was fearful that he would be unable to father Tom and hoped she could make him over by demanding he set limits for Kathie. Jane supported Karen in trying to make a better father of Adam but at times was defensive about the extremes of Kathie's behavior. She was glad to be free of Kathie when she visited the Rem household.

Present Situation

Kathie was doing poorly at school with peers, where she was too "bossy." At home with her biomother she was also parentified. Because of her mother's guilt over the divorce, she too was unable to set limits on the girl. Visiting with the Rem family became so bad, with so much conflict between Kathie and Karen, that the visits to the home had been stopped altogether and Adam was limited to seeing Kathie alone outside his home or at Jane's house. Even the exclusion of Kathie, however, had not solved the problem: Karen now felt the marriage was so shaky because of the girl, that she was considering taking Tom and leaving.

Goal Setting

After several evaluatory sessions and after the therapist's customary consultation with her colleagues, overall goals were established to enhance the quality of parenting of Kathie by the bioparents *and* her stepmother; to reconstruct a "holding environment" for Kathie, where she would be allowed to be a child again; to help the remarried couple reconstruct their relationship; and to help Jane move on individually in her work and love relationships.

Therapeutic Approaches

The therapy was set up so that the three adults would meet in relation to parenting concerns without Kathie present. Such issues as visitation, limit setting, providing structure, need for consistency, appropriate ways of sharing affection were addressed. This ultimately led to a re-entry of Kathie into the Rem home for visits, a process which took several months to achieve with other therapeutic work going on concurrently.

Karen and Adam were also seen for marital sessions (over five months' time) in which their expectations of each other were explicated through the use of couple contracts. It became very clear that what they wanted from each other was unrealistic: he wanted a wife to make amends for all the lacks of his former wife and his mother in their not always being there for him. Karen wanted Adam to be a perfect parent to their child, a very attentive, involved father to Tom and to herself also, in some way compensating for the actual desertion of her father. Once the couple became focused on each other, they released Kathie from being the scapegoat between them. Adam was helped to be more appropriately involved with Kathie: to set limits and to be reliable to the extent that he was able.

Kathie and her mother were also seen conjointly concerning the quality of their relationship. Out of her own guilt in depriving the girl of her father, Jane too was unable to set limits with Kathie, who was thereby able to run the household. She had also continued to try to make Adam the father for Kathie that she wanted, and protected Adam's image to Kathie. In several mourning sessions, both Kathie and Jane had to let go of that image and deal with the kind of limited parenting Adam could provide. In addition, Kathie was seen alone, as was her mother, where both had a chance to deal with their individual issues; Kathie with her dysfunctional peer relationships and Jane with her failure to return to work as a way to be around for Kathie, and her consequent financial dependence on Adam. The sessions with Kathie and Jane extended for a year's time, after Karen and Adam had improved their marriage and after the immediate Rem issues had been resolved. The overall goals were achieved: Kathie was less parentified in both houses, and her behavior settled in. She was able to relate appropriately to Karen and Tom, and then to another new baby who arrived after treatment ended. Her relationship with her biomother improved, as Jane became less guilt motivated and more of a parent to her. Jane also returned to work for the first time since Kathie's birth. Kathie had more success with her peers and her schoolwork improved somewhat. Preventive work was done with Tom in the sense that some of the parenting work with the Rem couple involved issues on how to raise him as well.

SUMMARY AND CONCLUSIONS

For children in Rem, the multiplicity of relationships, personalities, values and lifestyles can be extremely enriching. A child experiences a combination of home lives that he would never have been exposed to in our contemporary way of living where families move frequently, are cut off or at a distance from their extended families, have less children per family, and where both parents work and are just not at hand to form the kind of community ties which create a supportive network for the child. The result is often the nuclear or single-parent family in isolation. With remarriage, this system is opened up, with new family members added in the form of instant parents, siblings, and grandparents.

Increasing public awareness of the incidence of remarriage, and knowledge that the adjustment to Rem is difficult for all concerned, even under the best psychological and material circumstances, is reflected in the fact that parents now focus in on problems earlier, with some parents seeking preventive help before remarriage in the form of educational groups at community resource centers, health-oriented rap groups at clinics, and from self-help sources. In our clinical work with Rem, where more often than not the referral of a child and his family comes when problems are at a crisis level, we emphasize including all the involved family members in our therapy, so that the impact on the child's development will be meaningful and of long duration. With our systems approach, we find that to exclude noncustodial parents or ex-spouses and stepparents will usually mean that the therapeutic work will be short-circuited in some way. We take into account the stages preceding Rem and the current impact of "ghosts" of the past. We rely heavily on the therapist having solid family therapy skills as well as his knowledge of the special issues and problems of remarriage which affect the family before him. We also emphasize the therapist's personal qualities of awareness of himself, his attitudes, values, personal relationships, and emotional reactions which come into play in his work with Rem.

We recommend cotherapy with regular staff meetings at the best, or colleague consultation and/or supervision at the least, as ways to circumvent both depression, burn-out or unproductive counter-transferential-like reactions which therapists commonly experience when treating Rem. Optimally, the therapist should have a colleagual support group composed of other therapists treating Rem families with whom he gets personal and professional feedback, and where therapeutic problems are discussed and approaches are developed further. We favor opening up the therapist's work for scrutiny by his colleagues through the use of video-tape, one-way mirror, and in-person peer consultation. Our approach emphasizes flexibility, as we see our skills with Rem develop and change with an increased understanding of this complex family form.

REFERENCES

1. Bernard, J. *Remarriage: A Study of Marriage.* 2nd Ed. New York: Russell and Russell (1971).
2. Dicks, Henry V. *Marital Tensions,* New York: Basic Books (1967).
3. Duberman, L. Step-kin relationships. *Journal of Marriage and the Family.* 35(2):283–92 (1973).
4. Gardner, R. *Psychotherapy with Children of Divorce.* New York: Jason Aronson (1976).
5. Guerin, P. Evaluation of family system and genogram. In: *Family Therapy.* Guerin, P. (Ed.) New York: Gardner Press, 450–64 (1976).

6. McGregor, R. et al. *Multiple Impact Therapy with Families.* New York: McGraw Hill (1964).
7. Messinger, L. Remarriage between divorced people with children from previous marriages. *Journal of Marriage and Family Counseling.* 2(2):193–200 (1976).
8. Peck, B. The divorce remarriage family in psychotherapy. *A Family Therapy Notebook.* New York: Libra Publishers, pp 217–42 (1974).
9. Ransom, J. et al. A stepfamily in formation. *American Journal of Orthopsychiatry.* 49(1):36–43 (1979).
10. Sager, Clifford J. *Couple Contracts and Marital Therapy.* Brunner/Mazel, New York (1976).
11. Sandler, J. The background of safety. *International Journal of Psychoanalysis.* 41:352–356 (1960).
12. Schulman, G. Myths that intrude on the adaptation of the stepfamily. *Social Casework.* 53:131–39 (1972).
13. Tessman, L. *Children of Parting Parents,* New York: Jason Aronson (1977).
14. Visher, J. and E. Common problems of stepparents and their spouses. *American Journal of Orthopsychiatry* 2:252–62 (1978).
15. Visher, J. and E. *Stepfamilies.* Brunner/Mazel, New York (1979).
16. Winnicott, D. *The Maturational Process and the Facilitating Environment.* New York: International Universities Press (1965).

This chapter describes a family systems approach to the understanding of some of the speical characteristics of families of remarriage. Assessment and intervention strategies are discussed around setting the initial contract, clarifying the structural complexity and points of vulnerability of the step-family unit. Treatment strategy is looked at with particular attention to the patterns of the myth of the absent parent, the isolation of the stepparent, exclusion of the parental child and the scapegoating of the noncustodial parent.

318

14

A Family Systems Approach
With Families of Remarriage

Mary F. Whiteside, Ph. D.

As the number of couples deciding to separate and to divorce continues to increase, there is a corresponding increase in the number of remarriages, most of which involve children from previous marriages. Creative integration of these blended families is becoming one of the demanding challenges for family networks in United States communities. Both the popular literature[1,2,9,10,16] and the mental health literature[3,6,7,12,13] emphasize the structural, emotional, economic, and legal complexity of the stepfamily unit.* Out of this special complexity arise stresses which potentially can have significant impact on each family member. All are agreed that despite the overriding importance of a new loving relationship for the couple and the children, the task of constructing a workable remarried family is one which stretches the capabilities of even the most flexible, energetic, and highly motivated families. Because of the complexity and ambiguity of the roles and tasks in the stepfamily unit, family or group oriented modes of intervention are becoming acknowledged as extremely useful. They are used both as a mode of primary prevention in the form of seminars for couples planning a remarriage,[6,7] and also as a mode of intervention when

*See Walker, et al.[14] for an annotated bibliography of the remarriage literature through April 1978.

problems in the family seem so overwhelming that the family seeks professional help.[5,8,11,15,17] These problems may surface in the marriage, in relation to a child, or in relation to an individual adult.

Group-oriented modes of support are particularly useful because each family member is faced with forging new roles, models for which are not popularly available in wider society. Meeting with other couples struggling with similar experiences reduces the degree of anxiety, counters the tendency to feel that problems are internal ones, and opens new avenues for creative solutions. Family oriented modes of intervention make sense because it is not only the couple which is involved in the structural dilemmas of these families, but also the children from all marriages. Whatever mode of therapeutic or preventive intervention is chosen, a familiarity with some of the predictable patterns and dilemmas inherent in the remarried family structure is useful. On this basis, one can plan initial therapeutic contracts in such a way as to reduce anxiety, to avoid unintentionally reinforcing destructive defensive splits, and to aid in the clarification of problem areas, separating crisis-related conflicts from more chronically unresolved difficulties. This chapter will present the author's current stance in dealing clinically with families of remarriage. This position draws on the conceptual framework of family systems theory, on clinical work with families going through the process of marital difficulty, separation, divorce, and remarriage, and on a review of the remarriage literature.

INITIAL CONTACT

There are two basic clinical tasks which are critical in accurately assessing the nature of the presenting difficulties within the remarried family and in determining the appropriate form of intervention. The first is outlining and clarifying with the family the complexity of the remarried family structure and the ambiguity of the roles within this structure. The second is confronting the need to deal with the legacy of the past in order to weave securely the fabric of the family's future.

The initial contact with the clinician will be, of course, with only a part of the family of remarriage. Concern may be presented, for example, by a stepparent, harassed and complaining about a stepchild, or by a biological parent whose adolescent has suddenly started running away or has become defiant and depressed at home. The natural parent in this case may feel as if the child's responsibility is all on his or her shoulders and feels unsupported by the stepparent. Alternatively, one may have the marital couple calling wanting to understand the difficulties they are having with one another before they find themselves in another divorce. Usually the feelings are intense and the family is on the verge of taking precipitous action. They are pessimistic about available support from any quarter. They feel overwhelmed and harassed. Despite the family's feeling of urgency and their fear that they cannot work together about this problem, it is essential for the therapist to arrange on the first contact a meeting which places the therapeutic weight on the side of integration of the new family rather than one which supports already difficult splits within the family. One strategy is to support the parental unit in carrying out its responsibilities at the same time as keeping the door open to all other members of the family. For example, one may be talking with a mother who is very concerned about her own daughter and who says that the stepfather is not involved. If the first interview is set up with just mother and daughter, the therapist has increased the degree of the stepfather's noninvolvement. On the other hand, if the interview is set up for the mother and stepfather or for all the members of the family in the household, the therapist has challenged the dysfunctional arrangement and made it possible to see some more supportive alternatives. Inclusion of all the members of the remarried family group in the immediate unit—that is, wife, wife's children, husband, husband's children, and the children of the new marriage—has the immediate effect of strengthening the boundary around the remarried family and putting the therapeutic weight on the side of an integration which includes everyone. It is a message that all the members are part of the family in spite of their different histories and their different statuses. It also carries the expectation that everyone will be involved in coming up with solutions to the difficulties being faced.

As always, however, this initial period consists of a process of mutual negotiation between the therapist with his or her preference and values for the family, and the family's sense of what can be managed and what they want to change. The timing and sequence of meetings with various family members can vary widely. The therapist can expect that any path to be followed has the potential for being highly anxiety provoking for various members. Each marriage has a different pattern of strength and resiliency. For some remarried couples being seen alone together poses an expectation of commitment and intimacy which is very frightening. In these cases a focus on the children is a necessary first step. For others, the stepparenting is a task which cannot be attempted without the initial consolidation of the spouse relationship.

For example, one family came to the clinic after two years of marriage, distressed at the level to which their anger toward one another had risen. The couple came with very separate financial lives and very few positive alliances between the woman and her stepchildren or the man and his stepchildren. In addition, there was an active continuing ill-will towards the woman's first husband. Both were very independent persons, highly successful in their respective careers. They were active, energetic, and well informed. Although their presenting complaints included the whole range of family interactions, they were only willing to explore together, in a relatively protected environment, their potential for becoming more of a team. The idea of confronting the distance between them and the adolescents and risking anything with the ex-husband felt too explosive to them. The most helpful stance in this case was to broaden the base to include other family members very gradually, based on the couple's feeling of positive achievement. Initial expectations for change needed to be kept very small.

As a contrast, however, was another couple who came in on the verge of separation after six years of marriage. There again was distance between stepfather and son, and a certain degree of separate financial status. In addition, their longstanding marital distance had been exacerbated by the husband's job difficulties. In this case, the couple agreed to focus as a first priority on adjusting the relationship with the boy. The mother was able to step aside, allowing the stepfather to follow through some of his disciplinary decisions with the boy. She was able to listen to the criticisms of her which the boy was able to voice once he got his stepfather's support and had gained some sense that a divorce would not be over him. After just a few sessions, they were able to say clearly that more talk about the boy seemed to be an avoidance for them. They felt comfortable at that point tackling the more serious rifts in their own relationship. This initial period for them served the purpose of testing out the possibility of change on a subject one step removed, giving them some confidence to move further. It also established a family structure shift which was necessary to support the boy's movement into adolescence.

COMPLEXITY OF THE REMARRIED FAMILY STRUCTURE

After listening to the presenting story of the immediate source of pain and sense of crisis, one finds it then useful to obtain an assessment of the presenting situation in terms of all the actors in the drama. Sketching out a picture of the whole family—that is, the stepfamily, the ex-spouses and their families, and the grandparents involved—not only clarifies the family situation for the therapist but also becomes a supportive and clarifying move for the family. The general purpose is to concretize the complexity of such family arrangements and to obtain a clearer picture of the sources of support, the sources of stress, the strengths and the vulnerable points in the family structure. A useful device is to construct a family diagram, using genogram notation.[4] Asking about all family members in order to have a complete diagram allows the therapist to ask about sensitive areas in a relatively neutral way. This uncovers the persons who are rarely mentioned in the current family and obtains a brief overview of the history and current circumstances. This is an excellent way of pointing out an otherwise overlooked current development which is producing tension in the family system and affecting the presenting symptom. One common example would be remarriage of an ex-spouse. Everyone may be reacting to the resultant shift in family structure, but unaware of its relationship to their current stress. Having all members included on the diagram also presents a point of view which says that all the family members, despite separations and divorces, continue to be part of an extended family of a special sort. Separation does not end family relationships. It is a critical event in an ongoing process of change. In addition, one is proceeding with the basic therapeutic task of helping the family clarify and negotiate the nature of all the relationships in the family structure. An implicit goal is to integrate the history in such a way that members are not forced to deny what was meaningful to them. New members can be included in a way that does not rupture previous important relationships. Obviously there is no "correct" structure for a remarried family. Each family has the creative task of coming up with their own version of a satisfying and acceptable network.

The following is an example of a typical remarried family structure. Mr. and Mrs. Brown came to the clinic very concerned over Mr. B's son George, ten years old. Mr. and Mrs. B. had been married for five years, but George had just joined them the past summer. Before this George had lived with his mother and eight-year-old sister, Sonja, in a city about four hours away. They had agreed to take George to live with them when his mother felt she could no longer handle his fights, defiance, and school problems. These difficulties had continued in the new school, and Mrs. Brown, in particular, was beginning to feel desperate and very resentful at the new situation. Also living in the household were Tricia Merchant, age eleven, Mrs. B.'s daughter from her first marriage, and Heather Brown, age three, Mr. and Mrs. B.'s daughter. Tricia had adjusted well to the remarriage, and continued to visit her father, Mr. Merchant, every other weekend. Mr. Merchant also had remarried, and had a new baby from that marriage. Since George had arrived, however, Tricia had seemed more withdrawn. In addition, she and George were constantly bickering. Heather was a charming preschooler, the center of attention, adored by all members from both families. As they talked, the therapist sketched out the following diagram (Figure 14–1):

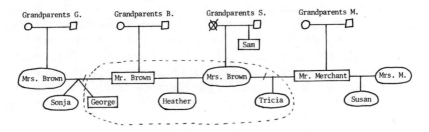

Figure 14–1. Geneological relationship of the Brown family.

She noted the strain of a continuing battle between Mr. B. and his first wife. In addition, she noted the separation of George and his natural sister, and the increased distance between Mr. B. and Sonja. On the other hand, there was a continuing positive tie between George, Sonja, and both sets of grandparents. Mrs. B. and Mr. Merchant had negotiated a cooperative ongoing coparenting relationship—a strong support for Tricia and a potential model for Mr. B. and his first wife. Adding to the current overload on Mrs. B., however, was the recent death of her mother and her feeling of responsibility for her brother Sam, who had just lost his job because of drinking problems. Heather clearly had a role of tying everyone together, a familiar stance for the "ours" child. Her presence did much to add an air of optimism, and to emphasize the loving support between Mr. and Mrs. B.

As one looks at even such a simple diagram, however, a number of the complications of living in a remarried family become evident. The many different people, connections among families, varied relationships within the same household are bewildering. For example, among the twenty-two potential dyads in this family, there are at least seven relationships which have no word for them in the English language. George had accompanied Tricia on a visit to the Merchants and was quite taken with the new baby. He struggled to find words to describe to the therapist the visit to the daughter of his father's wife's first husband.

The family's words for their relationships sometimes can be informative. The therapist's use of the word "stepparent" frequently evokes a strong reaction with an association to the myth of the evil stepmother. This reaction also can indicate a denial of the ambiguity of the role. A stepmother, complaining about a child's lack of respect, may also say, "I'm not a stepparent, I'm just a friend." On the other hand, a stepmother may believe she can do the impossible, saying, "The word stepparent makes me so uncomfortable. I've tried so hard to be a mother to them." Other families have words such as "extra parent" or "second mom" which acknowledge both the parental parts of the role and the shared responsibilities with a biological parent. One father discussed the differences for him among "biological parent," "substitute parent" (similar to a "substitute teacher"), and "real parent." For him it reflected the serious consideration most stepparents give to their very difficult role.

Not only are the relationships complex, but they have also changed recently. From being the oldest child in a three-person family unit, George has become a middle child in a five-person unit, with a stepsister and a half-sister. His closest natural sibling lives four hours away. The confusion and the cognitive complexity are important to remember, particularly from the child's point of view. The child's job in the new family is to construct a version of an extended family which meets his or her current developmental needs. Each child will do this in a way which reflects both his or her developmental level and also the nature of support and clarification received from the various adults involved. The appropriate degree of closeness and/or distance from various members will change as the child's needs change.

VULNERABILITY OF THE STEPFAMILY STRUCTURE

The goal of an adaptive, satisfying integration of this extended family unit is idealistic, outrageous, and realizable. It is implicit in the remarriage contract. However, this hope has to be seen in the context of potential vulnerabilities of the stepfamily structure. These vulnerabilities come in the areas of permeable external boundaries for the family, internal structural ambiguities and contradictions, a legacy of past hurt and bitterness which leaves a low fund of optisism, lack of extended family support, and lack of social network support.

External Boundaries

As discussed by Visher and Visher[12] and by Walker and Messinger,[13] the definition of membership in the stepfamily unit is ambiguous on legal, biological, psychological, and physical grounds. There are frequently differences of opinion within the same family as to who "really" belongs in the family. The family is not bounded by living quarters since in some families membership varies depending upon the day of the week and season of the year. Legal definitions are equally confusing. In many states the noncustodial parent continues to have legal responsibilities for the child, while the stepparent—living with the child a majority of the time—has none.[12] In the Brown family, only Heather was clear about where her primary home base was, and even she became confused when her "sister" Sonja came for a visit and then left.

Internal Structure

The psychological structure of the stepfamily system is equally ambiguous. Role relationships and responsibilities are overlapping and contradictory. Mrs. Brown continually struggled with the delicate balance of being ex-wife and coparent with Mr. Merchant. She had struggled hard to maintain appropriate emotional distance, while remaining cooperative in deciding what Tricia needed. Mr. Brown felt comfortable firmly enforcing with George the rules he and his wife determined were appropriate for preadolescents. However, although Tricia was very close to George in age, and was involved in many similar misbehaviors, Mr. Brown doubted whether his authority was legitimate or helpful to her. She was quite open about her preference for her natural father and her wish to return to the more peaceful times before the remarriage. She kept to herself her gradually increasing respect for her stepfather. Since George had arrived, however, Mrs. Brown had come to realize in a new way what her husband meant as he worried over what a stepparent should be. Still they both were continually feeling guilty over their awareness that they did not love their stepchildren, and frustrated that what had been successful with their biological children seemed always to fail with the stepchildren.

Low Fund of Optimism

As described by Peck,[8] remarried couples may not think of their attachment as a support for growth or nurturance. They feel they have risked a good deal in the past, and have been badly hurt, "used," "raked over the coals," every vulnerability exposed. They approach one another carefully, maintaining the lease on the bachelor apartment, keeping separate checking accounts. They reserve long-term commitment, protect emotional distance and independence. Positive emotions can feel as dangerous as negative ones. Any familiar criticism or argument carries with it not only the discomfort of present anger and difference, but brings up memories of a host of terribly difficult past events. There is not the same feeling of "we've been together for fifteen years—that has to be worth something," or "we've weathered past crises" that one sees with first married couples who may describe similar interactional difficulties. Moreover, there is not the same degree of trust or optimism one often sees in the early stages of first marriages. On the other hand, these couples have a good deal of experience with marriage and parenting and are aware of the potential pitfalls. There is a useful pragmatism which helps temper illusions of idyllic romance. In addition, the growth each partner has made through the period of separation often begins the marriage on a basis of a strong partnership, rather than on the basis of rigid dependence which many of them experienced in first marriages.

Extended Family Support

Frequently grandparents on both sides remain supportive and concerned throughout the divorce period and period of one-parent family. Although occasionally awkward, ex-in-laws frequently maintain their positive feelings and ties with both the children and the ex-spouse. However, ties with new stepgrandchildren, nieces, and nephews are more distant. On the other hand, in some families there may be history of divorce or severe marital stress in both the grandparent and the sibling families. The extended family members are then involved in their own problems, and may be relying on the client family for support. The added demands of extended family can make it even more difficult to clarify boundaries, priorities, and distribution of limited energy. In addition, there may be no family view of a successful, satisfying marital relationship, other than an idealized, unrealistic one. This leaves the couple easily vulnerable to feelings of failure and hopelessness.

Social Network

Finally, there may not be a strong, supportive social network available to the family. Many authors[2,9,12] cite the protectiveness of family members and their reticence to define themselves as a stepfamily. There remain in this country social stigma against divorce and a social awkwardness in many everyday situations encountered. For example, whom does the school call when the child is sick or hurt? Who gets invited to school conferences? Are former friends now divided into "his" or "hers"? In addition, there are now only the beginnings of a step-family network. Organizations such as Stepfamily Foundation[9,12] are just beginning to develop. But, as one stepmother said, "We're so busy dealing with what goes on at home, there isn't any time to make the contacts with other families."

In sum, an early therapeutic task is to establish the fact that the family is operating from a chronic baseline of overload and that they have a special family structure. Not only do they have to deal with the developmental tasks and everyday occurrences that a nuclear family has, but they have to do this in an extremely complex family situation which has its own family developmental tasks. The process of introducing the therapist to the extended family is one of general clarification, assessment, and anxiety reduction. Hopefully, this takes the initial edge off the feeling of crisis and slows down the urge to action. The clarification of areas of vulnerability and conflict refocuses their anxiety to an area where the family can more productively decide what changes they wish to make.

THERAPEUTIC STRATEGY

The clinical picture of stepfamily characteristics, of course, covers the same diagnostic range as that of any group of families. Technical interventions are adjusted accordingly. However, there are certain issues which can be kept in mind in regard to the therapeutic work. One important dimension is that for stepfamilies which seek clinical help, progress, paradoxically, can be particularly frightening. As the therapeutic work gets underway—clarifying boundaries, focusing issues, blocking displacement of conflict, and the like—the family reacts with an upsurge of anxiety. As Peck[8] puts it, "It is unavoidable that as the (divorced-remarried) family becomes more family-like, the more frightened everyone becomes" (p. 227). The couple is faced with the challenge of change in their relationship—a challenge which was met in the previous marriage with the decision that it would be more productive to separate than to change together. In addition, if the remarried couple can successfully make changes and resolve troublesome areas, it inevitably brings up the thought that the first marriage could have been saved after all. This thought threatens the carefully put together historical explanation and justification for the marriage breakup. For the children, despite the obvious advantages to them of an effectively functioning stepfamily, clear commitment between the remarried couple may also mean that all reunion fantasies must be given up. The loss of the old family is reexperienced. In addition, as the remarried couple becomes more comfortable at expressing their negative feelings toward one another, the children become very worried. An increase in tension between the spouses is reacted to with lightening speed by various anxious and disruptive behaviors from the children. It is useful here for the parents to be clear with the children about several points. They can be honest about thoughts of divorce. They can clarify that the problematic sources of disagreement belong to the spouses' difficulties, not to the children's actions. They are, of course, concerned about the children's actions and feelings, but one major task is for the adults to get together to deal with them. The child has not been the cause of either past divorces nor future ones. In addition, they can affirm their commitment to working together toward change. Children usually are greatly freed by their parents and stepparents assuming this responsibility. They continue testing them, but can proceed with their own work at clarifying their version of the family, establishing comfortable relationships, and proceeding with developmental tasks.

On the therapist's side it is useful to proceed with delicate care and to expect a high dropout rate. In addition, as described in Peck,[8] taking a very pessimistic rather than idealistic view can force the family into resisting the therapist by disproving his or her negativism. This only can be done by making progress.

Frequently Encountered Stepfamily Problematic Issues

Although each family presents its unique circumstances, adaptations, and difficulties, there are several commonly encountered constellations which can be expected. A few will be described here. Other excellent clincial examples are given by Goldstein,[3] Kaplan,[5] Peck,[8] Satir,[11] and Visher and Visher.[12]

The Myth of the Absent Parent. As the family discusses members living outside the household, one frequently hears the statement, "This person is out of the picture. He has not been seen or heard from in six or seven years." The assumption which follows from this is that because a person has not been physically available he, is not important or influential in understanding the current difficulties. There have been many examples in the author's clinical practice in which this has been dramatically proved not to be the case. Whatever the current availability of the noncustodial parent, he or she is irrevocably a part of the family history. For this reason he or she is at all times a highly salient person for the child in the family.

In addition, persons thought to be out of the picture frequently reappear on the scene. The absent person quite often is the father of the child, ex-husband of the wife. When one has such a father in treatment, it is clear that although many years have passed since he last saw his child, that child is still very much alive in his mind and affects his involvement both with his stepchildren and also with any further natural children. Although the lack of contact is usually maintained in order to protect the child and the child's new family, as well as to protect the father in his feelings of guilt and anger, the protection can backfire in the cost it takes on the father's current capacity for intimacy. Despite long years of separation, family members at different times make the decision to become reacquainted with one another and may appear "out of nowhere" and demand to be acknowledged.

Blended families have added to the basic mother-father-child triangles of the nuclear family a host of important new possibilities. There is wife-first husband-second husband, mother-stepmother-child, father-child-stepchild, mother-first husband-child, and so on. All the adults in the family are important both as potential models for identification and also as models for male-female relationships. This can serve as a useful range of choices for the child. The situation may simply multiply the possibilities for problematic triangulation. Issues of unresolved triangulation may be influential without the physical presence of all the members. The custodial parent, for example, may wish to minimize the importance of the ex-spouse. This person will state that mention of the past marriage or of attempts to deal with the ex-spouse currently only lead to increased upset and increased difficulty. This contradicts the child's need to continue a positive, open relationship with the parent outside of the home. Thus a history given from the custodial parent's point of view may strive to minimize the influence of the ex-spouse while the same history from the child's point of view serves to expand the child's available interpersonal options. In addition, open discussion of all the parents makes the child more comfortable and less likely to be overwhelmed by loyalty conflicts.

The parent outside of the home at one time obviously had an important complementary relationship with the custodial parent. This becomes particularly salient when children reach adolescence and begin to struggle with their own models of identity and interpersonal relationships with persons of the opposite sex. For example, one family came in over problems with a teenage daughter. There were struggles over what she did with peers. They had arguments about wild parties. Yet there was a lot of pressure on the girl for frequent dating relationships. Her mother was determinedly casual and unpretentious about her dress. The girl spent many hours with her hair, make-up and had shoplifted attractive clothes. The family unit had been a remarried one for many years and functioned as a stable family unit. However, as the dimensions of the issue were explored, one important element which emerged was the contrast between the two fathers in this girl's life. On one side she had the stern stepfather with closely cropped hair, lumberjacket informality, and intense moralism. On the other side, she had her handsome, well-dressed, yet irresponsible, natural father. In some ways they were polar opposites, each struggling with control issues and coming to different solutions. It was no surprise that control issues again became central as the girl moved into adolescence. In addition it became strikingly clear that the mother had also been very different with the two men. With her first husband she also had spent hours trying to please him by dressing in the latest fashion—behavior very similar to that which she was fighting so hard with her daughter.

Isolation of the Stepparent. A frequently cited stepfamily pattern is one in which there is a tight coalition between the biological parent and child, pushing the stepparent out to an isolated position. This pattern may be reflected in complaints by the mother that the marriage is breaking up because the spouse is so uninvolved, statements by the stepfather that he is continually being rejected, in control battles between child and natural parent, with the stepparent being seen as punitive or uninvolved, or battles between stepparent and child. Although the situation may be described in such a way that one person is identified as the problem, it can easily be seen that there are good reasons for each member to maintain his or her position.

Let us take, for example, a situation in which the biological mother and her son have come from a first marriage in which there had been many years of heated conflict, including physical abuse. Both the mother and the stepfather want to make up to the boy for those traumatic first years. The mother feels he must be continually reassured of her love. The stepfather would like to show him what effective, firm, and affectionate discipline can be, but immediately bumps up against a wall of protection. The mother feels she is protecting the boy from the additional hurt of exposure to an "unloving" stepparent. She moves into a role of comforter, nurturer, the parent who understands the boy. Both the stepfather and the biological father find themselves fitting into roles as punitive, angry, ungiving, critical parents. This pattern protects the mother from her own feelings of guilt and depression. She does not have to feel inadequate as a mother or angry at her son for being so difficult. The mother and son maintain the reassurance that they, at least, will always stick together, support one another, will not leave. When the spouses have withdrawn from the struggles of coparenting, they effectively avoid facing an important arena of difference between them. They maintain the myth that she is an ideal mother, despite the stepfather's opinion that she is not giving her son the space and clear limits he needs. The stepfather, in turn, is protected from the vulnerability of failure and rejection as a stepfather—if he does not try, how can he fail? But he is also protected from feelings of guilt and loss in relation to his natural children which may be stimulated by a positive contact with his stepson—what effective father would leave his own children? The boy remains with a heady sense of power and a tight grasp on his mother. He commands access to her and inhibits the flowering of the new marriage.

The drawbacks of the pattern come from the fact that it is based upon the presumption of fragility, vulnerability, and need for protection of each member. Despite their illusion of togetherness, the spouses argue and feel dissatisfied. In their attempts to prevent distance, they draw the child between them and end up farther apart. By protecting each other from feelings of failure and disappointment, by avoiding criticism, they also cannot use each other to stimulate satisfying change. Both parents feel they have failed because the family is not progressing as hoped. The boy is burdened by the protection and responsibility for the adults. He does not feel good about himself and is handicapped in making his needed progress in school and in moving out of the family towards involvement with friends and other neutral adults.

To modify this pattern, each member needs to give up some measure of security. In order for the mother to feel supported by the stepfather in her relationship with her son, she must modify her stance to incorporate some of his perceptions. The stepfather can gradually increase his disciplinary power on the basis of times of positive exchange, but only if the mother can hold herself back, allowing the two to work out their own differences. The mother needs to give up some of the special closeness with the boy, transferring the needs to her husband. At the same time the stepfather needs to recognize the boy's fear of abandonment and downplay his jealous, competitive feelings. The child needs to give up his hope of reuniting his biological parents, accepting a family which has three parents for him. He must give up the importance of being mother's protector, tolerating the new marital closeness, but receiving back the advantages of his stepfather's support, and the security that he can be critical without fearing exclusion from the family.

Exclusion of a Parental Child. In this constellation the family comes in with difficulties centering around a child, and very quickly brings up the imminent exclusion of one of the older children. The parents' feeling is that "we can no longer handle her. If she stays here any longer, she is going to destroy our marriage."

The Harris family came in with a group of five children—Mr. Harris' children: Amy age fourteen, Chris age twelve, and Jon age eight, and Mrs. Harris' children: Susan age ten, and Steve age eight. Jon was having particular problems in school, not paying attention, easily frustrated, getting into fights at the slightest provocation. The other younger children had all reacted to the new situation with various signs of tension and discomfort, but seemed to be settling down and feeling more comfortable. The parents were quite concerned about Jon's difficulties: he was always seen as more vulnerable, he had been very young when his mother had left, and had always been sensitive to the family emotions. He had quickly become attached to Mrs. H. Mrs. Harris, in addition, had a good relationship with the school social worker and saw her as being very helpful with Jon. His classroom teacher also had been responsive to suggestions about restructuring his work and giving special attention. What quickly emerged in the interview was a great deal of anger and bewilderment about Amy's latest behavior. They felt that they could handle Jon's problems, if only Amy wouldn't be so difficult. She was driving both of them to distraction. Before the marriage she had taken a great deal of responsibility in helping her father run the house and care for the younger children. Mr. Harris felt very proud of and close to her, although he worried that the extra responsibilities were making her miss out on many of the activities her friends were involved in. One of the very attractive qualities he had found in his new wife was her warmth and dedication not only to her own children, but also her commitment to his children. Amy had seemed to like her during the courtship period but in the past year it seemed the two of them hardly exchanged civil words. Mrs. Harris was finding her energy very taxed trying to maintain a smooth household for seven people. She felt Amy was constantly interfering with what she tried to do. Amy refused to eat the special meals she cooked, had been unreliable when babysitting for Jon and

Steve, and would not speak to her when she walked in the house. Mr. and Mrs. Harris had thought she would be pleased and relieved to have more time with her friends and to be freed of responsibilities. They could not understand her resentment and anger.

Amy had recently re-established contact with her mother, who had moved into an apartment in a nearby town. Mr. Harris felt that Amy was becoming more and more like her mother. Sometimes he found himself thinking, "Maybe those two deserve each other." On the other hand, he worried that the problems with Amy would be used by his ex-wife to reopen custody negotiations. He was sure that although she had recently established a somewhat more stable life than before, she would not be able to provide adequate mothering for the three children. Amy was feeling that there was nowhere she belonged. There were strong mixed feelings for her whether she was at her father's home or her mother's. She felt no one really wanted her and that somehow all this mess was her fault.

In the most recent emotional scene among Amy and Mr. and Mrs. Harris, Amy had threatened to run away and stay with her mother; Mrs. Harris out of desperation had shouted, "Why don't you just do that!" Amy had stormed out of the house, spending the night at a friend's, and Mr. and Mrs. Harris had spent the rest of the evening in the worst argument of their marriage. Mrs. Harris felt as if all her efforts were wasted, there was no way for her to reach Amy, she was ready to give up. Mr. Harris felt he had misjudged his wife, perhaps she wasn't going to be such a good mother after all, he felt that Amy was being damaged by the constant friction; he wondered if, in fact, the only way to preserve the marriage and help Amy, might be to send her to her mother's to live.

Two important tasks were brought out in the work with the family which enabled them to restructure the family situation in a manner which allowed Amy to find a livable space where she had some feeling of belonging and being important, which moved her out of the middle among the adults involved, concentrating their energy on helping Jon, and on forging their marital alliance.

The family began to realize that they had been expecting a quick and easy transition between two very different family structures. In the one-parent family, Amy's role had been essential and adaptive. However, there had been no allowance in the new family for the acknowledgment of the special responsibilities and authority she had had. Mr. and Mrs. Harris' agreement had been that Mrs. Harris would assume full parental responsibility for all the children, Amy had not been considered in this agreement, and had not been a part of planning on a more adult level for the transition. They began a more open negotiation of responsibilities: listening to Amy's observations and opinions about Jon's difficulties, not expecting her to babysit for her stepsiblings; Mrs. Harris set aside time to plan certain meals with Amy, in which Amy took responsibility for menus and Mrs. Harris supported her; and they planned activities in which Mr. Harris spent time just with his children and Mrs. Harris with hers.

Scapegoating of the Noncustodial Parent. A second important shift was to move the first Mrs. H. out of the position of a convenient external scapegoat. Since the time when she had left Mr. H. and the children, she had been viewed as a fragile, disturbed, neglecting, and rejecting mother. The second Mrs. H. was seen as just the opposite—a dichotomy which gave too rigid roles to both women. It allowed no room for the children to express their warmth and longings for their mother; their stepmother had no room for feelings of anger, inadequacy, or failure without evoking the corollary that she would leave. It was a convenient myth for the new couple to maintain. It allowed them to blame all his children's difficulties on his first wife's neglect. This protected Mr. H. from his own feelings of guilt and anger toward the children, and kept the couple from facing their own disagreements over parenting. Because of this constellation, Mrs. Harris was in the seemingly illogical position of supporting the intense, continuing contact between Mr. H. and his first wife. Their mixed feelings of bitterness and excited attraction toward one another made it a relationship the second Mrs. H. felt she had to compete with, but which also helped her maintain distance from her new husband. The first Mrs. H. also profited from the role, since her battles with Mr. H. protected her from the intense loneliness she found so intolerable, as well as maintained the image of a woman who would fight for her children.

Amy's provocations, however, provided an opportunity for all three adults to begin to disengage from the protective, but stagnating, triangle. Mr. H. was able to use his new wife's more dispassionate observations to see that his first wife was not so fragile as he feared, and that she had qualities which Army needed to see. With Mrs. Harris' support, he began to reconsider painfully the possibility of Amy's rekindling a strong positive tie with her mother. They set up regular times when Amy would stay with her mother on weekends, braced themselves for emotional storms when she returned on Sunday evenings and gradually moved toward a point at which the three adults and Amy could discuss the possibility of Amy staying with her in a planful way, based on a realistic consideration of her longing for her mother, her mother's wish to re-establish a mothering commitment, Amy's fierce competitive feelings towards her stepmother, and the overload in the Harris household. Mr. H. and his first wife were able, for the first time in years, to have short, face-to-face meetings, in which they limited their discussions to Amy and Jon, avoiding bitter recriminations from the old marriage. As they began to develop a more cooperative parenting alliance, Amy's emotional outbursts calmed dramatically. She was no longer sullen after her visits with her mother. Slowly, she began to test out the new situation by mentioning pleasant times with her mother and her mother's boyfriend. When these were tolerated, she also became free to explore her confusing, mixed feelings about these visits. In this way Amy was able to test out potential identifications with all the adults in her life, without risking losing the others. She was able to make her own observations and judgments about her mother as a person, without provoking emotional scenes and court hassles. The adults were able to work out a compromise which fit none of their original hopes, but which shared responsibility and lessened feelings of failure.

In conclusion, this chapter has suggested a possible stance in working with families of remarriage which approaches these families as a special form of extended family organization with a particularly complex network of biological, legal, and emotional ties. It has been put forth that blended family networks are faced with a continual balancing process between maintaining the distance necessary to develop clear boundaries and utilizing potential supports, important in minimizing the rupture of central attachments for the children. The examples have been suggestive only. They do not begin to cover the vast array of variation possible in the remarried family structure. Families vary in terms of the longevity of the first family, the stage of development of the children involved, how many different members and ages are to be accommodated, how long the remarriage has lasted, the circumstances surrounding the separation and divorce, and so on. In addition, drawing primarily on examples from clinical practice lends extra weight to an emphasis on stress, difficulty, feelings of hopelessness, and the outbreak of symptoms. The same issues have been described by other authors who have interviewed samples of nonclinic families.[6,9,10,16] However, there are as yet no systematic studies of well-functioning remarried families which look at effective patterns of external boundaries, internal structure, and network supports in everyday functioning and in handling particularly stressful times of change. It is hoped that the many issues described in this chapter will become quickly outdated as the complexities of the remarried family structure become more openly acknowledged and new spouse and parental role possiblities are publically supported.

BIBLIOGRAPHY

1. Dullea, G. Is joint custody good for children? *New York Times Magazine,* February 3: 32–46. (1980).
2. Franche, L. B., Sherman, D., Semiris, P. E., Abramsen, P., Zabarsky, M., Huek, J., and Whitman, L. The children of divorce. *Newsweek,* Feb. 11:58–63 (1980).

3. Goldstein, H. S. Reconstituted families: The second marriage and its children. *Psychiatric Quarterly.* **48**:433–440 (1974).
4. Hartman, A. Diagrammatic assessment of family relationships. *Social Casework* **59**:465–476 (1978).
5. Kaplan, S. L. Structural family therapy for children of divorce: Case reports. *Family Process* **16**:75–83 (1977).
6. Messinger, L. Remarriage between divorced people with children from previous marriages: A proposal for preparation for remarriage. *Journal of Marriage Family Counsel.* **2**:193–200 (1976).
7. Messinger, L., Walker, K. N., and Freeman, S. J. J. Preparation for remarriage following divorce: The use of group techniques. *American Journal of Orthopsychiatry* **48**:263–272 (1978).
8. Peck, B. *A Family Therapy Notebook: Experimental Techniques of Family and Couples in Psychotherapy.* New York: Libra Publishers (1974).
9. Roosevelt, R., and Lofas, J. *Living in Step.* New York: Stein and Day (1976).
10. Rosenbaum, L., and Rosenbaum, V. *Stepparenting.* New York: E. P. Dutton (1977).
11. Satir, V. *Peoplemaking.* Palo Alto, Calif.: Science and Behavior Books (1972).
12. Visher, E., and Visher, J. *Stepfamilies: A Guide to Working with Stepparents and Stepchildren.* New York: Brunner/Mazel, (1979).
13. Walker, K. N., and Messinger, L. Remarriage after divorce: Dissolution and reconstruction of family boundaries. *Family Process* **18**:185–192 (1979).
14. Walker, L., Brown, H., Crohn, H., Rodstein, E., Zeisel, E., and Sager, C. J. An annotated bibliography of the remarried, the living together, and their children. *Family Process.* **18**:193–212 (1979).
15. Weisfeld, D., and Laser, M. S. Divorced parents in family therapy in a residential treatment setting. *Family Process.* **16**:229–236 (1977).
16. Westoff, L. A. *The Second Time Around: Remarriage in America.* New York: The Viking Press (1975).
17. Whiteside, M. F., and Auerbach, L. S. Can the daughter of my father's new wife be my sister? Families of remarriage in family therapy. *Journal of Divorce* **1**:271–283 (1978).

Since 1972, each year has seen more than one million children affected by their parents' divorce. There is little public recognition of this and of its implications, and Joan Kelly traces its outcomes in relation to changing conceptions of children's visiting relationships with their noncustodial parent. What emerges from her research and her clinical experience is a new view of the complexity of this situation—and of the need to face its solutions realistically and flexibly.

The result of her concerns is a chapter that makes us more fully aware of the needs of the children themselves, as expressed in their own words, in their own feelings, and in their own behavior. She makes clear that any pattern of visitation that does not directly address itself to such needs is both unworkable at best, and unfair to the child at worst.

The Visiting Relationship After Divorce: Research Findings and Clinical Implications

Joan B. Kelly, Ph. D.

INTRODUCTION

The dramatic increase in the rate of divorce in the United States has shifted clinical and research attention during the 1970s to a newly emerging population at risk—children of divorcing parents. In each year since 1972, more than one million children have been affected by their parents' divorce, and this phenomenon is expected to continue into the early 1980s. Nearly thirty percent of children born in the 1970s are expected to experience at least one parental divorce before the age of eighteen, and the average child of divorce will live 5–6 years in a single parent family.[1] Most often, these children will reside with their mothers, for despite an increase in father custody, only 10 percent of children of separation and divorce live with their fathers.[7]

The rising divorce rate has been followed by a proliferation of studies investigating adults' adjustment to divorce[22,31] and to fathers' new roles as single parents.[6,21,24,27] Surprisingly few investigators have focused on the impact of divorce on children and adolescents during this same period, despite the large population affected. Yet, there is evidence that children of divorce are found in disproportionate numbers in mental health clinics and private practices in the United States.[5,15,33,34] The need for understanding all aspects of a child's divorce experience seems critical if we are to deal appropriately and sensitively with these troubled children when they appear in clinical settings. Attention must be directed not only to the initial stressful period following separation, but to the factors associated with psychological adjustment after the initial crisis has subsided.

Recent studies have confirmed that divorce is a major crisis in the lives of most children and adolescents. Except in families where parents engaged in intense conflict and interspousal violence, youngsters do not feel relieved initially by their parents' decision to divorce, nor do they approve of it.[39] The separation of the parents sets in motion a prolonged period of transition for children and parents alike, characterized by considerable disorganization, instability, and change.[11,12,39,40] The stress-engendered responses of children and adolescents to divorce in the first year after separation vary according to the youngster's age and developmental status,[12,17,35-37] may appear in varying intensities in the different settings of home, school, and clinic,[11,17,18,20,23,39] and differentially affect boys more than girls in the first two years.[13,39]

Few researchers have studied the course of the relationship between visiting fathers and children in the postdivorce period. Early studies of "father absence" searched for links between the absence of the father from the family household and the later psychological adjustment of children and adolescents from divorced families,[2-4,9,26,29,30,32] but the conceptualization of father absence was not sufficiently refined to adequately assess the meaning and impact of the postdivorce father-child relationship on the child or adolescent. While undoubtedly focusing on an important factor in the lives of divorced children, these studies did not consider the *degree* of father absence, the quality of the relationship between father and child *pre*divorce, or the quality of the *post*divorce relationship with the custodial parent in assessing outcome.

More recent studies[8,11,14,19,28,39] have examined in some depth the relationship between the availability of a noncustodial parent and the children's overall adjustment to divorce. The child's profound yearning for the noncustodial parent has been a particularly striking finding,[11,17,19,28,33,36,39] even when the predivorce relationship between parent and child was not especially gratifying, and the overall visiting relationship postdivorce has been found to be a significant factor in determining the outcome of children whose parents divorce.[8,11,12,39] Two studies reported that "unless the father is extremely poorly adjusted or immature, or the child is exposed to conflict between the parents, frequent availability of the father is associated with positive adjustment and social relations, especially in boys"(p. 856).[12] And a five-year longitudinal study of children of divorce found a significant relationship at eighteen months postseparation between infrequent visiting, poor academic functioning, and depression, a link especially strong in young boys.[39] The relationship between visiting frequency and psychological adjustment appeared as well at five years postseparation.[39] In particular, five years later, children whose fathers evidenced little or no interest in them, despite living nearby, became burdened by poor self-esteem, increased anger and, in some instances, chronic depression.

Because of the demonstrated importance to the child of the postdivorce relationship with the noncustodial parent, this chapter focuses on the visiting situation as it evolves after separation and continues on in the several years following divorce. Patterns of visiting, underlying factors promoting and interfering with visiting, attitudes toward visiting and the course of the visiting relationship over time will be discussed, as will clinical implications derived from these considerations.

Visiting After Separation

The visiting relationship is a new and awkward one for parent and child, involving changed roles for which there is no dress rehearsal and few directions. The parent moving out must restructure the relationship with his children along unfamiliar dimensions which include the new constraints of time and place. Children, too, must accommodate to the changes to ensure the success of the altered structure. For some parents, the constraints of visiting create a deep sense of loss and deprivation, while others welcome the release from the daily responsibilities and pressures of children. Restructuring the parent-child relationship into one characterized by "visiting" is a process which is influenced by many factors, some of them seemingly beyond control of the various participants. Thus, establishing a satisfying visiting relationship is more difficult than many envision, and there is little help offered along the way, either by practitioners in the fields of law and mental health, or by society at large. Because the long-term psychological well-being of children of divorce is affected by the visiting arrangements that are made soon after separation, it is important to understand how these visiting patterns typically evolve.

How Visits Are Established

Visiting patterns that evolve postseparation might expectably reflect the predivorce parent-child relationship, the child's wishes at the time of separation, and both parents' desire for continuity in the child's relationship with the noncustodial parent. Yet, none of these factors has been found to shape the visiting arrangements in any central way.[39] Forces external to the needs of children frequently predominate in influencing the frequency and ambience of the visits. The traditions of our society, the role of the legal profession, and the psychological response of each parent to the divorce itself are particularly powerful factors in determining the postdivorce visiting situation.

The Father's Diminished Role

Although at the turn of the century it was customary for fathers to retain full custodial rights of their minor children, the industrial revolution gradually brought about far-reaching changes in the role of the father within the family. As major responsibility for parenting shifted to the mother during this century, so too did society's view of the importance of the mother in the child's life. Theoreticians, clinicians, and researchers alike turned their attention to the mother-child relationship within the intact family with a resulting de-emphasis of the father-child relationship.

As the divorce rate spiraled, neither parents nor practitioners saw reason to alter the limited role of the father in the child's life. The belief in the primary importance of the mother to the child influenced decisionmaking in postdivorce arrangements as well, and it was deemed to be "in the best interests of the child" to be in the custody of mother and visit father. The traditional visiting pattern of twelve days with mother and two with father evolved as a symbol of the secondary importance of the father's role in the life of his child and in time became imbued with an aura of developmental and moral rightness. This traditional pattern has held despite enormous social and economic change which, by 1979, saw more than 60 percent of single mothers joining the work force. In retrospect, the failure of clinicians to question these traditional visiting arrangements was remarkable.

Legal Tradition and Practice

Not surprisingly, these cultural traditions have been reflected in and rigorously upheld by the practice of law and the courts in divorce matters. In the vast majority of divorces involving children, in which litigation over custody or visitation was not pending, "reasonable visitation rights" were awarded to the noncustodial parent. One would logically expect parents in such cases to determine the meaning of "reasonable" for their own children, based on the family's unique circumstances and the children's needs, and further, to consult the youngsters for their ideas about seeing the out-of-home parent. Unfortunately, such joint planning is more the exception than the rule. Instead, it is apparent that lawyers have an inordinate amount of influence in defining "reasonable visitation" for their clients, much more than was anticipated. Women are frequently advised to restrict fathers to alternating weekends and not give up anything more; men are told not to expect more than the usual pattern.

After listening to Mr. T.'s concerns about his children, the therapist asked how the twice-monthly visiting schedule was established. Mr. T. had solicited advice on this matter from his attorney and was told that "every other weekend is what fathers usually get. . . . I wouldn't push for more. . . . you're just asking for trouble." When asked by the therapist if the pattern was acceptable to him, Mr. T. expressed his considerable dismay about the length of time between visits: "I miss the kids terribly. . . . I think we're not as close as we used to be."

The issue of a parent's access to his or her children postdivorce has not been one which attorneys explored with their clients. This is true in part because decisions in law rely heavily on precedent, and there is much precedent in the area of visiting patterns. But, equally important, is the attorney's training and commitment to an ethical code which compels him to protect and fight for his client's wishes. If an angry custodial parent, for example, wants to severely limit visiting rights as part of a vendetta against a spouse seeking divorce, most attorneys feel bound to pursue this goal. Few attorneys question their client's motivation or judgment, nor do they see their function as involving a determination of the child's needs or wishes. Unfortunately, in bitter divorce proceedings, there is sometimes little relationship between the client's demands regarding his or her children and the youngster's actual developmental needs. Children are used as a vehicle for expressing rage and disappointment, and custody and visiting disputes frequently have, as a major component, the unconscious or conscious attempt to seek revenge. In such cases, the "best interests of the child" are more accurately a matter of the vested interest of the parent, as negotiated by his or her attorney. It is unfortunate that the field of family law seems to have diverged from other areas of legal practice in which active negotiation and compromise are routine.

Another factor complicating the process of visiting has been the widely held view that divorcing parents are unable to agree on arrangements that affect their children. "If they could agree about their kids, they wouldn't be divorcing." One study found, in fact, that a substantial number of parents had no real conflict about issues involving the children, despite their marital dissatisfaction.[39] Convinced that parents are unable to agree about anything, the majority of lawyers have firmly discouraged any informal contact between parents and view with suspicion the desire for some flexibility in the visiting schedule. Instead of encouraging attempts on the parents' part to communicate in a civilized manner concerning their children's needs, attorneys have directly or indirectly promoted lack of cooperation. Some encourage an absolute rigidity in a visiting schedule, specifying in a divorce agreement that any deviations in visiting be permitted with only written, advanced notice. Further, phone conversations regarding visiting plans are viewed as unwelcome and intrusive: "My client should have the right to lead her life without him calling all the time." Sometimes this restrictive attitude includes prohibiting phone conversations between noncustodial parent and child as well.

Within the context of the adversary system, arrangements about the children have too often been incorporated into the overall battle strategy of the divorcing spouse, and time with the children has been viewed as something to be yielded up, if need be, in the midst of battle.

With power legally and fully lodged in the hands of the custodial parent, the visiting parent has been the supplicant. Until recently, the visiting parent's efforts to alter patterns or unfair restrictions had been met with considerable resistance, even by that parent's attorney. Unless there were compelling reasons for a change of custody, the majority of attorneys took a dim view of such legal action, even where a visiting relationship was seriously eroded.

After Mr. P.'s ex-wife remarried, visiting arrangements that had been fairly routine were increasingly fraught with disruption. The three young children were placed outside the door to await the father, suitcases nearly empty and clothing inappropriate for the visit. The remarried couple, intensely hostile to Mr. P., abruptly canceled holiday weekends, claiming the children needed to be with their "family" on such important occasions. Although the divorce agreement specified Mr. P.'s right to call his children daily, the mother's attorney and the stepfather wrote abusive letters accusing the father of harassing them with his frequent calls. They demanded that he call only at a specified (and inconvenient) hour. In the face of the stepfather's hostility, Mr. P. had already drastically curtailed his phone contacts. During these now infrequent calls, the stepfather hovered nearby in an oppressive manner, and Mr. P. sadly noted his young son seemed much less communicative on the phone. Several months later, his ex-wife arbitrarily scheduled Saturday morning sports and music lessons, demanding that Mr. P. drive the long distance back for these events or curtail his visiting to Saturday overnights.

When Mr. P. asked his attorney for advice, he was asked: "What's so important about phone contacts?" Things weren't really that bad, he said. "Just wait until your children are invited to all those birthday parties!" The lawyer's failure to understand the importance of frequent contacts for fathers and children may be understandable, but more striking was an undercurrent of derision at Mr. P.'s efforts to maintain a meaningful relationship with his very responsive and enthusiastic children.

Counter-Transference Issues

Although there are recent encouraging changes, attorneys and mental health professionals, and society at large, continue to view with suspicion and hostility a father's desire for frequent visits. This is particularly so when a father expresses a desire for joint custody, but pertains as well to requests for midweek contacts and overnights. There are complex reasons, both conscious and unconscious, for the various responses of professional men and women to these increasing requests for greater contact between visiting parent and child. Perhaps the most difficult to identify and change are responses which can be best characterized as counter-transference phenomena, in which the lawyer or therapist is unconscious of hostility, or the reasons for resistance, to pursuing visiting requests. Women lawyers and therapists with children of their own, for example, may feel profoundly threatened by a father's desire for frequent access or custody (including joint custody). The potential for discouraging the father in his pursuit may be even greater if these professional women are themselves divorced with sole custody of their children. And, conversely, professional men may unconsciously view the father's desire for richness and continuity in his relationship with his children as a condemnation of their own fathering. The potential for rejecting or half-heartedly supporting the father's attempts to seek very frequent contact is especially great where an attorney or therapist has failed to maintain a gratifying relationship with his own children after divorce. The impact of counter-transference responses in family law and divorce-counseling work is insufficiently understood and seldom discussed, yet plays a key role in the various postdivorce arrangements which are made regarding the children of divorce.

The Parents' Influence

Conjoining with the traditions of society and law are the respective contributions of each parent to establishing visiting patterns. As indicated, a cooperative and conscious effort to plan visiting based on the child's developmental needs and wishes has more often been the exception than the rule. Often, intrapsychic factors compel, rather than shape, the visiting arrangements in the immediate postseparation period, particularly those factors associated with each parent's own psychological response to the divorce. In families with children, a mutually shared decision to divorce was found to be rare. More often, one spouse wanted to terminate the marriage, while the other opposed that decision in varying degrees.[16,39] This discrepancy in the extent to which each parent wanted the divorce was found to be responsible for much of the turmoil following separation, and contributed as well to difficulties in establishing meaningful visiting.

In a five-year longitudinal study of sixty divorcing families, the relationship between the parents' psychological response to divorce and the visiting relationship established after separation was examined. Reported elsewhere in detail,[39] the study found the father's attitude and feelings about the divorce more often took precedence in determining visiting arrangements than did the quality of the predivorce relationship with their children. Thus, fathers severely depressed about their spouses' decisions to divorce were significantly less likely to visit their youngsters on a regular and frequent basis. Depression interfered with the parents' ability to plan ahead and mobilize the energy needed to interact with their children. Further, the visits often exacerbated their intense feelings of loss and deprivation, and their wish to avoid further pain led to a decrease in visits.

Fathers who experienced guilt about leaving the marriage and the children were also less likely to visit frequently. Although initially some guilty fathers engaged in an intense flurry of visiting activity, this pattern did not hold beyond a few months, and the link between guilt and infrequent visiting was a significant one after the first year. A parent's guilt about leaving his children, especially strong where the children were left in the custody of a mother with significant psychological problems, seemed to be evoked anew with each visiting contact, and the resultant anxiety after visits acted as a deterrent to frequent visiting.

The intense angers of parents following separation also played a role in determining visiting arrangements. The embittered custodial parent, opposed to the divorce, attempted to severely limit visits or, failing that, to sabotage those that were legally scheduled. Such parents, unable to distinguish their rage at the offending spouse from the psychological needs of their children, attempted to offer their children more exciting alternatives during the time set aside for visiting, or scheduled exciting competing activities. In response, bewildered or angry children sometimes called the visiting parent to cancel or visited reluctantly.

Mrs. A. sent a letter to her ex-spouse explaining why the children should not come for their scheduled three-week Christmas visit. The reasons were legion: "it wasn't convenient. . . . they have dental and medical appointments scheduled. . . . they would miss their neighborhood friends." When Mr. A. insisted that they come, Mrs. A. sent the children with angry instructions not to forget the Christmas Eve party she had made reservations for at her church. When the father protested that they already had plans, she argued that the children wanted to go, she had paid the money and they should not be denied the right to participate in *her* church activities.

Such episodes are typically not isolated events, but are part of a continuing series of harassments designed to make the visiting parent's life difficult and miserable. Some fathers responded to such enduring and corrosive anger with a weary, sad retreat. As one father sighed after months of continual obstacles placed between him and his children: "I have to wonder whether it's all worth it. She makes it very hard to put the divorce behind me and get on with a new life. Do the children benefit enough for me to continue fighting to see them?" Rather than endure extreme frustration and a sense of impotence, such men often gradually withdraw from the lives of their children, some in anger, others with considerable reluctance.

Angry men, humiliated and in a rage about the wife's decision to divorce, also used the visiting to express their rage. They accused their wives of trying to prevent visits and turn the children against them, yet angrily shared with the children their condemnation of the attitudes and morals of the divorcing spouse. Threats of custody suits were often used as blackmail in getting their way. Such angry men typically refused to visit when they suspected the mother was dating or when it might be at all helpful to the ex-spouse: "She's not going to use *me* as a babysitter!" In their anger, these parents failed to recognize that any time spent with their children was potentially valuable and gratifying for both parent and child.

Consulting the Children

Children are rarely consulted for their ideas and input about visiting. While the general practice of refraining from asking young children to choose between parents in a custody dispute remains a sound one, it is perhaps generalized into a more unfortunate tradition of not consulting youngsters about *any* of the postdivorce arrangements that directly affect them. Many schoolage children and adolescents are upset that arrangements about visiting patterns are established without their input and consent. Some feel insulted that they have been so blatantly ignored; others find such exclusion from planning increases their loneliness. Further, it appears that youngsters are hesitant to volunteer their ideas at a time when their parents are likely to overreact emotionally to even simple questions and requests. Concerned about evoking bouts of crying or intense anger from the parents upon whom they are so dependent, these youngsters say nothing, but remain hopeful that someone will notice their agony.

How Often Do Visits Occur?

Information regarding visitation frequency after divorce is sparse. While the therapist of a parent or child may inquire about the amount of contact between visiting parent and child, there have been no systematic large-scale attempts to determine what regular patterns exist for a normal population of children of divorce. Only one study has reported visiting patterns as seen shortly after separation and followed the course of these visiting arrangements.

The initial postseparation patterns of visiting were examined in sixty families in the midst of divorce who came to the Children of Divorce Project for a six-week divorce-specific preventive intervention designed to facilitate the efforts of children and adolescents to cope with divorce.[18,38] Predominantly a middle-class white population, these families had 131 children between the ages of three and eighteen and had been married an average of eleven years prior to separation.* After the initial divorce counseling service contact, the families were seen for two subsequent follow-ups, one at eighteen months postseparation and again at five years' postseparation. The earliest visiting arrangements in these sixty families, as observed in the first few months following separation, have been reported in detail elsewhere.[19,39] They are summarized to serve as a comparison to the visiting patterns observed at the two follow-ups and elaborated in more detail in this chapter.

During the initial several interviews with children whose parents were divorcing, the amount of dissatisfaction expressed about the visiting situation was striking. Children who were visited frequently and infrequently alike complained about insufficient visiting. The intensity of their yearning for greater contact with the visiting parent was profoundly moving and mobilized a more careful scrutiny of visiting arrangements. While the frequency of visits is not in itself the hallmark of the quality of the parent-child relationship, it clearly serves as a powerful indicator to the child of a parent's interest.

Forty percent of the children and adolescents were seeing their fathers at least once a week, and nearly half of these youngsters, most often young schoolage boys, had even more contact. Yet, children in this group had complaints about the new constraints on their time with their dads and the inherent difficulties in bringing such contacts to fruition. Almost always, youngsters visiting this often did so with the implicit or explicit approval of their custodial parent, and tended to live very close to the father. Although these youngsters disapproved of their parents' divorce as strongly as their cohorts, they felt less hopeless and deprived than those children visited infrequently.

Tom was seven when first seen: "I hate that divorce. . . . it's really hard. I miss not having my dad around like it used to be." But Tom guessed that things would turn out all right in the long run because, "I can see him whenever I want." As for most youngsters whose parents divorce, the

*See Wallerstein and Kelly[39] for details of the research population.

departure of the father from the family home was a critical and central event.

More than one-quarter of the youngsters were visiting in accord with the traditional pattern of alternating weekends. Most of them were *not* initially staying overnight on those weekends, but instead were spending part or all of one weekend day with the noncustodial parent. Unfortunately for many children, "alternate weekends" often turned out to be a few hours twice a month, rather than the full weekend promised. Sometimes this occurred because the father had not moved to a living situation which comfortably included children.

Thus, in this study, more than two-thirds of the youngsters were visiting at a level defined by lawyers, courts, and society at large as "reasonable," but yet only 20 percent of all the youngsters were reasonably content with the visiting situation. Most often these were adolescents and several of the young school-age boys who biked to their dad's house casually and often during any given week. The degree of dissatisfaction with the infrequency and form of the visit in a group of normal children experiencing the divorce of their parents must be taken seriously if we are to continue to evoke the ideal of "the best interests of the child."

One-quarter of the children and adolescents were visited less than once per month, most often in an erratic and unpredictable pattern. This infrequent and erratic pattern was differentiated from an infrequent visiting pattern necessitated by geographical distance. Vacation or holiday visiting had different psychological meaning to the child from infrequent visiting where the father lived nearby. For children in this latter situation, their agony and intense yearning were painful to observe.

Although initially there were frequent and reliable visits, Todd's father gradually stopped calling. At the time of the counseling, Todd's birthday had just passed unnoticed by the father. Todd was close to tears as he observed that it had been seven weeks since his last visit: "He must be forgetting all about me."

In addition to frequency, the length of each visit was also an important dimension and disappointed many children. During the first few months postseparation, only one-quarter of the youngsters experienced overnight and weekend visits, most often the 6–12 year olds. Brief contacts of 2–3 hours were appreciated *only* if the child was also spending overnights, and if the contacts were many. Such a mixture of midweek and weekend meetings seemed to approximate the interaction between parent and child in the busy two-parent household and reassured the child of continuity in the father-child relationship. But, brief, infrequent visits were a bitter disappointment to almost all the youngsters, creating open sadness in younger children and considerable anger in youngsters nine years and older.

Genuine reluctance to visit was found in 11 percent of the children and adolescents, but these youngsters, almost all of them nine years or older, did in fact continue to visit. A few adolescents visited only because they felt their future support depended on it. Ann said of her father, "He is selfish and mean. . . . I see what he is like now that we don't live together. . . . but, I'd better be nice to him or he won't pay for college."

Only 5 percent of youngsters had no contact with their fathers. Aside from two children whose fathers completely abandoned them, the youngsters without contact were 9–12 year olds who formed alignments with their mothers and openly refused to visit. In each case, the mother's paranoid outrage at being abandoned was shared with the children, and the youngster's sadness and anger resonated and meshed with the mother's. Such alignments, discussed more fully elsewhere,[37,39] have as their intent the open and hostile exclusion of the other parent from the children's lives. Not only did such alignments have considerable power and longevity, but they frequently created permanent and insurmountable problems for the excluded parent in his or her attempts to maintain a parent-child relationship.[39]

VISITING IN THE YEARS AFTER DIVORCE

Although there are no data available on a large-scale basis regarding the course of visiting after divorce, visiting frequency between parent and child is thought to drop off precipitously within a year or two after separation. Some estimates suggest that perhaps only 25 percent of the children of divorce continue to have any reliable contact with their noncustodial parent. Certainly, the intervening years bring about economic, geographic, and psychological change, as parents take on new jobs or remarry and move to new locations.

Visiting Eighteen Months Postseparation

Among the families in the Children of Divorce Project seen for the first follow-up,[*] the visiting situation was stabilized or improved along nearly every dimension. This was an unexpected finding, perhaps owing in part to the brief intervention initially provided to the divorcing families. One central focus of the divorce counseling was the child's need for continuity in his relationship with both parents postdivorce. Work with fathers

[*]Fifty-eight of the original sixty families returned for follow-up interviews. See Reference 39 for follow-up method and details on parent and child adjustment.

specifically addressed the need to redefine, restructure, and enrich their roles as out-of-home parents postseparation. Frequent visiting was frankly encouraged, and the continuing importance of the father to the child was stressed with both parents. The intervention appeared more effective than was anticipated.

Changes In the Visiting Pattern

Nearly two-thirds of the youngsters continued to visit with their fathers at least 2–3 times a month. Some children actually spent more time now with their dads than before. Among the 2–8 year old group, for example, the percentage enjoying overnight or entire weekend visits had *doubled* in the intervening year. The increased time began to change the visiting relationship in advantageous ways. The intense excitement seen initially had diminished somewhat, replaced by a more comfortable feeling of secure contentment. These visits now seemed more "real," containing not just excited pleasure, but elements of frustration, boredom, disciplinary action, and conflict as well. Mr. B. described his relationship with his daughter: "I am less of a play daddy now. . . I am just back to being their dad. It feels good."

The number of children visiting their fathers weekly or several times a week decreased, yet altogether, 29 percent of the youngsters continued with at least once a week visits, down from 42 percent at counseling. Some of this diminution in very frequent visits was mutual and voluntary, particularly with adolescents. Very few adolescents eighteen months after separation spent an entire weekend with their fathers. They preferred a spontaneous meeting for a few hours to eat, chat, or perhaps swim, and relationships between fathers and teenagers seemed to thrive on such a basis. Adolescents were particularly content with these visiting arrangements when they continued to actively participate in determining the pattern. Slightly fewer youngsters, now just 16 percent, suffered erratic and infrequent visits by this first follow-up. Some fathers had been mobilized by the counseling service.

Nell did not see her dad for several months after the separation, at which point counseling began. Work with the father focused on the young child's need and longing for her father, new symptoms which seemed related to his absence, and the father's difficulties in his new marriage. Counseling enabled Nell's father to integrate his new family situation with his own children. At follow-up, Nell was delighted to be seeing her dad regularly, including frequent overnights. The father, too, was pleased with his responsible role in Nell's life. "The counseling was really helpful to me in that way." Where there was improvement in the visiting situation, youngsters tended to reinforce their father's efforts with expressions of open pleasure or begrudging appreciation.

When infrequent visits continued as a firm pattern, and it did more often with the 9–12-year-olds, the disappointment and anger of these youngsters continued unabated. It was no less hurtful one year later to think that one's father just didn't care.

When first seen, Todd was struggling with enormously painful feelings caused by his father's failure to visit. He couldn't understand why his previously devoted father seemed to be abandoning him in favor of a new family: "He must like *them* better now." Todd's depression was often masked by angry sarcasm, but tears would break through quickly as he talked.

One year later, Todd no longer reminisced over past adventures with his dad: "I don't think about him very much anymore." In place of the sadness, the angry disappointment, there were now growing disdain and feelings of bitterness toward his father. "Dad's wife has invited us over a couple of times, but I usually have other things to do. Besides, dad is usually not there when I *do* go over." Todd's struggle to achieve a sense of closure was reflected in his final comment: "I'm not really waiting any longer for him."

The number of children with no contact with their fathers remained small (8%). While families moved apart from one another, the distance was mostly within an hour's drive and did not deter visiting. No additional fathers had completely abandoned their youngsters during the intervening year, although, as we see in Todd's case above, some were close to doing so.

Thus at an average of eighteen months postseparation, a gradual move toward visiting patterns which more approximate the usual, that is, the "reasonable" visitation of twice-monthly weekends or overnight. And yet, the youngsters (29%) and fathers who continued, despite various barriers, to thrive on and enjoy really frequent access are a powerful indicator that for many the "usual" is not sufficient. When there were abrupt changes in the visiting pattern, one of two situations was observed. A few embittered fathers initially visited often, more to establish their right of access than out of genuine interest in the child. When given free access, they decreased their visits notably within a few months, and their erratic visiting pattern was a disappointment to some of the youngsters previously courted with such vigor. In a second instance, when the mother-daughter relationship was troubled and deteriorating, visits with the father increased partially at the initiative of the older girls involved. Perhaps these responsive fathers recognized the deficiencies in the mother-child relationship and more readily offered their support.

What Barriers Remained

Many of the obstacles interfering with gratifying visits were lessened in the intervening year. One of the most positive changes enhancing visits was a reduction of the hostilities attendant to visiting. The majority of parents had ceased their outright fighting; angry slurs and innuendos were becoming less common. The children were less often used as carriers of hostile messages. And, for many youngsters, scheduling the visit became easier. Phone calls to and from dad were less likely to stir up trouble, and most of the older youngsters arranged things themselves with their fathers, consulting mothers only if conflicting scheduling occurred.

Mothers were considerably less stressed by the visiting. They seemed to have recognized that the child's love for the father did not diminish that child's love for them. Thus, we saw greater flexibility in permitting visits and in varying their own schedules to accomodate father and child. Fathers, too, increasingly adapted to their offspring's needs. They offered fewer extravagant treats; they felt more secure in disciplining the children. As these youngsters were integrated into the household routines of two separate homes, they learned adeptly to handle whatever discrepancies in rules and lifestyles existed between both.

Sean talked of the differences at mealtimes. "My dad has a thing about manners. . . . we have to use our napkins on our laps and keep our elbows off the table. He gets mad at me if I forget. But my mom doesn't care about those things." Asked if the differences in the two homes were confusing, Sean shrugged, "Well, no, it's actually okay. . . . I just try to remember to do what they want. . . . it's no big deal."

But for some youngsters, problems still remained. Twenty percent of the mothers continued to see absolutely no value in the father's contact with his children and some of these embittered women stirred up continuous difficulties for father and child. While adolescents tended by now to ignore this unyielding hostility, younger children either continued to side in an alignment with their angry mothers or kept discussion of their fathers to an absolute minimum. "I've learned not to say anything about my dad." This need to isolate affects and thoughts seems a high price to pay for such young children, yet such a capacity may preserve intact the child's image of and identification with the father.

Children increasingly shared their visits with parents' dates or with new stepparents. By the first follow-up, one-fifth of the men had become engaged or remarried, and nearly half of the children visited father with his girlfriends. With the more steady partners, children gradually accepted the new person. Sharing the father with a succession of many dates, however, often created resentment and open disdain.

Dick mimicked his father: "Boys," he said in a high-pitched voice, "this is Marianne and she is very important to me." "Boys, this is Jane. I want you to like her. . . . she is very important." Dick hooted, "Each week it's a different lady!"

The younger the child, the less difficulty there was in admitting a stepparent or stepsiblings into their lives. If their own individual needs were met, younger children could find pleasure in sharing father with his new family. "I've got one daddy, two mommys and two dogs now!" This satisfied expression from one preschooler symbolized the nourishment such arrangements could offer to youngsters previously struggling with feelings of depletion.

Older youngsters had greater difficulties in accepting a stepfamily; often they felt deprived and jealous of stepbrothers and stepsisters living with *their* father. One ten-year-old plaintively said, *"They* get to see him all the time. You'd think on weekends I'd at least get to see him by myself sometimes. It's not fair—he's *my* father!"

Children's Feelings About Visiting

Remarkably little changed in the intervening year in the youngsters' attitudes towards visits. Those keenly disappointed by infrequent visits remained so; some others became newly disappointed and saddened by changes in visiting frequency. One-third of the youngsters expressed considerable disappointment that their fathers weren't sufficiently interested and available. The passage of time had not eased the pain of a father's rejection.

More relaxed than when first seen, Dana talked openly about the divorce. "It was better for my parents, but not especially for me. I wouldn't mind the divorce so much if my dad could visit one time a week like John's dad does. . . Or like if we had a system thing." Did she mean like a regular schedule? "Yes, but I guess that wouldn't really work for him." Dana's thoughts drifted off; her mood had become pensive and sad.

The age-related difference with which youngsters initially reacted to their father's inconstancy and rejection continued. Younger children longed for the father openly and without rancor. Older youngsters, nine and up, also yearned intensely for the erratic father, but defensively masked yearning with great anger. Some youngsters had made a transition developmentally in the intervening year. Open longing was no longer evident; in its place was bitterness, a new anger focused specifically on the father.

Ken was just nine years old when we first saw him. Throughout those early interviews, Ken sadly reminisced about wonderful times he and his father had shared before the divorce. But at the first follow-up, Ken said, "My father is off my list now." Actively angry at the father for his failings, Ken told us he wasn't out to hurt his father, but neither was he going to devote any more effort to liking him. "I plan not to speak to him anymore." Ken's anger at his dad served a protective function enabling him to cope with his pain and turn now with renewed energy to school, friends, and new relationships with male teachers.

Contentment about visiting had increased to include now one-third of the youngsters. Among this group were the adolescents noted earlier and young schoolage boys continuing multiple weekly visits with their dads. A small number of these satisfied youngsters were comfortable with a more attenuated relationship with their fathers that was made possible by the divorce itself.

Steve had made considerable developmental gain in the intervening year; his behavior at home and in first grade was now more age-appropriate. Without the daily presence of an angry and frightening father, Steve seemed happier, more independent, and less fearful. Although seeing his father just twice a month, Steve was quite content. Did he want to see his dad more? "No, it's just right the way it is." Like a small number of other fathers, Steve's dad was now able to be a warmer, more effective parent, and called at least weekly to keep in touch.

The youngsters, about 20 percent of the group, who earlier experienced conflict about visiting, continued in their anger at the father, especially when reinforced by the mother's enduring rage. Yet, their longing for more frequent contact was also undiminished, and despite the internal conflict, all continued to go on visits. And genuine reluctance to visit also remained unchanged in the small group of youngsters described earlier. They continued to find the visits boring, or their fathers harsh and overbearing, and they were just as happy to stay at home. Mostly they went, but did nothing to increase the frequency of visits and tried occasionally to cancel a visit by scheduling an important social occasion.

Thus, it appeared eighteen months postseparation that the youngsters' feelings about continued contact with the fathers were remarkably consistent with the attitudes expressed one year earlier at counseling. Like the visiting patterns themselves, feelings about the visiting situation develop soon after the separation, and while in some instances they are related to the predivorce relationship between father and child, they are just as likely to be determined by what happens in the aftermath of the separation.

Visiting at Five Years

For children, the emotional significance of the father continued in a powerful way in the five years following separation. In his presence or by his absence, the father had a major impact on the child's self-esteem and affected the child's sense of well-being.

Changes In the Visiting Pattern

Fathers and children continued to see each other in the intervening three years to a greater degree than expected. Rather than a sharp decline in the amount of visiting, there was a gradual change in the direction of fewer visits. Yet for one-third of the youngsters there was no change since the first follow-up, and 20 percent actually enjoyed more frequent visits.

Weekly visits continued for nearly 25 percent of the children and adolescents, some of whom continued the pattern of multiple-weekly contacts with their fathers. These latter children were fortunate in having fathers who not only loved them, but committed themselves to continuing in a challenging and sometimes ambiguous role. These men had sufficient maturity and psychological stability to give their children's needs high priority and to allow relationships to develop which kept apace with the child's increasing maturity and independence. One father told us: "I can't imagine seeing my kids only on vacations. I talk to them on the phone everyday and see them very often. Frequent contact is really important to stay in touch with what my children are thinking and doing."

The considerable contribution of the mother to these stable father-child relationships was her full recognition and acceptance of the child's need for the relationship, and her cooperation in allowing the relationship to flourish, change shape as needed, and be important to the child. For children, the demonstrated interest and investment on the part of both parents eventuated in good self-esteem and an overall postdivorce sense of sufficiency. These postdivorce families most approximated the joint or shared custody situation more recently receiving attention, although none had formally or legally labeled themselves as joint-custody families.

Twenty percent of the children and adolescents visited two or three times monthly, most often in the alternate weekend or overnight pattern. Another 20 percent visited monthly, and vacation or holiday visits necessitated by geographical distance occurred for a slowly increasing number of youngsters. The group of children experiencing erratic, infrequent visits remained essentially the same (17%), as did those with no contact. Thus, while there was a gradual trend towards fewer visits among those who started with a traditional visiting pattern, there was remarkable consistency in the years between the first and second follow-ups, particularly for youngsters enjoying either very frequent visits, or enduring erratic and infrequent visits.

All of the children took a larger role in shaping the time and content of the visit, and where the visiting arrangement was mutually viewed as a flexible one, subject to change without hurt feelings or anger, the youngsters were most pleased. The number of children generally content with the visiting situation had increased from one-third to more than one-half of the group. Where fathers and children had successfully integrated old life and new ways with an air of informality, youngsters felt satisfied. They were not burdened in their development by feelings of deprivation and rejection. Mary talked with us about her contentment: "Being with dad feels good, like it used to in the old days." Central to her pleasure was the sense that things with her dad were pretty much what they would have been if the divorce had not occurred.

In contrast, one-fifth of the children and adolescents did not like or find their visits pleasurable. Negative feelings were noted when the youngsters perceived their fathers as disinterested or selfish. They complained of parents "too busy" to visit, forgetful of birthdays, in a hurry to end the visit, or absorbed in other activities or people when the youngsters came over. These children and adolescents felt intensely hurt and rejected, and the passage of time seemed not to mute the pain. Adolescents in particular responded with an angry counter-rejection of the father and his values. And a second group of youngsters, initially involved in an intense alignment with the mother against the father, continued to view the visits negatively. Larry derisively catalogued his father's "dumb attempts" to regain the boy's affection. He had only one message for his dad: "Tell him there's no hope at all."

Infrequent and unpredictable visiting continued to cause disappointment for a large number of youngsters. The younger ones seemed unable to give up hope, and waited endlessly for some sign of love and interest. Unable to understand or accept the father's failings, these children continued to feel *they* were unworthy or uninteresting, a self-concept resistant to change, even in psychotherapy. A few youngsters gave insight into the father's problems as part of the increased perceptiveness of adolescence. While this eased their anger, it did not diminish the importance of the father in their lives.

Carrie showed us three tattered letters, her only contacts with her father in the previous year: "I cry everytime I get a letter from him. It's very depressing. He's a lonely man. . . . he doesn't know what he's doing. . . . he's not stable."

Overall, what remained as a notable aspect of the visiting situation five years after separation were the continuing strong desire for contact with the father, and concurrently, a sober acceptance of the attenuated relationship that resulted for the majority of youngsters and fathers who were not seeing each other regularly and very frequently. Sally, now age eleven, talked about the divorce: "I get to see my father some, so I don't miss him too much. It's not better now, but it's not worse."

CLINICAL IMPLICATIONS

Because the visiting relationship remains of central importance to the well-being of children and adolescents long after the parents' separation and divorce, clinicians must take the initiative in promoting postdivorce arrangements that will enhance rather than encumber the child's development. Such an initiative must include not only an examination of visiting issues within the therapeutic relationship, but extend beyond to larger educational efforts and program development specific to divorce.

Until recently, our knowledge of the impact of divorce on children has come from clinical case reports of troubled children who experienced divorce at some earlier point in their lives. Thus, for example, we have believed that "children always know their parents are going to divorce and are not surprised"; that children feel responsible for causing the marital rupture and are troubled by their guilt; that they approve of the parental divorce if the marriage was conflictual; and that an unhappy marriage is more damaging to the child's ultimate psychological adjustment than divorce. One study of 131 children and adolescents without a previous history of psychological difficulty found no significant support for the first three assumptions, and we learned that divorce may be as detrimental to a child's future development and mental health as an unhappy marriage if the postseparation ambience remains angry and chaotic, or if the postdivorce family arrangements reflect adult priorities and needs at the expense of the children's needs.[39] We must continue to expand our understanding of the normal, as well as the more pathological, divorce-related responses of children of different ages; and, as research increases our awareness of those postdivorce factors which impede or facilitate children's adjustment to divorce, clinicians must increasingly assume responsibility for exploring and promoting conditions which result in sound mental health.

We have, in the past, accepted rather than scrutinized the visiting arrangements of children seen in private practice or clinics. In part, working effectively with children of divorce demands a reevalutaion of clinicians' attitudes and a rethinking of traditional theories of child development and psychopathology. The concepts that have governed our thinking are legion: the literature of separation anxiety has led us to discourage overnight visits for infants and toddlers with their divorced fathers, regardless of the closeness of their relationship; theories of a child's need for stablility have led to statements that children need one toothbrush, one house. . . . two houses are too confusing; the child's cognitive and emotional capacity to cope with differences in the personality and style of parents in the intact family has been taken for granted, yet continued contact after divorce with a parent living a divergent lifestyle or with different goals and expectations has been pronounced confusing and potentially damaging; and, the concept of "*the* psychological parent" has led practitioners, lawyers, and parents to believe there is only one such parent per family, rather than two. But, in talking with and evaluating children of divorce over a protracted period of time, we observe that the practical effect of such wisdom is often real deprivation, that in saving the child from "anxiety" and "confusion," we have created anger, depression, and a deep sense of loss.

It is important to examine our clinical practices with a new lens focused on this newly burgeoning population of children experiencing divorce. Can we continue to accept one parent's claim that the other parent is "unsuitable" and should be denied visiting, without evaluating that other parent and his separate relationship with the child? Clinicians too readily have accepted a parent's assertion that the other parent is "not interested" in the child, *or* in coming for counseling, without determining this to be so themselves. Since the child of divorce clearly continues to view himself as a child of two parents, clinically we have the obligation to evaluate and facilitate his relationship with each.

Clinicians are often called upon to assist in determining what arrangements serve the best interests of the child in custody and visitation disputes. Such assessments have traditionally focused on the psychological stability of each parent and the quality of the predivorce relationship between parent and child. One important dimension of such custody determinations, so far given insufficient attention, must be the attitudes and feelings of each parent regarding the child's need for continuity postdivorce with the other parent. To what extent does that parent support a continuing relationship with the child's other parent? How much contact with the other parent does this parent think is beneficial for the child? How cooperative will this parent be in facilitating visiting, in allowing some flexibility in schedules? In making a recommendation about custody, the answers to these and related questions will be as important to the child's future psychological adjustment as the more traditional assessments of the parents' personalities, which may or may not speak directly to the quality of the parent-child relationship. When an angry, vindictive parent attempts to severely limit or destroy the child's relationship with the other parent, there must be serious question raised whether that parent can be considered "the better psychological parent," regardless of the quality of the predivorce relationship.

Increasingly, divorce cases appear before the court in which each parent petitions for custody and where the designation of "unfit parent" is clearly not applicable to either party. Such cases have the potential to push clinicians beyond the limits of current psychological knowledge and predictive capacity, and in so doing, render the clinician particularly vulnerable to decisions and judgments based primarily on a countertransference response. The turmoil, the angers, and the often driven need to defend vigorously against narcissistic injury characteristic of parents in the midst of divorce make it difficult for the clinician to remain honest, objective and nonaligned. But where each parent is deemed to be a "good enough parent," and each supports and encourages the child's relationship with the other parent, there is little basis in either law or psychological theory for making a rational choice in a custody dispute. In these families, the clinician can truly speak to the child's best interest by encouraging each parent to take an active postdivorce role in the child's life by sharing parental responsibility on an ongoing basis, in two separate locations.

Despite the increasing numbers of families experiencing the turmoil and uncertainties of divorce, programs to meet the needs of divorcing families have not developed at a similar pace, and parents have been left to fend for themselves. There have been few guidelines for divorcing parents to use in comprehending any of the aspects of the divorce experience for their children. How, when, and what to tell their youngsters, how to plan for the children's welfare after the divorce, and how to understand and deal with the varied responses of children of different ages to divorce—these and other important issues have more often been neglected than discussed. Yet, when given divorce-specific information and guidelines on postdivorce family arrangements, including visiting, parents can take an active and sensitive role in helping their children negotiate the divorce crisis.[18,38,39]

Opportunities abound for mental health practitioners to encourage and develop programs and services that will meet the needs of divorcing families at different points of stress in the postdivorce period. Certainly, broad educational efforts are needed to inform varied segments of the population dealing with divorce about the impact of the divorce experience on parents and children. Such education can be offered in separate programs, through educational workshops, media presentations, and consultation, or as an essential component of short-term preventive or early intervention programs which have the goal of preventing psychological damage in children not previously considered at risk. These new programs, in clinic, private practice, and court settings, must be not only highly available within the community, but visibly committed in their content and orientation to maintaining developmental progress and good psychological adjustment for children caught in the normative stress of divorce. With one million children each year experiencing their parents' divorce, the majority of whom are psychologically intact, but placed potentially at risk by the divorce, the mental health field must commit itself to new priorities which address this changed social and psychological reality.

REFERENCES

1. Bane, Mary J. Marital disruption and the lives of children. *In: Divorce and Separation: Context, Causes and Consequences.* Levinger, George, and Moles, Oliver C. (Eds.) New York: Basic Books (1979).
2. Biller, H. B. Father absence, maternal encouragement, and sex role development in kindergarten-age boys. *Child Development.* 40:539–46 (1969).
3. Drake, C. T., and McDougall, D. Effects of the absence of a father and other male models on the development of boys' sex roles. *Developmental Psychology.* 13:537–38 (1977).
4. Felner, R. D., Stolberg, A., and Cowen, E. L. Crisis events and school mental health referral patterns of young children. *Journal of Consulting and Clinical Psychology.* 43:305–10 (1975).
5. Gardner, Richard A. *Psychotherapy with Children of Divorce.* New York: Jason Aronson (1976).
6. Gasser, R. D. and Taylor, C. M. Role adjustment of single-parent fathers with dependent children. *Family Coordinator.* 25:397–401 (1976).
7. Glick, P. C. and Norton, A. A. Marrying, divorcing and living together in the U.S. today. *Population Bulletin,* 32:3–38 (1977).
8. Hess, R. D. and Camara, K. A. Post-divorce family relations as mediating factors in the consequences of divorce for children. *Journal of Social Issues,* in press.
9. Hetherington, E. M. Effects of father absence on personality development in adolescent daughters. *Developmental Psychology.* 7:313–26 (1972).
10. Hetherington, E. M., Cox, M., and Cox, R. Divorced fathers. *Family Coordinator.* 25:417–28 (1976).
11. Hetherington, E. M., Cox, M., and Cox, R. The aftermath of divorce. *In: Mother-Child, Father-Child Relations.* Stevens, J. H. Jr. and Matthews M. (Eds.), Washington, D.C.: National Association for the Education of Young Children (1978).
12. Hetherington, E. M. Divorce: A child's perspective. *American Psychologist.* 34:851–58 (1979).
13. Hetherington, E. M., Cox, M., and Cox, R. Play and social interaction in children following divorce. *Journal of Social Issues,* in press.
14. Jacobson, D. The impact of marital separation/divorce in children: Parent-child separation and child adjustment. *Journal of Divorce.* 4:341 (1978).
15. Kalter, N. Children of divorce in an outpatient psychiatric population. *American Journal of Orthopsychiatry.* 47:40–51 (1977).
16. Kelly, J. B. Divorce: The adult experience. *In: Handbook of Developmental Psychology.* Wolman, B. and Stricker, G. (Eds.), Englewood Cliffs, New Jersey: Prentice-Hall, in press.
17. Kelly, J. B., and Wallerstein, J. S. The effects of parental divorce: Experiences of the child in early latency. *American Journal of Orthopsychiatry.* 46:20–32 (1976).
18. Kelly, J. B., and Wallerstein, J. S. Brief interventions with children in divorcing families. *American Journal of Orthopsychiatry.* 47:23–39 (1977a).

19. Kelly, J. B., and Wallerstein, J. S. Part-time parent, part-time child: Visiting after divorce. *Journal Clinical Child Psychology.* **6**:51–4 (1977b).
20. Kelly, J. B., and Wallerstein, J. S. Children of divorce: The school setting. *National Elementary Principal.* **59**:51–8 (1979).
21. Keshet, H. F., and Rosenthal, K. M. Fathering after marital separation. *Social Work.* **23**:11–18 (1978).
22. Levinger, George and Moles, Oliver C. (Eds.). *Divorce and Separation: Context, Causes, and Consequences.* New York: Basic Books (1979).
23. McDermott, J. J. Parental divorce in early childhood. *American Journal of Psychiatry.* **124**:1424–31 (1968).
24. Mendes, H. A. Single fathers. *Family Coordinator.* **25**:439–44 (1976).
25. Norton, A. J. and Glick, P. C. Marital instability in America: Past, present, future. *In: Divorce and Separation: Context, Causes, and Consequences.* Levinger, G., and Moles, O. (Eds.) New York: Basic Books (1979).
26. Nye, I. F. Child adjustment in broken and in unhappy unbroken homes. *Marriage and Family Living.* **19**:356–61 (1957).
27. Orthner, D. K., Brown, T., and Ferguson, D. Single-parent fatherhood: An emerging family lifestyle. *Family Coordinator.* **25**:429–37 (1976).
28. Rosen, R. Children of divorce: What they feel about access and other aspects of the divorce experience. *Journal of Clinical Psychology.* **6**:24–27 (1977).
29. Santrock, J. Influence of onset and type of paternal absence on the first four Eriksonian crises. *Developmental Psychology.* **3**:273–74 (1970).
30. Santrock, J. Father absence, perceived maternal behavior and moral development in boys. *Child Development.* **46**:753–57 (1975).
31. Sell, K. D. Divorce in the 1970s: A subject guide to books, articles, dissertations, government documents, and film on divorce in the United States. Dept. of Sociology, Catawba College, Salisbury, N.C. (1977).
32. Sutton-Smith, B., Rosenberg, B. G., and Landy, F. Father absence effects in families of different sibling compositions. *Child Development.* **39**:1213–21 (1968).
33. Tessman, Laura H. *Children of Parting Parents.* New York: Jason Aronson (1977).
34. Tooley, K. Antisocial behavior and social alienation post-divorce: The man of the house and his myth. *American Journal of Orthopsychiatry.* **46**:33–42 (1976).
35. Wallerstein, J. S. and Kelly, J. B. The effects of parental divorce: The adolescent experience. *In: The Child in His Family,* Anthony, E. James, and Koupernik, Cyrille (Eds), New York: John Wiley Sons (1974).
36. Wallerstein, J. S., and Kelly, J. B. The effects of parental divorce: Experiences of the preschool child. *Journal American Academy Child Psychiatry.* **14**:600–16 (1975).
37. Wallerstein, J. S., and Kelly, J. B. The effects of parental divorce: Experiences of the child in later latency. *American Journal of Orthopsychiatry.* **46**:256–69 (1976).
38. Wallerstein, J. S., and Kelly, J. B. Divorce counseling: A community service for families in the midst of divorce. *American Journal of Orthopsychiatry.* **47**:4–22 (1977).
39. Wallerstein, Judith S., and Kelly, Joan B. *Surviving the Breakup: How Children and Parents Cope with Divorce.* New York: Basic Books (1980).
40. Weiss, Robert S. *Going It Alone: The Family Life and Social Situation of the Single Parent.* New York: Basic Books, 1979.

Index

363